Religious Experience Revisited

Studies in Theology and Religion

EDITED ON BEHALF OF THE
NETHERLANDS SCHOOL FOR ADVANCED STUDIES
IN THEOLOGY AND RELIGION (NOSTER)

Editors in Chief

Jan Willem van Henten (*University of Amsterdam/Stellenbosch University*)

Associate Editors

Herman Beck (*Tilburg University*)
Kees van der Kooi (*Vrije Universiteit Amsterdam*)
Daniela Müller (*Radboud University Nijmegen*)

Advisory Board

David Ford (*Cambridge*) – Ruard Ganzevoort (*Amsterdam*)
Maaike de Haardt (*Tilburg*) – Ab de Jong (*Leiden*) – Anne-Marie Korte (*Utrecht*)
Peter Nissen (*Nijmegen*) – Jeremy Punt (*Stellenbosch*)

VOLUME 21

The titles published in this series are listed at *brill.com/star*

Religious Experience Revisited

Expressing the Inexpressible?

Edited by

Thomas Hardtke, Ulrich Schmiedel and Tobias Tan

BRILL

LEIDEN | BOSTON

The Library of Congress Cataloging-in-Publication Data

Names: Hardtke, Thomas, editor.
Title: Religious experience revisited : expressing the inexpressible? /
    edited by Thomas Hardtke, Ulrich Schmiedel, and Tobias Tan.
Description: Boston : Brill, 2016. | Series: Studies in theology and religion,
    ISSN 1566-208X ; Volume 21 | Includes bibliographical references and
    index.
Identifiers: LCCN 2016033395 | ISBN 9789004328594 (hardback : alk. paper) |
    ISBN 9789004328600 (e-book)
Subjects: LCSH: Experience (Religion) | Religion—Methodology.
Classification: LCC BL53 .R449 2016 | DDC 204/.2—dc23
LC record available at https://lccn.loc.gov/2016033395

Want or need Open Access? Brill Open offers you the choice to make your research freely accessible online
in exchange for a publication charge. Review your various options on brill.com/brill-open.

Typeface for the Latin, Greek, and Cyrillic scripts: "Brill". See and download: brill.com/brill-typeface.

ISSN 1566-208X
ISBN 978-90-04-32859-4 (hardback)
ISBN 978-90-04-32860-0 (e-book)

Copyright 2016 by Koninklijke Brill NV, Leiden, The Netherlands.
Koninklijke Brill NV incorporates the imprints Brill, Brill Hes & De Graaf, Brill Nijhoff, Brill Rodopi and
Hotei Publishing.
All rights reserved. No part of this publication may be reproduced, translated, stored in a retrieval system,
or transmitted in any form or by any means, electronic, mechanical, photocopying, recording or otherwise,
without prior written permission from the publisher.
Authorization to photocopy items for internal or personal use is granted by Koninklijke Brill NV provided
that the appropriate fees are paid directly to The Copyright Clearance Center, 222 Rosewood Drive,
Suite 910, Danvers, MA 01923, USA. Fees are subject to change.

This book is printed on acid-free paper and produced in a sustainable manner.

Contents

Acknowledgements VII
Contributors IX

Introduction: Experience or Expression? A Puzzling Oversight 1
Thomas Hardtke, Ulrich Schmiedel and Tobias Tan

PART 1
Grasping the Ungraspable?

1 **How to do Transcendence with Words? The Problem of Articulation in Religious Experience** 15
Jörg Lauster

2 **Modern Trials and Tests of 'Experience': Plastic Commonplace and Managed Exception** 30
Yvonne Sherwood

PART 2
Imagining the Unimaginable?

3 **Fiercely Proselytizing and Feverishly Protective: Reading John's Revelation with Jacques Derrida** 59
Hannah M. Strømmen

4 **Religious Experience without Belief? Toward an Imaginative Account of Religious Engagement** 73
Amber L. Griffioen

5 **"Is that You?" Hearing God's Voice in the Words of a Stranger (Judges 6:11–24)** 89
Catherine Lewis-Smith

6 **Living with Invisibility: Emotion, Mind, and Transcendence** 106
Graham Ward

PART 3
Interpreting the Uninterpretable?

7   Navid Kermani's Poetic Hermeneutics of Religious Experiences   123
Johannes Kleine

8   The Complexity of Hermeneutical Experience: Transcendence and Transformation   137
Werner G. Jeanrond

9   "Mediated Immediacy": Karl Rahner and Edward Schillebeeckx on the Non-Reflective Element of Experience   154
Marijn de Jong

10   Supra-Religious? The Concept of Transcendental Experience and the (In-)Accessibility of the Absolute   173
Knut Wenzel

PART 4
Performing the Unperformable?

11   The Trouble with Trust in the Transcendent: Ernst Troeltsch's Reception of William James   187
Ulrich Schmiedel

12   The Corporeality of Religious Experience: Embodied Cognition in Religious Practices   207
Tobias Tan

13   Religious Experience in Fourteenth-Century Mystical Writing: The Revelations of Elsbeth von Oye   227
Johannes M. Depnering

14   Speaking of God: Ludwig Wittgenstein and the Paradox of Religious Experience   243
Brian Klug

Conclusion: Experience or Expression? Preserving the Puzzle   262
Thomas Hardtke, Ulrich Schmiedel and Tobias Tan

Index of Names   275
Index of Subjects   279

Acknowledgements

"When we reach the subject of mysticism, you will undergo so deep an immersion into these exalted states of consciousness as to be wet all over, if I may so express myself; and the cold shiver of doubt with which this little sprinkling may affect you will have long since passed away – doubt, I mean, as to whether all such writing be not mere abstract talk... set down *pour encourager les autres*. You will then be convinced, I trust, that these states of consciousness of 'union' form a perfectly definite class of experiences...." With these words, William James, a founding father of the turn to experience in the study of religion, warned the appreciative audience during his Gifford Lectures on *The Varieties of Religious Experience* about the effects and the side-effects experiences of mystical "immersion" might have.

By twisting James's warning a little, we are able to apply it to our own circumstances. During the international, interdisciplinary and interreligious conference, "Interpreting Experience – Experiencing Interpretation: Im/Possibilities of a Hermeneutics of Religious Experience", which we hosted at the University of Oxford in 2014, neither the lecturers nor the listeners got – as far as we could ascertain – "wet all over". But although a conference naturally and necessarily consists of "talk" (some of it "abstract" and some of it even more "abstract"), we gained the impression that the "immersion" into these experiences did indeed disperse a "cold shiver of doubt" – namely the doubt that the study of experience is hopelessly outdated, a raddled remnant of a historical and hermeneutical past prior to the linguistic turn, in which religious and non-religious experiences could be naively named "perfectly definite" subjects for study. Instead, we realized that interpretations and re-interpretations of these "states of consciousness" are a promising point of departure for the study of religion if experience and expression are neither totally connected nor totally disconnected. From the many excellent and exciting contributions delivered at the conference, we particularly selected those which provoke a critical and a creative tension between experiences and expressions of religion. And we "trust" that our selection might *"encourager les autres"*.

Thanks are due both to those who supported our conference and to those who supported our compilation. First and foremost, we are grateful to the Fritz-Thyssen-Stiftung für Wissenschaftsförderung, Germany. Without the generous funding they provided, we would not have been able to organize the conference. We are also grateful to the two neighboring institutions at the University of Oxford which hosted the conference: St Benet's Hall, Oxford, with its Master Werner G. Jeanrond as well as The Ertegun Graduate Scholarship Programme in the Humanities, Oxford, with its Director Bryan

Ward-Perkins. They provided a space for discussion and a place for dinner – both of which are essential to a successful conference – and much more. Thanks are also, of course, due to all those who participated in the conference; without the listeners and the lecturers, there would have been neither a conference nor a compilation.

Both the production and the publication of our compilation were supported by a dedicated and diligent team at Brill in Leiden: Mirjam Elbers, Ingrid Heijckers-Velt, and Bram Oudenampsen. The contributions were examined by two anonymous reviewers; we are grateful for their comments and critique which helped us to revise and refine the compilation. Last – not least – we would like to thank Jan Willem van Henten for including our compilation in the *Studies in Theology and Religion* (STAR) series.

Thomas Hardtke, Ulrich Schmiedel and Tobias Tan
Easter 2016
Berlin, Munich and Oxford

Contributors

Marijn de Jong
is a PhD candidate at the Catholic University of Leuven in Belgium. His dissertation compares the theological methodologies of Karl Rahner and Edward Schillebeeckx. Before coming to Leuven he studied corporate law and theology at Tilburg University, the University of Cambridge, and Boston College.

Johannes M. Depnering
is a teacher of German at Ampleforth College, Yorkshire. He gained his DPhil from the University of Oxford and was the Mellon Postdoctoral Fellow in Religious Writing in the German Middle Ages at Oriel College, Oxford. In his current research, he explores tactile experiences in late-medieval mystical writing. His doctoral dissertation deals with Latin and German sermon manuscripts and the Franciscan preacher Berthold von Regensburg.

Amber L. Griffioen
is a Margarete von Wrangell Research Fellow and Instructor at the University of Konstanz in Germany, where she works on issues in philosophy of religion, philosophy of action, and philosophy of sport. Her current research project is entitled "Faith Without Belief? Experience, Engagement, and the Religious Life".

Thomas Hardtke
is a PhD candidate at the Friedrich Schlegel Graduate School for Literary Studies at Freie Universität Berlin. He studied Protestant Theology and German Language and Literature at the Technical University of Dresden, at the Pontifical University Gregoriana in Rome, and at the University of Leipzig. His research interests include literature and insanity, narratology, literature and religion, museum studies, and literary education.

Werner G. Jeanrond
is Master of St Benet's Hall, Oxford. He has taught systematic theology as well as philosophical, theological, and literary hermeneutics at Trinity College Dublin, the University of Lund and the University of Glasgow. His publications, including his most recent English study *A Theology of Love* (2010), have been translated into many languages.

Johannes Kleine
is a PhD candidate at Friedrich Schlegel Graduate School for Literary Studies at Freie Universität Berlin. Having studied at the University of Erlangen and Nuremberg and the Technical University of Dresden, he conducted research at Rutgers University, Princeton University, and Gonville and Caius College at the University of Cambridge. He specializes in contemporary German literature.

Brian Klug
is Senior Research Fellow in Philosophy at St Benet's Hall, Oxford. He is a member of the Faculty of Philosophy at the University of Oxford, Honorary Fellow of the Parkes Institute for the Study of Jewish/non-Jewish Relations, University of Southampton, and Fellow of the College of Arts and Sciences, Saint Xavier University, Chicago. His research interests include the philosophy of Ludwig Wittgenstein, Jewish philosophy, and the philosophy of race (including anti-semitism and Islamophobia).

Jörg Lauster
is Professor of Systematic Theology, Philosophy of Religion and Ecumenical Studies at Ludwig-Maximilians-Universität München in Germany. His research focuses on philosophical and theological theories of religious experience, philosophical and theological hermeneutics, theology of religions, and the thought of Rudolf Otto. Recently he published a cultural history of Christianity entitled *Die Verzauberung der Welt: Eine Kulturgeschichte des Christentums* (2014).

Catherine Lewis-Smith
completed her doctoral studies at Lucy Cavendish College, University of Cambridge in 2016 and is a minister of the United Reformed Church in the United Kingdom. Her current research interests are conversation analysis in literature, and her thesis focused upon encounters with mal'ak YHWH (messenger of the Lord) in the book of Judges.

Ulrich Schmiedel
is a Postdoctoral Fellow in Systematic Theology at Ludwig-Maximilians-Universität München in Germany. He gained his DPhil in theology from the University of Oxford. His research interests include ecclesiology, the hermeneutics of experience, the concept of alterity in theological, sociological and philosophical thought, as well as the interdisciplinary oeuvre of Ernst Troeltsch.

Yvonne Sherwood

is Professor of Biblical Cultures and Politics at the University of Kent. Her research combines biblical studies and religious studies in conversation with continental philosophy. Most recently she published *Biblical Blaspheming: Trials of the Sacred for a Secular Age* (2012).

Hannah M. Strømmen

gained her PhD from the University of Glasgow in 2015. She is a Senior Lecturer in Biblical Studies in the Department of Theology, Philosophy and Religious Studies at the University of Chichester. Her research focuses on the intersections of the biblical archive with critical theory and Western culture, with a particular penchant for Jacques Derrida's work.

Tobias Tan

is a DPhil candidate in the Faculty of Theology and Religion at the University of Oxford. His research considers how embodied cognition might reshape theological methodology by broadening our conception of theological thinking. He is an alumnus of the Ertegun Graduate Scholarship Programme in the Humanities and is currently the Arthur Peacocke Graduate Scholar in Science and Religion at Exeter College, Oxford and the Hastings Rashdall Graduate Scholar at New College, Oxford.

Graham Ward

is Regius Professor of Divinity at the University of Oxford and Canon of Christ Church Cathedral. His broad-ranging work spans the intersections of theology with postmodernity, contemporary culture, politics, language, gender, and literature. His most recent study, *Unbelievable: Why We Believe and Why We Don't* (2014), examines the biological underpinnings of belief and brings these insights into discussions of belief in contemporary culture.

Knut Wenzel

is Professor of Fundamental Theology and Dogmatics in the Department of Catholic Theology at the Goethe-University Frankfurt in Germany. His research interests include the hermeneutics of Paul Ricoeur, narrative theology, theological aesthetics, the history, theory and theology of secularity, as well as the relationship between theology and contemporary culture.

Introduction: Experience or Expression?
A Puzzling Oversight

Thomas Hardtke, Ulrich Schmiedel and Tobias Tan

A paradoxical puzzle has haunted research on religion since William James's Gifford Lectures, *The Varieties of Religious Experience: A Study in Human Nature*, were delivered at the University of Edinburgh in 1901 and 1902.[1] In these lectures, James positioned 'experience' at the center of the study of religion. But the Jamesian concept of experience is puzzling. He argued that religious as opposed to non-religious experiences are marked by their inexpressibility, but his argument is rooted in expressions of the very experiences he characterized as inexpressible – 214 expressions of inexpressible experiences, to be precise.[2] In the wake of James's seminal Gifford Lectures, this paradoxical puzzle has permeated the study of religion, affecting an array of disciplines with dazzling diversity. Yet, what to make of James's paradoxical puzzle? What constitutes a religious experience? What constitutes a religious expression? And how are religious experiences and religious expressions related? The contributions to our compilation both raise and respond to questions like these in order to address the paradoxical puzzle of experience and expression.

Of course, our compilation cannot simply solve a puzzle which has haunted research on religion since James in one fell swoop. But it can take the (Jamesian) puzzle as a promising point of departure to map the possibilities as well as the impossibilities of a hermeneutics of religion. Rather than presuming that experience and expression are either totally connected or totally disconnected, our compilation pursues a hermeneutics which allows for critical and creative tensions between the two.

---

1 William James, *The Varieties of Religious Experience: A Study in Human Nature. Being the Gifford Lectures on Natural Religion Delivered at Edinburgh in 1901–1902*, The Works of William James, vol. 15, ed. Frederick H. Burkhardt, Fredson Bowers, and Ignas K. Skurupskelis (Cambridge, MA: Harvard University Press, 1987).

2 See Jeremy Carrette, "Passionate Belief: William James, Emotion and Religious Experience", in *William James and The Varieties of Religious Experience: A Centenary Celebration* (London: Routledge, 2005), 79–93.

The Pieces of the Puzzle

The puzzle of experience and expression runs through the study of religion.[3] It can be brought into sharper relief by considering two contrasting approaches. James tends to prioritize experiences, pitting them against expressions, while James's critics tend to prioritize expressions, pitting them against experiences. But can the puzzle of experience and expression be solved and settled by tackling experience instead of expression or expression instead of experience?

Elaborating on mysticism as the core of religion, James admits that he has not himself had an experience which could be characterized as mystical.[4] He refers to his approach to mysticism as "second-hand", drawing a distinction between a primary inward experience and a secondary outward expression.[5] James's approach to mysticism exemplifies his turn to experience in that he defines mystical experiences through their "ineffability".[6] And yet he describes these experiences not directly but indirectly, relying on the detour of their articulation and their interpretation – which is to say, their expression. Hence, according to his own theory, James's approach might miss the core of mysticism. Thus, a conundrum arises: on the one hand, he conflates experience and expression by assuming that the expression offers an unambiguous representation of the experience; and on the other hand, he draws a distinction between experience and expression which marshals 'authentic' first-hand experiences against 'inauthentic' second-hand expressions that offer but a faint echo of the original event.

James's conundrum has led a variety of critics to quarantine his concept of experience. Craig Martin's and Russell T. McCutcheon's *Religious Experience: A Reader* exemplifies such a strategy of confinement.[7] McCutcheon draws attention to experience and expression as alternatives.[8] In "I Have a Hunch", he

---

3 For a succinct survey of the literature see Ann Taves, "Religious Experience", in *Encyclopaedia of Religion*, vol. 11, ed. Lindsay Jones (Detroit, MI: Thompson Gale, 2005), 7736–7750. Wayne Proudfoot's *Religious Experience* (Berkeley: University of California Press, 1985) has functioned as a focus in the discussions between the 'perennialist' defenders and the 'constructivist' despisers of 'experience'.

4 James, *The Varieties of Religious Experience*, 302. However, James's son explained that the 'Frenchman' whose experience is examined in ibid., 134–135, refers to James's own experience. See John E. Smith, "Introduction", in ibid., xii–lii (xviii).

5 James, *The Varieties of Religious Experience*, 302.

6 Ibid., 303.

7 *Religious Experience: A Reader*, ed. Craig Martin and Russell T. McCutcheon with Leslie Dorrough Smith (Sheffield: Equinox, 2012).

8 Russell T. McCutcheon, "Introduction", in *Religious Experience: A Reader*, 1–16.

INTRODUCTION

argues that a concentration on experience as opposed to expression runs the risk of turning the study of religion into a "hermeneutics of hunches".[9] Martin's "William James in Late Capitalism: Our Religion of the Status Quo" elaborates on the dubious and dangerous consequences such a turn might have.[10] He argues that the distinction between inward experience and outward expression inherent in James's conceptualization of experience is "a building block" for a domestication of religion which advances capitalism.[11]

Although James repeatedly rejects essentializations of religion,[12] Martin's aim is to expose James's distinction between experience and expression as a rhetorical ploy which fosters and facilitates the essentialization of both individual religion and institutional religion.[13] He argues that the rhetoric of "naïve empiricism" overlooks the cultural constitution of both individual religion (which pairs with the Jamesian experience) and institutional religion (which pairs with the Jamesian expression).[14] On the Jamesian distinction, one allocates whatever one approves of in religion to an authentic individual experience as opposed to an inauthentic institutional expression. For Martin, such essentialism is at the core of James's "extremely superficial" theory of religion.[15] It has crucial consequences: "The discourse on religious experience normatively prescribes for us where religion belongs, what religion should and should not do . . .; and in so far as our 'religions' incorporate this discourse, they too are social technologies with a reach beyond the self".[16] James's theory anchors *"the norms of late capitalism"* in our souls, so to speak.[17] As soon as religion makes demands on us which criticize the consumerist and capitalist status quo, these demands are allocated to the institutional rather than the individual, to that which is not valuable as opposed to that which is valuable. Thus, James's concept of experience cements the status quo.

---

9   Russell T. McCutcheon, "I Have a Hunch", in *Religious Experience: A Reader*, 199–202 (202). For a critical account see Benjamin Y. Fong, "On Critics and What's Real: Russell McCutcheon on Religious Experience", *Journal of the American Academy of Religion* 82 (2014), 1127–1148.

10   Craig Martin, "William James in Late Capitalism: Our Religion of the Status Quo", in *Religious Experience: A Reader*, 177–196.

11   Ibid., 178.

12   James, *The Varieties of Religious Experience*, 30–31.

13   See also Robert H. Sharf, "The Rhetoric of Experience and the Study of Religion", *Journal of Consciousness Studies* 7 (2000), 267–287.

14   Martin, "William James in Late Capitalism", 185.

15   Ibid., 186.

16   Ibid., 195.

17   Ibid., 193.

Whatever we make of the way in which Martin 'capitalizes' on James's concept of religion, his argument revolves around the alternative of experience and expression. In as much as he conceptualizes religion as rhetoric, expression trumps experience. Thus, *Religious Experience: A Reader* culminates in the rejection of the concept around which it revolves. Martin concludes that James's "canonical status be retired at present; given the ease with which his work is appropriated into what amounts to vulgar rhetoric".[18] For Martin, James's Gifford Lectures ought to be seen as "a historical curiosity that is interesting in so far as it has informed the field of religious studies in the past, but – due to its embedded ideological assumptions – is presently not of much use to critical scholarship on religion".[19] James's concept of experience is "sophisticated propaganda".[20]

Even without critiquing James and his critics, the controversy between them plays out in the puzzle around which our compilation revolves. If we were to side with James, we ought to assume that experience is prior to its expression. Thus, we should concentrate our research on the primordial experience. If, however, we were to side with the critics of James, we ought to assume that expression is prior to its experience. Thus, we should concentrate our research on the primordial expression. But what if the alternative between experience and expression is a *false* alternative? In *Religious Experience Reconsidered*, Ann Taves discusses how the debates between those who emphasize experience and those who emphasize expression have shaped the study of religion since the linguistic turn.[21] She intends to "reframe" the study of experiences, but not by delineating "a middle ground" between the Jamesians on the one hand, and the critics of the Jamesians on the other.[22] Instead, Taves is interested in how some experiences come to be deemed religious or non-religious. How do subjects single out their experiences in order to deem them either this or that?

Applying Igor Kopytoff's concept of singularization to the study of experiences,[23] Taves argues that the attribution of something as religious might

---

18 Ibid., 196.

19 Ibid.

20 Ibid.

21 Ann Taves, *Religious Experience Reconsidered: A Building-Block Approach to the Study of Religion and Other Special Things* (Princeton, NJ: Princeton University Press, 2009). For the linguistic turn, see Steven Shakespeare, "Language", in *The Oxford Handbook of Theology and Modern European Thought*, ed. Nicholas Adams, George Pattison and Graham Ward (Oxford: Oxford University Press, 2013), 105–126.

22 Taves, *Religious Experience Reconsidered*, 94.

23 See ibid., 29–46, esp. the concise chart ibid., 45. See also Igor Kopytoff, "The Cultural Biography of Things: Commoditization as Process", in *The Social Life of Things: Commodities*

INTRODUCTION

start either with the experience (which triggers an expression of something as religious) or with the expression (which triggers an experience of something as religious).[24] Accordingly, she assumes that there is "some continuity" between the way things are experienced and the way things are expressed.[25] The assumption of continuity – an assumption which is neglected by both those who pit experience against expression and those who pit expression against experience – enables her to explore the impact of experiences on expressions and the impact of expressions on experiences.[26] According to Taves, the examination of "pre-hoc", "post-hoc" and "real-time" data equips scholars of religion to understand how experiences come to be attributed – which is to say, deemed – as religious rather than non-religious.[27] Taves admits that, in order to convince the defenders as well as the despisers of experience, her approach has to account for the subjects of experience who understand their experience as 'religious' rather than as 'deemed religious' – which is to say, subjects for whom transcendence is located in the experience rather than in the expression.[28] However, when she accounts for these subjects by arguing that "preconscious mental processes" make the subject feel that she or he "recognize[s]" transcendence, Taves tacitly theorizes expression as primary and experience as secondary.[29] The transcendence which the subject recognizes consciously is the transcendence which the subject created preconsciously (albeit on a different 'deeper' – namely the preconscious rather than the conscious – level). Thus, expression is prioritized over experience. Although Taves's *Religious Experience Reconsidered* is a significant step forward, it does not solve the puzzle of experience and expression which continues to haunt the study of religion.

---

    in Cultural Perspective, ed. Arjun Appadurai (Cambridge: Cambridge University Press, 1986), 64–93.

24   Taves, *Religious Experience Reconsidered*, 93–94.

25   Ibid., 63.

26   Ibid., 94. According to Taves, the impact of experience on expression overlaps with the influence of nature on culture (what she calls "bottom-up"), while the impact of expression on experience overlaps with the influence of culture on nature (what she calls "top-down").

27   Ibid., 68–71. See also ibid., 73–74 (our emphasis), where Taves asks scholars of religion "to *recast* the relationship" between experience and expression "*in terms of* the distinction" between these types of data.

28   Ibid., 20.

29   Ibid., 21.

Putting the Pieces Together

Given the nature of the puzzle, any engagement with the relation between experience and expression ought to be interdisciplinary. But definitions of controversial concepts such as 'experience' and 'expression' are contested in disciplinary and in interdisciplinary perspectives. Considering that James already warned his audience that a "theorizing mind tends...to the over-simplification of its materials", we, following his lead, are not so "pedantic" about "definitions" and "would-be definitions" as to "enumerate any of them to you now".[30] Instead, we have invited the contributors to define their core concepts in accordance with their disciplinary fields and with their interdisciplinary forays. We aim to avoid prescribing fixed and final definitions to our contributors when these definitions are precisely the matter which is up for discussion throughout our contribution. We will, however, return to the issues of conceptualization in the conclusion to take stock of both the convergences and divergences in the ways 'experience' and 'expression' are theorized.

Taking theology as a point of departure, our compilation aims to offer interdisciplinary engagements with religious experiences and religious expressions. Accordingly, we have resisted the temptation to organize our contributions along classical and conventional disciplinary lines. Instead, the contributions are grouped into four sections which blur disciplinary boundaries in order to provoke critical and creative methodological dissonances. The first section, 'Grasping the Ungraspable?', consists of two studies which explore the conceptualization of religious as opposed to non-religious experience. By providing theoretical and meta-theoretical perspectives, these studies offer a framework for the following sections. We examine the issue of imagination in the second section, 'Imagining the Unimaginable?', and the issue of interpretation in the third section, 'Interpreting the Uninterpretable?'. In the fourth and final section, 'Performing the Unperformable?', we elaborate on practices and performances of religion. Countering the false alternative between experience and expression, all of these sections illuminate the diverse features and the different facets of the (Jamesian) puzzle by putting experience back into its expression and expression back into its experience.

Grasping the Ungraspable?

Our compilation opens with two contributions which approach experience from theoretical and meta-theoretical angles – which is to say, they theorize about experience and they theorize about theorizing about experience. *Jörg*

---

30   James, *The Varieties of Religious Experience*, 30.

INTRODUCTION

Lauster advocates 'experience' as a core concept for the theological and the non-theological study of religion. Concentrating on Christianity past and present, he argues that the concept crystallizes religion in the subject. The subject is the one by whom the "breaking-in of transcendence" is simultaneously experienced and expressed. Thus, the subject – entangled as it is in historical and cultural networks of communication – provides *the* point of departure for a hermeneutics whose task it is to evaluate the accounts of experience past and present. Lauster suggests that the criterion for such an evaluation is that the expression of the experience confesses its confines: the in-breaking of transcendence can be conceptualized neither completely nor conclusively.

Turning to the tones and tenors of 'experience', *Yvonne Sherwood* explores how the core concept of experience has been utilized inside and outside academia. Countering the concentration on a strong and stable subject, she argues that 'experience' is neither a pre-modern nor a post-modern, but a distinctly modern concept. 'Experience' attempts to manage the unmanageable by trafficking between the secular and the sacred, or, as she pointedly puts it, between "fact-objects" and "fairy-objects". Through the category of experience, religion is made fit for modernized and modernizing politics. Pointing to the text and the legacies of the text of Abraham's attempt to sacrifice his son Isaac in the Bible, Sherwood highlights what might get lost in the sterilization of religion through the concept of experience.

Taken together, these two contributions map the terrain of uses and abuses of the concept of experience in the study of religion – a terrain which is navigated by the contributions that follow.

Imagining the Unimaginable?

The second section revolves around the issue of imagination. *Hannah M. Strømmen* takes up the meta-theoretical accounts of experience. Building on Jacques Derrida's notion of autoimmunity, she reads John's Revelation in order to expose how experience and expression are inextricably interwoven in John's "apocalyptic experience". Strømmen argues that the operations of "mediation" which are at the core of John's revelation cut both ways: by imagining ideas and images of the unimaginable, mediation publicizes and privatizes John's revelation at the same time. While the privatizing imagination "feverishly protects", the publicizing imagination "fiercely proselytizes". The notion of autoimmunity captures how the public and the private assume and attack each other.

Amber L. Griffioen pushes the issue of imagination further. Imagination, she argues, might be triggered regardless of whether a subject does or does not believe in the existence of what she imagines. Griffioen links the category of religious experience to the category of non-religious experience, concentrating on the variety of emotional responses to fiction. Retrieving a concept of faith without belief, she concludes that faith is less about what we imagine than about what we do with what we imagine.

Catherine Lewis-Smith grapples with the issue of believable or unbelievable imagination by exploring Gideon's theophany in Judges 6:11–24. Adopting Mikhail Bakhtin's concept of the superaddressee – the 'third' to which both the one who addresses and the one who is addressed address their speech – she examines Gideon's struggle (not) to hear God's voice in the voice of the stranger. She identifies how the stranger opens up the space for God in Gideon's imagination, tracing the textualization of the imagination of the unimaginable. The figure of Gideon thus exemplifies how imagination triggers self-transcendence and self-transformation.

Graham Ward concludes the investigation of imagination. His point of departure is the concept of the invisible in the phenomenology of Maurice Merleau-Ponty. While Merleau-Ponty confines the invisible to the immanent as opposed to the transcendent, Ward goes beyond this confinement, offering accounts of the invisible from the perspective of the cognitive sciences. Imagination is what opens humans to the invisible. Drawing together the consequences for theology, Ward argues that faith is belief in belief – a believing belief which would be impossible without imagination. Pointing to the articulation as well as the interpretation of experience, Ward thus leads us to the next section.

Interpreting the Uninterpretable?

Johannes Kleine pinpoints the paradox of articulation and interpretation which we explore in the third section. He analyzes the novel *Dein Name* ("Your Name"), published in 2011 by the German-Iranian author and academic Navid Kermani. Kermani's poetics stages mystical experiences and the expressions of mystical experiences simultaneously. Kleine explores and evaluates this simultaneity as a "meta-mystical poetics" which circles around what he calls the "mystical void". It is paradoxically and precisely the failure to speak of the unspeakable that produces expression after expression after expression.

This paradox is taken up as "hermeneutical experience" by *Werner G. Jeanrond*. Exploring the conceptualizations of experience in Friedrich D. E. Schleiermacher, Rudolf Otto, Mircea Eliade, and David Tracy, Jeanrond maps the field of theological and philosophical hermeneutics of religion. He distinguishes between a "hermeneutics of revelation" which attempts to approach the transcendent directly and a "hermeneutics of signification" which attempts to approach the transcendent indirectly. Only a hermeneutics of signification,

INTRODUCTION 9

he argues, is capable of examining the conditions which form and inform articulations and interpretations of experience. Such a hermeneutics recognizes and respects the plurality of possible expressions which is inherent in any experience of transcendence.

Marijn de Jong elaborates on the hermeneutics of experience when he compares how Karl Rahner and Edward Schillebeeckx engage with the issue of interpretation. De Jong argues that their engagements allow for a retrieval of the universality of the experience of religion after the linguistic turn in philosophy and theology. Through the concept of "mediated immediacy", he stresses that language is necessary in order to have an experience, religious or non-religious. But the necessity of language does not imply that the experience can be reduced to its expression. A conceptual combination of (unmediated) experience and (mediating) expression is vital for the public discussion of religious and non-religious claims to truth.

The concept of transcendental experience, as analyzed and assessed by de Jong, is at the core of *Knut Wenzel's* contribution. Taking inspiration from Rahner, Wenzel argues that the experience of the absolute in the relative is closely connected to what he calls "subject-experience", the subject's experience of subjectivity. Crucially, Wenzel likens transcendental experience to a "talk" without a "topic". The topic of the talk, he suggests, might be provided by religious and non-religious discourses alike, which is why he characterizes transcendental experience as "supra-religious". Essentially, Wenzel democratizes the experiences of the absolute in the relative, proposing human expressivity as the point of departure for a critical and constructive assessment of both religious and non-religious experiences. Wenzel's emphasis on expressivity takes us to the following and final section.

Performing the Unperformable?

Both practices and performances of religion are examined in the fourth and final section. By exploring and expanding on Ernst Troeltsch's reception of James, *Ulrich Schmiedel* characterizes religion as trust in the transcendent. Criticizing the interiorization and the individualization of the experience of religion in James, he argues that communities are indispensable for experiences of trust because they offer the space for encounters with the other. Alterity – the otherness of the other – encapsulates a spectrum of experiences from routine trust in the finite other to radical trust in the infinite other. However, trust creates trouble in communities because it counters closure and control. Driven by the expression of the inexpressible, the trouble with trust is a productive as opposed to a destructive trouble: it opens communities to the experience of the transcendence of both the finite and the infinite other.

Tobias Tan's examination of the corporeality of experience ties in with Schmiedel's critique of the interiorization and the individualization of religion. Challenging James's rejection of the physiological dimension of experience, Tan elaborates on the field of embodied cognition to enunciate how factors "beyond the brain", such as motor movements, impact cognitive processes. He argues that the physical performance of religion shapes the experience of religion. Tan concludes with a retrieval of Hans-Georg Gadamer's concept of tradition in order to offer a framework for the evaluation of the corporeality of experiences.

The corporeality of experience is taken up from a different disciplinary perspective by *Johannes M. Depnering.* In a paleographical re-assessment of the "revelations" of the medieval mystic Elsbeth von Oye which combines physiological and psychological perspectives, Depnering explores the impact of pain on the experience and the expression of mystical union. Elsbeth's texts are characterized as attempts of meaning-making in a situation of extreme stress. Depnering concludes that neither constructivist nor attributionist accounts of mysticism are adequate to capture such meaning-making. What is needed is a combination of both.

Brian Klug sketches such a combination in his examination of the significance of religion for Ludwig Wittgenstein's philosophy of language. Discussing the "philosopher with two personas", he argues that the paradox of experience and expression is at the core of Wittgenstein's work. Klug criticizes accounts of Wittgenstein which reduce his conceptualization of religion to a 'language' or a 'language game'. Building on Wittgenstein, he concludes that the paradox in our thinking and our talking about God is not to be resolved. It is to be lived – practiced and performed – as an unresolved and unresolvable puzzle. Hence, with Klug's contribution we return to the puzzle of experience and expression.

Preserving the Puzzle

The paradoxical puzzle of experience and expression is more than a curiosity in James's pioneering but problematic research on religion. The contributions to our compilation advocate that this paradox cannot be finessed as easily as James and the critics of James (mentioned above) would have it. To arrive at a hermeneutics of religion, experience and expression cannot be pitted against each other. Only if religion is conceived in terms of experience *and* in terms of expression, is it unshackled from the confining circumscriptions exemplified by James on the one hand and James's critics on the other.

INTRODUCTION

The contributions to our compilation allow us to understand both how experiences are expressed and how expressions are experienced. For the study of religion today it is imperative to explore the possibilities and the impossibilities of a hermeneutics of religion which takes experience and expression into account. To preserve and probe the paradoxical puzzle of experience and expression is a promising point of departure for such a hermeneutics.

Literature

Carrette, Jeremy, "Passionate Belief: William James, Emotion and Religious Experience", in *William James and The Varieties of Religious Experience: A Centenary Celebration* (London: Routledge, 2005), 79–93.

Fong, Benjamin Y., "On Critics and What's Real: Russell McCutcheon on Religious Experience", *Journal of the American Academy of Religion* 82 (2014), 1127–1148.

James, William, *The Varieties of Religious Experience: A Study in Human Nature. Being the Gifford Lectures on Natural Religion Delivered at Edinburgh in 1901–1902*, The Works of William James, vol. 15, ed. Frederick H. Burkhardt, Fredson Bowers, and Ignas K. Skurupskelis (Cambridge, MA: Harvard University Press, 1987).

Kopytoff, Igor, "The Cultural Biography of Things: Commoditization as Process", in *The Social Life of Things: Commodities in Cultural Perspective*, ed. Arjun Appadurai (Cambridge: Cambridge University Press, 1986), 64–93.

Martin, Craig, "William James in Late Capitalism: Our Religion of the Status Quo", in *Religious Experience: A Reader*, ed. Craig Martin and Russell T. McCutcheon with Leslie Dorrough Smith (Sheffield: Equinox, 2012), 177–196.

McCutcheon, Russell T., "I Have a Hunch", in *Religious Experience: A Reader*, ed. Craig Martin and Russell T. McCutcheon with Leslie Dorrough Smith (Sheffield: Equinox, 2012) 199–202.

McCutcheon, Russell T., "Introduction", in *Religious Experience: A Reader*, ed. Craig Martin and Russell T. McCutcheon with Leslie Dorrough Smith (Sheffield: Equinox, 2012), 1–16.

Proudfoot, Wayne, *Religious Experience* (Berkeley: University of California Press, 1985).

Shakespeare, Steven, "Language", in *The Oxford Handbook of Theology and Modern European Thought*, ed. Nicholas Adams, George Pattison and Graham Ward (Oxford: Oxford University Press, 2013), 105–126.

Sharf, Robert H., "The Rhetoric of Experience and the Study of Religion", *Journal of Consciousness Studies* 7 (2000), 267–287.

Taves, Ann, "Religious Experience", in *Encyclopaedia of Religion*, vol. 11, ed. Lindsay Jones (Detroit, MI: Thompson Gale, 2005), 7736–7750.

Taves, Ann, *Religious Experience Reconsidered: A Building-Block Approach to the Study of Religion and Other Special Things* (Princeton, NJ: Princeton University Press, 2009).

PART 1

Grasping the Ungraspable?

∵

CHAPTER 1

How to do Transcendence with Words?
The Problem of Articulation in Religious Experience

Jörg Lauster

As a Bavarian living close to the Alps, I have an extraordinary experience behind me this winter. This year we have had almost no snow to date! In Greenland, however, they have at least fifty words for snow. According to certain theories of human expression we can assume that these fifty words are the result of a long interaction between humans and snow in Greenland. In the evolution of Inuit culture, the encounter with an immense variety of snow created an immense variety of expressions for snow and, likewise, the immense variety of expressions for snow facilitates the Inuit experience of snow. The more words we have, the more constellations of sense experience we can represent to ourselves in consciousness. With their fifty words, Greenlanders can form more complex experiences of snow. I need not remark that this observation has significant import for our understanding of religious experience.

Why Religious Experience?

If we look at the general discussion in sociology, philosophy and theology, the category of religious experience is not the main topic of discourse.[1] After a long period of discussing the institutional aspects of religion, sociologists have placed emphasis on the social and the political dimensions of religion. The extensive research on the various kinds of fundamentalism illustrates this. Philosophers reflect on the idea of the origin of religious propositions as products of the human mind, which is quite close to what the neurosciences do when they consider religion as a function of the brain. For a long time, research in the study of religion was dominated by a detailed empirical description of religious practices, often under the guise of so-called 'scientific objectivism'. Even in theology, religious experience is not a self-evident

---

1 For the variety of possible approaches see Martin Riesebrodt, *The Promise of Salvation: A Theory of Religion*, trans. Stephen Rendall (Chicago: University of Chicago Press, 2012).

category. For example, it is well known that biblical theology plays a central role in Protestantism. But for the modern exegesis of the Bible, the main points of interest are philological and historical aspects of the texts on a structural level. To confront biblical scholars with the category of experience is like showing up to a twenty-first-century party in a nineteenth-century suit. Indeed, it is difficult to define the relation between experience and text. How could we trace back texts which were produced in a complex process of oral and written transmission to some original religious experience or experiences?

This very short overview of current debates in the research on religion demonstrates that we have to take some difficulties into consideration when we talk about religious experience. The category of religious experience was mainly introduced by prominent scholars of the nineteenth-century, such as Friedrich Schleiermacher, Ernst Troeltsch, Rudolf Otto, and, in the Anglophone tradition, Jonathan Edwards, Ralph Waldo Emerson and finally William James. They employed different descriptions but they fundamentally agreed on one point: whoever wants to understand religion must go back to the religious experience of human subjects, to their articulations and interpretations, and to the self-expressions and self-understandings of these experiences. For the study of religion, this is still the most important methodological argument: we do not learn more about religion if we look at it from the point of view of a 'scientific objectivism' which only wants to talk *about* religion. It is evident that this 'objectivism' is nothing but an ideological bias which shows a curious interest in the world of religion but which also seeks to exclude in advance any claim of the truth of this world. This is a classical and crucial methodological blind spot in the research on religion. The category of religious experience avoids this limitation. We learn more about religion, if we analyze the inward perspective of the religious subject.

The category of religious experience not only brings a methodological advantage, but it also corresponds to a deep conviction of modernity, namely, that we cannot conceive of the world in any mode other than that of our subjective perspectives. Personal experience is our window to the world.

Religious Experience as a Reference to Transcendence

The classical references from Schleiermacher to Otto and James have developed a variety of analytical instruments to shed spotlight on religious experience. As with all kinds of experience, religious experience also consists in personal engagement and involvement, it is something that *occurs* and cannot be directly produced. It is here that we can locate the *differentia specifica* of

HOW TO DO TRANSCENDENCE WITH WORDS?

religious experience: what is special about religious experience is that it is the experience of a break-through. The framework of our daily life is in some meaningful sense *transcended*. There is a movement from the mundane to a supermundane dimension. The *differentia* of the religious experience is *neither* the intensity *nor* the object of the experience; the *differentia* of the religious experience is the reference to the dimension of transcendence. It is fascinating to see how carefully the classical authors try to handle the category of transcendence. When they analyze the self-expressions of religious experience, they do not immediately claim an ontological or metaphysical proof of the transcendent. James is the most cautious in his famous definition: religion "shall mean for us the feelings, acts, and experiences of individual men in their solitude, so far as they apprehend themselves to stand in relation to whatever they may consider the divine".[2] The German tradition is, for well-known reasons, more closely affiliated with a metaphysical approach. Building on Schleiermacher's analysis of the religious consciousness, Troeltsch argues that religion is the "product of an impact".[3] Otto criticizes Schleiermacher's concept in his famous *The Idea of the Holy*, because it seems to him to be too limited by the bounds of human subjectivity. For Otto, the religious feelings represented in consciousness are a subjective "concomitant and effect", but basically they make "indubitably immediate and primary reference to an object outside the self".[4] Otto calls this the feeling of the numinous.[5] Although Troeltsch and Otto go further in their description of transcendence, we cannot call them pure realists. What they say in their initial approach is only that religious experiences are experiences which force the persons who have them to use the category of transcendence in their expression of the experience.

This short foray into classical concepts of religious experience allows us to arrive at an interim result. The category of religious experience leads us to a better understanding of what basically happens in religion. Religious expressions are neither projections nor simple reflections, nor idolatrous symbolizations of a divine reality. They are a special kind of human reaction and construction

---

2 William James, *The Varieties of Religious Experience: A Study in Human Nature* (Mineola, NY: Dover Publications, 2002), 31.

3 "Erzeugnis einer Einwirkung". Ernst Troeltsch, "Die Selbständigkeit der Religion", in *Kritische Gesamtausgabe*, vol. 1, ed. Christian Albrecht (Berlin: De Gruyter, 2009), 359–535 (428), my translation.

4 Rudolf Otto, *The Idea of the Holy: An Inquiry into the Non-Rational Factor in the Idea of the Divine and Its Relation to the Rational*, trans. John W. Harvey (Oxford: Oxford University Press, 1969), 10.

5 See ibid., 11.

which attempts to express particular events and experiences. The reference to transcendence is the central element of religious experience. The subject of religious experience makes a reference to transcendence. Transcendence is a *result* of the interpretation of religious experience; transcendence is a mode of articulation of religious experience.

Experience and Interpretation

To conceive of transcendence as a result of interpretation leads us immediately into the eye of the storm. Where do the articulations with reference to a transcendent dimension come from? In earlier discussions we might find a repetition of the radical dilemma between religion as an answer and religion as an illusion. We could assume that it is the event which produces the articulation; religious experience would then be the result of something like an epiphany and, according to this model, its expression would be a necessary consequence.

In opposition to this simple impression-expression model of experience we find a radical culturalism, according to which there is no pre-linguistic event or experience: everything we experience is formed by cultural signs such as language. As far as I can see, no one sides with either extreme of this radical opposition in the current debate on experience and religious experience. There is no pure event, no pure pre-linguistic act without any interpretation, and there is no interpretation without any encounter with something. So the question is how experience and interpretation work together. How does the experience influence the interpretation, and how does the interpretation form the experience?

A Theory of Articulation

Here it may be useful to consult contemporary theories of the articulation of human expressions. One of the most inspiring theories in the German context can be found in the work of philosopher Matthias Jung.[6] His claim is that

---

6   See Matthias Jung, *Der bewusste Ausdruck: Anthropologie der Artikulation* (Berlin: De Gruyter, 2009). It is interesting to see that Jung started his academic career with a theory of religious experience and then came to the theory of articulation. See Matthias Jung, *Erfahrung und Religion: Grundzüge einer hermeneutisch-pragmatischen Religionstheorie* (München: Alber, 1999).

expression is an *anthropological constant*. Human beings tend to express themselves in order to handle their experiences in relation to other human beings. Any form of expression has its starting point in inward consciousness, and expression is just the articulation of what someone is experiencing. We accompany everything we experience with a 'film of words' in ourselves, so to speak, a running commentary, but our feelings are also a constant commentary on our experiences. Only in a second step, expression goes outwards, in verbal and non-verbal communication. It is as banal as it is interesting that human beings must learn to articulate themselves. Language is the most evident example. This is one of the strongest arguments against any idea of an immediate, pre-linguistic experience. Articulation is a part of a complicated process of cultural education and formation which is the result of a long process of interactions between the inward mind and the outward world. The fifty words for snow in Greenland are an excellent example of this interaction.

Transcendence – Toward a Mediated Realism

The Greenlanders help us slip between the horns of the dilemma between experience and interpretation with regard to religious experience. Religious experience is, as I have argued, characterized by its reference to transcendence. This reference is the result of a long cultural evolution in which human beings built up different modes of expressing their experiences of something that goes beyond their daily experiences and opens the horizon to a dimension interpreted by them under the category of transcendence. And the variety of these expressions increases the possibilities of representing these experiences in the human mind. This circular model of religious experience and interpretation is based on what we might call an 'indirect realism' (*vermittelter Realismus*) regarding transcendence. It occupies a middle ground between the two extremes of immediate realism and culturalism. Indirect or, phrased differently, mediated realism argues that we do transcendence via procedures of interpretation, but that we do so because something in the experience of the world activates a long cultural and religious history of expressions of transcendence.

Transcendence and Words: The Plurality of Religious Expressions

The modes to express our experiences of transcendence are inconceivably diverse. We should distinguish psychological and anthropological perspectives on the one hand, and cultural and historical perspectives on the other. If we trace the history of both perspectives, we end up bringing together the psychological tradition – culminating in James – with the continental tradition of the history of religion.

With respect to psychology, we can distinguish between reason and feeling as different modes of representing transcendence in the human mind. From simple words to the cathedrals of religious thought, we can find modes of cognitive articulation of religious experience. But this is, of course, not the only mode of religious expression. Actions such as religious rituals also express religious experiences in performances. More recent discussions have emphasized the importance of religious feelings. Feeling produces an evaluative representation in the human mind.[7] Instead of merely providing an objective description, this kind of symbolization emphasizes the importance of that which is experienced *for* the subject; it accentuates how the subject itself is engaged with the world. Hence, religious feelings, such as gratitude, humility and penitence, articulate the centrality and the consequences of the religious experience for the subject.

With respect to history, we can observe the cultural context, the development and the variety of cultural forms which religious experience uses to express itself. Art, architecture, music and literature might all be ways of expressing religious experience. Thus, we can say that we do transcendence with words, but not only with words. Human beings use a complex variety of expressions. Reason and feeling are the most important vehicles for expression, and they also employ a multitude of cultural forms to express themselves.

The Order of Plurality: "Nothing is ever lost" (Robert Bellah)

This immense plurality of religious expressions raises the question of how these modes of articulations are related. The prominent models at the beginning of the modern pursuit of religious studies were largely hierarchical. Georg W. F. Hegel's philosophy of religion is an impressive example of considering religion as a development in both psychological and historical terms. With respect to psychology, he describes the evolution of religion in the human mind from feeling as the lowest, imagination as the middle, and conceptual articulation as the highest form. With respect to history, he attributes these forms to concrete religions like Greek religion, Judaism, Buddhism and Islam, and considers Christianity as the most sophisticated in terms of its

---

7 See Sabine A. Döring, *Philosophie der Gefühle* (Frankfurt am Main: Suhrkamp, 2009), 14.

HOW TO DO TRANSCENDENCE WITH WORDS?

conceptual articulation and therefore as the highest form in the history of religion. In contemporary debates on religion, Hegel is not particularly well-received. His systematic thought and also his metaphysical theory of the world and the human mind as forms of the self-realization of the absolute spirit are considered somewhat out of fashion. His Eurocentric preference is against all rules of political correctness. Nevertheless, his claim of a systematic order of religious articulations still presents a great challenge for us today.[8]

That there is a variety of religious expressions for religious experiences goes without saying; the question is, how do they come together? I consider Robert Bellah's fruitful but unfortunately final book, *Religion in Human Evolution*, to be an impressive attempt to accept the challenge which Hegel brought into the contemporary thinking on religion. The book is the sum of Bellah's life work, full of inspiring nuggets. I would like to summarize his striking statement "Nothing is ever lost".[9] Bellah concludes his discussion by considering the idea that there is a hierarchy of articulate modes of religious experience. According to Bellah, approaching transcendence means understanding the variety of religious expressions not as a hierarchy but as a network of articulations which all attempt to interpret religious experience. To comprehend fully what religious experience calls 'transcendence' we have to complete the variety of articulations. Bellah has used this idea to analyze the ancient religions up to the axial ages in a fascinating manner. I would like to carry this approach into a theological analysis of Christianity.[10]

The Christian Universe of Articulations: The Program of a Cultural History of Christianity

As with all religions, Christianity uses an immense variety of religious expressions to articulate the central experience of what Christianity actually means: the break-through of divine transcendence into the world of common experience. In order to understand the Christian concept of transcendence, we have

---

8   See Georg W. F. Hegel, *Phänomenologie des Geistes*, Werke 3, ed. Eva Moldenhauer and Karl M. Michel (Frankfurt am Main: Suhrkamp, 1998), 495–574; Georg W. F. Hegel, *Vorlesungen über die Philosophie der Religion I–II*, Werke 16–17, ed. Eva Moldenhauer and Karl M. Michel (Frankfurt am Main: Suhrkamp, 1986).

9   Robert N. Bellah, *Religion in Human Evolution: From the Paleolithic to the Axial Age* (Cambridge, MA: Harvard University Press, 2011), 13; 267; 284; 489; 501.

10   For the following see Jörg Lauster, *Die Verzauberung der Welt: Eine Kulturgeschichte des Christentums* (Munich: Beck, 2014).

to analyze the sum of its various articulations. First, the biblical writings alone represent a universe of religious expressions with narrative, poetic and also – if we think of Paul's letters – conceptual interpretations of transcendence. And the fact that the first Christians accepted not only one but four gospels underlines the multiple approaches to transcendence. Second, the rise of Christian theology in ancient and medieval times is the result of various conceptual interactions with ancient philosophy. Christian theologians are always at the same time the heirs of Plato and Aristotle. Among Protestants the bashing of scholastic theology is a common sport – an unjustified cliché. The scholastic's endeavor to conceive of transcendence with the logical power of rational concepts deserves our admiration even today. A third classical form of Christian expression is the liturgy, a kind of enacting representation of the sacred. These expressions were embodied in institutions with a special organization of their communal life. These common forms alone demonstrate the broad framework necessary for religious articulation.

It is not only in the Bible, the dogmatic tradition, the liturgy, and the traditional institutions, where we find adequate expressions of religious experience. Since its very beginning, Christianity has also employed iconic and musical modes of articulation. I would not go as far as Marshall McLuhan in his famous statement that "the medium is the message",[11] but Christianity surely employs various forms of media in its transmission of religious experience. It can make use of the advantages of each medium. Images fulfill a deep religious desire of concrete visualization of the sacred – against all the theological criticisms of the iconoclastic tradition. It is not a coincidence that the rise of Western art took place during the Renaissance when Francesco Petrarca and others discovered the power of the subject. From Giotto to Michelangelo, visual art is full of attempts to conceive of the sacred so concretely that it can produce a real experience in the spectators. One could call to mind the extraordinary success of Giotto's crucifix in the church of Santa Maria Novella in Florence. Never before had the Florentines seen the suffering of Christ in such a realistic representation. Alternatively, one could consider Michelangelo's Pietà, which we can admire today in the St. Peter's Basilica. It made the young artist famous overnight with its perfect iconic symbolization of charity. While art enables the religious imagination, music addresses the emotions and represents the invisible and the ineffable dimension of transcendence. The discussion in the nineteenth century on "absolute music" was about the interesting question of whether music is the most appropriate medium to represent

---

11   Marshall McLuhan, *Understanding Media: The Extensions of Man* (Cambridge, MA: MIT Press, 1964), 7–21.

transcendence.[12] Finally, we may add literature as a medium of religious articulation. It is an amazing fact that the modern novel was born under the English Dissenters. John Bunyan's *Pilgrim's Process* and Daniel Defoe's *Robinson Crusoe* are impressive examples of the power of literature as a form of religious articulation. Even if the English puritans were skeptical of all forms of fiction, the novel brought immense advantages in describing inward religious feelings; it can express more precisely what individuals actually think and feel. For example, the Protestant esteem of the Bible is, dogmatically speaking, a very abstract thing. If one reads what happens to Robinson Crusoe after he brought a Bible, which he found in the wreckage, to his island, one understands why Protestants admire the Bible. Robinson takes the words of the Bible as words spoken by a divine authority directly into his life, full of the power of orientation, encouragement and consolation. I cannot imagine a better description of the Protestant spirituality of the Bible than in Robinson Crusoe. Literature has the capacity to bring religious articulations very close to individual life-experience, offering interpretations of what happens to us. In a certain sense it is still valid: we admire good books and good authors because they can express our own experiences in a deeper way and can offer us a broader range of interpretations of life.

In sum, Christianity expresses and transmits the experience of transcendence through the evolution of various forms. It makes no sense to create a hierarchy. Why should we attempt to choose between Thomas Aquinas and Wolfgang Amadeus Mozart, or between Michelangelo and Daniel Defoe as the only and exact articulation of the heart of the Christian experience? What counts is the interaction between the forms, the ways in which they make use of their own means of expression to compensate for the lack in other means of expression. Art and music are no better than other means of expression. The best way to understand the Christian concept of transcendence is the program of the cultural history of Christianity.

Secularization as a Transformation of Religious Articulation

If we understand the necessary plurality of means of expression, we may also comprehend Christianity in the modern world in more detail and more depth. Recently, it has become a broad conviction that 'secularization' is a watchword

---

12   Carl Dahlhaus, *Die Idee der absoluten Musik* (Kassel: Bärenreiter, 1994). See also Mark Evan Bonds, *Absolute Music: The History of an Idea* (Oxford: Oxford University Press, 2014).

to assess this complex process.[13] I cannot enter into the immense discussion of this problem, but the program of a cultural history of Christianity enables us to conceive of secularization not simply as a loss of the importance of Christian articulations, but as a deep transformation in these articulations. It is a kind of tragic misunderstanding to identify Christianity only with the classical and somehow canonical forms of religious articulation in the Bible, dogma and liturgy. Both the Enlightenment and Romanticism are protest movements against this identification.

Take, for example, the essay by Scotsman Thomas Carlyle entitled "The State of German Literature",[14] which was full of admiration for German literature and philosophy. Together with Madame de Staël's book on Germany, it is one of the sources of the myth that Germany is a country of poets and philosophers, *Dichter* and *Denker*.[15] But Carlyle is more interesting for us in another respect. He gives one of the most impressive examples of the new self-awareness of literature as a mode of religious articulation:

> Literary Men are the appointed interpreters of this Divine Idea; a perpetual priesthood, we might say, standing forth, generation after generation, as the dispensers and living types of God's everlasting wisdom, to show it in their writings and actions, in such particular form as their own particular times require it in.[16]

Not the theologians, not the official priests – it is literary men who are the new priesthood with their capacity to express and to interpret religious experience in a more adequate manner. The cultural history of the nineteenth century is full of examples in which artists, musicians or writers attempted to offer a deeper and broader articulation of religious experience. So what is often simply called 'secularization' is, from a certain point of view, something which regards the problem of articulation as at least a process of three steps. First, we can observe the emancipation from the traditional modes of articulation. The biblical, dogmatic and liturgical expressions are no longer the only acceptable modes of expression. From Caspar David Friedrich through Ludwig van Beethoven to Thomas Carlyle we can find supporters of this process. The

---

13   See Hans Joas and Klaus Wiegandt (eds), *Secularization and the World Religions*, trans. Alex Skinner (Liverpool: Liverpool University Press, 2009).

14   See Thomas Carlyle, "The State of German Literature", in *Complete Works*, vol. 13 (New York: John B. Alden, 1901), 26–84.

15   See Germaine de Staël, *De l'Allemagne* (Paris: Charpentier, 1844).

16   Thomas Carlyle, "The State of German Literature", 56–57.

second step is emancipation not only from Bible, dogma and liturgy but from Christian expressions altogether. But these emancipated forms of articulation are still religious, they only attempt to conceive of transcendence with new concepts. Their background is apophatic theology. Transcendence should be more than only one religious tradition can express. Modern art and literature are full of these religious hints which we might call secular epiphanies. Only at the third step can we observe the radical denial of any transcendent dimension – with sometimes tragic and banal consequences for contemporary art and literature, but this would be a topic for another contribution.

Interaction of Articulations: Dancing Plastic Bags

All these modes interact with each other. I would like to give one example. In the film *American Beauty*, Sam Mendes shows us the famous scene of a plastic bag dancing in the wind. For about three minutes one sees only the dance. It is a clip filmed by a teenager who presents his film to his girlfriend. He introduces the clip in the following terms:

> Do you want to see the most beautiful thing I ever filmed? It was one of those days when it's a minute away from snowing. And there's this electricity in the air, you can almost hear it, right? And this bag was just...dancing with me...like a little kid begging me to play with it. For fifteen minutes. That's the day I realized that there was this entire life behind things, and this incredibly benevolent force that wanted me to know there was no reason to be afraid. Ever. Video is a poor excuse, I know. But it helps me remember...I need to remember...Sometimes there's so much beauty in the world...I feel like I can't take it...and my heart is just going to cave in.

This comment is evidently full of religious hints, "benevolent force", "no reason to be afraid", "to cave in". Such forms of articulation are improbable, even impossible, without any interaction with the classical expressions of religious traditions, in this case especially the mystical tradition. That does not mean that the teenager must have read Meister Eckhart before watching the dance of the plastic bag; it means only that he has to live in cultural contexts which still provide him with articulations for the experience of transcendence. This enables him to interpret the dance of the plastic bag. His articulation provides a concrete example of how we might experience what Christian doctrine calls 'creation' and what the content of the religious feeling of cosmic gratitude and thankfulness might look like. That does not mean that we should rewrite our dogmatic tradition, inserting a chapter on plastic bags in the tracts on the doctrine of creation. The interaction between the forms of articulation is a process of reciprocal compensation and supplementation.

The Limits of Religious Articulation

This example leads us back to our original question of the interaction between experience and interpretation. Millions of people have seen plastic bags dancing in the wind, but only a few tend to interpret them as an epiphany of a benevolent force in the world. When I talk about this, I always have in mind a colleague of mine, a philosopher who is a famous expert on the atheistic tradition. He loves opera, and when he reports from his most recent visit to the opera house, his description of the experience sounds to me very close to that what I would call a religious experience or at least an experience where the category of transcendence would assist us to understand what happened. My colleague, however, categorically denies all references to transcendence or – even worse for him – to a religious experience. But at least we can discuss these experiences and we can learn more adequate or more appropriate modes of description from each other – which is not nothing. But we must accept our limits. There is no way to prove the necessity of a religious interpretation of experience. It is difficult to accept this limit. This is one reason why religions tend to be violent.

The Plausibility of Religious Articulation: The Task of Hermeneutics

I finally come to the task of hermeneutics. The discipline of hermeneutics has an interesting story over the previous two centuries. In the nineteenth century hermeneuts served as a priesthood of interpretation. They claimed that they could deeply empathize with the expressions of other persons and other epochs, that they could understand authors better than they understood themselves. They could endow every incident, every event and every story with a meaning like ketchup to chips. So the revolt against interpretation in the second half of the twentieth century is quite easy to understand. But we should not throw the baby out with the bathwater. Understanding the nineteenth-century attitude toward hermeneutics as a descriptive and analytical theory of

HOW TO DO TRANSCENDENCE WITH WORDS?

experience and interpretation enables us to understand religious experience and the interaction between experience and interpretation. Hermeneutics is an analytical theory of what happens in religious experience.[17]

To explain this interaction, we must start with a point which is far away from the task of hermeneutics; it is a rather banal observation. The possibility of a religious interpretation is necessarily linked to the existence of forms of religious articulation. We can see what this tautology means in parts of Eastern Europe where for over a generation communist governments tried to suppress all forms of religious articulation. If religious experience represents the interaction between experience and interpretation, we extinguish all reference to transcendence when we extinguish the forms of articulation of the transcendent. Religious education and the public presence of religion are necessary conditions for religious experience. As children in Greenland have to learn fifty words for snow to enjoy a rich experience of snow, so too must our children learn the plurality of religious articulations to create a deeper experience of their lives and the world. According to the program of a cultural history of Christianity, this means not only the classical articulations but also other forms in art, music and literature, and it also means a profound interest in so-called 'secular epiphanies'.

The task of hermeneutics is to reveal the meaning of these articulations and – importantly – to discover the limits of meaning. A theological hermeneutics can attempt to explain a word of the gospel, the dogma of Chalcedon, a painting of Michelangelo, Johann Sebastian Bach's Passion of St. Matthew or a poem by Emily Dickinson, but all these explanations must make clear that the gospel, the dogma, the Michelangelo painting, the Bach piece and the Dickinson poem expressed more than we can express with our words. The dimension of the ineffable, the emotive sphere, is an important aspect of all religious articulations. So hermeneutical explanation begins a process of inward and complex interpretation, but it does not bring it to an end. This entails that hermeneutics is no longer just a theory of translation. The so-called 'old' theological hermeneutics tried to translate religious expressions from former times into what they thought a modern human could conceive. Rudolf Bultmann's program of demythologization is a famous example. Now Bultmann has made a lot of important points and it is not so easy to get rid

---

17   See Jörg Lauster, *Religion als Lebensdeutung: Theologische Hermeneutik heute* (Darmstadt: Wissenschaftliche Buchgesellschaft, 2005), 9–30.

of his program,[18] but from Bellah and others we have learned that all kinds of religious expressions fulfill a certain function in the system of religious articulation.

This leads us to the special task of hermeneutics. Bellah's "Nothing is ever lost" brings a risk with it. Are all religious articulations equal and equally helpful in interpreting experience? George Steiner wrote in his fascinating "Ten (Possible) Reasons for the Sadness of Thought" that we have no way to discern the religious importance of the rites of a Voodoo-priest from the writings of Thomas Aquinas.[19] I would not agree, but I know that this is a delicate point. It is not only that the 'Political Correctness Police' are watching, it is also the deeper problem of all kinds of plurality. The classical expressions of Bible, dogma and liturgy have a traditional privilege. Opening the door to a cultural universe of expressions raises the importance of an evaluative system – an evaluative system does not mean a hierarchy. An important criterion for the evaluation of religious expressions comes from the religious experience itself. Experiencing transcendence produces acts of interpretation which, according to the traditions of apophatic and cataphatic theology, combine what we can say and what we cannot say. The best interpretations of the experience of transcendence contain in themselves the limits of their own interpretation, they produce the attitude that we can say this, but that there is much more that we cannot articulate and yet is also unspeakably present in our minds.

Finally, we reach arguments for the plausibility of religious interpretations of experience. The main task of hermeneutics is to argue that there are good reasons to give a religious interpretation to certain constellations of experience. Good reasons are reasons for an interpretation which provide a broader and deeper understanding of that which is experienced. Arguing with the spectator of the dance of the plastic bag or with my philosopher colleague who loves music, we might explain that 'doing transcendence' helps us to understand the meaning of the moment in more depth and in more detail, and that this could create an attitude and life-orientation which is open to the transcendent dimension of our world and our life. This is, of course, not a proof, not an irresistible argument, but it is a good reason for a religious interpretation – and that is much more than nothing.

---

18   See Jörg Lauster, "Das Programm 'Religion als Lebensdeutung' und das Erbe Rudolf Bultmanns", in *Hermeneutische Theologie – heute?*, ed. Ingolf U. Dalferth, Pierre Bühler and Andreas Hunziker (Tübingen: Mohr Siebeck, 2013), 101–116.

19   George Steiner, "Ten (Possible) Reasons for the Sadness of Thought", *Salmagundi* 146/147 (2005), 3–32 (31).

Literature

Bellah, Robert N., *Religion in Human Evolution: From the Paleolithic to the Axial Age* (Cambridge, MA: Harvard University Press, 2011).

Bonds, Mark Evan, *Absolute Music: The History of an Idea* (Oxford: Oxford University Press, 2014).

Carlyle, Thomas, "The State of German Literature", in *Complete Works*, vol. 13 (New York: John B. Alden, 1901), 26–84.

Dahlhaus, Carl, *Die Idee der absoluten Musik* (Kassel: Bärenreiter, 1994).

de Staël, Germaine, *De l'Allemagne* (Paris: Charpentier, 1844).

Döring, Sabine A., *Philosophie der Gefühle* (Frankfurt am Main: Suhrkamp, 2009).

Hegel, Georg W. F., *Phänomenologie des Geistes*, Werke 3, ed. Eva Moldenhauer and Karl M. Michel (Frankfurt am Main: Suhrkamp, 1998).

Hegel, Georg W. F., *Vorlesungen über die Philosophie der Religion I–II*, Werke 16–17, ed. Eva Moldenhauer and Karl M. Michel (Frankfurt am Main: Suhrkamp, 1986).

James, William, *The Varieties of Religious Experience: A Study in Human Nature* (Mineola, NY: Dover Publications, 2002).

Joas, Hans, and Klaus Wiegandt (eds), *Secularization and the World Religions*, trans. Alex Skinner (Liverpool: Liverpool University Press, 2009).

Jung, Matthias, *Der bewusste Ausdruck: Anthropologie der Artikulation* (Berlin: De Gruyter, 2009).

Jung, Matthias, *Erfahrung und Religion: Grundzüge einer hermeneutisch-pragmatischen Religionstheorie* (München: Alber, 1999).

Lauster, Jörg, "Das Programm 'Religion als Lebensdeutung' und das Erbe Rudolf Bultmanns", in *Hermeneutische Theologie – heute?*, ed. Ingolf U. Dalferth, Pierre Bühler and Andreas Hunziker (Tübingen: Mohr Siebeck, 2013), 101–116.

Lauster, Jörg, *Die Verzauberung der Welt: Eine Kulturgeschichte des Christentums* (Munich: Beck, 2014).

Lauster, Jörg, *Religion als Lebensdeutung: Theologische Hermeneutik heute* (Darmstadt: Wissenschaftliche Buchgesellschaft, 2005).

McLuhan, Marshall, *Understanding Media: The Extensions of Man* (Cambridge, MA: MIT Press, 1964).

Otto, Rudolf, *The Idea of the Holy: An Inquiry into the Non-Rational Factor in the Idea of the Divine and Its Relation to the Rational*, trans. John W. Harvey (Oxford: Oxford University Press, 1969).

Riesebrodt, Martin, *The Promise of Salvation: A Theory of Religion*, trans. Stephen Rendall (Chicago: University of Chicago Press, 2012).

Steiner, George, "Ten (Possible) Reasons for the Sadness of Thought", Salmagundi 146/147 (2005), 3–32.

Troeltsch, Ernst, "Die Selbständigkeit der Religion", in *Kritische Gesamtausgabe*, vol. 1, ed. Christian Albrecht (Berlin: De Gruyter, 2009), 359–535.

CHAPTER 2

Modern Trials and Tests of 'Experience': Plastic Commonplace and Managed Exception

Yvonne Sherwood

Everything depends on the register and sedimented histories of a word and the particular freedoms that the word permits. The obligatory ritual dictionary trawl gives as substitutes for 'experience', 'incident', 'event', 'test', 'trial', 'exploit', 'encounter', 'happening', 'coming into contact with', 'running into', 'being faced with' or 'being forced to contend with'. But the contributions to this compilation would read differently had the conversation been staged as 'religious incidents', 'religious tests', 'religious trials', 'contacts with the religious', 'religious happenings', 'religious encounters' or 'religious events'. Unlike these other terms, experience has the *kudos* of being a fundamental modern concept. It belongs to modernity; it comes from and with modernity. As a modern commonplace, experience benefits from a certain self-evidence. Experience has a close relationship to the empirical. Experience is equally at home in, and traffics between, the religious and the scientific, and the religious and the secular. It even promises something of a bridge, or ferry service, between these isolated domains. Derived from Latin *experientia*, 'trial, proof or experiment', experience has very respectable family ties to empiricism and the scientific experiment – which were not born, of course, out on the pure island of 'the secular'. Aristotelianism, Thomism, and the nominalist emphasis on *haecceitas* all fed into the turn to experience. For example, the belief that phenomena should be described in their distinct particularity according to the evidence of the senses, led sixteenth century Franciscan missionaries to produce startlingly proto-modern ethnographies of the New World.[1]

---

1 See for example the little-known work of Bernardino de Sahagún, *General History of the Things of New Spain: Florentine Codex*, trans. Arthur J. O. Anderson and Charles E. Dibble, 13 vols (Salt Lake City: University of Utah, 1950–1982), as discussed in Yvonne Sherwood, "Prophetic Postcolonialism: Performing the Disaster of the Spanish Conquest on the Stage of Jeremiah", in *Congress Volume 2013: 21st Congress of the International Organisation for the Study of the Old Testament*, ed. Christl Maier (Leiden: Brill, 2014), 300–332.

MODERN TRIALS AND TESTS OF 'EXPERIENCE' 31

It is a commonplace – voiced by, among others, Hans-Georg Gadamer, Peter Fenves and Martin Jay – that experience is one of modernity's most popular, 'potent', 'auratic' and 'obscure' keywords.[2] I want to explore in a little more detail why this is the case. The verdict usually goes little further than the observation that 'obscurity' somehow contributes to the cult, myth or idolatry of experience. Fenves suggests that the word operates rather like 'freedom'.[3] But I think that 'experience' is differently potent, and differently free – which is to say differently vague. The success of freedom relies on its operation as the quintessential modern virtue, to be invoked in all contexts and on all occasions. In contrast, experience is so essential and successful because it has been used to negotiate – which is also to say fudge – the fundamental split between the subject and the object that defines the modern age.

Experience and the Factish

The time of modernity is the time when 'man frees himself to himself'; the time when the base ground of metaphysics, that which-lies-before, the *hypokeimenon* or *subiectum*, is relocated to the subject as I. Subjectivism finds its corollary in objectivism and the "reciprocal conditioning of one by the other" defines the modern age.[4] Henceforth modern thinkers will find themselves caught between discovery and invention; passivity and agency; the given and the constructed/projected/man-made. Bruno Latour takes us to the heart of the man-made conflict by minting the amalgam the *factish*: the combination of the fact and the fetish. In his *On the Modern Cult of the Factish Gods* (a pun on Voltaire's friend's, President Charles des Brosses's, *On the Cult of the Fetishistic Gods* of 1760) Latour makes the term 'factish' to invoke the strange symmetry between the logic of the fact and fetish. This symmetry is more than hinted at in the French *le fait*, which means both 'what nobody has fabricated' and 'what somebody has fabricated': the manufactured thing.[5] Landing on the Gold Coast in Guinea, the Portuguese coined the term *fetish* to describe

---

2   Martin Jay, *Songs of Experience: Modern American and European Variations on a Universal Theme* (Berkeley, CA: University of California Press, 2006), 1–2.
3   Peter Fenves, "Foreword: From Empiricism to the Experience of Freedom", in Jean-Luc Nancy, *The Experience of Freedom* (Stanford, CA: Stanford University Press, 1993), xiii–xxxi.
4   Martin Heidegger, *The Question Concerning Technology and Other Essays*, trans. William Lovitt (New York: Harper Touchstone, 1977), 128.
5   Bruno Latour, *On the Modern Cult of the Factish Gods* (Durham, NC: Duke University Press, 2011).

the materially-manufactured gods that they encountered, and subjected their creators to a typically modern interrogation scene.[6] Are these gods, or are they works of your own hands? Did you build it, or is it real? "Stunned silence", says Latour from the indigenous peoples "who failed to see any contradiction", having not yet developed agile modern brains.[7] The modern critical thinker is proud of himself. Having demolished the idols and the fetishes, he has set the stage for the apparition of the real. The revelation is that "only human action gives voice and power to objects".[8] "The fire that Prometheus had stolen from the gods" has been "stolen back from Prometheus himself by critical thinking. [Henceforth] fire would come from humans, and from humans alone".[9] But this is only the first round in the dialectic tussle:

> Sobered up, freed, de-alienated, the subject takes back the energy that used to belong to him and refuses to grant his imaginary constructions an autonomy that they can never again recapture. The work of denunciation does not stop here, however; it starts up again, but now in the other direction. The free and autonomous human subject boasts, a little too soon, that he is the primal cause of all his projections and manipulations. Fortunately, the critical thinker, who never sleeps, [now] reveals how determination works, beneath the illusion of freedom. The subject believes that he is free, while 'in reality' he is wholly controlled. In order to explain the determinations involved, we must take recourse to objective facts, revealed to us by the natural, human, or social sciences. The laws of biology, genetics, economics, society and language are going to put the speaking object, who believed himself to be master of his own deeds and acts, in his place.[10]

"Like an earnest lawyer who has to divide an estate where there is no will and no heir, the critical thinker never knows to whom he should restore the power that was mistakenly attributed to the fetishes".[11] We do not know quite where to put the power that has been displaced. We need both revelations (the brute

---

6   For another brilliant reflection on the aporiae of the fetish see Tomoko Masuzawa, "Troubles with Materiality: The Ghost of Fetishism in the Nineteenth Century", in *Religion: Beyond a Concept*, ed. Hent de Vries (New York: Fordham University Press, 2007), 647–667.

7   Latour, *On the Modern Cult of the Factish Gods*, 3.

8   Ibid., 9.

9   Ibid.

10 Ibid., 13.

11 Ibid., 10.

MODERN TRIALS AND TESTS OF 'EXPERIENCE' 33

fact and the projection) to be operative. We want to be protected from the nasty contradiction of the factish. So we divide the world into 'fairy-objects' on the one hand and 'fact-objects' on the other, so that the two counter-dramas of revelation do not collide. We put everything in which we do not believe in the list of fairy-objects. On this list goes religion and its even more dubious twin, superstition, but also (for example) fashion, ideology, mass media, popular culture. Into the filing cabinet of fact-objects or cause-objects, go economics, sociology, genetics, geography, neuroscience, and mechanics: causes and forces which genuinely exceed us, which exist. Aspects of the subject that are dear to us – responsibility, liberty, inventiveness, intentionality, and so forth – go on 'the credit side of the ledger'. Everything that we deem useless or artificial – mental states, affects, fantasies, and so forth – are chalked up as debt.

Experience – that pliable miraculous stuff – has proved so alluring and important in modernity because it allows us to move between fairy-objects and fact-objects, facts and fetishes. Experience serves as shorthand for the uneasy sense of moving between construction/projection and the given; subjecthood and subjection; passivity and agency. That beautifully flexible term 'experience' flits between subject and object, naming what is being experienced and the subjective process of experiencing. On the side of experimentation and fact-objects (experiential/experiments) experience promises the observation of the real, the object as such. This can be recorded by flesh-and-blood witnesses (kenotically emptied of all preconceptions) or, even more reliably, by objective instruments, precise and impartial prosthetic devices.[12] In *Infancy and History*, Giorgio Agamben observes how modernity "responds to loss of certainty by displacing experience as far as possible outside the individual: on to instruments and numbers".[13] But experience also, by definition, folds back self-reflexively into the subject. Intrinsic to the word experience is a sense of eluding perfect capture by even the best observers or observing instruments. An experience is not something that can be had vicariously. Experience "gestures towards precisely that which exceeds concepts and even language itself".[14] It stands as a marker of that which is so "ineffable and individual" (or so specific to a particular group) that it cannot be rendered in conventionally communicative terms to those on the outside.[15] Experience seems to segue naturally into the religious because it carries more than a hint of the ineffable

---

12 See Jay, *Songs of Experience*, 37.
13 Giorgio Agamben, *Infancy and History: The Destruction of Experience*, trans. Liz Heron (London: Verso, 1993), 17.
14 Jay, *Songs of Experience*, 5.
15 Ibid., 5.

(as Samuel Beckett liked to joke, that which cannot be 'effed'.) Experience supports the idea of insider and outsider; emic and etic. The inside is secreted, protected. The observer-outsider never gains complete access. The outsider is like the merkavah mystic, thwarted and tortured in her desire to access the inner circle of the divine palace; or the one who knocks on the door and waits (forever), knowing that she does not have the passcard of the god who sees all secrets and searches the inmost heart (see Jer 17.10; Heb 4.13). Experience functions like a secularized translation of the god of monotheism: inimitable, incomparable, unique.

Certain commonplace words operate like little conceptual drawers in which we store our sense of fundamental impasses, or contradictions, in shorthand. Problems to which philosophers and theorists devote book length studies are gestured to, in passing, in strangely plastic words. 'Experience' is a particularly revealing example. Ambitious in the extreme, it leaps between the active and the passive; the particular and the general; the individual and the universal; the subject and the supra-subject; the quotidian and the marvelous, the exception, the excess. Many scholars of religion, including Ann Taves, James Cox, Russell McCutcheon and Timothy Fitzgerald, have criticized traditional studies of religious experience for questing for the common core of the world religions, following a liberal ecumenical agenda.[16] But this is not just a unique problem for religion. The word experience has always ranged between the ephemeral happenings of singular life and universal truth. Experience dwells with this-ness, the particular, the exceptional, the singular subject – but also the supra-subject, the supra-individual (as both the transcendent *and* the collective).[17] Though it has its home in the subject in the modern sense, it names (in Martin Jay's telling phrase) an "encounter with otherness, whether human or not".[18] Where experience is, there is always an other, an outside: communal or divine. Experience is a game of twos; of alterity. Experience also knows itself by contrast. It is actualized by a whole host of opposites, including theory, dogma, theology – and innocence.[19] Experience is also, as Hans Joas puts it, "unchosen and yet voluntary".[20] It is rooted in the subject, but evokes pathos: that which

---

16   Craig Martin and Russell McCutcheon with Leslie Dorrough Smith (eds), *Religious Experience: A Reader* (London: Routledge, 2014).

17   See Hans Joas on the supra-individual and self-transcendence; for example in Joas, *The Genesis of Values*, trans. Gregory Moore (Cambridge: Polity Press, 2000), 1; 51.

18   Jay, *Songs of Experience*, 7.

19   See ibid., 6.

20   Joas, *The Genesis of Values*, 5. The English translation gives "ineligible and voluntary" which differs from the German "nicht wählbar und doch freiwillig", Hans Joas, *Die Entstehung der Werte* (Frankfurt: Suhrkamp, 2006), 16.

MODERN TRIALS AND TESTS OF 'EXPERIENCE'   35

happens, that which one suffers and endures, that which befalls one without being sought or desired. Experience bisects and exceeds the subject like the old word passion. It operates like a modern secular update of the term passion. Derived from Latin *passiōn-em* and Greek *pathos*, passion evokes the "fact or condition of being acted upon or affected by an external agency" (Oxford English Dictionary), but also that which originates inside, and spills outside, with a force gestured to by prefixes like 'out' or 'over'. Thus passion is an 'over-mastering' zeal or an 'out-reaching' of the mind.[21] This compilation would have had a very different flavor if it had been staged as an enquiry into 'religious passion'. But, like passion, experience carries a sense of exceeding *and* intensifying the subject – making us both more and less than ourselves.

Religious Experience as the Secular Rehabilitation of Religion

What is the relationship between religion and experience? Is religious experience a particular subset or species of experience: 'We all experience, and there are particular experiences that can be classified as religious'? Or is the term 'religious experience' a way of smoking out a residual religious element in this term 'experience', which has always been perceived as somewhat 'mystical', 'potent', 'auratic' and 'obscure'? Is there not an automatic and privileged association between religion and experience, given that we think of experience as an "encounter with otherness, whether human or not"?[22] Experience makes the subject both more and less than itself – and does so in a humdrum, workaday fashion. Similarly, in the same innocuous fashion, 'experience' resurrects and revivifies the old religious terms and ghosts, as if smuggling them back in through the back door.

In the traditional ways of playing the modern philosophical games of given-ness and projection, discovery and invention, religion has ended up in the place of the spectral and the un-real, as the fairy-object par excellence. How useful, then, to have the term 'religious experience' which is able to rehabilitate the religious in a way that all can acknowledge and access. To return to my opening point, if we were to get together to talk about 'religious encounters', 'religious happenings', 'contacts with the religious' or 'tests of the religious', we would instantly find ourselves at a gathering that was more sectarian and specialist.

---

21   I explore the deep ambiguities of passion further in Yvonne Sherwood, "Passion-Binding-Passion: sacrifice, masochism and the subject", in *Biblical Blaspheming: Trials of the Sacred for a Secular Age* (Cambridge: Cambridge University Press, 2012), 195–226.

22   Jay, *Songs of Experience*, 7.

These very different ways of phrasing the question are relatively dangerous in that they beg the question of the numinous, the dubious: the divinities that do not exist in modernity in the sense that they do not exist for all. Experience is more resilient than the gods because it is connected to the modern subject. Experience is a very handy strategy for thinking religion in terms that all can acknowledge. Because experience roots religion in the subject, it stands on the ground which all not only acknowledge, but also valorize.

Though the idea of experience pays its dues to that which exceeds the subject and changes the subject, it still belongs to the subject. It begins with and returns home to the subject. This relation to the subject is what gives religious experience credibility and solidity in an unevenly and debatably 'secularized' age. That there are experiences, religious experiences, and religious subjects, who speak of these experiences, is not just indisputable. It is part of the virtue of democracy – with its defining commitment to religious freedom – to *celebrate* these experiences. Religious experience does not simply rehabilitate the suspected 'religious'. As religious experience, the religious is re-sacralized. This is because in modernity sacrality has not disappeared, but been relocated to the human person, the subject. In late modernity, reverence has been earthed as respect.[23]

According to the traditional trailblazers in the phenomenology of religion such as Gerardus van der Leeuw, Joachim Wach, Mircea Eliade, Ninian Smart, and Rudolf Otto, the essence of religion lay in a unique form of experience of the sacred. The terminology was somewhat tautological ('the essence of religion is the religious') and deliberately designed to preserve the *sui generis* status of religion, but let us leave that problem to one side for now. The essence of religion was revealed in moments of hyper-experience: Moses removing his sandals before the burning bush; Paul divinely ambushed on the road to Damascus; the *mysterium tremendum et fascinans*.[24] Contra the popular myth, late modern democracies have not eliminated the 'sacred' and made all profane. They have relocated the boundary marker between the sacred and the profane. The Holy of Holies, the inner sanctum, is no longer the divine with which we might have encounter, but the inviolable core of the religious subject, marked off as worthy of reverence or respect.

---

23   On the secularization of reverence as respect, see further Sherwood, *Biblical Blaspheming*, 49–66.

24   I am referring, of course, to Otto's famous treatise on *Das Heilige: Über das Irrationale in der Idee des Göttlichen und sein Verhältnis zum Rationalen* of 1917. See Otto, *The Idea of the Holy*, trans. John W. Harvey (Oxford: Oxford University Press, 1968).

MODERN TRIALS AND TESTS OF 'EXPERIENCE'

The valorization of religious experience is related to the highlighting of religious identity as one of the core identities that citizens of modern democracies are charged to notice, cherish and respect. Essential to the idea of democracy is equal representation: the substitutability of one individual for another; the notion that we are all the same. But potentially this makes for a bland, faceless idea, or one that seems dismissive or cavalier in respect of our particular personhoods, reducing us all to one person, one vote. So, to counterbalance this, democracies use particular faces, groups, identities as signs of democracy's concern or investment in care. In the mechanics of democracy, an elected MP represents his/her constituents. In the *symbolism* of democracy, an iconically protected person or group represents the desire to give all people protection and respect. The modern democratic state represents the promise of a perfect inclusivity that will, one fine day, be perfectly realized. Since it can never be fully realized, the desire to protect every identity needs to be crudely and synecdochally represented in the interim. The good faith of a democracy is displayed in the protection of core identities: representatives of *religion, sexuality/gender* and *ethnicity* or race. Good democracies must make a show of listening, patiently and empathetically, to 'religious experience', 'women's experience', 'gay experience' – in all their manifestations – whether this is done in good or bad faith. One must hearken to the experience with all the attention that we once gave to hearing, recording, archiving, treasuring and interpreting the voice of the gods. And as with the words of the gods, one must not expect to gain easy access to the 'ineffable and individual' songs and canons of experience. One may hear and hear and not understand these experiences, which may well, and by definition, "exceed concepts and even language itself".[25] In our late modern understanding, experience – or certain marked experience – is given the same existential and political position as rights: inalienable, a personal possession, the secret of identity. "No one can take my experiences away from me".[26]

Experience is related to what sociologists term 'ascriptive identity', which functions as a distinctly modern twist in the concept of tolerance.[27] For early moderns like John Locke (who also played a major role in the turn to experience),[28] tolerance was necessary because man was, and should be, free to choose the form of his belief or unbelief. In this understanding 'man' was

---

25   Jay, *Songs of Experience*, 5.

26   Ibid., 7.

27   Wendy Brown, *Regulating Aversion: Tolerance in the Age of Identity and Empire* (Princeton, NJ: Princeton University Press, 2006).

28   Most famously in the *Essay Concerning Human Understanding* (1690).

seen as a universal creature, only contingently divided by language, culture, nation or religion. Late modern politics (or public management strategies) revolve around the idea of 'ascriptive identities': identities understood to be rooted in inner nature or manifested in external bodily attributes. The task is to manage core (intractable) differences: of sexuality, ethnicity, and religion.[29] As Wendy Brown has argued, we have witnessed a major shift "from a universal subject imagined to arrive at particular beliefs or values through revelation or deliberation to a particular subject (of sexuality, ethnicity, etc.) who is thought to have these beliefs or values by virtue of who he or she is".[30]

This has profoundly changed our understanding of religion and religious experience. In modernity, we talk about being or not being religious in a way that we would not talk about being or not being feminist or Marxist. The verb 'to be' here seems to have a certain power, a certain relation to essence. The habitually-used phrase 'deeply-held convictions' is used as automatically by vociferous opponents of religion such as Richard Dawkins or Christopher Hitchens as by religious representatives in the public realm. In modernity, Religion can never have the same weight as a term like Politics or History or Literature. Sometimes 'religious' is lighter than terms like 'historical' or 'political' or 'literary'; sometimes it is heavier. The particular role that religion has played in balancing out modernity means that the category 'religion' can never be of equal weight. In this case, in the politics of ascriptive identity, religion and religious experience prove to be heavier. Terms like 'political experience', 'historical experience', or 'literary experience' do not carry the same weight as 'religious experience'. They are not capable of being understood as of permanently marking the subject, or as going as deep as the ascriptive identity markers of ethnicity or sex.

Religion has become increasingly reified in modern 'secular' public discourse and accompanying legislation.[31] For the sake of public argument, religion is understood as defining or exceeding the individual, operating on him/her as an incontestable given that operates just like the intractable givens of sexuality or ethnicity/race. The UK Equality Act of 2010 offers the following series of *experientia* of religion, in the sense of legal trials or tests of religion. Religion is understood as 'belief', though the terms and conditions are

---

29   Brown, *Regulating Aversion*, 47.

30   Ibid., 46.

31   See for example Yvonne Sherwood, "On the Freedom of the Concepts of Religion and Belief" in *The Politics of Religious Freedom*, ed. Winnifred Fallers Sullivan, Elizabeth Shakman Hurd and Saba Mahmood (Chicago: University of Chicago Press, 2015), 29–44.

MODERN TRIALS AND TESTS OF 'EXPERIENCE'

transferrable to experience, as I will explain. In order to qualify the 'religion or belief', the 'religion or belief'

> must be genuinely held.
>
> must be a belief and not an opinion or view based on the present state of information available.
>
> must be a belief as to a weighty and substantial aspect of human life.
>
> must attain a certain level of cogency, seriousness, cohesion and importance.
>
> must be worthy of respect in a democratic society, not incompatible with human dignity and not in conflict with the fundamental rights of others.[32]

Belief is strangely weighty and weightless. It floats above knowledge or information or the verifiable. If it did not, it would not qualify as belief (or religion). But then, unlike a lifestyle 'choice' or a political 'opinion' or 'viewpoint', religion is not seen as something ephemeral, susceptible to change. Belief is the kind of thought that comes as if from outside, and takes to the deepest recesses of the inside. It seems it is the kind of thought that reaches the parts that other thoughts cannot reach. Compare the strange status of experience, and particularly religious experience, as 'voluntary and unchosen': a property of the subject that originates in that which exceeds or transcends the subject. Belief is a form of thought so strong that it appears that it has chosen us, rather than that we have chosen it.

'Experience' is a word that operates like 'belief'. Like belief, it sounds like an innocuous commonplace. It is not a neologism like 'deconstruction', 'governmentality' or 'subjectivization', provoking us and tempting us to reject a new piece of 'jargon'. We are all at home with experience. Experience is well bedded in. Religious experience and religious belief provide habitual placeholders for in-breaking transcendence. Within a 'secular' order, they give us normative and habitual names for encounters with the gods – which are by definition anything but normative. These encounters (or beliefs or experiences) are understood as a place of paradox and danger: volatile, voluntary and unchosen; absolutely deep and absolutely free.

Attempting to capture the free force that they have accommodated – or even invented – Western states impose trials to guard the entrance to the category 'religion'. In order to qualify for public reverence-respect and protection,

---

32 The Employment Equality (Religion or Belief) Regulations 2003, as incorporated into the Equality Act of 2010. See http://www.legislation.gov.uk/uksi/2003/1660/contents/made (accessed 17 December 2014).

the gods, the religions and those acknowledged to be 'religious' must confirm back to us the public liturgies of religious identity. A space in law is granted for the experience of the divine, provided that we can offer a reciprocal assurance that the true gods lead us only to do certain things and only speak from a particular kind of script. Note how in the trials of religious belief, the first four criteria create and unleash 'belief' as a floating vague force – and the fifth tries to squeeze the genie back into the bottle. Only if it is worthy of respect can religious belief (tautologically) be respected. Respect and respectability impose trials of ethics and aesthetics. A belief (or experience) will be admitted as valid if it does not assault the values of others; if it is not too specious, exotic, weird.

In order to enter the public realm experience, and above all religious experience, must be a managed category, like belief. But as Michael Oakeshott complains, "[e]xperience of all the words in the philosophic vocabulary is the most difficult to manage".[33] As a good philosopher of a particular kind, Oakeshott takes it upon himself to purge the ambiguities. Martin Jay, as intellectual historian and cultural critic, smiles at Oakeshott's lack of imagination and prefers to let the ambiguities run free. But freedom can be allowed free reign if one is dealing (as Jay is) with literature, antiquarian exotica, intellectual history as the cabinets of dead, stuffed ideas. For those who take on the headier task of negotiating between experience, particularly religious experience, and the modern state – or those responsible for presenting the public face of religion – it is imperative to think about the propriety of experience and to manage experience carefully.

William James's Managed Eccentricities

Consider, for example, the excruciatingly careful treatment of 'religious experience' by the founding father of the turn to religious experience, William James. Eschewing institutional religion as "dull habit", or "second-hand religion", James puts the spotlight on "peculiarities which are ordinarily classed as pathological".[34] In a gentle, careful assault on the *sui generis* status of religious experience, James demystifies these experiences as indeed pathological – while at the same time carefully managing and directing the response of his learned audience in Edinburgh, and taking exquisite care of the public face of

---

33   Michael Oakeshott, *Experience and Its Modes* (Cambridge: Cambridge University Press, 1933), 9; see Jay, *Songs of Experience*, 9.

34   William James, *The Varieties of Religious Experience: A Study in Human Nature* (London: Routledge, 2002), 27.

MODERN TRIALS AND TESTS OF 'EXPERIENCE' 41

religion and religious experience in the public realm. He piles on the reassurances. First, his own labors of demystification are mild compared to the 'nothing but' demystifications of 'medical materialism' that would attribute Paul's vision on the road to Damascus to a "discharging lesion of the occipital cortex", diagnose George Fox with a disordered colon, and deem Theresa of Avila a hysteric.[35] (James' own assessment of Paul would be that, like all who experience instantaneous conversion, he was a particular kind of subject whose "conscious fields" did not have a "hard rind of a margin that resists incursions from beyond it" allowing "leaks" or "incursions" from the highly developed subconscious field).[36] Second, origin is firmly separated from outcome and *telos* – and *telos* is far stronger. Like higher critics of the Bible, James exposes torment at the origin. As biblical scholars expose split sources and incongruities, so he finds, at the origin of religious authority, "borderland insanity, crankiness, insane temperament, loss of mental balance, psychopathic degeneration" – and, relatedly, "genius".[37] But just as the exposure of the (as he puts it) natural and existential conditions for the production of a Bible does not harm assessments of supernatural value, so the revelation of pathological origin does nothing to harm religious experience which is *known by its fruits*.

More specifically, the value of experience is proved by certain conditions, tests or proofs: *"immediate luminousness", "philosophical reasonableness", "moral helpfulness", "good consequential fruits for life"*, and *"serviceability for our needs"*.[38] Appealing to the robust mental health of his audience, James announces: "You must be ready now to judge the religious life by its results exclusively, and I shall assume that the bugaboo of morbid origin will scandalise you no more."[39] We should not speak disparagingly of "feverish fancies", since for "aught we know to the contrary 103 or 104 degrees fahrenheit might be a much more favourable temperature for truths to germinate and sprout in, than the more ordinary blood heat of 97 or 98 degrees".[40] If it were to fail the tests of 'immediate luminousness', 'philosophical reasonableness' and 'moral helpfulness' (and later in the book James more than hints that it would), Saint Theresa's theology could not be saved even if she were to exhibit the "nervous system of the placidest cow".[41] (Actually James's own assessment of Theresa

---

35   Ibid.
36   Ibid., 197.
37   Ibid., 27.
38   Ibid., 37; 39.
39   Ibid., 42.
40   Ibid., 21.
41   Ibid., 22.

might lead her to prefer the medical materialists, who would merely dismiss her as a hysteric. "In the main her idea of religion seems to have been that of an endless amatory flirtation ... between the devotee and the deity". The type of experience experienced by Theresa expels her beyond the pale of the 'human'. There is "absolutely no human use in her", or any "general human interest", "apart from helping younger nuns to go in this direction".)[42] Experientia or 'trials' of experience indeed.

Though James's study (and the very word experience) leads him to 'eccentricities and extremes', these are carefully chosen 'eccentricities and extremes' – which must and must not be "corrected and sobered down and pruned away".[43] He introduces awkward self-consciousness into the lecture hall:

> All of you are sitting with a certain constraint at this moment, and entirely without express consciousness of the fact, because of the influence of the occasion. If left alone in the room, each of you would probably involuntarily arrange himself, and make his attitude more 'free and easy'. But proprieties and their inhibitions snap if any great emotional excitement intervenes.[44]

We can imagine how this rhetorical gesture turned his audience's attention to the theatre of 'the lecture' and their role as gentleman audience in the prestigious Gifford Lectures on Natural Theology at the University of Edinburgh. I imagine them awkwardly wondering, whether or not to cross or uncross their legs – and also feeling, surely, a frisson of expectation: the promise of social conventions radically deranged and rearranged. But what comes next is not the anticipated carnival of deranged sociality. Instead James parades the most modest transgressions of the lines between public and private space. At the cry of 'Fire!' we might see, on the street, a woman in her nightie, or a 'dandy' with shaving foam on his face.[45] Presumably not even mortal danger would lure a gentleman out onto the street before he had washed the shaving foam from his face!

It turns out that saintliness's capacity or desire to disorder society is minimal – thanks be to god, or more accurately, thanks be to the proper definition of religion and its experiential core. Truly repugnant excesses, or

42   Ibid., 278.
43   Ibid., 48.
44   Ibid., 212.
45   Ibid., 212.

morbidities, are privatized. Expressions of intense theopathy, self-laceration and erotic encounters with god are all pathologies that turn in on the individual, without doing much damage to society- or politics-at-large. There is no trace of the kinds of 'overlordly' ones feared by Immanuel Kant: not a trace of those who, having been in a private tête-à-tête with God, think themselves monarch, Führer, messiah.[46] If the aim of the *Verwissenschaftlichung* ('scientization') of religion as a state-sponsored object of study was "to head off religious extremism" and turn "fundamentalists" into "liberals",[47] this is dramatically performed here, in this study of religious experience from which the millenarianists, mystagogues and messiahs have already disappeared. The social scandals produced by true saintliness are no more unnerving than a woman or a dandy slightly shamed in public – or the Quakers who, following the lead of George Fox, provoke controversy by refusing to doff their hats. These modest counter-cultural gestures can easily be rehabilitated as saintly opposition to the world of surfaces and sham.

I once attended a conference on religious experience in Oxford – the conference where this paper was presented. There were several intimations of personal experiences, but no-one appeared in their nighties or with shaving foam on their face. Experience was assumed to be that which was exceptional, personal: Diltheyan *Erlebnis* as event, occurrence, adventure. 'Religious experience' was certainly not understood as the accumulated experience of a trained practitioner: the kind of 'years of experience' that one presents on a curriculum vitae. And yet the instances of personal adventures were liturgically formalised. Perhaps the Oxford ambience – not unlike the aura of the Edinburgh Gifford Lectures – nudged participants to share experiences of synod, drinking merlot, and walking in the hills ...

Similarly, there is something rather narrow about James' canon and chronicles of 'religious experience'. His example of Fox crying "Wo to the Bloody City of Lichfield" and his vision of the streets running with blood might make one think of biblical prophets and apocalyptic. But James does not. James creates a corpus of largely nineteenth century testimonials as a surrogate

---

46 Immanuel Kant, "On a Newly Arisen Superior Tone in Philosophy", trans. Peter Fenves, in *Raising the Tone of Philosophy: Late Essays by Immanuel Kant, Transformative Critique by Jacques Derrida*, ed. Peter Fenves (Baltimore, ML: Johns Hopkins University Press, 1993), 51–82.

47 Wilfred Cantwell Smith, "The Study of Religion and the Study of the Bible", in *Rethinking Scripture: Essays from a Comparative Perspective*, ed. Miriam Levering (Albany: State University of New York Press, 1989), 18–28 (19); Michael C. Legaspi, *The Death of Scripture and the Rise of Biblical Studies* (Oxford: Oxford University Press, 2012), 38.

canon: a sampling of experience. But his book (in my edition, big, heavy and black, like a Bible) contains no visions of the heavenly chariot with all those wheels and beasts and eyes, no visions of "locusts... like horses equipped for battle... with lions teeth, human faces, women's hair, and crowns of gold... and stings in their scorpion tails that can harm people for precisely five months" (Rev. 9.7–11); no brutal murder of the whore of Babylon or the blood from the angel's winepress that forms a lake as high as a horse's bridle for up to two hundred miles (14.20; 17.16; 19.17–21). What is so scandalous about such examples is "der mystische Takt"[48] which scandalizes thinkers like Kant by turning the voice into *contact*, something one might touch: a beast, a mutant locust, a wheel full of eyes. There is something properly immaterial about canonized religious experiences. The turn to experience is a turn from the institution and the text to lived, embodied experience – *Erlebnis* – but the sphere of 'life' is highly circumscribed. There is no chance that Daniel Paul Schreber, who was busy writing his *Memoirs of My Nervous Illness* in the same years that James was delivering his Gifford Lectures, would make it onto the stage as a more mutant variety of religious experience. One suspects that James, who condemns the stories of the saints for being "encrusted with a heavy jewellry of anecdotes which are meant to be honorific, but are simply abgeschmackt and silly", would not have found much useful experience in the visions of John of Patmos, Ezekiel or Zechariah.[49] We can tolerate the *Mystagogein* who say that "they are in immediate and intuitive relation to the mystery",[50] provided that their accounts are given as penetrable biography, not encrypted codes; provided that they present their experience *qua* 'experience': experience being that which gestures towards that which is beyond concept and communication, without being so consumed by that beyond that the experiencer can only babble. We do not want to make it too difficult for ourselves to translate these experiences into the voice of reason *"that speaks equally in each and maintains the same language for all"*.[51] As Steven Shapin argues, truth and credibility have always been established by a certain "epistemological decorum".[52] Truth is a matter of aesthetics and society: a question of tone, voice, style. James articulates these experiences at perfect pitch. And while expecting less

---

48   Kant, "On a Newly Arisen Superior Tone in Philosophy", 62.

49   James, *The Varieties of Religious Experience*, 274.

50   Jacques Derrida, "Of an Apocalyptic Tone Recently Adopted in Philosophy", trans. John P. Leavey, *Oxford Literary Review* 6 (1984), 3–37 (9).

51   Derrida, "Of an Apocalyptic Tone", 12.

52   Steven Shapin, *A Social History of Truth: Civility and Science in Seventeenth-Century England* (Chicago: University of Chicago Press, 1994), 193.

of his sources (who by definition can commit minor transgressions against the gentlemanly social scene of truth) they are not permitted to scream, screech, wail, or retreat into aphasia or silence, like Zechariah, Ezekiel or John.

I am, of course, not pretending to be surprised that there is so little Bible in *The Varieties of Religious Experience*. With growing momentum since Friedrich Schleiermacher, experience/*Erlebnis* has been seen as a more authentic ground for religious belief than the increasingly problematic archives of doctrinal theology and the Bible. In raising the question of the textuality of experience, this compilation forces text and experience out of their habitual oppositional space. Other zones of the Humanities may imagine themselves to be staging a liberation from recent linguistic constructivism and "unearth[ing] experience from the thick sedimentary strata of language covering it".[53] But in Religious Studies, there is a much older pedigree to this story of the quest for emancipation from the prison house of the text. Religious Studies and the quest for religious experience was defined as a much-needed rebellion from Theology and Biblical Studies: those way-too-bookish disciplinary parents, obsessed with piling carefully finessed nuance around the Trinity, or patiently teasing out (as if with tweezers) the sedimented strata of a small square of biblical text.[54]

But without expecting biblical varieties to be included in James's new canons of experience, we can observe that the recorded and exegeted voices of experience come in at a very different frequency to transmissions of 'experience' in the Bible. The Hebrew Bible knows nothing of the modern subject. The media conditions and styles and tests of 'truth' are entirely different. The word 'experience' does not seem to fit. When prophets take up humiliating self-defeating postures (such as lying on one's side for hundreds of days and cooking over excrement), or complain with Jeremiah that they have been raped or abused by God, it does not seem quite right to say that they are having an experience or testifying to experience. The characters in the Bible are not subjects, but characters that shade into written characters. Ezekiel lies on his side and does crazy things with his hair and Isaiah makes a sign, and also has a son, called Maher Shalal Hash Baz ("The spoil speeds, the prey hastens") because in cultures where writing is regarded as a magical technology, and cannot be expected to attain to the status of anything so grandiose as a codex or a corpus, they are functioning as ciphers, living text. It would be as strange

---

53 Frank Ankersmit, *Sublime Historical Experience* (Stanford, CA: Stanford University Press, 2005), 14.

54 For a more detailed study of the agonistic relationship between 'Bible', 'Theology' and 'Religion', see Ward Blanton and Yvonne Sherwood, "Bible/Religion/Critique", in *Religion/Culture/Critique*, ed. Richard King (New York: Columbia University Press, forthcoming).

to think these scenes as centralized around 'their experience' as it would be to think that having a child in order to make that child signify 'disaster' is an abuse of her/his human rights.

Rather than create head-on conflict with the biblical-Christian corpus, James selects the much more common option in modernity, to evoke Bible-lite. Invoked as a distant foundation which has long relinquished most of its problematic textuality, the Bible as icon is made to conform to certain standards, standards arranged around the subject. For James, Job's typical slogan is "Though he slay me yet I will trust in him" (Job 13.15) and this expresses a proper religious attitude to be opposed to the stoicism of Marcus Aurelius.[55] There is no trace of the wild Job of the poetry who, in a visceral experience of in-breaking transcendence, rages against a God who hunts him like a lion (10.16); slashes open his kidneys (16.13); pours him out like milk and curdles him like cheese (10.10). The biblical Job is not a modern novelistic 'character', but a figure who/that dissolves into written characters, a test case in a cosmic experiment, a hypothetical 'what if...'. But for James a carefully filleted and thoroughly modernized Job stands for the essence of the true religious attitude. In a summary that might make us suspect that he is disciplining and managing the biblical Job, James announces:

> There must be something solemn, serious and tender about any attitude which we denominate religious. If glad, it must not grin or snicker; if sad, it must not scream or curse... The divine shall mean for us only such a primal reality as the individual feels compelled to respond to solemnly and gravely, and neither by a curse or a jest.[56]

The tests or trials of genuine experience are not just moral, but aesthetic, just like the legal criteria we examined earlier. Recall that to count as belief, a belief must attain a level of "cogency, seriousness, cohesion" (which rules out John of Patmos and the biblical prophets) and "must be a belief as to a weighty and substantial aspect of human life".

Or as James puts it, "all religious phenomena" must be subjected to the "golden mean".[57] This puts him in a paradoxical relation to his already carefully selected eccentricities and excesses. On the one hand, they provide the living experience and essence of religion which peters out into empty orthodoxy when the wellspring of inwardness runs dry. As soon as the singular

---

55 James, *The Varieties of Religious Experience*, 42.

56 Ibid., 39.

57 Ibid., 270; 272.

MODERN TRIALS AND TESTS OF 'EXPERIENCE'

becomes collective, it is in danger. Experience dissipates when it is passed from hand to hand and becomes second-hand. Experience is threatened when it is institutionalized and shared. "The basenesses so commonly charged to religion's account are thus, almost all of them, not chargeable at all to religion proper, but rather to religion's wicked partner, the spirit of corporate dominion."[58] A foundational religious experience must be so strong that it has the strength to found a movement. But the movement turns against it, in an auto-immune gesture, and destroys the energy from whence it came.

But James is also actively involved with the socialization and modification of experience, which he laments. Even though the recorded eccentricities are not always very scandalous, we still need to tone them down, test and sift them, to get to a more moderate and true religious core:

> Having the phenomenon of our study in its acutest possible form to start with, we can shade down as much as we please later. And if in these cases, repulsive as they are to our ordinary worldly way of judging, we find ourselves compelled to acknowledge religion's value and treat it with respect, it will have proved in some way its value for life at large. By subtracting and toning down extravagances we may thereupon proceed to trace the boundaries of *its legitimate sway*.[59]

The irony here is beautiful. The study of experience takes James into the zone of the exceptional, idiosyncratic and excessive. But even in a study such as this, exceptional acts and nominalist theologies are out of fashion – for humans and especially for gods. The kind of gods and subjects modernity needs are those who, of their own grace and volition, have decided to restrict their revolutionary whimsical powers and subject themselves to law: moral, social and 'natural' (or in James' words 'human'). James imposes this discipline, where the subjects have not imposed it on themselves. By "toning down extravagances", we can trace the "*boundaries*" of functional, legitimate, religion; or religion's *legitimate sway*. In practice, this involves setting up operational distinctions between, for example, what James calls "devoutness" (which is good) and "fanaticism", which is deviant excess, loyalty carried to a "convulsive extreme".[60] (Compare Kant's efforts to distinguish *Enthusiasmus* from *Schwärmerei*.)

Toning down extravagances also involves praising *moderate* praise. Though praise is by definition 'exaltation' and 'adoration', praise should stop short of

---

58   Ibid., 270–271.

59   Ibid., 48.

60   Ibid., 273.

excesses in which "vocabularies are exhausted and languages altered in the attempt to praise him enough".[61] No place here for glossolalia or speaking in tongues, or the testimony of Rabbi Ishmael that he has direct from the fiery angel Metatron, who is the transmogrified Enoch (now there is an experience!), written up, in cryptic notes, as the *Shiur Qomah*: the report of the astronomical dimensions of the divine body and screeds of divine-name-code churned out like computer code. True religion and the essence of true religious experience must be protected from the sectarian, the martyr and the zealot. Separating 'devoutness' from 'fanaticism' as one separates fact-objects and fairy-objects, James puts on the fanatical side of the ledger the aberrations where "death is looked on as gain if it attracts [the deity's] grateful notice" or where "the personal attitude of being his devotee becomes what one might almost call a new and exalted kind of professional speciality within the tribe".[62] Religious experience, bound to the subject, becomes a means for policing the proper boundaries of religion. I think of Kant's "police in the realm of the sciences [*die Polizei im Reiche der Wissenschaften*]".[63] It functions as a device for keeping the peace and keeping the tone. Religious experience, bound to the subject, becomes a way of prescribing the "kind of subjectivity that a secular culture authorizes, the practices it deems as truly (versus superficially) spiritual – the forms of religion that it will tolerate – and the relationship to history that it prescribes".[64]

Dying Gods

Though he becomes rather more circumspect when he gets closer to the Christian tradition, James is quite explicit about the fact that *we kill gods* (and dusty old records of moribund and morbid-excessive experiences related to those gods) and that *we should kill gods*. His narrative makes space not only for the observable phenomenon of loss of faith, but the perhaps even more observable phenomenon of the dying gods. James acknowledges the "numerous backslidings and relapses" in religious experience, even though he wants to affirm (if somewhat anxiously) that the most "striking conversions" are

---

61   Ibid., 273.

62   Ibid., 273.

63   Kant, "On a Newly Arisen Superior Tone in Philosophy" as discussed in Derrida, "Of an Apocalyptic Tone", 31.

64   Saba Mahmood, "Secularism, Hermeneutics, and Empire: The Politics of Islamic Reformations", *Public Culture* 18 (2006), 323–47 (328).

MODERN TRIALS AND TESTS OF 'EXPERIENCE'

"permanent" – or that at least "the persons who have passed through conversion, having once taken a stand for the religious life, tend to feel themselves identified with it, no matter how much their religious enthusiasm declines".[65] He compares the memory of an association held despite dwindling enthusiasm to a dying marriage, still manifesting the public face of marriage. The analogy undermines more strident ideas of religious identity promoted in public and legal discourse over a century later. Our contemporary static ideal of 'religious identity' is far more secure than James's account of religious experiences. James would not relapse as easily as we do into clichés of religious identity as permanently 'deep' and impervious to change.

Strangely, contemporary truisms about deeply held religious identities are more secure even than the gods, as understood by James. In his attempt to chart the 'mutations of theological opinion' James produces a striking inventory of the dying gods. I want to quote this remarkable passage at some length:

> Nothing is more striking than the secular alteration that goes on in the moral and religious tone of men, as their insight into nature and their social arrangements progressively develop. After an interval of a few generations the mental climate proves unfavourable to notions of the deity which at an earlier date were perfectly satisfactory: the older gods have fallen below the common secular level, and can no longer be believed in. Today a deity who should require bleeding sacrifices to placate him would be too sanguinary to be taken seriously. Even if powerful historical credentials were put forward in his favour, we would not look at them. Once, on the contrary, his cruel appetites were of themselves credentials. They positively recommended him to men's imaginations in ages when such coarse signs of power were respected and no others could be understood. Such deities were then worshiped because such fruits were relished.
>
> Doubtless historical accidents always played some part, but the original factor in fixing the figure of the gods must always have been psychological. The deity to whom the prophets, seers and devotees who founded the particular cult bore witness was worth something to them personally. They could use him. He guided their imagination, warranted their hopes, and controlled their will – or else they required him as a safeguard against the demon and a curber of other people's crimes. In any case, they chose him for the value of the fruits he seemed to them to yield. So soon

---

65   James, *The Varieties of Religious Experience*, 208.

as the fruits began to seem quite worthless; so soon as they conflicted with indispensable human ideals, or thwarted too extensively other values; so soon as they appeared childish, contemptible, or immoral when reflected on, the deity grew discredited, and was erelong neglected and forgotten. It was in this way that the Greek and Roman gods ceased to be believed in by educated pagans; it is thus that we ourselves judge of the Hindu, Buddhist and Mohammedan theologies; Protestants have so dealt with the Catholic notions of deity, and liberal Protestants with older Protestant notions; it is thus that the Chinamen judge of us, and that all of us now living will be judged by our descendants. When we cease to admire or approve what the definition of a deity implies, we end by deeming that deity incredible.

...Not only the cruelty, but the paltriness of character of the gods believed in by earlier centuries also strikes later centuries with surprise. We shall see examples of it from the annals of Catholic saintship which make us rub our Protestant eyes. Ritual worship in general appears to the modern transcendentalist, as well as to the ultra-puritanic type of mind, as if addressed to a deity of the most absurdly childish character, taking delight in toy-shop furniture, tapers and tinsel, costume and mumbling and mummery, and finding his 'glory' incomprehensibly enhanced thereby; – just as on the other hand the formless spaciousness of pantheism appears quite empty to ritualistic natures, and the gaunt theism of evangelical sects seems intolerably bald and chalky and bleak. Luther, says Emerson, would have cut off his right hand rather than nail his theses to the door at Wittenberg, if he had supposed that they were destined to lead to the pale negations of Boston Unitarianism ...

...The gods we stand by are the gods we need and can use, the gods whose demands on us are reinforcements of our demands on ourselves and on one another...[66]

Gods can be killed off suddenly and spectacularly by conquest or iconoclasm. But in James's litany they tend to die less spectacularly, quietly "neglected and forgotten", killed off by degrees. They die from "historical accidents" that they could not anticipate and defend themselves against. Above all, they die from changes in "mental climate" and changes in "*tone*". When the tone, the aesthetic-moral register of a community, changes, the air/atmosphere changes and the old gods find it hard to breathe. They asphyxiate as human experience moves on and judges the old gods according to new conceptions of justice, utility,

---

66   Ibid., 264–266.

MODERN TRIALS AND TESTS OF 'EXPERIENCE'

serviceability, community and worth. The old gods die by the same principles that disqualify some experiences from the category of religious experience. They die when their "fruits begin to seem quite worthless", when they "thwart too extensively other values", or when they are discredited as "childish, contemptible, or immoral". Deities become "incredible" when we move to a higher tone that makes former praise seem unworthy; when we can no longer praise because we can no longer "admire or approve". On one level, the line of divine corpses is entirely predictable. The classical, Hindu, Buddhist, "Mohammedan" and Catholic deities croak according to an evolutionary schema that culminates in liberal Protestant theology. But the comfort is at least partially illusory. For we are invited to imagine, in turn, our gods asphyxiating under the scrutiny of our descendants and the Chinese.

Whereas late moderns tend to decorously and discretely neglect and forget the old gods without drawing vulgar attention to their forgetting, eighteenth and nineteenth century writers were engaged in a far more active struggle. In a quintessentially modern development of the battle between the 'spirit' and the 'letter' (which has always been a problem for the gods who took to writing and committed themselves to scriptures), Gotthold Ephraim Lessing argued that the Bible manifestly contained more than belongs to religion, which is not to say it contained no religion, but that the difference between the two was like the difference between gross and net.[67] It is as if we are getting a chance to peek behind the scenes into the counting house that produced the idea of religiously-inspired value, at least a century before value was understood as 'value judgment', German *Werturteil* or social principle (a term first coined in English in 1889). Lessing's taxation metaphor stays close to older senses of 'value' such as 'the degree to which something is useful or estimable,' or 'price, moral worth; *standing, reputation*'. The writing gods and prophets have left us with an archive or memory stock that transcends immediate use, parts of which now seem to cry (or scream and screech) out to be sealed off safely in the museum cases of the past. Like a book-keeper doing his taxes, the citizen theologian makes deductions at source. He takes the gross – in both senses of the word 'gross' – and produces the essence, the net. He gives to historical context what belongs to historical context, and to the true gods and religions what belongs to them.

---

67   Gotthold Ephraim Lessing, *Cambridge Free Thoughts and Lessons on Bibliolatry*, trans. H. H. Bernard (London: Trübner, 1862), 23, near the beginning of a section "The Bible manifestly contains more than belongs to religion". See 32: "there was religion ere the least part thereof was committed to writing – before one single book of that Bible existed, which is now made equivalent to Religion itself".

Not by accident, modern historical biblical criticism has developed as an active forgetting of the moral and social dimension of these decisions. We write as if we have only ever been making disinterested, philological decisions about sources. We forget the aesthetic and social dimension of integrity that was lost – and not just by accident – when biblical scholars isolated the question of textual 'integrity' in a purely formal sense. For early moderns such as Pierre Bayle, the Third Earl of Shaftesbury (Anthony Ashley Cooper) and Immanuel Kant, the primary explicit concern was the integrity of biblical characters and the Bible's morality, social standing and political effects.[68] The interrogation of biblical *characters* (in the double sense of personae and letters) was bound to a consideration of the Bible's 'character' and 'manners' and its role as political and social exemplar, as assessed according to principles of etiquette and gentlemanly politesse.

This led to a radical re-reading of even the most foundational experiences at the heart of the Judeo-Christian tradition – such as, and not just as one example among others, Abraham's near sacrifice of his son. If experience is "knowledge gained by repeated trials" and "an event or occurrence which leaves an impression on someone, that affects one",[69] then surely this story qualifies as an experience *par excellence*. In Jewish tradition it stands as the pinnacle of Abraham's ten trials. Though feeling is backgrounded, it is hard to imagine that it did not make something of an impression on Abraham – and, particularly, Isaac. This is also an experience that foregrounds all those connotations of journey, trial and danger that linger around words like *Expereri* and *Erfahrung*.[70] Symptomatically, dictionaries seem to run towards pain and danger as they struggle to define experience. Though "enjoyable experiences" are of course possible, they tend to favor examples such as "a harrowing experience"; "to learn a lesson by painful experience"; and (my personal favorite) "My encounter with the bear in the woods was a frightening experience."[71]

---

68 See further Sherwood, *Biblical Blaspheming*, 89–95; Stephen D. Moore and Yvonne Sherwood, *The Invention of the Biblical Scholar: A Critical Manifesto* (Minneapolis, MN: Fortress, 2011), 49–64; Yvonne Sherwood, "Early Modern Davids: From Sin to Critique", in *The Oxford Handbook of the Bible in England, 1520–1700*, ed. Kevin Kileen, Helen Smith and Rachel Willie (Oxford: Oxford University Press, 2015), 640–658.

69 See the key definitions that emerge from googling 'experience' at https://www.google .co.uk/#q=experience+definition+ Note also the graph of occurrences – with an exponential rise in the uses of experience from 1900 to 1950 and again from 1950 to 2010.

70 *Erfahrung* carries the same root as *periculum* or 'danger' notes Jay, *Songs of Experience*, 10.

71 See http://dictionary.reference.com/browse/experience (accessed 14 December 2014). This site also sees 'religion' as a primary object of experience, and makes 'experiencing religion' a category that stands alone.

MODERN TRIALS AND TESTS OF 'EXPERIENCE' 53

We seem to feel about experience the way that Nietzsche felt about conscience. The most powerful experiences, the ones most likely to make an impression, or indent, are painful experiences (such as 'harrowing' encounters with marauding bears.)

Though Abraham is prepared to give body to his experience of God by burning the child of his body, this is not an experience or testimony that modern Christians and Jews can easily accept. *Only by de-authenticating Abraham's experience can we save religion from the gross of the text.* Abraham genuinely believed that he heard God tell him to sacrifice his son, granted, but this 'God' must have been a phantasm, an illusion, or an effect of context – for example an effect of the influence of the child-sacrificing Canaanites, Abraham's neighbors, from whom he learnt a false idea of what the true gods want. "No matter if angels, dreams, visions, voices from heaven" affirmed it, "the moral unfitness of the action ... was a stronger reason against the divinity of the command, than any of those extraordinary ways in which that command was conveyed to him could possibly be for it."[72] The point is the value, the outcome, the utility – not the temperature of transmission, not the level of fever, not the angels, miracles or special effects.

Modernity is not simply the time when the doubters impiously messed with the traditional reception of 'the voice of God', suggesting that they were sound-tricks projected by "speaking trumpets" and "oracle machines".[73] It is also the time when, *in order to save and protect religion*, believers and experiencers circumscribed founding characters as having had an idiosyncratic experience, valorized (for what it was to them), but detached from true religion as such. Regrettably, for the greater cause of morality and good citizenship, Abraham's experience must be localized as simply Abraham's experience. In the modern reading, Abraham becomes a religious subject, undergoing an experience. This was his experience. He certainly seems to have experienced self-transcendence, a feeling of "I can do no other",[74] but the experience can only be translated into value if, bypassing all that Søren Kierkegaard says in *Fear and Trembling*, we abstract it and take it in the general sense of self-abnegation, extending the self beyond the self, or giving one's best. Effectively, in this now standard modern pious reading, Abraham's God becomes a 'fairy-object', not

---

72 Thomas Chubb, "Treatise XIX: The Case of Abraham with Regard to his offering up Isaac in sacrifice, re-examined, In a Letter to a Clergyman," in *A Collection of Tracts on Various Subjects* (London: 1730), 244.

73 Leigh Eric Schmidt, *Hearing Things: Religion, Illusion and the American Enlightenment* (Cambridge, MA.: Harvard University Press, 2000), 115.

74 See Joas, *The Genesis of Values*, 5.

a 'fact-object' – *but this is still Abraham's experience*. The text still works at the level of the subject, even if that subject errs.

Infinitely pliable, experience expands and contracts. It can contract as 'his experience' – or open out into the broader arena of community and/or transcendence, ultimate truth. Both levels are valorized, but in different ways. His religious experience is his religious experience and as such must be revered/respected. But confined and segregated as 'his experience', it has no ramifications for community, truth, or religion as such. This is the secret of the plasticity of 'experience'. This is what makes it so useful. Experience contracts into our subjectivity, but also offers at least the possibility of transcendence/community. With experience, in our experience, we are bounded in a nutshell – and also count ourselves kings (and queens) of infinite space.[75] Experience bridges the abyss between the secular and the religious; subjects and objects; the active and the passive; the individual and the universal; facts and fairies; the real and the not-real. 'Experience' manages irruptions of religion in modern space.

Literature

Agamben, Giorgio, *Infancy and History: The Destruction of Experience*, trans. Liz Heron (London: Verso, 1993).

Ankersmit, Frank, *Sublime Historical Experience* (Stanford: Stanford University Press, 2005).

Blanton, Ward and Yvonne Sherwood, "Bible/Religion/Critique", in *Religion/Culture/Critique*, ed. Richard King (New York: Columbia University Press, forthcoming).

Brown, Wendy, *Regulating Aversion: Tolerance in the Age of Identity and Empire* (Princeton, CA: Princeton University Press, 2006).

Chubb, Thomas, "Treatise XIX: The Case of Abraham with Regard to his offering up Isaac in sacrifice, re-examined, In a Letter to a Clergyman," in *A Collection of Tracts on Various Subjects* (London: 1730), 244.

Derrida, Jacques, "Of an Apocalyptic Tone Recently Adopted in Philosophy", trans. John P. Leavey, *Oxford Literary Review* 6 (1984), 3–37.

Fenves, Peter, "Foreword: From Empiricism to the Experience of Freedom", in Jean-Luc Nancy, *The Experience of Freedom* (Stanford, NJ: Stanford University Press, 1993), xiii–xxxi.

---

75   With due credit to William Shakespeare, and Hamlet's famous soliloquy in Act II, scene II.

MODERN TRIALS AND TESTS OF 'EXPERIENCE' 55

Heidegger, Martin, *The Question Concerning Technology and Other Essays*, trans. William Lovitt (New York: Harper Touchstone, 1977).

James, William, *The Varieties of Religious Experience: A Study in Human Nature* (London: Routledge, 2002), 27.

Jay, Martin, *Songs of Experience: Modern American and European Variations on a Universal Theme* (Berkeley, CA: University of California Press, 2006).

Joas, Hans, *Die Entstehung der Werte* (Frankfurt: Suhrkamp, 2006).

Joas, Hans, *The Genesis of Values*, trans. Gregory Moore (Cambridge: Polity Press, 2000).

Kant, Immanuel, "On a Newly Arisen Superior Tone in Philosophy", trans. Peter Fenves, in *Raising the Tone of Philosophy: Late Essays by Immanuel Kant, Transformative Critique by Jacques Derrida*, ed. Peter Fenves (Baltimore, ML: Johns Hopkins University Press, 1993), 51–82.

Latour, Bruno, *On the Modern Cult of the Factish Gods* (Durham, NC: Duke University Press, 2011).

Legaspi, Michael C., *The Death of Scripture and the Rise of Biblical Studies* (Oxford: Oxford University Press, 2012).

Lessing, Gotthold Ephraim, *Cambridge Free Thoughts and Lessons on Bibliolatry*, trans. H. H. Bernard (London: Trübner, 1862).

Mahmood, Saba, "Secularism, Hermeneutics, and Empire: The Politics of Islamic Reformations", *Public Culture* 18 (2006), 323–47.

Martin, Craig and Russell McCutcheon with Leslie Dorrough Smith (eds), *Religious Experience: A Reader* (London: Routledge, 2014).

Masuzawa, Tomoko, "Troubles with Materiality: The Ghost of Fetishism in the Nineteenth Century", in *Religion: Beyond a Concept*, ed. Hent de Vries (New York: Fordham University Press, 2007), 647–667.

Moore, Stephen D. and Yvonne Sherwood, *The Invention of the Biblical Scholar: A Critical Manifesto* (Minneapolis, MN: Fortress, 2011).

Oakeshott, Michael, *Experience and Its Modes* (Cambridge: Cambridge University Press, 1933).

Otto, Rudolf, *The Idea of the Holy*, trans. John W. Harvey (Oxford: Oxford University Press, 1968).

Sahagún, Bernardino de, *General History of the Things of New Spain: Florentine Codex*, trans. Arthur J. O. Anderson and Charles E. Dibble, 13 vols (Salt Lake City, UT: University of Utah, 1950–1982).

Schmidt, Leigh Eric, *Hearing Things: Religion, Illusion and the American Enlightenment* (Cambridge, MA: Harvard University Press, 2000).

Shapin, Steven, *A Social History of Truth: Civility and Science in Seventeenth-Century England* (Chicago: University of Chicago Press, 1994).

Sherwood, Yvonne, "Early Modern Davids: From Sin to Critique", in *The Oxford Handbook of the Bible in England, 1520–1700*, ed. Kevin Kileen, Helen Smith and Rachel Willie (Oxford: Oxford University Press, 2015), 640–658.

Sherwood, Yvonne, "On the Freedom of the Concepts of Religion and Belief" in *The Politics of Religious Freedom*, ed. Winnifred Fallers Sullivan, Elizabeth Shakman Hurd and Saba Mahmood (Chicago: University of Chicago Press, 2015), 29–44.

Sherwood, Yvonne, "Prophetic Postcolonialism: Performing the Disaster of the Spanish Conquest on the Stage of Jeremiah", in *Congress Volume 2013: 21st Congress of the International Organisation for the Study of the Old Testament*, ed. Christl Maier (Leiden: Brill, 2014), 300–332.

Sherwood, Yvonne, *Biblical Blaspheming: Trials of the Sacred for a Secular Age* (Cambridge: Cambridge University Press, 2012).

Smith, Wilfred Cantwell, "The Study of Religion and the Study of the Bible", in *Rethinking Scripture: Essays from a Comparative Perspective*, ed. Miriam Levering (Albany: State University of New York Press, 1989), 18–28.

PART 2

Imagining the Unimaginable?

∴

CHAPTER 3

Fiercely Proselytizing and Feverishly Protective: Reading John's Revelation with Jacques Derrida

Hannah M. Strømmen

"We must begin wherever we are", Jacques Derrida writes. "Wherever we are: in a text where we already believe ourselves to be".[1] The book we call the Bible is one such textual landscape from which the questions of religious experience, its articulation and interpretation, still arise. In reflecting on religious experience, the apocalyptic – or what has become associated with the apocalyptic – is a notorious and niche aspect of religious experience, often associated with bizarre revelations, peculiar sects with prophetic leaders, extraordinary ceremonies and rituals. Signifying an uncovering, laying bare, or revelation, ἀποκάλυψις has come to denote a genre of literature, both biblical and extra-biblical.

As one particularly influential source of the apocalyptic the book of Revelation – or John's Apocalypse – is at one and the same time a blueprint for religious experience and at its extreme edges. In many ways, Rudolf Otto's characterization of religious experience as "that which is quite beyond the sphere of the usual, the intelligible, and the familiar"[2] aptly describes the uncanny scenes of the book of Revelation. It surely could be said to be a text that provokes "blank wonder and astonishment".[3] But – or perhaps, because of this – this book is also associated with the madder end of religious experience, its dangerous fringes, falling too easily into sheer lunacy and dragging the good name of religion down with it into the murky depths of revelatory irrationality, inciting violence and extremism.

The issue of interpretation, and its relationship to religious experience, appears on the scene of the book of Revelation somewhat like an advisory straightjacket to eschew what Frank Kermode calls "embarrassing literalism".[4]

---

1   Jacques Derrida, *Of Grammatology* (Baltimore, ML: John Hopkins University Press, 1998), 162.
2   Rudolf Otto, *The Idea of the Holy*, trans. John W. Harvey (Oxford: Oxford University Press, 1968), 26.
3   Ibid.
4   Frank Kermode, "Millennium and Apocalypse", in *The Apocalypse and The Shape of Things to Come*, ed. Frances Carey (Toronto: University of Toronto Press, 1999), 19.

© KONINKLIJKE BRILL NV, LEIDEN, 2016 | DOI 10.1163/9789004328600_005

It provides an ordering apparatus to grapple with this mad patient and attempt to put it on the straight and narrow. If the Bible is something of a wolfish corpus, as Robert Carroll warned,[5] Revelation would perhaps be the teeth-baring part. Much scholarship on Revelation takes its starting point in such an attitude as to curtailing the potency of John's apocalyptic experience and its expression, as if its fangs could all too easily cause religious rabies. For example, in *Revelation and the End of All Things*, Craig R. Koester writes: "The power of a book can be seen in what it does to people, and few books have affected people more dramatically than Revelation".[6] Koester cites everything from sermons, art, theology, to the "rise of the modern state of Israel, the outbreak of the Persian Gulf War, volcanic eruptions, and oil spills".[7] He notes that many readers are repelled by this book, and some suggest that revelation might be "best kept on the shelf, sealed and unread".[8] Michael Gorman urges "responsible" readings of Revelation, and writes that the book is frequently approached with fear and suspicion, "some would even call it dangerous".[9] Tina Pippin too writes of biblical apocalypse as something that "scares and scars".[10] The religious experience recorded in the book of Revelation is in some sense treated as dangerously infectious; by implication, 'proper' interpretations are called on to safeguard its content and usage.[11]

As already intimated, apocalyptic experience is heavily associated with the scenes depicted in Revelation. Yvonne Sherwood facetiously lists what "by cryptic or overt citation signals 'apocalyptic'" as, amongst other things:

---

5   With his allusion to the Bible as a wolf in the sheepfold, Carroll is warning against the ways in which the diverse and complex set of texts referred to as the Bible have been used and abused in being read as sacred scripture, "made to serve the powerful as weapons". Carroll suggests that the task of critically reading the Bible today is to identify its accounts and expressions in its various versions, understanding these accounts in their historical contexts, and evaluating such texts from where we are now. Robert P. Carroll, *Wolf in the Sheepfold: The Bible as Problematic for Theology* (London: SCM Press, 1991), 5, 32.

6   Craig R. Koester, *Revelation and the End of All Things* (Grand Rapids, MI: William B. Eerdmans, 2001), 1.

7   Ibid.

8   Ibid.

9   Michael J. Gorman, *Reading Revelation Responsibly: Uncivil Worship and Witness: Following the Lamb Into the New Creation* (Eugene, OR: Cascade Books, 2011), 1.

10 Tina Pippin, *Apocalyptic Bodies: The Biblical End of the World in Text and Image* (London: Routledge, 1999), xii.

11 Gorman suggests that interpreting this text is a "serious and sacred responsibility, not to be entered into lightly", as some readings risk being "unchristian and unhealthy." Gorman, *Reading Revelation Responsibly*, xiii–xiv.

FIERCELY PROSELYTIZING AND FEVERISHLY PROTECTIVE

angels; lampstands; seals; the number seven; the whore of Babylon; a noxious cocktail of hail, fire, blood, famine and pestilence; the bowls of God's wrath; the woman clothed with the sun; the four beasts; the ten horns; ... the New Jerusalem; Satan thrown into the lake of fire and sulphur; death on a pale green horse; Wormwood the great falling star; the battle between the dragon and the archangel Michael; the scroll and the lamb; the new heaven and the new earth; the 144,000 ...

all of which can be found in Revelation.[12] This would be religious experience at its wildest, a Box-Office hit, ready-made for 3D screens and Imax theatres, for pop-corn munching audiences eager to replace the dreary quotidian with an intense experience of the more virile, action-packed spectrum of the religious imagination. But rather than an example of the sheer madness and imaginative overflow of religious experience, I would like to show how the book of Revelation also documents the idea of religious experience within a determinedly textual landscape – one that both anxiously and desirously demands incessant interpretation. The signatory of the book, John, describes an experience that is both already a kind of text, and that aspires to survive as a text. I argue that this dramatic and notorious example of a revelatory religious experience is a much drier landscape than is often thought. Not only "flashes of lightning, and rumblings, and peals of thunder" (4:5) or "hail and fire, mixed with blood" (8:7), it is at the same time anxious, self-conscious and contradictory about the relationship between experience, its articulation and interpretation. This relationship is muddled, or, to put it differently, experience on the one hand and articulation as well as interpretation on the other are not two different facets that can be temporally or substantially distinguished. Rather, experience is always already caught up in a mesh of signs and traces that must themselves be experienced, articulated, interpreted and reproduced.

No Outside-Text?

Jacques Derrida's work has by many been met with "blank wonder and astonishment".[13] Although notably lauded as an apocalyptic and prophetic

---

12 Yvonne Sherwood, "'Napalm Falling like Prostitutes': Occidental Apocalypse as Managed Volatility", in *Abendländische Apokalyptik: Kompendium zur Genealogie der Endzeit*, ed. Veronika Wieser, Christian Zolles, Catherine Feik, Martin Zolles, and Leopold Schlöndorff (Berlin: Akademie Verlag, 2013), 39–74 (41–42).

13 Otto, *The Idea of the Holy*, 26.

Patmos figure à la John of the book of Revelation,[14] Derrida has received much flak, particularly for the widely misinterpreted line "Il n'y a pas de hors-texte" ("There is no outside-text").[15] Put plainly, the panicked assumption seemed to be that Derrida was suggesting we are stuck in a postmodern vortex where the 'real' has given way to a flimsy text-world in which fictions and semantics would reign over truth and nature. Of course, Derrida's point was rather that what is considered the 'real', or 'truth' and 'nature', is always already caught up in discursive apparatuses that construct the worlds in which we live; these worlds are "more or less stable".[16] This is "language in the broad sense, codes of traces being designed, among all living beings, to construct a unity of the world that is always deconstructible, nowhere and never given in nature."[17] Turning John P. Manoussaki's quip about Derrida as a Patmos-prophet around, we might see John of Patmos as something of a Derridean. The writer of Revelation might be similarly accused of there being nothing outside the text, or no outside-text, with his entanglement with the words, writing and textuality of his religious experience. The book of Revelation begins with a certain "John" on the island of Patmos (1:9), whose narrative is based on a religious experience: he is visited by an angel who shows him spectacular scenes, in order for John to be a witness "to the word of God" (1:1–2). According to the much-cited John J. Collins definition of apocalypse, it

> is a genre of revelatory literature with a narrative framework, in which a revelation is mediated by an otherworldly being to a human recipient, disclosing a transcendent reality which is both temporal, insofar as it envisages eschatological salvation, and spatial insofar as it involves another, supernatural world.[18]

---

14   John P. Manoussakis, 'The Revelation According to Jacques Derrida', in *Derrida and Religion: Other Testaments*, eds. Yvonne Sherwood and Kevin Hart (London: Routledge, 2005), 309.

15   Derrida, *Of Grammatology*, 158–59.

16   Derrida, *The Beast and the Sovereign, Volume II*, trans. Geoffrey Bennington, ed. Michel Lisse, Marie-Louise Mallet and Ginette Michaud (Chicago: University of Chicago Press, 2011), 8, 9.

17   Ibid.

18   John J. Collins, "Introduction: Towards the Morphology of a Genre", *Semeia* 14 (1979), 1–20 (9).

FIERCELY PROSELYTIZING AND FEVERISHLY PROTECTIVE 63

As Leonard Thompson puts it, "John becomes merely a link in the chain from God and Jesus Christ".[19] If William James describes religious experience as a person's individual and ineffable encounter with the divine,[20] the apocalyptic genre is characterized precisely by *mediating* the experience of the transcendent, the other-worldly, to disclose or unveil this reality to others within a narrative framework. In other words, at the heart of apocalypse is not only the exceptional experience of God unveiled, but the experience of *unveiling* this event by mediating it to others. In John's apocalypse there is little sign of a prior, originary experience of an unmediated God or revelation; rather, the entire experience is caught up in a mesh of traces given or withheld, as if every experience is always already mediated, caught up in systems of signs that demand interpretation and further mediation.

The attention to writing and reading in John's apocalyptic experience can be traced throughout Revelation, marking a textual trajectory running through the author's depiction of the revelatory experience. In 1:11 a voice tells John to "Write in a book what you see and send it to the seven churches", which is repeated in 1:19, "write what you have seen, what is, and what is to take place after this". Chapter 2 begins with a voice dictating the letters John writes. In 3:7, the narrative is interrupted with a comment that "These are the words of the holy one, the true one", reminding us that this experience consists in words shown or given to John to record and reproduce in writing. In 5:1–6 John's writing is interrupted by his exclusion from the opening of a scroll as if to emphasize the lack of immediacy to his experience. Finally, from the sixth seal comes an earthquake, and the "sky vanished like a scroll rolling itself up" (6:12–14) as if John's experience is further deferred in the signifying tremors erupting from the scroll's pages, thus causing the experience he is supposed to be writing down to elude him like a rolled up scroll. In 10:1–5 an angel comes with a scroll in his hand, and John says "I was about to write" but is told "do not write it down" (10:4), while in 14:13 he is emphatically told "Write this"; and again in 19:9: "Write this", with the confirmation added "These are the true words of God". In 21:5 one seated on a throne tells John, "Write this, for these words are trustworthy and true", repeated in 22:6–7 by an angel: "These words are trustworthy and true". At the end of the book John is told not "to seal up the words of the prophecy of this book" (22:10).

---

19 Leonard L. Thompson, *The Book of Revelation: Apocalypse and Empire* (Oxford: Oxford University Press, 1990), 178.

20 William James, *The Varieties of Religious Experience: A Study in Human Nature*, ed. Eugene Taylor and Jeremy Carrette (London: Routledge, 2002), 29–30; 295.

What these references show is the reading and writing activity inexorably bound to John's experience. In John's unveiled – apocalyptic – state, to see is to read signs and to reproduce them in writing. These references convey the way in which the word of God in this experience is not an unmediated event prior to textuality. Rather, the experience hinges on the erratic mediation of words, the readability of signs in scrolls, of voices announcing words and producing texts for John to read, hear, understand, and transcribe. The textuality of the apocalypse, then, is not a secondary and separate facet, but is co-constitutive with the very experience of revelation for John as a series of signs to be read, understood and written. Apocalypse, or unveiling, is both what happens *to* John and what John himself does in reading and writing his experience: both are mediated events. To unveil here is not simply a drawing back of the curtain that hides transcendence and truth, then, rather it is to see traces and texts, experience their intelligibility or lack of intelligibility, to read signs or remain illiterate, to experience and express them *in medias res*.

Autoimmune Responses

But there are repercussions for this demonstration of religious experience as an experience of signs read and reproduced further by John, in a mesh of traces continuously referred and deferred. These repercussions are relevant to the relationship between religious experience, its articulation and interpretation. Derrida argues that a text is not "a finished corpus of writing, some content enclosed in a book or its margins, but a differential network, a fabric of traces referring endlessly to something other than itself, to other differential traces".[21] John's experience of revelation is a testimony to such a fabric of traces. He attempts to transcribe his experience faithfully so that it will become a book that will live on, its network of signs referring onwards, thus *keeping testifying* to the word of God given to him in his apocalyptic religious experience.[22] John's function as a testimonial writing hand in his apocalyptic experience is to 'keep' the word of God by disclosing and transcribing it faithfully. But also, what the

---

21 Jacques Derrida, "Living On", in *Deconstruction and Criticism*, trans. James Hulbert, ed. Harold Bloom et al. (New York: Seabury Press, 1979), 84.

22 Jacques Derrida, "Signature, Event, Context", in *Limited Inc*, trans. Samuel Weber and Jeffrey Mehlman (Evanston, IL: Northwestern University Press, 1988), 1–24 (10). Derrida extends what holds for writing to experience more generally – at least if experience is characterised as never consisting of *pure* presence but of a "chain of differential marks". Ibid.

FIERCELY PROSELYTIZING AND FEVERISHLY PROTECTIVE

apocalyptic experience divulges is a salvation grounded in *keeping* the word of God. Salvation is upheld for those who *keep* the word of God as it is presented in *this* book that will be posted out to readers, outlined most emphatically at the beginning and end of the book, with the prologue 1:3 "blessed are they who hear, read aloud and *keep* the words of the prophecy" and "what is written in it", and in the epilogue of 22:18, 19 to not alter the words of this book. John's function as the writer of such an apocalyptic religious experience, then, is to testify to such a 'keeping' of God's word.[23] This testimony is suspended between past and future. Drawing on Derrida's thought, Nicholas Royle describes texts as "an effect of traces and remnants" marked by a ghostly logic of survival or "living on".[24] It is this living on that John's apocalyptic experience hinges on as a testimonial endeavor. At issue is – as Derrida argues – a "structure of repeatability".[25] A book would be the thing, the support, the surface of inscription that ensures the possibility of readability and repeatability of traces:

> For writing to be a writing it must continue to 'act' and to be readable even when what is called the author of the writing no longer answers for what he has written, for what he seems to have signed, be it because of temporary absence, because he is dead or, more generally, because he has not employed his absolutely actual and present intention or attention, the plenitude of his desire to say what he means, in order to sustain what seems to be written 'in his name'.[26]

Albeit a truism, writing, and writing *in* a book, thus lives on, outliving its author and perhaps its intended readers, although such a survival of its traces is not guaranteed in the potential of a book to be lost, burnt, archived away and given

---

23   Testimony and keeping the word of God is portrayed as heroic: victims of the testimony to the "word of God", "for the testimony they had given" are mentioned in 6:9–10; "the word of their testimony" is linked to the blood of the lamb and defeating the serpent-dragon-Satan in 12:11. In 12:17 the dragon will make war on those who "hold the testimony of Jesus", and the angel in chapter 19 calls himself a fellow-servant to John and his comrades "who hold the testimony of Jesus", saying further that "testimony of Jesus is the spirit of prophecy" (19:9,10); 20:4 speaks again of those who "had been beheaded for their testimony to Jesus and for the word of God". The book closes in chapter 22 with a repetition of the claim that "I, Jesus", was the one who "sent my angel to you with this testimony for the churches" (22:16). To keep the word of God is thus to testify to the other and for the messianic Jesus to come.

24   Nicholas Royle, *Jacques Derrida* (London: Routledge, 2003), 64.

25   Derrida, "Signature, Event, Context", 7.

26   Ibid., 8.

over to physical decay or destruction. But it is also haunted by the absence of a determined signified meaning, and of the context and intention of the signification.[27] Considering the degree of distaste directed at John's book of Revelation as not 'Christian' enough, the fragility of survival concerning books and the survival of this book as a testament to a particular apocalyptic experience is pertinent.[28]

Because the book and its text live on beyond the author's control, the 'keeping' of the word of God in this context sets in motion an 'autoimmunity' at the heart of John's religious experience. Drawing upon Derrida's use of autoimmunity, it is when the very thing that is desired to be kept safe and sound is destroyed, and destroyed in the name of *keeping* it safe. In other words, it is when something "can spontaneously destroy, in an autonomous fashion, the very thing within it that is supposed to protect it against the other, to immunize it against the aggressive intrusion of the other".[29] Testifying to the word of God in writing demands the *keeping* of words: this entails the demand to protect them from harm, contamination, erasure, and, at the same time, to proselytize them faithfully and spread them as traces in the world. This evokes the ambiguity of 'keeping' words as an orientation towards an originary text: a word of God already written that must be safeguarded. At the same time, as already mentioned, John's keeping of words is a proselytizing act oriented towards the future, inscribing the traces of testimony for a future; this involves the risk of consigning them to an unknown destination that is potentially destructive.[30] A text and its traces, as Derrida writes, risks overrunning the limits assigned to it.[31] It subsists in the fact that it does not exhaust itself in the instant of

---

27   Ibid., 10.

28   Håkan Ulfgard writes that Revelation "is one of the biblical books that offers the greatest difficulties for its interpreters, and it has often been regarded as the least 'Christian' book of the New Testament", recalling Rudolf Bultman's assessment on it as "weakly Christianized Judaism". Håkan Ulfgard, "Reading The Book of Revelation Today: Respecting its Originality while Recognizing its Lasting Message", in *Is the World Ending?* ed. Sean Freyne and Nicholas Lash (London: SCM Press, 1998), 32–33. Early commentators identified this John with John the apostle, leading to an assumption of legitimization that could be seen as somewhat destabilized now that most scholars agree that the book of Revelation was written by an otherwise unknown prophet-figure in Asia Minor.

29   Jacques Derrida, *Rogues: Two Essays on Reason*, trans. Pascale-Anne Brault and Michael Naas (Stanford, CA: Stanford University Press, 2005), 123.

30   For a discussion of a recent example of a vandalised Bible and the stir this caused, see the first chapter of Yvonne Sherwood's *Biblical Blasphemings: Trials of the Sacred for a Secular Age* (Cambridge: Cambridge University Press, 2012), 9–95.

31   Derrida, "Living On", 84.

FIERCELY PROSELYTIZING AND FEVERISHLY PROTECTIVE

its inscription; it can signify in the absence of any determined addressee and beyond the presence of the one who has produced it.[32] It is part of the very structure of the written sign that it carries with it a force that breaks with its context or any predetermined future context.[33] Every sign in the possibility of its repetition or citation – put between quotation marks – can break with any given context and as such engender new contexts in a way that is not limitable. "There are only contexts without any centering, or absolute anchoring".[34] Michael Naas argues that every written trace is testamentary – to the other.[35] "Because the trace is always testamentary, destined for a future beyond both the addressee and the addressor, its fate is always uncertain, a living on that is always *to be determined*".[36] Mastery of the word, its *keeping*, in its plenitude, presence and one's possession, is the impossible. Derrida argues that it "is inherent to a trace that it is always being erased and always capable of being erased".[37] "But the fact that it *is* erased, that it can always *be* erased or erase *itself*, and this from the first instant of its inscription, through and beyond any repression, does not mean that someone, God, human, or animal, can be its master subject and possess the power to erase *it*".[38] For Revelation, this marks what Derrida calls "the finitude of a God who doesn't know what is going to happen to him with language".[39]

The tension in the double mission in John's religious apocalyptic experience – a mission to both protect and proselytize – shows an autoimmune reaction. It is a reaction to the tensions between *unveiling* a given text (that is, John's experience) and giving it over to interpretive volatility. John must answer to the demand in his apocalyptic experience and keep these words of God, to mediate them in writing as testimonial traces to others. But to reproduce them is precisely to forego the possibility of such keeping as possession or protection, and to give them over to a vulnerable future of interpretive flux. This is of course a flux that John has already showed himself to participate in, in his own experience in reading and reproducing the signs he sees, that are never wholly present or simply given. Arguably, one autoimmune

---

32 Derrida, "Signature, Event, Context", 9.

33 Ibid.

34 Ibid., 12.

35 Michael Naas, *Taking on the Tradition: Jacques Derrida and the Legacies of Deconstruction* (Stanford, CA: Stanford University Press, 2003), 4.

36 Ibid., 8.

37 Jacques Derrida, *The Animal That Therefore I am*, trans. David Wills, ed. Marie-Louise Mallet (New York: Fordham University Press, 2008), 136.

38 Ibid.

39 Ibid., 17.

moment in Revelation is when John is commanded to take a scroll and eat it: "Take it, and eat; it will be bitter to your stomach, but sweet as honey in your mouth" (10: 8–10). "So I took the little scroll from the hand of the angel and ate it; it was sweet as honey in my mouth, but when I had eaten it, my stomach was made bitter" (10:10). It is thus sealed in John's stomach, safe from 'outside' harm but simultaneously destroyed, making it illegible. The fate of any written artefact could be the digestive tract, thus made unreadable, autoimmunely saving it from the other who might threaten its sacred words but in thus 'saving' it destroying its potential to be read, disseminated, to keep meaning. Another autoimmune gesture appears at the end of the book:

> I warn everyone who hears the words of the prophecy of this book: if anyone adds to them, God will add to that person the plagues described in this book; if anyone takes away from the words of the book of this prophecy, God will take away that person's share in the tree of life and in the holy city, which are described in this book (22:18–19).

It would be impossible to read, hear or speak these words and not add or take away *something*, that is, to add interpretations or remove interpretations, precisely because these words are not entirely stable self-identical signifiers. In translation, reproduction, duplication, copying, reading aloud, in adding one's own tone, meaning, understanding, emphasis, comments and context to them, would one not always risk adding or taking away something, that is, be guilty of interpretation? As surely John already is from his own inevitable interpretation of the signs shown him? As Derrida puts it: "every reading is not only anachronistic, but consists in bringing out anachrony, non-self-contemporaneity, dislocation in the taking-place of the text".[40] Like the structure of repeatability inherent in the traces of writing, to treat the events this book describes as a pure presence or to gather the signs of the book in their plenitude would be to announce the end – lights out, curtains down – with no possible understanding or literacy. This would foreclose the further dissemination of John's religious experience as a testimonial mediation. Gayatri Spivak explains that the sign cannot be taken as a homogeneous unit bridging an origin (referent) and an end (meaning). Rather, there is a heterogeneity at work that always already refers the signs of writing to other signs and ensures their continued signifying powers.[41] This is interpretive practice; but not as an add-on to the presence of experience, but as constitutive of experience itself as a network or mesh of

---

40   Derrida, *The Beast and the Sovereign, Volume II*, 8.

41   Gayatri Spivak, "Translator's Preface", in Derrida, *Of Grammatology*, ix–lxxxvii (xxxix).

FIERCELY PROSELYTIZING AND FEVERISHLY PROTECTIVE

traces. To announce the signification of John's experience as wholly present would be to deny the injunction to "Come!" announced in the opening of a scroll (6:1, 3, 5, 7) and in the pages of this book and concede the uselessness of further books of testimony as the end has already arrived; whereas, what John's religious experience testifies *to* is an experience of traces for a future still to come, a text still being read and interpreted with unknowable effects. Like the messiah, the signifiers of the text have not yet finally come, they are *to come*. In the name of safeguarding them, John's warning in the epilogue impedes the potency of the words to be spread in the world as proselytizing, readable missives to come. The threat of the epilogue, then, is an autoimmune attempt to safeguard the words of this book, to keep them safe and sound, but in doing so, the epilogue attempts to sterilize their potency as testimonial traces. One would barely dare read these words in the fear of adding an extra syllable or accidentally dropping out a word or letter.

Religious Experience as Event

If an occurrence worthy of the term *event* is to arrive or happen, Derrida argues, it must, beyond all mastery, affect a passivity.[42] The same might be said for a religious experience. It cannot be programmed in advance. Rather, it touches on an "exposed vulnerability", and so can only take place somewhere "without absolute immunity", "there where it is not yet or is already no longer possible to face up to the unforseeability of the other".[43] In other words, the religious experience presented as the source and content of the book of Revelation may 'happen' as an event, coming like a surreptitious thief (3:3) as precisely such an unforseeability, in its powers as a text to influence its readers and live on. Facing up to the unforseeability of the other could be explained in terms of Derrida's notion of the 'messianic', not as a particular prophetic prefiguration, but as an "opening to the future", an exposure to surprise and otherness, being prepared "for the best as for the worst, the one never coming without opening the possibility of the other".[44] The vulnerability and unforseeability in the face of a future to come could be characterized as the element of anxiety and autoimmunity that the book of Revelation shows in regard to its destination. But in regard to this exposed vulnerability Derrida posits that "autoimmunity is not

---

42 Derrida, *Rogues*, 152.

43 Ibid.

44 Jacques Derrida, "Faith and Knowledge: The Two Sources of 'Religion' at the Limits of Reason Alone", in *Acts of Religion*, ed. Gil Anidjar (London: Routledge, 2002), 40–101 (56).

an absolute ill or evil", as it "enables the exposure to the other, to *what* and to *who* comes – which means that it must remain incalculable".[45] This book and the signs of its religious experience are still potentially 'living' and waiting to 'happen' as a structure of signs awaiting the unsealing of its pages, the reading, hearing, speaking of its traces.

By revealing its own anxieties as an interpretive and testimonial endeavor in reading and reproducing the signs of this experience, the book of Revelation conveys religious experience as never unmediated or wholly present. Rather, religious experience operates within a system of signs that demand mediation, articulation, interpretation, and is thus subject to slipperiness, otherness, deferral, but also longevity and survival. This marks the success of the book of Revelation as a testimony to a religious experience that lives on; but the author's anxiety at the text being erased or corrupted, risking becoming a rarely watched B-grade movie rather than a cult classic, haunts this success. The significance of my reading of the book of Revelation is that the apocalyptic experience described in this book does not assume an access to God and his word as an unmediated or absolute presence; rather, the very experience itself is always already caught up in systems of signs and acts of mediation.

According to my reading of John's Apocalypse, there can be no privileged access to a pure presence outside of mediation or devoid of traces that demand interpretation, despite its spectacular scenes and dramatic register. The unveiling experience for John is haunted by the attempt to read and reproduce signs; revelation is "spectral" as Richard Kearney puts it, rather than simply "revealed", residing in the possibility of (knowing) an event of revelation rather than the knowledge of the event revealed.[46] The book of Revelation both annuls its own eventfulness by autoimmunely resisting interpretative flux, and produces incalculable effects in announcing the "Come!" (22:17, 20) that invites readers to read and keep its words, without knowing where or to whom this book will eventually arrive, what earthquakes might erupt in unsealing its pages, or what future this book will have had.

If part of religious experience, as demonstrated by this text, is to continuously grapple with the tensions between trying to read, understand and preserve the signs of a religious experience on the one hand, and to write and proselytize them by mediating them to others on the other, then such experience must abide in an erratic movement of mourning and exultation, loss and

---

45   Derrida, *Rogues*, 152.

46   Richard Kearney, 'Deconstruction, God, and the Possible', in *Derrida and Religion: Other Testaments*, eds. Yvonne Sherwood and Kevin Hart (London: Routledge, 2005), 304.

gain, vulnerability and vitality. Most of all, perhaps, the book of Revelation exemplifies that what is essential to religious experience is the *impetus* for continuous interpretive activity in grappling with signs and symbols, in embodying a mediating activity that never rests, in the desire to grasp at the traces of experience even as such traces roll up and out of sight. Interpretation is thus the faithful enterprise of keeping the word of God alive and mediated as an event constantly being unveiled and withdrawn, an enterprise that is not immune to faithlessness, frustration, loss and illiteracy, but that continuously resists prematurely turning off the lights, in order to keep reading on.

Literature

Carroll, Robert P., *Wolf in the Sheepfold: The Bible as Problematic for Theology* (London: SCM Press, 1991).

Collins, John J. "Introduction: Towards the Morphology of a Genre", *Semeia* 14 (1979), 1–20.

Derrida, Jacques, "Living On", in *Deconstruction and Criticism*, trans. James Hulbert, ed. Harold Bloom et al. (New York: Seabury Press, 1979).

Derrida, Jacques, "Signature, Event, Context", in *Limited Inc*, trans. Samuel Weber and Jeffrey Mehlman (Evanston, IL: Northwestern University Press, 1988), 1–24.

Derrida, Jacques, *Of Grammatology*, trans. Gayatri Spivak (Baltimore, ML: John Hopkins University Press, 1998).

Derrida, Jacques, "Faith and Knowledge: The Two Sources of 'Religion' at the Limits of Reason Alone", in *Acts of Religion*, ed. Gil Anidjar (London: Routledge, 2002), 40–101.

Derrida, Jacques, *Rogues: Two Essays on Reason*, trans. Pascale-Anne Brault and Michael Naas (Stanford, CA: Stanford University Press, 2005).

Derrida, Jacques, *The Animal That Therefore I am*, trans. David Wills, ed. Marie-Louise Mallet (New York: Fordham University Press, 2008).

Derrida, Jacques, *The Beast and the Sovereign, Volume II*, trans. Geoffrey Bennington, ed. Michel Lisse, Marie-Louise Mallet and Ginette Michaud (Chicago: University of Chicago Press, 2011).

Gorman, Michael J., *Reading Revelation Responsibly: Uncivil Worship and Witness: Following the Lamb Into the New Creation* (Eugene, OR: Cascade Books, 2011).

James, William, *The Varieties of Religious Experience: A Study in Human Nature*, ed. Eugene Taylor and Jeremy Carrette (London: Routledge, 2002).

Kearney, Richard, 'Deconstruction, God, and the Possible', in *Derrida and Religion: Other Testaments* (London: Routledge, 2005).

Kermode, Frank, "Millennium and Apocalypse", in *The Apocalypse and The Shape of Things to Come*, ed. Frances Carey (Toronto: University of Toronto Press, 1999).

Koester, Craig R., *Revelation and the End of All Things* (Grand Rapids, MI: William B. Eerdmans, 2001).

Manoussakis, John P. 'The Revelation According to Jacques Derrida', in *Derrida and Religion: Other Testaments* (London: Routledge, 2005).

Naas, Michael, *Taking on the Tradition: Jacques Derrida and the Legacies of Deconstruction* (Stanford, CA: Stanford University Press, 2003).

Otto, Rudolf, *The Idea of the Holy*, trans. John W. Harvey (Oxford: Oxford University Press, 1968).

Pippin, Tina, *Apocalyptic Bodies: The Biblical End of the World in Text and Image* (London: Routledge, 1999).

Royle, Nicholas, *Jacques Derrida* (London: Routledge, 2003).

Sherwood, Yvonne, *Biblical Blasphemings: Trials of the Sacred for a Secular Age* (Cambridge: Cambridge University Press, 2012).

Sherwood, Yvonne, "'Napalm Falling like Prostitutes': Occidental Apocalypse as Managed Volatility", in *Abendländische Apokalyptik: Kompendium zur Genealogie der Endzeit*, ed. Veronika Wieser, Christian Zolles, Catherine Feik, Martin Zolles, and Leopold Schlöndorff (Berlin: Akademie Verlag, 2013), 39–74.

Spivak, Gayatri, "Translator's Preface", in *Of Grammatology* (Baltimore, ML: John Hopkins University Press, 1998), ix–lxxxvii.

Thompson, Leonard L., *The Book of Revelation: Apocalypse and Empire* (Oxford: Oxford University Press, 1990).

Ulfgard, Håkan, "Reading The Book of Revelation Today: Respecting its Originality while Recognizing its Lasting Message", in *Is the World Ending?* ed. Sean Freyne and Nicholas Lash (London: SCM Press, 1998), 31–39.

CHAPTER 4

Religious Experience without Belief? Toward an Imaginative Account of Religious Engagement

Amber L. Griffioen

> *Our dreams are more romantic*
> *Than the world we see*
> *And if the things we dream about*
> *Don't happen to be so*
> *That's just an unimportant technicality*
> FROM THE SONG 'MAKE BELIEVE' IN *SHOWBOAT: THE MUSICAL*

It is commonly supposed that a certain kind of belief is necessary for religious experience. This claim gets cashed out in various ways in the philosophical and theological literature. For example, on some accounts religious experience is claimed to be subjectively self-verifying – that is, one cannot have a religious experience without in some sense believing in the existence of the intentional object of the experience.[1] On other, more nuanced accounts, religious experience always minimally involves a belief about the causal origin of the experience. That is, it is not possible to have an experience *of God* if one sincerely judges the experience to be purely naturalistically explicable.[2] Yet it is not clear that this must be so. In what follows, I will defend the possibility that a subject could have a genuine emotional religious experience without thereby necessarily believing or coming to believe that the purported object of her experience corresponds

---

[1] Rudolf Otto might hold a version of this view. For Otto, it seems that although genuine religious experience itself is technically non-conceptual and non-discursive, experiencing *mysterium tremendum et fascinans* still appears to involve a belief in the existence of the "numinous". See Rudolf Otto, *The Idea of the Holy*, trans. John W. Harvey (London: Oxford University Press, 1958).

[2] See, for example, Wayne Proudfoot, *Religious Experience* (Berkeley, CA: California University Press, 1985).

to reality and/or is the cause of her experience. In so doing, I will put forward what I call an *imaginative account of religious engagement.* Imaginative engagement, I will argue, may evoke emotional religious experiences that may be said to be both genuine and appropriate, despite not necessarily including beliefs of the aforementioned kind. Indeed, I maintain that such religious engagement is compatible not only with non-belief but also with *dis*belief. (For purposes of brevity, however, I will usually simply refer to the distinction between 'believers' and 'non-believers', which is meant to include not only those who remain agnostic or who lack a belief one way or the other but also those who reflectively disbelieve or deny the truth of the relevant propositions.)

Religious Engagement: An Imaginative Account

We often set up the terms 'imagination' and 'reality' as contrasts. Yet this can be misleading. In many instances, imagination is required for us to represent things we take to really exist or have happened, as when we represent very large or small things (like galaxies or DNA) to ourselves or when we picture spatially or temporally non-present events (as when we imagine what Mardi Gras in New Orleans or the Battle of the Bulge must be/have been like). Engagement with religious concepts, too, requires a significant degree of imaginative activity, even for those who believe such concepts correspond to reality. Engaging with concepts like 'God', 'the Transcendent', 'Ultimate Reality', 'the beatific vision', and so on – as well as being able to understand and meaningfully utter sentences like 'The Holy Spirit proceeds from the Father and the Son' – seems not only to require imagination but also to take us to the very limits of what we as finite human subjects can represent to ourselves. Likewise, regardless of whether any particular religious story is true or not, to understand the whole of the history of the world as a kind of 'divine narrative' – one featuring, for example, the interaction of natural and supernatural agents, a struggle between good and evil, or an eschatological resolution – requires an imaginative narrative understanding that goes beyond mere claims about certain historical or empirical 'facts'. Moreover, participation in religious ritual, be it in the form of celebrating the Eucharist, engaging in merit-making, or even simply *praying*, involves opening oneself up imaginatively to the idea of something which putatively transcends our empirical understanding, even if it is also limited by our own conceptual constraints. In all these ways, the imagination is no stranger to the sphere of religion. If anything, it appears an essential part of it.[3]

---

3   Garrett Green makes a similar claim in *Imagining God: Theology and the Religious Imagination* (San Francisco, CA: Harper & Row, 1989).

RELIGIOUS EXPERIENCE WITHOUT BELIEF? 75

Yet such imaginative activity is not restricted to believing subjects. Non-believers, too, can employ their imaginations in the service of religious participation and engagement, even if they do not believe the propositions involved in such engagement are literally true or that the content of the concepts they employ corresponds to something actual. Indeed, it seems perfectly possible that a subject may have (good) practical reasons for pursuing a life of religious participation, despite finding herself unable (or unwilling) to be completely confident of the truth of that particular tradition's content.[4] For example, an epistemically cautious subject may suspend judgment regarding certain articles of faith and yet consistently adopt a hopeful or optimistic attitude toward them. One may even believe these propositions are, strictly speaking, *false*, yet imaginatively engage with the relevant concepts in ways similar to those in which we engage with fictional entities and settings. In fact, I think this is something we commonly see when we look at what many religious adherents 'on the ground' actually do, as opposed to focusing on more abstract philosophical and theological treatments of the religious life.

Of course, the religious believer employs her imagination to represent something she thinks actually exists. She thinks that when she says, 'God is omniscient', she says something that is *true*. What about religiously-engaged non-believers like those in the examples above? On one understanding (e.g., that put forward by certain versions of theological fictionalism),[5] the non-believer thinks that the statement 'God is omniscient' is literally false, but she 'pretends' or 'makes believe' that the statement is true. She acts 'as if' there were such a being as God who knows everything there is to know. Now surely there is something right about this picture of the religious non-believer, in the sense that she does willfully enter into a certain imaginative context, one which employs concepts and makes claims that she thinks do not necessarily correspond to reality. Yet there is no need for us to say that just because the non-believer takes these statements not to refer to really existing entities and states of affairs she must take them to be false *tout court*. Just as there is a sense in which the claim 'Jane Eyre is a governess' is true (it is wrong, for example, to say that Jane Eyre is a professional baseball player), there is a very legitimate sense in which, when the religiously committed non-believer says 'God is omniscient', she likewise says something that is *true* – at least from within the context of certain monotheistic traditions. Similarly, the statement

---

4   There are several candidates for such reasons, ranging from moral to aesthetic to purely prudential, and (as I discuss below) many corresponding attitudes that one might adopt (such as hope, optimism, acceptance, etc.).

5   See, for example, Robin Le Poidevin, *Arguing for Atheism* (London: Routledge, 1996) and Andrew Eshleman, "Can an Atheist Believe in God?", *Religious Studies* 4 (2005), 183–199.

'God is triune' is false from within Jewish or Muslim contexts, just as the statement 'Captain James T. Kirk was born in Minnesota' is false in the Star Trek Universe.[6] So there is no need here to say that religious believers and non-believers within a certain tradition are necessarily talking past each other when they engage in religious discourse. In fact, if we accept that many or most religious concepts require a certain degree of imaginative engagement on the part of all religious subjects, we might be in a better position to examine how dialogue within a certain religious context can get off the ground in the first place.[7]

So just what is the difference between the religious believer and non-believer in such imaginative contexts? From within the religious context, the gap might not be as great as we may have first thought. Still, there will be a relevant distinction between the two. One possible way of understanding this difference is to say whereas believers believe (and thereby accept) that p, non-believers *merely accept* that p. What is the difference? According to William Alston, whereas belief is a non-voluntary dispositional state in which we simply 'find' ourselves, acceptance involves a voluntary mental act. Alston claims that both believers that p and 'mere acceptors' that p will be disposed to behave in similar ways as far as action regarding p is concerned (e.g., affirming p in relevant action-contexts, using p as a premise in their theoretical and practical reasoning, and so on), with one minor difference: for the non-believer, "[t]he complex dispositional state engendered by accepting p will definitely *not* include a tendency to *feel* that p *if the question of whether p arises*", whereas for believers this tendency is present.[8] But, importantly, the question of 'whether p', as a question that calls

---

6 According to the Star Trek canon, Captain Kirk was (or will be) born in Iowa.

7 The notion of 'true or false within a religious context' will, of course, raise interesting questions regarding religious disagreement and interreligious dialogue. See, for example, some of the problems raised in Victoria Harrison, "Philosophy of Religion, Fictionalism, and Religious Diversity", *International Journal for the Philosophy of Religion* 68 (2010), 43–58. I do not have space to go into these issues here, but I think a more detailed discussion of what inter- (and intra-) religious disagreement and dialogue might look like on a fictionalist account – or on any antirealist picture, for that matter – is warranted. For the germs of such an approach to theological semantics, see Amber Griffioen, Prolegomena zu einer jeden künftigen '(Nicht-)Metaphysik' der Religion: (Anti-)Realismus, (Non-)Kognitivismus und die religiöse Imagination", in *Gott ohne Theismus*, ed. Rico Gutschmidt and Thomas Rentsch (Münster: Mentis, 2016), 127–147.

8 William Alston, "Belief, Acceptance, and Religious Faith", in *Faith, Freedom, and Rationality*, ed. Jeff Jordan and Daniel Howard-Snyder (Lanham, MD: Rowman & Littlefield, 1996), 10–27 (10), additional emphasis mine.

RELIGIOUS EXPERIENCE WITHOUT BELIEF? 77

for ontological or metaphysical speculation (or one about whether some event actually happened), is not necessarily or even commonly a question taken up from *inside* the religious tradition. And where it is taken up from within the tradition, what does it matter if some individuals lack a tendency to 'feel' that *p* in these contexts? It does not mean they *never* feel that *p* – rather, it is only from the standpoint of ontological speculation that they differ in feeling from their believing counterparts. But this is simply to affirm that there is sometimes a phenomenological difference between believers and non-believers when it comes to ontology, which is, of course, exactly what we would expect. So acceptors need not believe that *p*, though presumably they must *approve* of *p* in some sense. As Daniel Howard-Snyder notes, belief that *p* is not required for what he calls "propositional faith", but rather only a positive cognitive and affective/conative stance toward *p*.[9] One such stance, as James Muyskens has suggested, might be that of hope.[10] Thus, as hinted at above, perhaps the non-believer need merely hope that *p* be true, even if she does not believe it.[11] In any case, it seems clear that one can practically commit oneself to religious propositions without having to believe them to actually 'match up' one-to-one with reality.[12]

Likewise, one can sincerely accept and adhere to religious *norms* without belief, which may involve one's being further committed to engaging in certain religious practices and rituals. For example, we can imagine someone committing herself to wearing the Hijab without believing that it is actually divinely ordained – perhaps because it encourages religious devotion, modesty, and humility. Or we can imagine a Taoist burning joss paper during Ghost Month, even though he is unsure whether his deceased ancestors are actually

---

9   Daniel Howard-Snyder, "Propositional Faith: What It Is and What It Is Not", *American Philosophical Quarterly* 50 (2013), 357–372. Howard-Snyder puts forward a few other criteria for propositional faith as well, with which I take some issue, but that is not relevant to my discussion here.

10   James Muyskens, *The Sufficiency of Hope: Conceptual Foundations of Religion* (Philadelphia, PA: Temple University Press, 1979).

11   Of course, hoping that *p* requires believing that *p* is at least possible, and I would argue that even this need not be the case on an imaginative account of religious engagement. However, as Greg Landini has pointed out in personal conversation, even if a person believes that *p* is metaphysically impossible, she might still hope *that she is wrong* about this.

12   Moreover, even among believers there are many different ways in which one can *understand* or *interpret* religious propositions – literally, analogically, metaphorically, narratively, mythologically, and so on. Thus, once we move beyond straightforward literal interpretation of religious propositions, the gap between the believer and the non-believer appears very narrow indeed.

benefitted by such a practice. In neither case need the practitioner be convinced of the truth of the relevant propositions, though he or she may certainly accept or hope or act as if they are. Further, as I have intimated, I think sincere religious engagement is compatible even with disbelief. This is because what is required for sincerity in the case of religious engagement has more to do with the strength of one's *practical* commitment to the relevant aspect of the religious tradition than with that of one's *epistemic* commitment to it. To be sure, the latter often does strongly inform the former – and sincere religious engagement may, as a matter of contingent psychological fact, generally be less effortful for the believer than the non-believer. But even this does not follow with necessity. For one may have a strong belief that p and yet be hostile or uncommitted to acting on it.[13]

So perhaps the relevant distinction between the religiously committed believer and non-believer is that, although both may be equally practically committed to certain religious propositions and concepts, when the former steps 'outside' of the strictly religious context or examines it from a critical standpoint, she affirms that, for example, God is an actually existing feature of the universe, whereas the latter denies this. Another way to put this is that when the believer engages in ontological or metaphysical speculation – when she thinks about what there really is and how it is constituted – she affirms that the statements she makes within the religious contexts really refer. The non-believer, on the other hand, denies this. But although this may be one way to engage with religion (critically, from the outside), it is certainly not what religion is centrally *about*. Put a bit differently, although metaphysical speculation or natural theology may be an important – perhaps even essential – feature of engagement within some religious and mystical traditions, it does not seem to me that the essence of religion *per se* is to be found in existence-assertions regarding correspondence with reality.[14]

Still, one might claim that for the 'truly' religious individual, there is no 'stepping outside' the religious context. Religion, one might argue, colors *all* aspects of experience, such that anyone who can compartmentalize and view her religious tradition 'from the outside' cannot be said to be sincerely religiously engaged. It is easy (and appropriate), the objector might claim, to step out of the fictional Jane Eyre or Star Trek universe once in a while, but it is not

---

13   As James 2:19 states, "The demons also believe and shudder". But surely they do not count among the religiously faithful.

14   This is not to say that religious propositions never perform an explanatory function. It *is*, however, to deny that a concern for explanation is at the heart of the religious life, even if some "proto-religions" may have their origin in efficient-causal explanatory attributions.

RELIGIOUS EXPERIENCE WITHOUT BELIEF? 79

so simple (nor ought it be) to step outside of a particular religious context. Yet this is to confuse the matter. Although it is true that, ideally, religion is more than a set of practices – it is a *form of life*, a *way of being* – this does not mean one cannot step outside it or consider it from alternative perspectives. If it were, then interreligious dialogue and dialogue between the non-religious and the religious would be doomed from the outset. (I know there are those who support this view, but I find it overly pessimistic.) Second, even though the religious believer and non-believer affirm inconsistent things about the make-up of the universe in extra- or supra-religious contexts, this does not mean that their experience within that context is relevantly different, or that their lives as a whole cannot be equally enriched by engagement with a religious form of life.

However, in order to make this latter assertion plausible, I will have to defend the claim that religiously engaged non-believers are capable of having genuine religious experiences of the kind relevant to a meaningful religious life. For although the level of religious *commitment* may be the same between certain believers and non-believers, if the latter are – by virtue of their non-belief – incapable of genuine religious *experience*, this may count as a strike against the kind of imaginative model I am proposing here.

Applying the Imaginative Account: The Case of Religious Experience

First, we must say a bit more about what we mean by the term 'religious expe-rience'. On the view I am advocating here, in order to count as a specifically *religious* experience, the subject has to view her experience in light of some particular religious tradition or conceptual schema, and that particular tradi-tion or schema must enter in some way into the content of her experience. Thus, a mere feeling of contingency might not count as a straightforwardly religious experience, but the "feeling of absolute dependence" understood in Friedrich Schleiermacher's sense or the "creaturely feeling" we find in Rudolf Otto might, assuming they are interpreted from within a religious framework.[15] Otherwise they might count as mystical or spiritual (but not specifically reli-gious) experiences. In other words, although I am not taking a position on whether there is some perennial element independent of interpretation and

---

15   See Rudolf Otto, *The Idea of the Holy*, and Friedrich Schleiermacher, *The Christian Faith*, trans. Hugh R. Mackintosh and James S. Stewart (London: T&T Clark, 1999).

common to all experiences of a 'spiritual' nature, I do think that to count as religious, an experience must be viewed through the conceptual lens of some particular religious tradition or traditions.[16] However, little of what I am going to say here hinges on this (admittedly vague) account being correct.

Further, when I say 'genuine' religious experience, I do not mean that it must be understood *factively* – as only genuine if it was, in fact, caused by what it is about. (Though 'what it is about' is sometimes more difficult to get at than we might think. I return to this below.) Finally, I should note that I am focusing on an important subset of religious experiences, namely those experiences that are fundamentally affective or emotional in nature. The term 'religious experience' may encompass a wider set of experiences than the merely affective (such as intellectual apprehensions, visions and auditions, sensed presences, out of body experiences, and so on), but these are not my concern here. What concerns me is whether the religiously engaged non-believer can genuinely experience religious emotions, and how (if at all) they might differ from the religious emotions of believers.

Engaging with religious concepts and propositions requires some cognitive accomplishment on the part of the religious subject, yet I have claimed that this cognitive role a) may (and perhaps must) involve the religious imagination and b) need not involve full doxastic commitment, or belief. I have also hinted at the idea that the non-believer – who doubts that such concepts and propositions refer to actually existing entities – might engage with them in a way similar to the way we engage with concepts and propositions in fictional settings.[17] It will be helpful here to examine this idea a bit more closely. When we engage with fiction sincerely – that is, when we immerse ourselves in a piece of fiction or otherwise 'take it seriously' – it is not as though we *forget* or somehow *fail to realize* that we are dealing with situations we take to be non-actual. Yet we do tend to distract ourselves from reflecting too heavily on this fact. Indeed, fictional engagement often requires a kind of a temporary 'letting go of' or psychologically 'distancing oneself from' certain aspects of (perceived) reality that might conflict with our being able to take the fiction seriously.[18] And this is something we do successfully on a regular basis without

---

16   By 'religious tradition' I have in mind something social, institutional, and historical. But I am aware that there are competing scholarly understandings of religion. Still, I think most of these theoretical accounts are compatible with the idea of religion as a kind of 'lens' or 'orientation' through which an experience may be interpreted.

17   This is not the only way one may imaginatively engage as a non-believer, but it is the one I will focus on in the remainder of this essay.

18   For example, in order to enjoy the television show "24", one must perhaps not reflect too heavily on the fact that mere mortals do not generally exemplify the physical resilience

RELIGIOUS EXPERIENCE WITHOUT BELIEF?

much cognitive difficulty or dissonance: we bracket certain metaphysical and ontological presuppositions in order to be able to properly enjoy the fiction with which we are engaging.

But why do we *care* about being able to enjoy fiction? What *value* might it have for our lives? There are various answers one might provide here: that engaging with fiction allows us to expand our imaginative horizons, making us more flexible in our everyday lives; that it increases our sense of empathy by allowing us to engage with characters we will likely never meet; that it allows us to travel imaginatively to places and times to which we have not been (nor perhaps has anyone else).[19] Or perhaps engaging with fiction, like playing sports or music (or doing philosophy!), is enjoyable *for its own sake*. In any case, we would be hard-pressed to find someone who thinks that engaging with drama, literature, film, and the like does not contribute in any way to human flourishing. In fact, I think most people would agree that their lives are in some way 'enriched' by their engagement with fiction.[20]

Still, there are some persons for whom suspending disbelief, bracketing metaphysical considerations, or otherwise mentally compartmentalizing may be more difficult. And for such people, enjoying certain fictions (or being able to take them seriously) will not come as easily as for others. Then there are those persons who take fiction more seriously than their more skeptical counterparts. Role-playing games, cosplay, fan fiction, historical re-enactments, and other similar activities represent ways in which fiction and pretense may take on a more concrete role in one's everyday life. But such enthusiasts need not be characterized as delusional or pathological – they merely engage with fiction in a more concrete fashion than those of us who simply leave the book on the nightstand. Of course, most of us fall somewhere in the middle of this spectrum.[21]

---

of a Jack Bauer, or be willing to accept that one can make it across Los Angeles in ten minutes during rush hour.

19   Keith Oatley, for example, argues that engaging with fiction can have beneficial results in the "exploration of the minds of others, investigation of relationships, dynamics of interactions in groups, and grappling with the problems of selfhood". Keith Oatley, *Such Stuff as Dreams: The Psychology of Fiction* (Oxford: Wiley, 2011), 167.

20   It is important here to note that certain types of fictional engagement may, in fact, be *harmful*, depending on the nature and content of the fiction with which one engages (see Keith Oatley, *Such Stuff as Dreams*, 167). But the same may be said for religious engagement. Still, nothing about what I say here regarding the possibility of religious experience by engaging imaginatively with religious concepts hinges on this. One could also have religious experiences within a religion which is morally bad.

21   Similarly, there are often particular fictional contexts with which we find ourselves more able and/or willing to sincerely engage than others. I might be a huge "Battlestar Galactica"

Yet regardless of where we find ourselves on this continuum, assuming we are capable of 'letting go' enough to enjoy fiction in some capacity, we will also notice that we appear to be capable of being emotionally affected by it. We cry when a beloved character dies; our flesh crawls when we watch a creepy horror film; we feel torn and upset when a character faces a moral dilemma; and we rejoice when the hero overcomes a difficult obstacle to triumph over evil. Still, we might wonder whether such phenomena represent *genuine* emotions and, if so, whether such emotions might not be irrational, misplaced, or otherwise *inappropriate*, given that they have as (at least part of) their content non-existent entities and states of affairs. The answer that we give to this question will affect the way we view the experiences of committed non-believers in imaginative religious contexts.

In a seminal piece on this question, Kendall Walton has argued that the feelings we experience when we encounter fiction are not really emotions at all – they are better understood as *quasi-emotions*.[22] Although they bear certain similarities to 'genuine' emotions, they differ in that they do not require the existence of their objects and that they do not appear intrinsically tied to motivation and action. Colin Radford, on the other hand, has argued that the emotions themselves are genuine, but they are misdirected or irrational, since their objects do not exist.[23] However, Tamar Szabó Gendler and Karson Kovakovich have (I think persuasively) argued against both of these positions, and with good reason.[24] First, they note, it simply begs the question to assume that genuine emotions are only those whose objects exist or that all emotions with non-existent objects are, by virtue of this fact, irrational. Both claims threaten to reduce the debate to a mere lexical dispute.[25] Further, they argue that it is false that fictional emotions are not linked to action. They cite a series of studies by Antonio Damasio which conclude that imagining certain (non-actual) practical consequences of hypothetical behavior triggers

---

fan, where you find it difficult to take science fiction seriously. Perhaps you prefer historical fiction or romance novels. This may have important parallels in the religious case, since aesthetic preferences can and do play a role in one's ability and willingness to sincerely participate in certain religious traditions or practices.

22 See Kendall Walton, *Mimesis as Make-Believe* (Cambridge, MA: Harvard University Press, 1990), 195–202.

23 See Colin Radford, "How Can We Be Moved by the Fate of Anna Karenina?", *Proceedings of the Aristotelian Society*, supp. vol. 49 (1975), 67–80.

24 See Tamar Szabó Gendler and Karson Kovakovich, "Genuine Rational Fictional Emotions", in *Contemporary Debates in Aesthetics and the Philosophy of Art*, ed. Matthew Kieran (Oxford: Blackwell, 2005), 241–256.

25 See ibid., 249.

RELIGIOUS EXPERIENCE WITHOUT BELIEF? 83

emotional mechanisms that serve as "somatic markers" which then assist in guiding future behavior. And the "simulated emotions" in play here are not significantly different from the emotions we encounter when engaging with fiction. Thus, emotions that have as their objects entities or states of affairs the subject herself takes not to exist may not only motivate behavior; they might be crucial for the successful exercise of practical reasoning in the first place.[26]

Further, regarding Radford's claim, it seems wrong to say that every 'fictional emotion' is irrational by virtue of being targeted at and/or triggered by a fictional object. There certainly seem to be *inappropriate* emotional responses with regard to fiction. (We would think it inappropriate for someone to take joy in the moral dilemma in which the title character of *Sophie's Choice* finds herself.) But the fact that there appear to be inappropriate emotional responses to fiction implies that there are also *appropriate* ones. Indeed, there would appear to be no possibility of a substantive debate about the appropriate way to feel within certain fictional contexts if all such emotions are *per se* irrational or inappropriate.

What is the upshot of this discussion? If Gendler and Kovakovich are right, and we can "respond with genuine, rational emotions to targets that we believe to be fictional",[27] then it does not seem all that far-fetched to extend this conclusion to religious emotions in the case of the non-believer. Now, it *might* be the case that the believer experiences such emotions more vividly or intensely than the non-believer (just as the death of a close friend affects me more strongly than the death of a beloved fictional character), but this is an empirical matter – one which I am not sure would be borne out in every case of religious emotion. Even if it were, however, it would only demonstrate that there is a *quantitative*, not a *qualitative*, difference in emotion between the religious believer and non-believer. Further, as with our engagement with fiction, engagement with religion might open us up to *new* ways of seeing the world and ourselves: it might allow us to develop a "sense and taste for the infinite"[28] – to *see* the universe *as* disclosing transcendence, *as* a matter of "Ultimate Concern"[29] – to understand our own contingency and our special place in the world. Viewing an occupation as a vocation, a calling, instead of a

---

26 See Antonio Damasio, *The Feeling of What Happens: Body and Emotion in the Making of Consciousness* (New York: Harcourt, 1999), cited in Tamar Szabó Gendler and Karson Kovakovich, "Emotions", 247–248.

27 Tamar Szabó Gendler and Karson Kovakovich, "Emotions", 253.

28 See Friedrich Schleiermacher, *On Religion: Speeches to Its Cultured Despisers*, trans. Richard Crouter (Cambridge: Cambridge University Press, 1988).

29 See Paul Tillich, *Dynamics of Faith* (New York: Harper Collins, 2001).

84 GRIFFIOEN

mere job may imbue our lives with a sense of meaning, even if we take there to be no one who has actually called us. Viewing our moral duty as divinely ordained may help us develop characters that are more virtuous and more loving, even if we think there is ultimately no 'divine commander'.[30] Indeed, emotions in simulative contexts might not only be important for practical reasoning – they may be necessary for us to view ourselves as agents-in-the-world in the first place, and religious emotions have their place in this schema too. In any case, I think a case can plausibly be made that the imaginatively-engaged religious life can and does (at least in some instances) contribute positively to human flourishing.

What Kind of Religious Emotion?

However, one might object here that I am too hasty and too vague with my characterization of religious emotions. One might argue that while we may feel 'basic' emotions like joy, sadness, anger, amusement, fear and so on in response to fictional characters and states of affairs, the emotional states characteristic of religious experience are not those we typically experience in fictional contexts. So what should we say here? Are the paradigmatic religious emotions of a kind that can (non-pathologically) be experienced by a non-believer? To begin, I think that at least some paradigmatic religious emotions are not particularly problematic for the non-believer. Awe, wonder, fear, mystery, Otto's *mysterium tremendum et fascinans*, even Schleiermacher's "feeling of absolute dependence"[31] – I think all of these can be fairly straightforwardly experienced by the imaginatively-engaged non-believer. Indeed, imaginative engagement with particular religious concepts in certain contexts might be the exact kind of thing that makes such experiences possible for any subject, believer or not.

Interestingly, in none of the cases just mentioned is the actual target of the emotion *God*. I feel awe in response to a magnificent Alpine landscape; I wonder at the expanse of the night sky; I tremble at the uncanny stillness of an empty church; I thrill at the swelling of a choir's voices; I feel 'creaturely' and dependent when I imagine myself as a tiny speck in a greater universe; and so on. In these kinds of emotional experiences, the direct target of my

---

30   Further, we can imagine a philosophically-minded theist who finds theological intellectu-alism more theoretically persuasive – yet who is (rightly) concerned about the sources of normativity – adopting a divine voluntarist model as a "useful fiction" to motivate action or serve as a practical guide to everyday life.

31   See Rudolf Otto, *The Idea of the Holy*, and Friedrich Schleiermacher, *The Christian Faith*.

RELIGIOUS EXPERIENCE WITHOUT BELIEF? 85

experience (and, in many cases, its proximate cause) is something worldly and immanent, something *existent*. In the latter case, it may even be my own self that is both the subject and the object of the emotion. Even for the believer, there is no *direct* perception of God here – indeed in many religious traditions, it would be heresy to maintain that such a thing is even possible. Where God is 'perceived' by the believer in religious experience, God becomes present only *indirectly*, via the actual target of the experience.[32] In any case, what makes these experiences religious has more to do with their being interpreted from within the framework of a religious tradition in which one is willingly and sincerely engaged, their being articulated with the use of religious terms and propositions, and their being colored by these concepts in a way that non-religiously interpreted experiences are not.

This is a kind of experience that both the believer and the non-believer can 'make' (to speak, as the Germans do, of *Erfahrung machen*). And while such experiences may be correlated with a belief in the existence of the divine, they need not be. The inferences that one draws from a religious experience may be vast and wide-ranging. Thus, *pace* Wayne Proudfoot, I do not think that the noetic quality of a religious experience – its informative, cognitive aspect – must involve an explanatory judgment about the causal origin of the experience. Proudfoot maintains that were I to provide a wholly naturalistic explanation of my experience, I could not view it as religious.[33] Yet anyone who has taken a hallucinogenic substance knows that one can be genuinely afraid of something they 'know' is a drug-induced hallucination. Instead, I would argue, the noetic quality of emotional religious experience has more to do with a kind of *self-knowledge* – one perhaps combined in some cases with a deeper sense of one's relation to others – than with beliefs about the existence of a divine reality.

Still, one might argue, there are further paradigmatic religious attitudes – interactive, second-personal attitudes like those of gratitude, trust, and love –

32 This is, of course, in contrast to such accounts of religious or mystical experience that purport to be 'direct perceptions' of God. See, for example, William Alston's *Perceiving God: The Epistemology of Religious Experience* (Ithaca, NY: Cornell University Press, 1991). While I leave it open that such experiences may be possible, I do not think they are common within everyday religious practice.

33 See Wayne Proudfoot's discussion of William James in his chapters on "Mysticism" and "Explanation" in *Religious Experience*. Proudfoot's analysis of the explanatory feature of religious experience is much more nuanced and subtle than I can reproduce (or refute) here. However, suffice it to say that I part ways with him (and, apparently, with James and others) in claiming that an explanatory judgment is not necessary for religious experience.

that may be closed off to the non-believer. Of course, unlike experiences of awe and wonder, none of these latter attitudes is, strictly speaking, a discrete emotional state. They involve larger complexes of cognitive, affective, and volitional states and activities that extend over time. I may feel thankful toward someone, but ultimately gratitude is something I *show*. I may 'feel trusting' toward someone, but trusting (and especially *en*trusting) is something I *do*. Something similar may be said for love. So engaging here goes beyond merely responding emotionally to a stimulus. It also involves something active, temporally extended, and volitional.

But can the religious non-believer feel and do such things? In principle, I do not see why not. To be sure, such attitudes are not typical responses to fiction. It sounds odd to talk about 'trusting' Harry Potter or being 'grateful' to Daenerys Targaryen. And we would think it borderline pathological if someone were to say that she, like Jane Eyre, were 'in love' with Mr. Rochester. Yet simply because we do not generally display interactive attitudes toward fictional characters does not mean we cannot display such attitudes toward nonexistent entities, at least within contexts in which such attitudes are appropriate. First, as with the non-interactive attitudes discussed above, displaying these latter attitudes will also require a stretch of the imagination on the part of the believer. If 'trust', 'gratitude', and 'love' have a univocal (or even analogous) meaning in religious and non-religious contexts, then even the religious believer must conceive of God as a creative, providential, *personal* being – an anthropomorphization that might require bracketing other things she takes to be true of God (like God's eternality or immutability).[34] Second, although we do not generally experience such attitudes when we engage with literary or dramatic fiction, it does not mean we are incapable of taking up an imaginative second-person stance. Children often address imaginary persons in play, and even many adults engage in imaginary dialogues (including self-dialogues, in which we take the self as an Other). So it is not really a stretch to think that such imaginative second-person stances are psychologically possible.

Thus perhaps taking on a certain kind of imaginative, second-personal stance may make room for the possibility of a non-believer's adopting the above kinds of attitudes. When we undertake an imagining of the world *as* created by a benevolent being, we may be able to view our lives as though they were gifts from God, allowing us to respond with a form of gratitude. The same type of imaginative stance may allow us to take on a kind of 'willing passivity', a trusting commitment to accepting what may befall one. Love is not far

---

34   This is one way of expressing the tensions between apophaticism and cataphaticism or between God's immanence and God's transcendence in certain monotheistic contexts.

RELIGIOUS EXPERIENCE WITHOUT BELIEF? 87

behind here.[35] If one can cash out these attitudes in this way, then, it seems that religious engagement may help foster such feelings in believers and non-believers alike and that the imaginative employment of religious concepts may help to flesh them out or to give them more substance.[36]

Conclusion: Religious Experience without Belief

In summary, I think there is a way of making sense of emotional religious experience that does not require belief in the existence or truth of the relevant religious concepts or propositions involved in that experience. There is certainly more to be said here, and a full-fledged account of the religious imagination still needs to be provided.[37] But I hope to have shown that what is central to religious engagement is not necessarily belief, but rather a kind of volitional, imaginative commitment. The experiences that result from such commitment will involve a certain level of imaginative 'interpretation' (or *Deutung*) – a way of seeing things through a religious 'lens', as it were – but this need not threaten their (in-)genuineness. Furthermore, if I am right that certain forms of religious engagement may contribute positively to human flourishing, it would seem we should start rethinking the way we approach religious faith as well.[38] Indeed, perhaps religious faith is less about what we *believe* and more about what we *do* with what we *imagine*. And if those things we imagine "don't happen to be so", perhaps "that's just an unimportant technicality".[39]

---

35   The idea of taking on an imaginative second-personal stance will be especially important in fleshing out an account of what might be going on in prayer as well.

36   For a fascinating example of exercises in pretense and play intended to cultivate a sense for second-personal interaction with God, see: Tanya M. Luhrmann, *When God Talks Back* (New York: Vintage Books, 2012).

37   For a few helpful sources on the religious imagination and belief, see: Garrett Green, *Imagining God*; Douglas Hedley, *Living Forms of the Imagination* (London: T&T Clark, 2008); and, more recently, Graham Ward, *Unbelievable: Why We Believe and Why We Don't* (London: I. B. Tauris, 2014).

38   This paper serves as a precursor to the account of religious faith I am currently developing. Unfortunately, I will have to save the intricacies of this view for another occasion.

39   I would like to thank Ulrich Schmiedel, Tobias Tan, and Thomas Hardtke for the organization of the conference at which an earlier version of this paper was presented. I would also like to thank Jörg Lauster, Graham Ward, Scott O'Leary, Ian James Kidd, David Cooper, Clare Carlisle, Dina Emundts, Jochen Briesen, Ursula Renz, Evan Fales, Greg Landini, Daniel Schumacher, Arie Griffioen, and all the others who have given me helpful feedback on some of the central ideas of this paper.

Literature

Alston, William, "Belief, Acceptance, and Religious Faith", in *Faith, Freedom, and Rationality*, ed. Jeff Jordan and Daniel Howard-Snyder (Lanham, MD: Rowman & Littlefield, 1996), 10–27.

Alston, William, *Perceiving God: The Epistemology of Religious Experience* (Ithaca, NY: Cornell University Press, 1991).

Damasio, Antonio, *The Feeling of What Happens: Body and Emotion in the Making of Consciousness* (New York: Harcourt, 1999).

Eshleman, Andrew, "Can an Atheist Believe in God?", *Religious Studies* 4 (2005), 183–199.

Green, Garrett, *Imagining God: Theology and the Religious Imagination* (San Francisco, CA: Harper & Row, 1989).

Griffioen, Amber, "Prolegomena zu einer jeden künftigen '(Nicht-)Metaphysik' der Religion: (Anti-)Realismus, (Non-)Kognitivismus und die religiöse Imagination", in *Gott ohne Theismus*, ed. Rico Gutschmidt and Thomas Rentsch (Münster: Mentis Verlag, 2016), 127–147.

Harrison, Victoria, "Philosophy of Religion, Fictionalism, and Religious Diversity", *International Journal for the Philosophy of Religion* 68 (2010), 43–58.

Hedley, Douglas, *Living Forms of the Imagination* (London: T&T Clark, 2008).

Howard-Snyder, Daniel, "Propositional Faith: What It Is and What It Is Not", *American Philosophical Quarterly* 50 (2013), 357–372.

Le Poidevin, Robin, *Arguing for Atheism* (London: Routledge, 1996).

Luhrmann, Tanya M., *When God Talks Back* (New York: Vintage Books, 2012).

Muyskens, James, *The Sufficiency of Hope: Conceptual Foundations of Religion* (Philadelphia, PA: Temple University Press, 1979).

Oatley, Keith, *Such Stuff as Dreams: The Psychology of Fiction* (Oxford: Wiley, 2011).

Otto, Rudolf, *The Idea of the Holy*, trans. John W. Harvey (London: Oxford University Press, 1958).

Proudfoot, Wayne, *Religious Experience* (Berkeley, CA: California University Press, 1985).

Radford, Colin, "How Can We Be Moved by the Fate of Anna Karenina?", *Proceedings of the Aristotelian Society*, supp. vol. 49 (1975), 67–80.

Schleiermacher, Friedrich, *On Religion: Speeches to Its Cultured Despisers*, trans. Richard Crouter (Cambridge: Cambridge University Press, 1988).

Schleiermacher, Friedrich, *The Christian Faith*, trans. Hugh R. Mackintosh and James S. Stewart (London: T&T Clark, 1999).

Szabó Gendler, Tamar, and Karson Kovakovich, "Genuine Rational Fictional Emotions", in *Contemporary Debates in Aesthetics and the Philosophy of Art*, ed. Matthew Kieran (Oxford: Blackwell, 2005), 241–256.

Tillich, Paul, *Dynamics of Faith* (New York: Harper Collins, 2001).

Walton, Kendall, *Mimesis as Make-Believe* (Cambridge, MA: Harvard University Press, 1990).

Ward, Graham, *Unbelievable: Why We Believe and Why We Don't* (London: I. B. Tauris, 2014).

CHAPTER 5

"Is that You?" Hearing God's Voice in the Words of a Stranger (Judges 6:11–24)

Catherine Lewis-Smith

The story of Gideon's encounter with a messenger of YHWH possesses one highly startling feature: a single stranger comes to Gideon, but two voices are heard in this one body.[1] A messenger of YHWH initiates a conversation with Gideon (Judg. 6:12), but YHWH voices the stranger's second and third speeches (6:14,16).[2] Another speech is ascribed only to a masculine pronoun (6:18), but as the narrated action resumes, it is clearly the messenger who moves and mobilizes the action.[3] In the final conversation of this encounter, Gideon prays directly to YHWH and receives direct answer (6:23), which raises the question of why a mediating figure was necessary. Perhaps the confusion over who is speaking, and how many voices are present, arises from an attempt to represent the experience of recognizing the divine word in the voice of another.

In this paper, I use discourse analysis tools developed by Mikhail Bakhtin to show that Gideon's initial encounter with God is mediated by Gideon's experience as a user of language. Gideon is a skilled speaker, and adeptly employs double-voiced speech to its full effect.[4] I suggest, however, that Gideon's preference for double-directed words causes him to seek double-meaning in the stranger's words, and it is this hermeneutic of suspicion which creates the narrative crisis of this encounter – could Gideon fail to recognize the divine when directly and intimately addressed?

---

1 In Hebrew one cannot distinguish whether מלאך יהוה is 'the' or 'a' messenger of the LORD. As one should not assume that all instances of *mal'ak YHWH* have a single referent, I prefer the indeterminate construction.
2 I use 'the stranger' to signal both Gideon's confusion and the instability of referent in the narrative frame.
3 However he is called both messenger of God (6:20) and messenger of YHWH (6:21, 22).
4 Bakhtin distinguishes two major categories of double-voiced speeches. The first is the use of a character's speech by an author to convey authorial perspectives, whilst the second is an individual speaker's use of language to create polysemous utterances. Mikhail M. Bakhtin, *Problems of Dostoevsky's Poetics*, trans. Caryl Emerson (Minneapolis, MN: University of Minnesota Press, 1984), 185–186; 191–199. In this article I will exclusively focus upon the latter form of double-voiced speech.

© KONINKLIJKE BRILL NV, LEIDEN, 2016 | DOI 10.1163/9789004328600_007

As the encounter begins Gideon suspects that Israel has been abandoned by its God. I will read Gideon's perception of divine disinterest and his dawning awareness of immediate divine presence in relation to Bakhtin's image of the 'superaddressee', a hypothetical and necessary third party in all discourse, who is always presumed to be present and whose absence instills terror.[5] As we will see, the primary role of the superaddressee is to hear and adjudge every utterance in discourse, but Bakhtin also explores scenes in which the words of the superaddressee are heard in an utterance spoken by another, human interlocutor.[6] Perhaps, then, the superaddressee provides a critical model for hearing two voices in a single speaker.

Bakhtin's value to the literary critic is his careful consideration of the role and function of dialogue within a text. In Judges 6:11–24 dialogue is the primary evidence available to Gideon as he attempts to establish the identity of the stranger, his intentions, trustworthiness, status, and so on. Dialogue is also the reader's primary means of discerning Gideon's interpretation of the encounter.[7] I will read Gideon's evolving perception of the divine in relation to Bakhtin's distinction of the self-account, the "accounting rendered to oneself for one's own life," and the confessional self-account.[8] In a confessional self-account the author, i.e. the one accounting for herself, comes to realize that "my own word about myself is in principle incapable of being the last word, the word that consummates me."[9] Thus an awareness of the divine emerges in the need for consummation, in the forms of "forgiveness and redemption."[10] My analysis will show that the stranger provokes Gideon to

---

5   The superaddressee is introduced in Mikhail M. Bakhtin, *Speech Genres and Other Late Essays*, ed. Caryl Emerson and Michael Holquist, trans. Michael Holquist and Vern W. McGee (Austin, TX: University of Texas Press, 1986), 127. Two helpful recent discussions of its value in discussing religious experience are Peter Slater, "Bakhtin on Hearing God's Voice", *Modern Theology* 23/1 (2007), 1–25 and Frank M. Farmer, "'Not Theory...But a Sense of Theory:' The Superaddressee and the Contexts of Eden", *Symplokē*, 2 (1994), 87–101.

6   Bakhtin, *Problems of Dostoevsky's Poetics*, 255–256.

7   As Jack Sidnell observes, "a response displays a hearing or analysis of the utterance to which it responds." Jack Sidnell, *Conversation Analysis: An Introduction* (Chichester: Wiley-Blackwell, 2010), 66.

8   The confessional self-account emerges in Mikhail M. Bakhtin, *Art and Answerability: Early Philosophical Essays by M. M. Bakhtin*, ed. Michael Holquist and Vadim Liapunov, trans. Vadim Liapunov (Austin, TX: University of Texas Press, 1990), 138–148.

9   Ibid., 143.

10   Ibid.

HEARING GOD'S VOICE IN THE WORDS OF A STRANGER 91

re-evaluate and reject the self-account he holds at the beginning of the encounter, characterized by cynical and sarcastic speech. Destabilized by the apparent interruption of the divine in the words of the stranger, a 'place for God' opens up in Gideon's imagination, which is represented by the narrator in direct, unmediated prayer dialogue between Gideon and YHWH.[11] Thus discourse is not only the means by which the divine is experienced in Judges 6:11–24, but also the means by which transformation of the self is represented.

Angel Encounter or Theophany?

Although it is commonplace in the study of Gideon's narrative to assume that the messenger of YHWH is a form in which YHWH appears, this paper does not share that assumption.[12] As Samuel Meier noted, the extent to which biblical authors identify the messenger with YHWH is both perplexing and inconsistent.[13] James Barr suggested that the messenger "might be better understood as the accompaniment of the anthropomorphic appearance rather than as a dilution of it."[14] Thus 'messengers' accompany YHWH in a theophany as an additional concrete anthropomorphic presence, and not as anthropomorphic representations of the divine.

Frank Polak focused his discussion of theophany on its genre expectations, but his inclusion and exclusion of features in the "the supra-textual matrix" of theophany nonetheless determines the categories of religious experience which can be so defined; Polak excluded dreams and visions from the category of theophany, arguing that "concrete, outside perception" was a necessary feature.[15] Polak concluded that divine speech mediated by a prophet or human

---

11 Ibid., 144.

12 Recent readers of Judges 6 who treat the encounter as a theophany include: Daniel Block, *Judges, Ruth* (Nashville, TN: Broadman & Holman, 1999), 258; Benjamin D. Sommer, *The Bodies of God and the World of Ancient Israel* (Cambridge: Cambridge University Press, 2009), 43, Barry G. Webb, *The Book of Judges* (Grand Rapids, MI: Eerdmans, 2012), 228–29.

13 Samuel A. Meier, "Angel of Yahweh", *Dictionary of Deities and Demons in the Bible* (Leiden: Brill, 1999), 54–55.

14 James Barr, "Theophany and Anthropomorphism in the Old Testament", *Congress Volume: Oxford, 1959* (Leiden: Brill, 1960), 31–38 (34).

15 Frank Polak, "Theophany and Mediator: The Unfolding of a Theme in the Book of Exodus", in *Studies in the Book of Exodus: Redaction, Reception, Interpretation*, ed. Marc Vervenne (Leuven: Leuven University Press, 1996), 113–147 (113). The exclusion of dreams and visions

messenger is not a theophany,[16] but Polak offered no perspective on divine speech mediated by angel messengers, as the messengers of Exodus do not speak.[17] George Savran's project similarly depends upon literary resemblance to select the experiences of divine which belong to the category 'theophany';[18] his analysis includes some messenger encounters but excludes others.[19] Of particular significance to this paper, Savran claims that the messenger is intimately connected to a theophany's reception: "the presence of the *malakh* serves as a signal that there will be a delay in recognition."[20]

Thus a messenger introduces an experience of the divine which is vulnerable to rejection by its addressee. The as-though human form and speech of the messenger leads to the interpretation of his words and actions through a frame of human-to-human social convention, which can result in misunderstanding or mistrust. Misunderstanding and delayed recognition emphasize the distance between addressee and deity. The messenger signifies both the drawing close of divinity to humanity and the distance normally perceived between them.[21] In Judges 6:11–24 the narrator needs, and exploits, the distinction between messenger and LORD to establish the *anagnorisis* plot which generates its narrative momentum.[22] The presence of two voices within one body intensifies the drama of misrecognition: it is unfortunate for the messenger to go unrecognized, but scandalous to fail to recognize YHWH. The reader is made acutely aware of two voices so that the risk and comedy of misrecognition can be exploited to the full.

---

from theophany is discussed by Nicolaas F. Schmidt and Philip J. Nel, "Theophany as Type-Scene in the Hebrew Bible", *Journal for Semitics* 11 (2002), 256–281 (259).

16   Polak, "Theophany and Mediator", 113.

17   Although the Israelites are told to listen for the voice of 'my messenger' (Exod. 23:20–33), no utterance is assigned to him.

18   George W. Savran, *Encountering the Divine: Theophany in Biblical Narrative* (London: T&T Clark International, 2005).

19   Savran excludes scenes in which a messenger is heard but not seen, e.g. Gen. 21:14–19, 22:1–19, but also the messenger who comes to Bochim (Judg. 2:1–5). Presumably these excluded texts lack features which Savran considers essential to the genre. Savran, *Encountering the Divine*, 5, 30.

20   Ibid., 78.

21   Ibid., 17.

22   Anagnorisis is a moment of recognition, "a change from ignorance to knowledge". Roger W. Herzel, "Anagnorisis and Peripeteia in Comedy", *Educational Theatre Journal* 26/4 (1974), 495–505 (500).

HEARING GOD'S VOICE IN THE WORDS OF A STRANGER

The Superaddressee

Bakhtin distinguishes three roles in dialogue: speaker, addressee, and superaddressee.[23] A speaker desires to be understood. She specifically addresses herself to one or more persons, casting them in the role of addressee.[24] In most dialogues, the roles of speaker and addressee will pass back and forth between participants. Whoever is speaker hopes for and aims to foster 'responsive understanding' in the addressee.[25] Though there are three roles, Bakhtin places no limit upon the number of persons in the dialogue taking the first and second roles.[26]

The third role is that of superaddressee, whose task is "to supply just and responsive understanding."[27] The 'superaddressee' is Bakhtin's term for the role played in dialogue by an actual or abstract hearer whom both speaker and addressee presume to attend to their communication, and pass judgment upon it.[28] This presumption is, Bakhtin suggests, an intrinsic feature of utterance, as discourse longs for understanding: "the word always wants to be *heard*, always seeks responsive understanding, and does not stop at *immediate* understanding but presses on further and further (indefinitely)."[29] We should observe that the superaddressee is imagined to be beyond the immediate, and the understanding which it supplies is greater than that of the primary addressee.[30] The superaddressee is distant, whether distant in time or metaphysically different.[31] Bakhtin identifies the following in a non-exhaustive list of superaddressees: "God, absolute truth, the court of dispassionate human conscience, the people, the court of history, science."[32] Bakhtin nonetheless

---

23 Bakhtin, *Speech Genres*, 95–96; 126–27.

24 Ibid., 126.

25 Ibid., 69.

26 Ibid., 126.

27 Ibid.

28 Ibid.

29 Ibid., 127.

30 As Frank F. Farmer observes, "The superaddressee thus offers a 'loophole' for a perfect understanding elsewhere, and a hedge against the dangers of a consummated misunderstanding here". Farmer, "Not Theory", 96.

31 Ibid., 126.

32 Ibid. Though, as Warren Midgely observes, the first and second participants in a discourse need not be addressing the same superaddressee. Warren Midgley, "Look Who's Listening: Using the Superaddressee for Understanding Connections in Dialogue", in *Creating Connections in Teaching and Learning*, ed. Lindy Abwai, Joan M. Conway and Robyn Henderson (Charlotte, NC: Information Age Publishing, 2011), 153–163.

does not permit simple identification of God and superaddressee, and expressly rejected the idea that the superaddressee can, in material reality, be a deity: "the third party is not any mystical or metaphysical being (although, given a certain understanding of the world, he can be expressed as such)."[33] My assertion that 'superaddressee' is an appropriate term for the divine is not based therefore on the "Problem of the Text", in which the concept arises,[34] but on the observation that Bakhtin's discussion of the role of God in the texts of Fyodor Dostoevsky describes God's activity in terms which anticipate the role of the superaddressee.[35] Importantly, the absence of a superaddressee is too awful to contemplate. Bakhtin observes that for discourse itself as for "the human being", "there is nothing more terrible than a *lack of response*."[36]

Gideon's attitude to the superaddressee changes dramatically across his encounter. At first the hero suspects that Israel has been abandoned by its superaddressee. Indeed, Gideon rejects the stranger's greeting "YHWH is with you" (6:12) with a lengthy rebuttal of the stranger's claim (6:13) which reveals his fear that YHWH has abandoned Israel. By the time Gideon leaves the winepress, however, he has begun to recognize a divine voice within the conversation. When he requests "a sign that it is you who is speaking with me" (6:17) Gideon seeks to distinguish the second speaker, his immediate addressee, and the 'third' voice in the dialogue, that is, God as superaddressee. The implicit question "is it you speaking" cannot be addressed to an ordinary addressee. That the second speaker has spoken cannot be in doubt. Instead, Gideon seeks to distinguish another voice.

The narrator and reader know that this second speaker is YHWH but this knowledge is unavailable to Gideon unless he can discern it from the content or quality of the stranger's speeches. My translation of the dialogue of 6:12–17 is presented below, as though a transcription of the conversation:

> *STRANGER*   YHWH is with you, mighty warrior.
>
> *GIDEON*   Please sir, if YHWH is with us, why has all this happened to us? And where are all his marvelous deeds of which our fathers told us, saying 'Did not YHWH bring us up from Egypt?' But now YHWH has cast us off, and given us into the hand of Midian.

---

33   Bakhtin, *Speech Genres*, 126.

34   Ibid., 103–31.

35   See Bakhtin, *Art and Answerability*, 143–146; Bakhtin, *Problems*, 216–217. Slater concludes that when Bakhtin chooses to employ God language in his texts he does so theistically. Slater, "Bakhtin on Hearing", 9.

36   Bakhtin, *Speech Genres*, 127. Emphasis as per this edition of the text.

STRANGER	Go, in this your strength and deliver Israel from the hand of Midian. Am I not sending you?
GIDEON	Please, my Lord, how can I save Israel? Look, my clan is the least in Manasseh and I am the weakest in my father's household.
STRANGER	Because I will be with you, you will strike down Midian as though one man.
GIDEON	Please, if I have indeed found favor in your eyes, perform a sign for me that it you who is speaking with me.

The Masoretic text of Judg. 6:15 clearly asserts that Gideon recognizes the change of speaker immediately; whereas Gideon responded to the stranger's arrival with an irony laden "please, sir", his second speech employs an address proper only to God, "please, my Lord."[37] This subtle distinction between "sir" and "Lord" is achieved by a single change in vocalization of the Hebrew text, from בִּי אֲדֹנִי to בִּי אֲדֹנָי. This ostensibly respectful address to the divine is, however, dissonant with the plot. At 6:17 Gideon hesitates to claim that he hears a third voice. This uncertainty is incoherent with the address to the stranger as God one speech act earlier. Moreover, the moment of recognition which fulfils the *anagnorisis* plot does not come until after the act of sacrifice and the departure of the messenger (6:22). Narrative logic suggests that Gideon has partial recognition of divine address when he asks for a sign, but lacks full recognition of the encounter until the messenger has departed.

A Confessional Self-Account

My argument that Gideon has not recognized the divine voice in the stranger's voice at 6:15, and that the reader may therefore read with the plot against the Masoretic vocalization, will be built with reference to two further Bakhtinian concepts: the confessional self-account and penetrant speech. In its idealized form, the confessional self-account is an aesthetically pure activity.[38] It is,

---

37 On this point the Masoretic text is supported by Targum Jonathan to the Prophets. However, the Septuagint traditions erase the interplay of divine voices entirely.

38 The confessional self-account emerges as a thought experiment about the possibility of an aesthetic act in which the author, by which Bakhtin means a speaking subject, produces a work in which overcomes "all the transgredient moments of justification and valuation that are possible in the consciousness of other people." Bakhtin, *Art and Answerability*, 142. That the confessional self-account nonetheless provides a helpful framework for describing the role of confessee and God is demonstrated by Patricia K. Tull, "Bakhtin's

and is *only*, "that which I myself can say about myself."[39] Once the confessee acknowledges that she cannot be justified by the judgment of human others,[40] nor can she supply her own justification,[41] she comes to realize "the need for religious justification."[42] As Les W. Smith puts it, "confession *of* begins to yield before confession *that*."[43] At the outset of his encounter, Gideon does not desire to make a confessional self-account, but at its conclusion he does finally, speak honestly of himself before God. Perhaps, then, Bakhtin can help us speak with insight on this transformation.

An ordinary self-account is, however, polluted by awareness of the judgments of others which is manifest in fear of the opinions of others and fear of being shamed. These arise when the self-account is shaped by 'self-abasement', in submitting to the opinion of the other.[44] The internalization and acceptance of the judgment of others means that a person values herself on terms that reflect her value in the eyes of others: reputation, esteem, shame and favor.[45] In contrast, the speaker of a confessional self-account acknowledges the possible judgments of others against the self, but refuses to accept them; resistance to divine judgment is 'theomachy' whilst 'anthromachy' is rejection of human judgment.[46] Bakhtin suggests that the presenting symptoms of such resistance are "tones of resentment, distrust, cynicism, irony, [and] defiance."[47]

Resentment, resistance, cynicism and defiance could stand as a description of Gideon's response to the stranger's greeting, which is frequently described in terms of sarcasm and cynicism.[48] Although the stranger's greeting is ostensibly straightforward and appropriately respectful, Gideon rejects the assertion "the Lord is with you" and transforms it into negatively framed rhetorical question:

Confessional Self-Accounting and Psalms of Lament", *Biblical Interpretation* 13 (2005), 41–55; see also Les W. Smith, *Confession in the Novel: Bakhtin's Author Revisited* (Madison, NJ: Fairleigh Dickinson University Press, 1996), 32–37.

39 Bakhtin, *Art and Answerability*, 141.

40 Ibid., 143–144.

41 Ibid., 143, discussed above.

42 Ibid.

43 Les W. Smith, *Confession in the Novel*, 34.

44 Bakhtin, *Art and Answerability*, 141–142.

45 Ibid., 142.

46 Ibid., 146.

47 Ibid.

48 Roger J. Ryan, *Judges* (Sheffield: Sheffield Phoenix Press, 2007), 48, observes sarcasm and cynicism. Daniel Block describes the reply as a 'cheeky and sarcastic response, Block, *Judges, Ruth*, 260. See also Lillian R. Klein, *The Triumph of Irony in the Book of Judges* (Decatur, GA: Almond Press, 1988), 52.

"But if the Lord with us, why have these things happened to us?"[49] Gideon's speech is saturated with the judgment of others, judgments belonging to God and the community of Israel. Indeed, at this moment, and when it suits his rhetorical purposes, Gideon subsumes his self-account, his understanding of his own life, into the community account of rescue from Egypt by God's marvelous deeds.[50] This is, however, deliberate rhetorical positioning. Gideon adopts the language of community, as a means to resist the stranger's attempt to enlist him against the Midianites, and his narrative of corporate and personal nonworth should be approached by the reader with suspicion.

Gideon's self-account has a second community-orientated aspect, as his words echo the expression of the covenant relationship voiced by the prophet who appears immediately before Gideon's angel encounter (6:7–10). But Gideon quotes and re-accents these divine judgments in a theomachic fashion. Selective quotation of the prophet's words allows Gideon to omit the accusation "you have not listened to my voice" (6:10), and replace it with an accusation of divine silence. The shame which the prophet sought to engender is masked by Gideon's tone of defiant resentment, which nonetheless reveals that Gideon is acutely aware of his own, and Israel's, humiliation. Gideon's socio-spatial location at the outset of the encounter is emblematic of the tribes' plight, the could-be "mighty warrior" is hiding, attempting to work unseen by enemy raiders who would plunder his harvest (6:2–4, 11). Gideon's claim of abandonment, "YHWH has cast us off", and totalizing lament "why have these things happened to us", transform his experience of humiliation into accusation.

Gideon's response, which turns the stranger's words against their surface meaning, indicates that Gideon feels threatened by the stranger. The honorific "mighty warrior" (6:12) is utterly at odds with Gideon's location and

---

49   Lillian Klein suggests that "the use of the *waw* conversive ($w^e y\bar{e}\check{s}$) – literally 'And (is/exists) Yahweh with us?' lends an ironic, even sarcastic tone" to Gideon's response. Ibid., 53.

50   One of my readers raised the important question of whether Gideon's experience can be discussed in terms that arise from the enlightenment notion of an autonomous individuals. Colleen Shantz recently addressed this concern: "Concerns about anachronism have led to repeated lip service to the idea that ancient people were far more oriented to group identity than we are [...] Nonetheless, those corporate values and social sensibilities have to be received by individuals somehow in order for them to function. We cannot simply replace individual consciousness with corporate identity and assume that we have done justice either to the events themselves or to the complex process of enculturation". Colleen Shantz, "Opening the Black Box: New Prospects for Analyzing Religious Experience", in *Linking Text and Experience*, ed. Colleen Shantz and Rodney A. Werline, *Experientia*, 2 (Atlanta, GA: Society of Biblical Literature, 2008), 1–16 (7).

activity, which Block caricatured with the description "fearful farmer."[51] The reader could interpret the name as a performative utterance which inaugurates Gideon's career as deliverer-judge,[52] but Gideon's robust rebuttal of "YHWH is with you" as though a theological statement suggests that he interprets these words as "double-voiced speech", as a speech-act with hidden polemic in which Gideon is ostensibly praised but actually parodied.[53]

Double-voiced speech is a key discourse feature in Gideon's self-account. Gideon is a master of, and highly attuned to, double-voiced speech; the presence or absence of this discourse feature thus furnishes the reader with a means of distinguishing Gideon's perception of the stranger, and a critical tool to account for Gideon's initial recognition of a numinous aspect within the encounter. In Bakhtin's analysis, double-voiced speech is speech with more than one agenda.[54] Double-voiced speech includes parody, the "transmission of someone else's words with a changed accent", i.e. repetition which alters meaning, speech with hidden polemic and "any discourse with a sideward glance at another person's word".[55] It includes speech which seems on the surface to be a direct, linear, and final word on a subject but which contains a loophole, which leaves open the possibility that the author will "change its tone and its ultimate meaning".[56]

Gideon's reply betrays that he identifies hidden polemic in the stranger's greeting. His extended rebuttal of "the Lord is with you" exposes Gideon's ostensibly polite phrase, "please, sir," as a hollow formality. Intriguingly, however, Gideon rebuts only the claim of divine presence; he does not reject the status of "mighty warrior," and thus even Gideon's silence is double-voiced. By his reply, Gideon exposes his self-account and self-justification to the stranger, but also exposes himself to the stranger's judgment by his temporary acceptance of the title.

To find resistance of the deity in Gideon's second response contradicts a type-scene analysis of this theophany, which read the second pair of speeches as a commission and a humble response.[57] However, to interpret Gideon's

---

51   Daniel Block, *Judges, Ruth*, 261. See also J. Clinton McCann, *Judges* (Louisville, KY: John Knox Press, 2002), 64.

52   See Trent C. Butler, *Judges* (Nashville, TN: Thomas Nelson, 2009), 202.

53   Bakhtin, *Problems*, 193–99.

54   Ibid., 199.

55   Ibid., 199.

56   Ibid., 234.

57   Using Gideon as archetype, Norman C. Habel argued that the newly-appointed prophet or leader should humbly resist his calling. Norman C. Habel, "The Form and Significance

second response as a confession of humility is to aestheticize the discourse, importing concepts and contexts which are available to the reader but not to Gideon. From Gideon's perspective, the stranger's speech is poised on the boundary between monological speech and double-voiced mockery.[58] The stranger asserts that Gideon is strong, but in the absence of evidence on which to found the claim, Gideon has grounds to doubt its sincerity.

A second problem is the rhetorical question, "am I not sending you?" (6:14), which further obscures the stranger's identity. J. Alberto Soggin astutely observed this conundrum: "the rhetorical question does not make any sense here, given that Gideon could not know who was commanding him."[59] The words point to YHWH as speaker, but only when observed with the "surplus of seeing" available to the narrator and reader.[60] As Charles F. Burney observed, the words spoken by YHWH are not sufficient in themselves "to convince Gide'on that he was actually the spectator of a theophany."[61] Thus from Gideon's discourse-immanent perspective, the referent "your strength" points either to Gideon's audacious rebuttal of the stranger or else to Gideon's lack of strength, thereby extending the parody of the fearful farmer as a man of might. Both readings suggest the stranger has spoken a double-voiced speech.

By his ostensibly humble reply (6:15) Gideon once again seeks to resist the stranger's words. Gideon's self-construction cannot be reconciled with his social construction in the narrative which follows (6:25–32);[62] thus Gideon's second answer resembles his first. Gideon's supposed self-account is a self-parody in which Gideon appeals to the supposed judgments of others in order to resist being made subject to them.[63] Such self-destruction liberates the speaker from the power of those in whose eyes he is now debased. As a person of no regard, surely Gideon will be seen as a person on whom neither hopes

---

of the Call Narratives", *Zeitschrift für die Alttestamentliche Wissenschaft* 77 (1965), 297–323 (299–300).

58   Mark E. Biddle argues that the messenger's command is ironic and sarcastic, *Reading Judges: A Literary and Theological Commentary* (Macon, GA: Smyth and Helwys, 2012), 80.

59   J. Alberto Soggin, *Judges: A Commentary* (London: SCM Press, 1987).

60   "Surplus of seeing" is a more nuanced description of a narrator's knowledge than the notion of omniscience it seeks to displace. Bakhtin, *Problems*, 72–73.

61   Charles F. Burney, *The Book of Judges* (London: Rivington, 1918), 188.

62   Gideon's family are wealthy, Gideon possesses ten men-servants, and his father has sufficient social standing to refuse the demands of a lynch mob. Discussed in Butler, *Judges*, 203.

63   Gideon thus resembles Dostoevsky's underground man, whose self-destructive speech represents a "desperate effort to free oneself from the power of the other's consciousness". Bakhtin, *Problems*, 232.

nor obligations should be placed. Gideon's self-account is thus motivated by a desire for independence and marked by skillful manipulation and re-narration of the judgments of others.

Penetrant Speech

I have suggested that Gideon's cynical double-voiced speeches in 6:13 and 6:15 encourage us to dispute the Masoretic claim that Gideon recognizes YHWH as the third voice in this dialogue after YHWH's speech of 6:14. Rather it is the penetrant quality of YHWH's speech at 6:16 which reveals the superaddressee. Bakhtin identifies penetrant speech in a scene from *The Brothers Karamazov* in which Alyosha claims to speak divine speech when revealing to his brother something the latter has concealed from himself, declaring "God has sent me to tell you so" and "God has put it into my heart to say this to you".[64] These words are penetrant not because they are attributed to the divine but because of their discourse function. Penetrant speech speaks "actively and confidently" into the interior discourse of another.[65] It lacks the double-voiced quality of most ordinary dialogue and, unlike other modes of speech, penetrant speech can cause "the reconciliation and merging of voices", within a dialogue, or within a single speaker.[66] Its characteristic marks are directness, authenticity, and the capacity of such speech to provoke healing.

The stranger's declaration, "I will be with you" (6:16), does indeed address Gideon's deepest concern and seek to heal his perception of divine abandonment. His opening assertion "YHWH is with you" is transformed by being recast as first person speech, and now incorporates a revelation of divine presence; the words create an explicit intertextual connection with the call of Moses, in which the same promise "because I will be with you" is provided as an assurance, and anticipates the divine name (Exod. 3:12). Without using the words 'penetrant speech', Webb describes its presence and its purpose when he concludes that the stranger's third speech is "an unsubtle way of forcing into Gideon's consciousness the awareness that he is having an encounter with God himself, and is being given a commission he cannot refuse".[67] We cannot adjudge whether Gideon hears this utterance as the first person speech of a

---

64   Fyodor Dostoevsky, *The Karamazov Brothers*, trans. Ignat Avsey (Oxford: Oxford World Classics, 2008), Part 4, Book 11, ch. 5. Discussed in Bakhtin, *Problems*, 255–256.

65   Ibid., 242.

66   Ibid., 249.

67   Webb, *The Book of Judges*, 231.

HEARING GOD'S VOICE IN THE WORDS OF A STRANGER   101

third speaker (the superaddressee) or as reported speech in the voice of the second (the addressee), but we can posit, on good grounds, that Gideon finds in them his superaddressee.

Though the principal role of the superaddressee is to hear and judge each utterance, the superaddressee can gain a more active role in dialogue; Peter Slater observes that the superaddressee is heard "on the boundary between what is said and not said, on the brink of communication."[68] Most significantly for our investigation, Slater finds that the superaddressee can only emerge "in a dialogue that generates wholeness", in which the discourse partners cease role-playing thereby permitting, to quote Bakhtin, "the full and final emergence of the word into the plane of reality."[69] The capacity to hear God in discourse is therefore dependent upon the attitude of the speaker and addressee. If one or both are orientated towards 'wholeness' the potential for the superaddressee to emerge within the discourse is increased. A refusal to emerge from role-playing and its associated power games would, however, diminish the possibility that the superaddressee be heard.

Gideon's discourse strategy changes once he suspects the presence of the superaddressee. Gideon caresses his speech with volitional phrasing (אסֿ־נא at 6:17, אל־נא at 6:18) to signal a new humility; he also seeks confirmation that he has indeed discerned the divine voice. By offering a מנחה which could be interpreted as either a sacrificial offering or a gift,[70] Gideon carefully respects the addressee whilst communicating his awareness of the superaddressee.[71] The ambiguity is deliberate. If Gideon's discernment of two voices were incorrect, the gift would not offend propriety,[72] but it is also an acceptable offering to YHWH. The messenger co-operates with Gideon's test, and dedicates the food gift as a sacrifice; yet even then Gideon does not fully recognise the divine presence. Although the messenger pointed Gideon towards the existence, and active interest, of the superaddressee, its presence delays Gideon's ability to

---

68   Slater, "Bakhtin on Hearing", 9.

69   Slater, "Bakhtin on Hearing", 12 discussing Bakhtin, *Problems*, 261.

70   Soggin, *Judges*, 116, 121, observed that meat, broth and bread does not resemble any known cult offering. The quantities would, however, be excessive for a meal for two.

71   The narrator further signals Gideon's threshold awareness of the superaddressee by depicting the presentation of the מנחה with the verb וַיִּגַּשׁ (6:19). If the verb is a simple qal, then וַיִּגַּשׁ would simply translate "he [Gideon] approached". If, however, the verb is a pausal hif'il then it would connote Gideon's presentation of himself and/or his offering in a cultic space.

72   To erroneously greet a human stranger as if a god would be scandalous. Consider Manoah's unfortunate attempt to greet a messenger as though an honoured human guest (Judg. 13:15–16).

recognize the divine. The messenger must depart before the *anagnorisis* plot culminates. Uninhibited by the messenger's presence, Gideon finally recognizes that he has met a messenger of YHWH and, more crucially, that he is in the presence of YHWH. It is this awareness which provokes Gideon to a new confessional self-account.

Gideon's Confessional Self-Account

Bakhtin suggests that the nearer a self-account approaches to the ideal but unattainable solitary self-account, "the clearer and more essential is one's referredness to God".[73] But for Gideon the inverse proposition is true: the clearer Gideon's referredness to God becomes, the nearer he attains to a pure self-account. The moment at which Gideon finally recognizes that he has stood face to face with a messenger of God is the moment at which Gideon's speech loses its double-voiced character (Judg. 6:22). Bakhtin describes the theophanic potential of the confessional self-account in a parenthetical aside: "Where I overcome in myself the axiological self-contentment of present-on-hand being, I overcome precisely that which concealed God, and where I absolutely do not coincide with myself, a place for God is opened up".[74]

The climax of Gideon's encounter could be described as an inversion of Bakhtin's thesis: when YHWH overcomes the self-justificatory account by which Gideon has concealed God, Gideon's self-contentment of present-on-hand-being is overcome, and thus a place for God is opened up. It is YHWH's persistent action towards a resistant Gideon which leads Gideon to a purer self-account, in which he addresses himself to the deity in petitionary and penitent tones.[75] The stranger provokes Gideon on multiple levels: he provokes an adversarial response; he provokes recognition of the divine; he provokes Gideon's humility and thereby Gideon's resubmission to the God of Israel. Gideon is mobilized to the role of deliverer through a dialogue in which the possession of truth is contested and Gideon's double-voiced speech is elicited and then exposed by the words of the stranger. This is Gideon's only monological speech act. Although fearing for his life, Gideon no longer seeks to control or limit God. Aware of his dependence upon God's mercy, Gideon now understands himself as an "other for God" whereas he had once suspected that he lived as a self without God.

---

73 Bakhtin, *Art and Answerability*, 144.

74 Ibid.

75 Ibid.

Conclusion

I suggested earlier that the presence of two voices in one body, and the misalignment of the narrator's and Gideon's perception of the doubled voice, may arise from the attempt to represent in dialogue the experience of recognizing the divine word in the voice of another. Gideon interprets the stranger as a threat to be resisted but suddenly suspects the presence of the divine speaker, when the stranger quotes and reapplies words from the call of Moses. Peter Slater captured this process in his account of how the superaddressee is heard to speak in dialogue: "if God is heard through the reporting [speech reported as divine speech], the hearer hears God addressing him or herself directly in the utterances of an actively engaged dialogue partner."[76] Gideon recognizes the superaddressee whose presence he doubted when the stranger invokes a sentence from Gideon's cultural heritage, which is repurposed to address not only Gideon's apparent anxiety about suitability for military service, but his deeper anxiety concerning divine abandonment.

The narrator and the reader perceive YHWH's address even earlier. From their experience-external perspective the change of speaker represents an intensification of effort by the divine self-revealer. The divine word has been resisted when mediated by a prophet (6:7–10), and both the messenger of YHWH and even YHWH receive an initially hostile reception. Thus the vulnerability of the divine word to an indifferent (human) addressee is foregrounded in Gideon's religious experience. This vulnerability is consequent upon the role of experience in interpretation of religious and spiritual experience; YHWH's revelation is dependent upon Gideon's reception of that revelation to find its meaning.

Just as Gideon's sensitivity to dialogic speech, particularly his capacity to perceive double-voiced meanings, creates the narrative crisis of this scene – the possibility that the divine revelation will go unnoticed – so that sensitivity provides the means by which recognition can begin. Nonetheless, Gideon's hermeneutic of suspicion forces a modulation of the divine voice, the adoption of a new discourse strategy in the assurance "because I will be with you". This utterance is simultaneously double-voiced *and* penetrant, as the words fitted to another context and hearer are redeployed to achieve both their original and an additional purpose. Gideon hears both familiar words from the narrative of the fathers and the reassurance necessary to the present day. The assurance of the divine presence prompts within Gideon a reorientation towards the stranger, and towards his longed-for superaddressee. Thus the stranger

---

76   Slater, "Bakhtin on Hearing", 9.

successfully challenges Gideon's deceptive self-account, and provokes a renewed relationship between speaker and superaddressee, which enables Gideon, at last, to speak with the "petitionary and penitent tones" of an ideal confessional self-account.

Literature

Bakhtin, Mikhail M., *Problems of Dostoevsky's Poetics*, trans. Caryl Emerson (Minneapolis, MN: University of Minnesota Press, 1984).

Bakhtin, Mikhail M., *Speech Genres and Other Late Essays*, ed. Caryl Emerson and Michael Holquist, trans. Michael Holquist and Vern W. McGee (Austin, TX: University of Texas Press, 1986).

Bakhtin, Mikhail M., *Art and Answerability: Early Philosophical Essays by M. M. Bakhtin*, ed. Michael Holquist and Vadim Liapunov, trans. Vadim Liapunov (Austin, TX: University of Texas Press, 1990).

Barr, James, "Theophany and Anthropomorphism in the Old Testament", in *Congress Volume: Oxford, 1959* (Leiden: Brill, 1960), 31–38.

Biddle, Mark E., *Reading Judges: A Literary and Theological Commentary* (Macon, GA: Smyth and Helwys, 2012).

Block, Daniel, *Judges, Ruth* (Nashville, TN: Broadman & Holman, 1999).

Burney, Charles F., *The Book of Judges* (London: Rivington, 1918).

Butler, Trent C., *Judges* (Nashville, TN: Thomas Nelson, 2009).

Dostoevsky, Fyodor, *The Karamazov Brothers*, trans. Ignat Avsey (Oxford: Oxford World Classics, 2008).

Farmer, Frank M., "'Not Theory . . . But a Sense of Theory:' The Superaddressee and the Contexts of Eden", *Symplokē*, 2 (1994), 87–101.

Habel, Norman C., "The Form and Significance of the Call Narratives", *Zeitschrift für die Alttestamentliche Wissenschaft* 77 (1965), 297–323.

Herzel, Roger W., "Anagnorisis and Peripeteia in Comedy", *Educational Theatre Journal* 26 (1974), 495–505.

Klein, Lillian R., *The Triumph of Irony in the Book of Judges* (Decatur, GA: Almond Press, 1988).

McCann, J. Clinton, *Judges* (Louisville, KY: John Knox Press, 2002).

Meier, Samuel A., "Angel of Yahweh", *Dictionary of Deities and Demons in the Bible* (Leiden: Brill, 1999), 54–55.

Midgley, Warren, "Look Who's Listening: Using the Superadressee for Understanding Connections in Dialogue", in *Creating Connections in Teaching and Learning*, ed. Lindy Abwai, Joan M. Conway and Robyn Henderson (Charlotte, NC: Information Age Publishing, 2011), 153–163.

Polak, Frank, "Theophany and Mediator: The Unfolding of a Theme in the Book of Exodus", in *Studies in the Book of Exodus: Redaction, Reception, Interpretation*, ed. Marc Vervenne (Leuven: Leuven University Press, 1996), 113–147.

Ryan, Roger J., *Judges* (Sheffield: Sheffield Phoenix Press, 2007).

Savran, George W., *Encountering the Divine: Theophany in Biblical Narrative* (London: T&T Clark International, 2005).

Schmidt, Nicolaas F. and Philip J. Nel, "Theophany as Type-Scene in the Hebrew Bible", *Journal for Semitics* 11 (2002), 256–281.

Shantz, Colleen, "Opening the Black Box: New Prospects for Analyzing Religious Experience", in *Linking Text and Experience*, ed. Colleen Shantz and Rodney A. Werline (Atlanta, GA: Society of Biblical Literature, 2008), 1–16.

Sidnell, Jack, *Conversation Analysis: An Introduction* (Chichester: Wiley-Blackwell, 2010).

Slater, Peter, "Bakhtin on Hearing God's Voice", *Modern Theology* 23 (2007), 1–25.

Smith, Les W., *Confession in the Novel: Bakhtin's Author Revisited* (Madison, NJ: Fairleigh Dickinson University Press, 1996).

Soggin, J. Alberto, *Judges: A Commentary* (London: SCM Press, 1987).

Sommer, Benjamin D., *The Bodies of God and the World of Ancient Israel* (Cambridge: Cambridge University Press, 2009).

Tull, Patricia K., "Bakhtin's Confessional Self-Accounting and Psalms of Lament", *Biblical Interpretation* 13 (2005), 41–55.

Webb, Barry G., *The Book of Judges* (Grand Rapids, MI: Eerdmans, 2012).

CHAPTER 6

Living with Invisibility: Emotion, Mind, and Transcendence

Graham Ward

In this essay I will discuss the relationship between affective embodiment, mind, and transcendence drawing together several different forms of intellectual enquiry: phenomenology, biology, neuroscience, and theology. The way these separate disciplines have recently begun to interact enables us to gain a much better overall perspective of what it is to be human – a perspective that a theological anthropology could not provide us within itself. From work in the history of science by Mary Poovey[1] to Judith Butler's examination of how matter always matters,[2] empirical facts have come to be recognized as far from ambivalent, simply 'out there' or stable. So I will approach the relationship I am investigating here by examining the way the invisible (like the workings of the mind in the process of interpreting one's experience in the world) pertains to what is visible, perceived, and physiologically processed.

The Invisible: Transcendence in Phenomenology

I shall start with phenomenology for it has always been concerned with how the invisible production of meaning or significance adheres to our reception of the world. In his last-published essay, *The Visible and the Invisible*, the French phenomenologist Maurice Merleau-Ponty insists that he is not treating "an absolute invisible" such as God, "but the invisible of *this* world, that which inhabits this world, sustains it, and renders it visible".[3] His examination is not into transcendence *per se*, but rather intentional transcendence. To understand the difference we can take an example that the German phenomenologist

---

1 Mary Poovey, *The History of the Modern Fact: Problems of Knowledge in the Sciences of Wealth and Society* (Chicago: University of Chicago Press, 1998).

2 Judith Butler, *Bodies that Matter: On the Discursive Limits of "Sex"* (London: Verso, 1993).

3 Maurice Merleau-Ponty, *The Visible and the Invisible*, trans. Alphonso Lingis (Evanston, IL: Northwestern University Press, 1968), 151.

© KONINKLIJKE BRILL NV, LEIDEN, 2016 | DOI 10.1163/9789004328600_008

LIVING WITH INVISIBILITY: EMOTION, MIND, AND TRANSCENDENCE   107

Edmund Husserl used in his *Cartesian Meditations*: a cube.[4] Husserl writes that when we see a cube we do not and cannot perceive its six sides. We can only see two or three. And yet we know that a cube to be a cube has to have six equal sides. In seeing the cube then we 'project' the missing sides in making sense of what we see. We see *as*. In Husserl's technical vocabulary this is "apperceptive transcendentalism". It is 'apperception' because it is a perception that makes possible a further, correlated but unpresented perception. It is transcendental because it affirms what is beyond and external to the perceiver and what is perceived and provides a 'condition for the possibility of' its appearance. Apperceptive transcendentalism provides the conditions for the possibility that what is perceived is meaningfully recognized as a cube. The three or four invisible sides of the cube are actually present along with the other sides that we can see, but they are concealed *in* the visibility of what is seen. This 'projection' or 'expectation' that posits as co-present in an object that which is invisible *in* its visibility is intentional transcendence – because the meaning of the object goes beyond what is perceived of the object in itself (if indeed we can even see any object at all in itself).

Merleau-Ponty develops this recognition of intentional transcendence into what he calls "perceptual faith" (*la foi perceptive*):

> Meaning is *invisible*, but the invisible is not the contradictory of the visible: the visible itself has an invisible inner framework (*membrure*), and the in-visible is the secret counterpart of the visible, it appears only within it, it is the *Nichturpräsentierbar* [unpresentable] which is presented to me as such within the world.[5]

'Perceptual faith' is the seeing of meaningful form through intentional expectation and projection. If it is 'faith' in an invisible *logos* that opens horizons of meaning within *phusis* or belonging to natural phenomena, it is not then some intellectual assent to the unknown that denies material reality. It is a 'faith' that is co-posited with perception itself. The use of the German term *Nichturpräsentierbar* is curious use of a negative *Nicht* prefixed to the noun presentable (*Präsentierbar*) in a manner that is affirmative since it is this unpresentable which makes possible what is presented (and *vice versa*). 'Unpresentable' is my translation and it is a poor one which, for the time being,

---

4 Edmund Husserl, *Cartesian Meditations*, trans. Dorion Cairns (The Hague: Nijhoff, 1960), 39–41.

5 Merleau-Ponty, *The Visible and the Invisible*, 215.

I cannot better. What the word points to is far deeper than the 'unpresentable'. The German prefix *ur* in *urpräsentierbar* indicates an origin, a source, more primordial that subtends what is unpresentable. This draws Merleau-Ponty's 'unpresentable' into the proximity of what in the monotheistic faiths is termed 'negative theology'. But this is exactly the point where we have to recall the dangers of analogy: proximity is not identity. And who is there that can measure the proportions of sameness and difference with respect to that proximity?

Nevertheless, in an important lecture to the *Société française de philosophie* in 1946, having outlined his thesis on the relationship between the visible and the invisible, transcendent horizons within the immanent, Merleau-Ponty draws a direct comparison between phenomenology and the Christian worldview:

> My viewpoint differs from the Christian viewpoint to the extent that the Christian believes in another side of things where the *"renversement du pour au contre"* takes place. In my view this 'reversal' takes place before our eyes. And perhaps some Christians would agree that the other side of things must already be visible in the environment in which we live.[6]

Indeed some Christian theologians would agree – Marie-Dominique Chenu and Henri de Lubac, to name but two – and any number of Christian phenomenologists influenced by Merleau-Ponty (most of them French). For these philosophical theologians there is no *renversement* as such, for there is nothing in the transcendent *contre* to the world as it is. Nevertheless, this is a remarkable statement by Merleau-Ponty – a statement that begins by distinguishing phenomenology from Christianity but ends by re-framing both intellectual projects.

The statement was picked up in the discussion that followed the lecture, leading Merleau-Ponty to spell out one of the implications of his analysis. "As to mystical experience, I do not do away with that either",[7] he told his audience. If we accept the 'mystical experience' as the experience of what is invisible and *Nichturpräsentierbar*, the enigma within and inseparable from the material, then, on Merleau-Ponty's phenomenological terms, who *a priori* can

---

6 Merleau-Ponty, "The Primacy of Perception and its Philosophical Consequences", in *The Merleau-Ponty Reader*, eds. Ted Toadvine and Leonard Lawlor (Evanston, IL: Northwestern University Press, 2007), 89–118 (103).

7 Ibid., 111.

LIVING WITH INVISIBILITY: EMOTION, MIND, AND TRANSCENDENCE

decide whether with such an experience we are treating not "an absolute invisible" such as God, "but the invisible of *this* world"?

This question is particularly prominent, since Merleau-Ponty himself recognized that the phenomenological enquiry is and will always be incomplete: "the most important lesson which the reduction teaches us is the impossibility of a complete reduction".[8] So while judgments always concern the visible, the invisible itself cannot be circumscribed. And if the visible is endlessly open to the invisible and can never be grasped as such without "a complete reduction"; if the visible is not contained but is saturated with an invisibility that continually leaks from it: then towards what does it tend? Quite simply, it cannot be divorced from and pitted against a construal of an absolute transcendent.

In that late essay *The Visible and the Invisible*, Merleau-Ponty described the flesh of the world as "a pregnancy of possibles, *Weltmöglichkeit*".[9] One can admit, as Edmund Husserl does explicitly in #58 of his *Ideas*, that absolute transcendence or the transcendence of God must be excluded from the study of phenomenology, which treats only a field of pure consciousness. But then, even monotheistic theologians would admit that God is not an object in this world; or a proper name for that matter. From the position of the fourth century Patristic Christian theologian, Gregory of Nyssa, the term 'Godhead' is significant of operation, a Trinitarian operation.[10] So, again, who can draw the line between absolute and intentional transcendence, and claim the invisible begins here and ends there? Who can strictly announce that the invisible is *only* the invisible of this world? Consider the observation of a more recent French phenomenologist, Jean-Louis Chrétien, who, while respecting that the business of phenomenology is not to prove the existence of God, nevertheless wishes to examine, as early Martin Heidegger did, religious phenomena phenomenologically: "The invisible before which human being shows itself can range from the radical invisibility of the Spirit to the inward sacredness or power of the visible itself, like a mountain, a star, or a statue".[11] Of course, the corollary in this line of thought is that what moves us beyond phenomenology

---

8 Merleau-Ponty, *The Phenomenology of Perception*, trans. Colin Smith (London: Routledge, 1989), xiv.

9 Merleau-Ponty, *The Visible and the Invisible*, 250.

10 Gregory of Nyssa, "On 'Not Three Gods'", in *Select Writings and Letters of Gregory, Bishop of Nyssa*, vol. 5, ed. William Moore and Henry Austin Wilson (Oxford: Parker and Company, 1893), 331–336.

11 Jean-Louis Chrétien, "The Wounded Word: The Phenomenology of Prayer", in *Phenomenology and the 'Theological Turn': The French Debate*, ed. Dominique Janicaud, (New York: Fordham University Press, 2000), 147–175 (150).

and towards a theology of phenomena (which is nothing more or less than a doctrine of creation) is the corporeal itself, the mystery of embodiment, the mystery of both flesh and its ability to perceive.

Imagination: The Transcendence of Mind

To the invisibility that adheres to visibility in perception and the invisibility that adheres to intentional consciousness, we come to a second mode of the invisible: the working of the mind. I shall focus on a particularly cognitive operation, imagination, since the workings of the imagination is the nearest we come to the co-operation between left and right hemisphere processes.[12] Most analytical approaches to the philosophy of mind are left hemisphere dominated. The imagination is not just a matter of having thoughts; it integrates thoughts with affective and more primordial levels of brain function: emotions, desires, and drives. It is not just a matter of the meaningful and how we come to project it, or the intentional operations of consciousness we found in Merleau-Ponty. For example: No one has ever been to Minas Tirith with its thick walls and its tall towers. No one has ever strolled down its arched streets, climbed its steep cobbled alleys, or sketched its pillared porches of grey and weathered stone. No tourists have rested their arms on the moss-flecked battlements and balustrades looking east across the Pelennor fields to the ruins of Osgiliath or north-west towards Rohan and the distant forest of Fangorn. While imagination always works with the textures of the world, it can also create worlds that never existed and engage our belief in them through cognitive processes with profound emotional effect. If, returning to Merleau-Ponty, the flesh of the world is "a pregnancy of possibles, *Weltmöglichkeit*", then imagination creatively plays with, extends and inhabits those "possibles". This capacity could be viewed as an aspect of phenomenology's 'projection' and 'anticipation', except with time and memory imagination operates backwards as well as forwards. Neither the past nor the future is visible as such, while we continually live with the implications and consequences of their invisibility.

In preparation for a meeting with a colleague I may generate any number of scenarios none of which will coincide with the facts of the situation when I engage in it. It does not stop me anticipating and engaging with those 'possibles'. There is a sense, as Heidegger observed, that because we see *as* we create

---

12   See Iain McGilchrist, *The Master and His Emissary: The Divided Brain and the Making of the Western World* (New Haven, CT: Yale University Press, 2009).

LIVING WITH INVISIBILITY: EMOTION, MIND, AND TRANSCENDENCE 111

the worlds that we inhabit, singly and collectively. But we also create imaginary worlds within those worlds.

To phenomenology's 'intentional transcendentalism' then, and its mode of invisible visibility, we have to add what I want to call 'transcendental freedom'. That is, the ability through the imagination to transcend our perspectives and intentional perception. Of course, the two other modes of invisible visibility are the conditions for the possibility of imagination's 'transcendental freedom', but with this freedom we engage with what Jean-Paul Sartre, in his attempt at a phenomenology of the imagination, called the 'irreal'. The 'irreal' for Sartre cannot be seen, touched, smelled except irreally. Sartre himself relates belief to this freedom to imagine:

> [O]ne of the essential factors of the imaging consciousness is belief. This belief aims at the object of the image. All imagining consciousness has a certain positional quality in relation to its object. An imaging consciousness is, indeed, consciousness of an *object as imaged* and not consciousness *of an image*. But if we form on the basis of this imaging consciousness a second consciousness or reflective consciousness, a second species of belief appears: the belief in the existence of the image.[13]

The image is not an *image of* but an *object imaged*. Sartre is explicitly referring to an art form he was fully acquainted with, the novel. In the space of possibles opened by the imagination we encounter the transcending invisibility of our freedom (in which lies our hope). It is not an unbounded freedom. It is not a freedom without determination of some sort, to some extent. Though none of us can articulate to what extent – and this itself is freeing.

Faith: Transcendence in Religion

And finally there is a third mode of invisibility that the author of the *Letter to the Hebrews* draws attention to: "[f]aith is the substance of things hoped for, the evidence of things not seen (Ἔστιν δὲ πίστις ἐλπιζομένων ὑπόστασις, πραγμάτων ἔλεγχος οὐ βλεπομένων.)" (Heb. 11.1). Allow me to examine what is going on in the articulation of these complex and balanced antitheses for the Christian faith. In Greek the sentence begins with the verb in the present

---

13   Jean-Paul Sartre, *The Imaginary: A Phenomenological Psychology of the Imagination*, trans. Jonathan Webber (London: Routledge, 2004), 86.

tense, the third personal singular of 'to be'. In grammatical terminology: before we have the subject of the sentence (faith) we have the ontological conditions within which the subject is located. Then we have the subject, transliterated as *pistis*. We can translate it either as 'faith' or 'belief'. There is no object, only a second subject which, transliterated, is *hypostasis*. This is a word with a long and complex history in Christian Patristic debates, but all that is in the future for the author of this letter. 'Substance' is the right translation, but 'essence' might be slightly better, because this word has ontological freight and relates back directly to the verb 'to be' that opens the sentence. Poised exactly between these two subjects in the nominative (which, grammatically, means they can be converted into or stand in one another because they name the same thing) is the present passive participle of the verb 'to hope', and it is in the genitive. That is, hope is what belongs to and is a property of both 'belief' and 'essence'.

Having defined belief as fundamental to being itself and as possessing the future-orientated disposition to hope, then, we come to the sub-clause "the evidence of things not seen". The sub-clause begins with the subject, *pragma* (from which we get the word 'pragmatic'). It is translated here vaguely as "things" because it is in the plural, but it could be translated with greater specificity: acts, deeds, facts, affairs, enterprises, or issues. It is not vague or abstract in any way; rather it is active and highly concrete. It is also in the genitive, like the participle for hoping (though that is singular and refers to belief). It is the object of the present passive participle which is in the negative at the end of the sentence, transliterated as *ou' blepomenōn* – "not being seen". These activities of what is unseen belong to something and that is 'evidence'. They are the very properties of this 'evidence'. Here the nominative subject of the sub-clause is sandwiched emphatically between the two characteristics it possesses (like belief and essence in the main clause). The word is, transliterated, *elegchos* and it does bear the sense of 'evidence' if we understand that term not scientifically but legally. It is related to and can be translated as trail, conviction, judgment, examination or proof.

Now I realize this is all very technical, but attention to the technical is important if we are to understand something about the nature of religious belief, the nature of the visible and the invisible expressed here. Believing cannot be disassociated from hoping; and those facts and actions that are not seen are still evident in the very examination and trial of the facts and actions themselves. The invisible therefore is not divorced from the visible. It does not demand a leap beyond what is real and actual (both translations of *pragma*). The invisible is a property of the visible and religious believing is an act of response to that invisible in the visible; a response that cannot be separated from the affect hope. As St. Paul puts it: "For the invisible things of [God] from the creation of

LIVING WITH INVISIBILITY: EMOTION, MIND, AND TRANSCENDENCE   113

the world are clearly seen, being understood by the things that are made, even his eternal power and Godhead" (Rom. 1.20).

Given that a paradox – and not necessarily a contradiction – is articulated by the author of the *Letter to the Hebrews* and St. Paul, what then can we say here? There are two prominent possibilities. First, religious faith, in pursuing the invisible that is *beyond* the invisibilities that adhere to the visibilities we have been outlining, is a self-conscious acceptance of believing as a fundamental disposition that in hoping and desiring orientates itself towards an ultimate and absolute *telos* – the divine – outside this world. Certain rational theologies developing out of natural philosophy from the writings of Philipp Melanchthon onwards, referred to the Pauline text in their cosmological proofs for the existence of God. But the God who 'exists' here is only the extrinsic Architect of creation, beyond and exterior to all that is visible. The second option is that religious faith is a response to an invisible that operates always *within* the visible, always calling forth believing as seeing *as* and moving us then *beyond*. For a Christian theologian, I confess, no choice is necessary for – and here comes St. Paul again (as cited in the *Acts of the Apostles*) – "in God we live and move and have our being" (Acts 17.28). The visible is created and the hallmark of divine authorship permeates it.

So belief in a divine invisibility, Merleau-Ponty would say an "absolute transcendence", is founded upon an intuition of being created. Of course, we could have been created by aliens from a distant galaxy. This would be our contemporary equivalent to God as Architect. But the religious intuition is founded upon our having been created by the loving and therefore personal God. And it has to be accepted that such an account of creation does fly in the face of red-tooth-and-claw Darwinian evolution, which is random if not downright cruel and highly inefficient if not indeed wasteful in its selective process. Even the teleology of so-called 'teleosemantics' and 'natural teleology', proposed by contemporary biologists like Ruth Millikan,[14] where meaning is rooted in the biological at the cellular level because in the single cell there is a 'proto-mentality' – even that teleology recognizes that any design that emerges in which there is a resemblance between dispositional properties of cells, digestive systems, adrenalin flows and human beliefs "are the upshot of prior processes of selection. A trait has a function if it has been designed by some process to produce some effect ... the selection process will be non-intentional natural selection".[15]

---

14 See Ruth Millikan, *Language: A Biological Model* (Oxford: Oxford University Press, 2005).

15 Graham MacDonald and David Papineau, "Introduction: Prospects and Problems for Teleosemantics", in *Teleosemantics*, ed. Graham MacDonald and David Papineau (Oxford:

Many are the theological minds that have been exercised in attempting a reconciliation here, because the stakes are high. As William Carlos Williams opens one of his most famous poems: "So much depends..." Without reconciliation a dualism opens up between the material and the spiritual which some religious traditions (Judaism? Islam?) might be happy to embrace, but because of the doctrine of the incarnation not Saint Paul and not Christianity. But following this exploration of those second and third modes of invisibility adhering to the visible, what can we observe about religious believing as it relates to religious experience? We can observe that with religious believing we encounter belief in belief itself. That is, not only a recognition and acceptance of the fact of invisibility as it pertains to our everyday existence, but an investment (of trust and emotion) in the meaningfulness, value and significance of that invisibility.

And other animals are not capable of doing this. Well, not according to one of the most important studies on the way the world is experienced by our nearest mammal kin, the chimpanzee.[16] This is not to deny both consciousness and a limited self-consciousness to chimpanzees.[17] But the extent of that self-awareness is still a matter of much debate, because it is we, the human observers, who identify, measure, and interpret that awareness. It is the observer who has to discern the difference between conditioned, reflexive, and willed behavior. As a primatologist Daniel Povinelli emphasizes, this assessment and evaluation of awareness in other animals, including chimpanzees, is by analogy. And the problem is that by our drawing analogies and emphasizing the proportions of the similarity over difference when it comes our experience of the world and the way the world is experienced for a chimpanzee we are treating again what is fundamentally invisible. We cannot see the world in the way a chimpanzee sees it because we are not chimpanzees.[18] We can only observe, in close detail, aspects of their behavior: *we* conclude and see *as* significant. So we project and anticipate levels of intentionality with respect to these observations; intentions that may or may not be there. The limited self-consciousness

Oxford University Press, 2006), 1–22 (10). For views on life as information processing, teleodynamics and the molecular interpretation of teleonomy, see the work of Terrence W. Deacon, *Incomplete Nature: How Mind Emerged from Matter* (New York: W. W. Norton & Company, 2012).

16   See Daniel J. Povinelli, *Folk Physics for Apes: The Chimpanzee's Theory of How the World Works* (Oxford: Oxford University Press, 2000) and, more recently, *World without Weight: Perspectives on an Alien Mind* (Oxford: Oxford University Press, 2012).

17   Gordon G. Gallup, "Self-awareness in Primates", *American Scientist* 67 (1979), 417–421.

18   Of course, this observation is only rephrasing the question governing Thomas Nagel's famous article "What is it like to be a bat?", *The Philosophical Review* 83 (1974), 435–450.

LIVING WITH INVISIBILITY: EMOTION, MIND, AND TRANSCENDENCE 115

in these animals is episodic, whereas in human beings it is continually available. Without that capacity to transcend their own consciousness then Sartre's 'second consciousness' is not possible. 'Second consciousness' plays with and extends the immediate environment by transcending it. So all the inventiveness and creativity of imagination working on intentional perception is not available to them. Reflective consciousness is not available either and this is fundamental both to inferring causation (from effect) and employing this inference more generally in tool-making, technology, and developments of the concept of 'tool'. They have limited access to symbolic activity and no recognition that this activity is symbolic. Chimpanzees and other animals will have both emotions and dispositions because these are biologically intrinsic to being embodied, possibly even down to the cellular. But they have not the capacity to evaluate emotions, as feeling. And so our nearest animal cousins may have dispositional beliefs but because they cannot transcend and reflect upon those beliefs they cannot have religion – self-conscious belief in believing.

But, there is no advantage for religious studies in positing a divinity in the 'gaps' not yet explained by the various sciences, including primatology. And the fact that we cannot fully account for belief, unconsciousness, consciousness or even perception, because of the invisible adhering to the visible, is not in itself an index of a grounding religious world-view. It is of no advantage either for religious studies to surrender to a dualism between the invisible and inexplicable powers of mind (our mind or the divine mind) and the material properties of objects and processes in the natural world. Nevertheless, what is yet to be explained or understood does return us to certain aspects of the examinations that raise the question of some intrinsic relationship between belief as a primordial disposition inextricably bound to our embodied experienced of being in the world and the religious commitment to transcendence.

There is a certain transcendence involved in self-consciousness itself and recognitions of the meaningful outside oneself (even if, at first, this 'outside' is the perspective of perceiving oneself as an object in the world). The neuroscientist, Raymond Tallis, would concur, at least up this point. It is the fulcrum upon which he wishes to refute the reductiveness of biological materialism: "the mind transcends, and so it not identical with, activity in the brain".[19] It is not insignificant that the first signs of belief among hominids were religious signs (burial of the dead) and intentional, purposeful behavior (the domestication of fire). We need to examine the implicit relationship between belief and

---

19 Raymond Tallis, *Aping Mankind: Neuromania, Darwinitis and the Misrepresentation of Humanity* (Durham: Acumen, 2011), 338.

transcendence further with respect to both the notion of the bounded 'self', the understanding of a meaningfulness external to it, and intentionality.

Conclusion: The Transcendent Subject

So what are the requirements for transcendence that have emerged from our inquiry into the invisibility intrinsic to visibility? Here are four.

First, as we have already noted, there needs to be a recognition of an exteriority – that I am not a tree, a chair, etc. This is not a pure exteriority, an objectivity exteriority. There is no objectivity insofar as not one of us can get outside ourselves to know what Immanuel Kant called "things in themselves". We see *as* which means that the external world is always mediated to us through our body's perception of it – a perception colored by a thousand variables from memory and anticipation, to the way the light falls on it. In Manchester there is an internationally recognized Emotional Intelligence Academy founded by the psychologist Paul Ekman. It is a private concern. It runs workshops training people in emotional intelligence, and the courses begin by getting people to recognize their own habits of blocking out, of not seeing, certain aspects of the objects and events that surround them. They enable people to understand the way they have been socialized to perceive. The "recognition of an exteriority" is not a passive registration by our ears and eyes, our fingers and our taste buds (the most direct appropriation by the senses is thought to be smell). An object scanned by my retina, triggering sensations processes through the visual cortex in terms of cause and effect becomes, at some unidentifiable point, a 'recognition' by me of that object. As we have already examined, in that recognition there is a level of both anticipation and intentionality: the object is meaningful to me. My perception itself is intentional. We noted this above in the phenomenological work of Merleau-Ponty.

Secondly, transcendence both constitutes and requires a subject who perceives. This subject is a necessary condition for the 'recognition'. Materialistic accounts that conflate mind with brain view this 'subject' as illusory. Like 'consciousness' it is epiphenomenal. But this evades, because it cannot explain, the mechanisms whereby a notion of the 'self' is co-present with all perception. Daniel Dennett's idea that the necessary "intentional stance" has evolved because it is the brain's efficient way of simplifying endless possibilities that arise from neural processing is, at best, a hypothesis.[20] And a hypothesis

---

20   Daniel Dennett, *Consciousness Explained* (Harmondsworth, UK: Penguin Books, 1991), 76–77; 162–167.

LIVING WITH INVISIBILITY: EMOTION, MIND, AND TRANSCENDENCE 117

that does recognize intentionality exists, even if its inconvenience to a materialist account of nature demands extraordinary lengths to explain it away. But its illusory nature is a hypothesis; he cannot demonstrate that that is the case. Furthermore, in many of the accounts of the 'self' as an epiphenomenon intentionality is smuggled in as we have seen. It is there in the very fact Dennett is able to author his sentences, his books and have a hypothesis that is and is not shared by other people. And he is aware that other people do not share it, as much of his work is a polemic against the reasoning of these other people. In wishing to exorcize the ghost in the machine the machine stills needs to be programmed to operate in the way it does. Dennett turns the single ghost into a legion of demons working chaotically in the synaptic gaps armed with neurotransmitters. Intentionality is denied by the materialists and then smuggled in to facilitate the accounts they wish to argue for.

Thirdly, this subject is not just conscious. Other animals possess consciousness, but transcendence requires a consciousness of the contents of one's consciousness in order to affirm what I am not – the very distance and difference that characterizes transcendence. The degree of self-awareness makes possible the recognition that other people too have mental states. This is the basis for symbolic activity between people that is the foundation for communication. The otherness of the other person is not an incommensurate otherness; a pure otherness. If that were the case there could be no shared understanding. The other would be incomprehensible to me. But the 'mutuality' recognized and created in and through the recognition enables there to be a community of embodied minds – and there is no culture, politics, city-building, or civilization without such a community issuing from that recognition.

Fourthly and finally, as a requirement, a characteristic and a consequence of transcendence the subject must be free. Transcendence constitutes the subject in his or her freedom (and hope) because it expands consciousness by opening up the world before us. When we move from a closed room in which we recognize 'I am not this chair' and the chair is perceived as distant and different we might not gain from this experience a sense of our freedom. But consider moving out of that room and standing at the top of Goat Fell, the highest peak on the Isle of Arran in the Hebrides. A vast stretch of water opens between the island and the mainland, an even greater stretch opens between the island and the Atlantic Ocean, and other islands in the vicinity mark out distance and distinction. Now we experience the freedom that is a concomitant of transcendence. Insofar as we transcend our environment this is a freedom bestowed and discovered. If the immensity solicits our wonder, what philosophers like Kant recognized as the sublime, then we also must understand wonder as the foundational affect in worship. But, as we saw such an experience can also become creative freedom, an exercise of freedom in which freedom is not limited to questions of choice but an invitation to play; an invitation for imaginative acts in which believing is both engaged and expressive.

These four requirements for transcendence point to how transcendence is written into the way human beings perceive *as*. That does not mean that the human capacity to perceive in this way is not a product of our evolution, from hominid to *Homo sapiens*, but something changed radically when one animal form evolved such a capacity. And things have not been the same since. Such an account of transcendence does not demonstrate or even require the existence of God; a divine mind. But such a notion cannot be ruled out *a priori*. The question arises: in our exploration of the meaningful in and through our ability to transcend ourselves why stop at just the human level? Or what we take to be the human level? Because the diachronic structures of believing operate always with cultural and historical construals of what it is to be human. And with materialist and frequently non-reductive materialist accounts (Tallis's, for example) we are working within a secular understanding of what it is to be human. Another way of putting this is: if the meaningful is not simply a human construct but as aspect of the world in which human beings both create and discover the meaningful, then from where does the meaningful come?

> [T]o explain not merely the possibility but the actuality of rational beings, the world must have properties that make their appearance not a complete accident: in some way the likelihood must have been latent in the nature of things. So we stand in need of both a constitutive explanation of what rationality might consist in, and an historical explanation of how it arose ... Such an explanation would complete the pursuit of intelligibility by showing how the natural order is disposed to generate being capable of comprehending it ...

writes Thomas Nagel.[21] As Nagel also points out, even an evolutionary account of the place of reason presupposes reason's validity and "cannot confirm it without circularity".[22] If this is the case – and we would have to square this with the blind, cruel wastefulness of the evolutionary process (not at all easy) – why should human self-transcendence cul-de-sac with a secular understanding of what it is to be human? Religious believing, inseparable from experiencing the world religiously, points beyond that cul-de-sac. Why *a priori*

---

21 Thomas Nagel, *Mind and Cosmos: Why the Materialist Neo-Darwinian Conception of Nature is Almost Certainly False* (Oxford: Oxford University Press, 2012), 86.

22 Ibid., 81.

LIVING WITH INVISIBILITY: EMOTION, MIND, AND TRANSCENDENCE

should it be viewed as having transgressed some limit? Whose limit is it anyway? We return to a question I raised at the beginning of this essay with respect to Merleau-Ponty: Given that transcendence as we experience it is profoundly related to the adherence of the invisible to the visible, who can circumscribe the invisible?

Literature

Butler, Judith, *Bodies that Matter: On the Discursive Limits of "Sex"* (London: Verso, 1993).
Chrétien, Jean-Louis, "The Wounded Word: The Phenomenology of Prayer", in *Phenomenology and the 'Theological Turn': The French Debate*, ed. Dominique Janicaud (New York: Fordham University Press, 2000), 147–175.
Deacon, Terrence W., *Incomplete Nature: How Mind Emerged from Matter* (New York: W. W. Norton & Company, 2012).
Dennett, Daniel, *Consciousness Explained* (Harmondsworth, UK: Penguin Books, 1991).
Gallup, Gordon G., "Self-awareness in Primates", *American Scientist* 67 (1979), 417–421.
Gregory of Nyssa, "On 'Not Three Gods'", in *Select Writings and Letters of Gregory, Bishop of Nyssa*, vol. 5, ed. William Moore and Henry Austin Wilson (Oxford: Parker and Company, 1893), 331–336.
Husserl, Edmund, *Cartesian Meditations*, trans. Dorion Cairns (The Hague: Nijhoff, 1960).
MacDonald, Graham, and David Papineau, "Introduction: Prospects and Problems for Teleosemantics", in *Teleosemantics*, ed. Graham MacDonald and David Papineau (Oxford: Oxford University Press, 2006), 1–22.
McGilchrist, Iain, *The Master and His Emissary: The Divided Brain and the Making of the Western World* (New Haven, CT: Yale University Press, 2009).
Merlau-Ponty, Maurice, "The Primacy of Perception and its Philosophical Consequences", in *The Merleau-Ponty Reader*, eds. Ted Toadvine and Leonard Lawlor (Evanston, IL: Northwestern University Press, 2007), 89–118.
Merleau-Ponty, Maurice, *The Phenomenology of Perception*, trans. Colin Smith (London: Routledge, 1989).
Merleau-Ponty, Maurice, *The Visible and the Invisible*, trans. Alphonso Lingis (Evanston, IL: Northwestern University Press, 1968).
Millikan, Ruth, *Language: A Biological Model* (Oxford: Oxford University Press, 2005).
Nagel, Thomas, "What is it like to be a bat?", *The Philosophical Review* 83 (1974), 435–450.
Nagel, Thomas, *Mind and Cosmos: Why the Materialist Neo-Darwinian Conception of Nature is Almost Certainly False* (Oxford: Oxford University Press, 2012).
Poovey, Mary, *The History of the Modern Fact: Problems of Knowledge in the Sciences of Wealth and Society* (Chicago: University of Chicago Press, 1998).

Povinelli, Daniel J., *Folk Physics for Apes: The Chimpanzee's Theory of How the World Works* (Oxford: Oxford University Press, 2000).

Povinelli, Daniel J., *World without Weight: Perspectives on an Alien Mind* (Oxford: Oxford University Press, 2012).

Sartre, Jean-Paul, *The Imaginary: A Phenomenological Psychology of the Imagination*, trans. Jonathan Webber (London: Routledge, 2004).

Tallis, Raymond, *Aping Mankind: Neuromania, Darwinitis and the Misrepresentation of Humanity* (Durham: Acumen, 2011).

PART 3

Interpreting the Uninterpretable?

∵

CHAPTER 7

Navid Kermani's Poetic Hermeneutics of Religious Experiences

Johannes Kleine

Contextualizing Kermani's Poetics in the History of Writing with Mystical Intentions

Navid Kermani is a German-Iranian writer of novels and essays, a distinguished scholar in Islamic studies and a public intellectual. His literary writings have not yet attracted much scholarly attention, although his poetic technique and epistemological interest leads German contemporary literature onto new paths. In order to contextualize Kermani and to point out what distinguishes his literary works from the texts of his contemporaries a few characteristics of mystical writing traditions will have to be revisited first, focusing only on those Kermani appropriates in his work.

Locating mystical discourse in modern literature has often led to the disclosure of elements of negative theology, such as the common use of paradoxes or negations in approaching the ineffable.[1] Many scholars focused on a tradition of apophasis that reaches from Dionysius the Areopagite to Hegel, Nietzsche, and Heidegger and is unlikely to end with contemporary thinkers like Hent de Vries and Alain Badiou.[2] Thinking in the Areopagite tradition often meant talking about God as the similar and the dissimilar at the same time: While the Numinous generates echo and afterimage, it at the same time cannot be satisfactorily communicated, be it poetically or logically. The negative predicates, however, bear more eligibility than any affirmative approaches for they signify the ultimate alterity of God. These three elements: negations, paradoxes and

---

1 See Martina Wagner-Egelhaaf, "Mystische Diskurse. Mystik, Literatur und Dekonstruktion", *Modern Austrian Literature* 28 (1995), 91–109.
2 See the concise overview William Franke, "Apophasis as the Common Root of Radically Secular and Radically Orthodox Theologies", *International Journal for Philosophy of Religion* 71 (2012), 57–76, and William Franke, "Apophasis and the Turn of Philosophy to Religion. From Neoplatonic Negative Theology to Postmodern Negation of Theology", *International Journal for Philosophy of Religion* 60 (2006), 61–73. For a perspective from Islamic Studies with a special focus on Sufi traditions see Michael Sells, *Mystical Languages of Unsaying* (Chicago: University of Chicago Press, 1994).

© KONINKLIJKE BRILL NV, LEIDEN, 2016 | DOI 10.1163/9789004328600_009

the attempt to communicate the incommunicability were influential in shaping those poetical discourses with *mystical* intentions, and they are effective in Kermani's writing as well.

The description of experiences of unification – the well-known *unio mystica* – is also part of a long standing tradition, especially when using nuptial metaphors, a tradition that goes back to the Song of Songs.[3] In his famous *Aurora*, for instance, Jakob Böhme uses such Christian-mystical bridal metaphors to describe moments of demise of the old and emergence of a new identity in various ways. Although the attempt to describe the ineffable, indescribable and invisible is the main theme of Böhme's work, the narrator reflects that the words of the text remain pale and shapeless as compared to the actual transcendent sensation. With this meta-reflexivity, *Aurora* stands as an archetype for mystical poetry that is often self-aware of its own inadequacy. What is very significant, it seems, is the fact that after hundreds of pages the text simply stops before describing the actual moment of epiphany.[4] Kermani's postmodern autofictions[5] follow quite similar paths in that they use metaphors of unification and perform their own epistemological inadequacies. In order to understand the literary and epistemological traditions Kermani also relies on, a quick look at German Romanticism shall be helpful.

One significant idiosyncrasy of Romanticism is its expansion of the enthusiasm and momentousness of a single and ineffable moment of unification to various moments in life, whether religiously connoted or not. This trend famously found its manifestation in Friedrich Schlegel's and Novalis's attempts to found an artificial religion, or rather, the Kunstreligion, the religion of arts. This is why one must recognize the poetics of Romanticism, with its tight bonds between aesthetic and mystical epistemology, to find traces of mystical poetry in Kermani's texts. The most important method was the *Zauberstab der*

---

3 Francis Landy, "Song of Songs", in *The Literary Guide to the Bible*, ed. Robert Alter and Frank Kermode (Cambridge, MA: Harvard University Press, 1987), 305–319, and Daniel Boyarin, *Sparks of the Logos. Essays in Rabbinic Hermeneutics* (Leiden: Brill, 2003), esp. 89–113. For the term 'metaphorology' see Hans Blumenberg, *Paradigms for a Metaphorology*, trans. Robert Savage (Ithaca, NY: Cornell University Press, 2010).

4 Jakob Böhme, *Aurora*, trans. Andrew Weeks and Günther Bonheim (Leiden: Brill, 2013). See Gisela Discher, *Das Sichtbare haftet am Unsichtbaren. Mystische Spuren in Kunst und Dichtung der Moderne* (Berlin: Philo, 2005), 11–12.

5 The term 'autofiction' has become popular for fictitious texts that play with the thin line between fact and fiction when it comes to autobiographical material and references to the actual environment of the author. See Serge Doubrovsky, "Textes en main", in *Autofictions & Cie*, ed. Serge Doubrovsky, Jacques Lecarme and Philippe Lejeune (Nanterre: Université Paris X, 1993), 207–217.

NAVID KERMANI'S POETIC HERMENEUTICS   125

Analogie, Novalis's magic wand: It stands for his obsessive use of analogies, not only as a poetic device, but also as a means to gesture towards the unintelligible by approximation.[6]

Novalis's premise is that the same patterns work in all layers of nature and conscience. Since he intends to compare the rules and structures effective in both mind and material world, *analogy* becomes the most important operation of cognition. For Novalis, the ecstatic experience that would formerly have been called mystic now becomes a metonymy for all kinds of perceptions that allow for the achievement of intensive emotional conditions.

This and the need for paradoxes when thinking what is yet unthinkable find systematic equivalents in the poetics of Novalis's texts. The *coincidentia oppositorum* indeed became his means to overcome the 'language of differences' Novalis so much desired to leave behind eventually. Our differentiating language, Novalis thought, could only circle around the ineffable core of what was actually desired to be uttered. Thus, poetic discourse was obliged to go astray, to leave the ways of causally determined logics. His idea of the recurrence of structures on various layers of the knowable reality led to a poetic of self-similarity and the use of poetic *mises-en-scène*. The plot of his novel *Heinrich von Ofterdingen*, for instance, is mirrored in a narrative found by the protagonist in an ancient book within the plot of the novel. The fictitious book remains fragmentary – just like the one the reader holds in his or her hands. The recursive structure of the novel is therefore reminiscent of a fractal; a structure that shows repeating patterns at various scales.[7]

Well beyond Modernism, God, or the Absolute, remained unidentifiable and inaccessible; but the very fact that the ineffability remains irreducible generated innumerable poetic encounters with this very problem of being ineffable. Far from being comprehensive, this very short history of mystical writing shall find an end here because the genealogy of the basic principles of Kermani's poetics have been sketched.

Within the last fifty years religiously-informed literature or even a poetic that strives after expressing religious experiences has become a rare thing in

---

6   Novalis, 'Die Christenheit oder Europa', in *Schriften. Die Werke Friedrich von Hardenbergs, vol. 3*, ed. Richard Samuel, Hans Mähl and Gerhard Schulz (Stuttgart: Kohlhammer, 1984), 506–524 (518). See Jürgen Daiber, "Die Suche nach der Urformel. Zur Verbindung von romantischer Naturforschung und Dichtung", *Aurora* 60 (2000), 75–103. See also the chapter "Der Zauberstab der Analogie. Kant, Swedenborg und Novalis" in Gisela Discher, *Das Sichtbare haftet am Unsichtbaren*, 174–205.

7   Novalis, "Heinrich von Ofterdingen", in *Schriften. Die Werke Friedrich von Hardenbergs, vol. 1* ed. Paul Kluckhohn and Richard Samuel (Stuttgart: Kohlhammer, 1960), 181–369.

German literature. Until 1970, Christian authors like Gertrud von le Fort or Reinhold Schneider as well as Jewish authors like Nelly Sachs or Paul Celan wrote texts that were interspersed with mystic threads of thought and based on religious themes.[8] However, the contemporary scene is strikingly different with only few authors addressing religious topics in their work. Because of this decline in mystically- and religiously-interested literature there has been nearly no interest within literary studies in dealing with the issue of theopoetics[9] in contemporary literature.[10] Navid Kermani challenges this development as he tries to think poetically of a way to present a hermeneutic of religious experiences, or rather of a way to communicate such instances in the first place. This is why a look at the texts of this writer, born to Iranian parents in 1960s Germany, will illustrate the persistent *longue durée* of mystical and theological thinking in the German literary tradition. The following examinations will not only show how Kermani transposes the poetic means that have just been explored in literary history into modern prose (negation, paradoxes, analogies between unio and intercourse, between world and the I, between different cultural spheres, etc.). I will especially try to find out how his texts perform an approximation to the ineffable while they describe such attempts of approximation of others, thus creating a meta-mystic kind of literature of sorts.

Contextualizing Kermani within the Literary Field

Kermani represents the intersection of theology and literature. As indicated earlier, this intersection has been neglected by German studies in the past, but recently things have begun to change, not least because of the emergence of German literature written by Muslims. For example, the latest collaborative

---

8   See, e.g., Gertrud von le Fort, *The Veil of Veronica*, trans. Conrad M. R. Bonacina (New York: AMS Press, 1970); Reinhold Schneider, *Imperial Mission*, trans. Walter Oden (New York: The Gresham Press, 1948); Nelly Sachs, *Collected Poems 1944–1949*, trans. Michael Hamburger and Ruth Mead (Los Angeles, CA: Green Integer, 2011) and Paul Celan, *Threadsuns*, trans. Pierre Joris (Los Angeles, CA: Green Integer, 2006).

9   Amos N. Wilder was the first to use the term 'theopoetics' in order to categorise coincidences of poetry and worship, literature and prayer: Amos Nive Wilder: *Theopoetic. Theology and the Religious Imagination* (Philadelphia, PA: Fortress, 1976).

10 Some exceptions may indicate a change in this trend: Sibylle Lewitscharoff's 'Poetikdozentur' at the University of Frankfurt intertwines religion and poetics. See Sibylle Lewitscharoff, *Vom Guten, Wahren und Schönen* (Berlin: Suhrkamp, 2013). Patrick Roth's lectures had a similar topic, but he did not elaborate on it in a similarly systematic manner. See Patrick Roth, *Ins Tal der Schatten* (Frankfurt am Main: Suhrkamp, 2002).

NAVID KERMANI'S POETIC HERMENEUTICS 127

work between theologians Karl-Josef Kuschel and Georg Langenhorst, and literary scholars – formerly interested in Christian and Jewish literature solely – examines the literature of writers with Muslim backgrounds, including Emine Sevgi Özdamar, Feridun Zaimoglu, and Navid Kermani.[11] As a result, scholars in literary studies are rediscovering the religious dimension of literature. Only recently, Georg Langenhorst and Christoph Gellner have considered how much Muslim authors in particular owe to the mystical-poetic traditions of Islamic cultural history.[12]

Kermani not only attempts to use literature as a means to explore poetically the effects of religious experiences, but he also works on the reception history of mystical poetry and the Quran itself as a poetic endeavour in his academic work. As a scholar, Navid Kermani, together with thinkers like Angelika Neuwirth, Stefan Wild and others, represents a movement in Islamic Studies which reads the Quran with a historical-critical approach.[13] Confronted with the problem of reconciling faith and scholarship, Kermani applies and popularises the works of Egyptian scholar Nasr Hamid Abu Zaid.[14] Abu Zaid's perception of the Muslim term *waḥy*, 'revelation', stresses the impossibility of verifying the historical reality of the revelations that the prophet Muhammad received.[15] According to this movement, verifiability is simply not a part of scholarly work, and therefore scholars may apply themselves to studying the aesthetic effects of belief rather than its historical foundations.[16] Some literary scholars may be perplexed that this prerequisite of research in aesthetics is still

---

11 *Islam in der deutschen und türkischen Literatur*, ed. Michael Hofmann and Klaus von Stosch (Paderborn: Schöningh, 2012).

12 Christoph Gellner and Georg Langenhorst, *Blickwinkel öffnen. Interreligiöses Lernen mit literarischen Texten* (Ostfildern: Patmos, 2013).

13 See Angelika Neuwirth, *Der Koran als Text der Spätantike. Ein europäischer Zugang* (Berlin: Verlag der Weltreligionen, 2010), which summarises Neuwirth's work. For a general view see also Thomas Bauer, *Die Kultur der Ambiguität. Eine andere Geschichte des Islams* (Berlin: Verlag der Weltreligionen, 2011); *The Qur'an as Text*, ed. Stefan Wild (Leiden: Brill, 1996); and Kermani's dissertation *Gott ist schön. Das ästhetische Erleben des Koran* (München: Beck, 1999) as well as his 'Habilitation' *Der Schrecken Gottes. Attar, Hiob und die metaphysische Revolte* (München: Beck, 2011).

14 Nasr Hamid Abu Zaid, *Reformation of Islamic Thought. A Critical Historical Analysis* (Amsterdam: Amsterdam University Press, 2006) and *Rethinking the Qur'ān. Towards a Humanistic Hermeneutics* (Utrecht: University of Humanities, 2004).

15 Kermani already did so in his first academic monograph *Offenbarung als Kommunikation. Das Konzept waḥy in Nasr Hamid Abu Zaids Mafhum an-nass* (Frankfurt am Main: Peter Lang, 1996).

16 See Nasr Hamid Abu Zaid, *Ein Leben mit dem Islam* (Freiburg: Herder, 1999), 98–165.

under discussion in the twenty-first century. But we should remember that the *Bible as Literature* movement in British literary studies had to debate the very same issue some thirty years ago. Frank Kermode frequently had to defend his readings of the Bible as a literary text until the late-1980s.[17]

Kermani has written three academic monographs. Both here, and in various articles, he primarily focuses on the literary quality and poetic beauty of the Quran together with other foundational texts of Islam and their reception history. For Kermani, the poetic quality of the Islamic tradition actually marks a basic difference to the other Abrahamic religions. While the descriptions of great conversions from Paul to Augustine, from Blaise Pascal to Martin Luther often focus on moral and ethical messages for the individual, post-Quranic experiences are described as overwhelming due to great beauty. Indeed, the poetic power and beauty of the Quran's Arabic is taken as the verification for it being composed by God. Thus, there is no *incarnation* in Islam but an *inlibration*, if you will.[18]

Kermani was interested in analysing phenomena of transgressions in those margins of Muslim cultural history that tended toward mystic ideas. For instance, he explored the works of Ahmad ibn Muhammad Al-Thaʿlabī. This medieval scholar wrote a short text about those believers who, on hearing Quranic language being recited, died by being overwhelmed ecstatically by its beauty. But Kermani also uses his knowledge about Al-Thaʿlabī's poetic strategies for his own literary endeavours. Al-Thaʿlabī's book is titled *Qatlā l-Qurʾān*, 'The Book of Those Who Died Listening to the Quran'. Kermani subsequently entitles his book *Das Buch der von Neil Young Getöteten*, 'The Book of Those

---

17 As a summary of their work see the influential *The Literary Guide to the Bible* (see footnote 3). Daniel Weidner and Andrea Polaschegg still in 2012 have to ask the academic public in Germany: "Denn ist nicht die Bibel selbst ein Teil der Literatur, ist sie nicht selbst ein Text, der alle Zeichen der Literarizität trägt und daher offensichtlich auch als Literatur gelesen werden kann?" ("Isn't the Bible a piece of literature in the end, a text showing all signs of poeticity and therefore recognizable as literature?") in the introduction to their anthology *Das Buch in den Büchern. Wechselwirkungen von Bibel und Literatur*, ed. Andrea Polaschegg and Daniel Weidner (München: Fink, 2012), 9–35 (33).

18 In *The Philosophy of the Kalam* (Cambridge, MA: Harvard University Press, 1972), 244, Harry A. Wolfson writes that the Quran constitutes the 'inlibration' of God (as opposed to the Christian incarnation). This is not an idiosyncrasy of European approaches, Iranian philosopher of religion Seyyed Nasr is also applying such a 'reader-response criticism'; see Angelika Neuwirth, "Der Prophet Muhammad. 'Ikone' eines Rebellen im Wahrheitsstreit oder 'Tabula rasa' für den Empfang göttlicher Wahrheit", in *Prophetie und Prognostik. Verfügungen über Zukunft und Wissenschaften, Religionen und Künsten*, ed. Daniel Weidner and Stefan Willer (München: Fink, 2013), 229–239 (231).

NAVID KERMANI'S POETIC HERMENEUTICS

Who Died Listening to Neil Young'. Instead of providing an academic description of what Muslim mystics had written in earlier ages, Kermani turns toward an *appropriation* of their writing and thinking techniques. Furthermore, he opens this semantic sphere of descriptions of religious encounters in Muslim cultural history to those in Western or Christian tradition. Even more significant is Kermani's survey of the similarities of those descriptions to accounts of receptions of works of art from all backgrounds and eras.

The survey at the beginning of this paper examined that three principles were crucial for approaching the ineffable via language. First, negative theology is only a systematised version of a thread of thought that assumes the ineffable could best be approximated by relating it to what it is not. The use of paradoxes, as a second principle, is not only one conceivable method of expressing the inexpressibility but also figures as a means to poetically circle the semantic point that is desired to be addressed. The third basic means found in mystic accounts is analogy; by analogizing a religious experience either to accounts of other's experiences or to accounts of aesthetic experiences, the ineffable is often being approached. All these poetical methods only approximate or gesture towards the ineffable. With the exception for some attempts in Romanticism, they always take into account the impossibility of ever achieving their desired goal. Nevertheless, this impossible exercise relentlessly generates poetic and other written attempts.

Navid Kermani uses all three of these methods in his poetic texts while reflecting upon the former uses of these techniques in various cultural traditions and semantic spheres. He thereby creates a meta-mystic of sorts, for at the very core of his poetic system is a strong resemblance to and reflection about decidedly mystical accounts, expressed in texts that vary widely in genre, tone, and topic.

Kermani references other writers' descriptions of mystic or aesthetic encounters in roughly four categories: First, he refers to early Muslim mysticism and Sufi-inspired poetry, from the ecstatic poetic prophecy of Hafez to sober descriptions of the biographies of certain Sufi masters. Second, he is interested in mystically inspired ways of writing from many other backgrounds far beyond the Abrahamic confessions, from Zen Buddhism to the most recent esoteric movements. Third, he extensively analogizes mystical encounters with overwhelming effects of material culture and artistic performances. Fourthly, Kermani describes the interaction between descriptions of artistic immersions – such as the contemplative power of an improvizing music group – and religious experiences.

Often, Kermani mixes the use of these categories, for instance in his forty short stories written for a German newspaper under the title *Vierzig Leben,*

Forty Lives in 2004.[19] These stories also show how far Kermani's literature follows up, and in a way fulfils, his academic work in the area. *Vierzig Leben* relates terms such as 'Glück' (bliss), 'Leidenschaft' (passion) or 'Übung' (exercise) to snippets and anecdotes from the lives of various people. The book begins with a quote from Khwaja Abdullah Ansari, a Sufi master from Herat in what is now Afghanistan, from the eleventh century. In his dissertation, Kermani calls Ansari the systematic theologian of Sufism whose taxonomy assists Kermani to determine the exact Quranic meaning of abstract terms like 'ḥawf'. Translated literally, the term means 'fear' or 'anxiety', but in the Quran, things are more complicated: 'ḥawf' is rather an empty-word, or the least inaccurate term for something that cannot really be captured in a single word.[20] This is why Kermani the scholar tells us that in the Quran the terms have to be charged with a narrative, an emotion, an aesthetic sublimation. This is exactly what the poet Kermani does – not with Quranic Arabic – but with contemporary German abstract nouns in his story-collection *Vierzig Leben*.

Dein Name

Even more important in terms of creating a hermeneutics of religious experiences than the re-description of poetic structures from Muslim cultural tradition is Kermani's attempt to analogize religious encounters with aesthetic experiences. Here is where the concept of meta-mystical poetics is put into play. The giant novel *Dein Name*[21] brings together all of Kermani's previous attempts and threads of thought. The text from 2011 resembles the diary of a protagonist named 'Navid Kermani'. Using the author's name as the protagonist's is a technique Jean Paul famously introduced to the German literary tradition.[22] Kermani's tremendous journal-like autobiographical novel *Dein Name* reflects upon the most diverse kinds of people, artefacts, social phenomena and political issues, many of which Kermani reported on as a journalist. The text contains several obituaries of deceased persons whom Kermani knew or was influenced by who died within the narrative time from 2006–2009 and it tells the story of the decline of the narrator's marriage. This novel could thus

---

19   Published in one volume as: Navid Kermani, *Vierzig Leben* (Zürich: Ammann, 2004).

20   Kermani, *Gott ist schön*, 385.

21   Navid Kermani, *Dein Name. Roman* (München: Hanser, 2011).

22   Famously in his second novel and first big success *Hesperus*. Jean Paul, *Werke. Historisch-kritische Ausgabe. Vol. I: Hesperus oder 45 Hundsposttage*, ed. Barbara Hunfeld (Tübingen: Max Niemeyer, 2009).

NAVID KERMANI'S POETIC HERMENEUTICS

be read as a modern version of Jean Paul's writings, but as we will see, its poetic structure differs in a decisive way.

Structurally, the extended novel is a hyper-textual homology: As a homology, it links various analogies between descriptions of experiences from different semantic layers within the story to its own poetic structure. Thus, the text reduplicates the workings within its microstructure on a macro-logical level. By doing so, the novel describes former accounts of experiences – literary or otherwise – and at the same time, it is itself an approximation of the void of mystic encounters. This is how it manages to be deeply concerned with the question of how a theistically structured worldview could be transmitted in a literary text and how encounters with the ineffable could be transformed into poetic approximations without simply relying on loose metaphors, allegories or vague allusions. Kermani attempts to rely solely on a poetics of structure and writes a mystical novel in a very sober and plain language, and he still uses the basic means of mystical poetry as worked out earlier: negations, paradoxes and analogies. He writes meta-mystic literature in that he reflects upon the use of mystical linguistic elements in literary language while applying them to the structural composition of his therefore poetic text. The term 'hyper-textual structural homology', however, should be further elucidated.

Gérard Genette, the most influential theorist on how texts relate to one another, calls commentaries on texts *metatexts*. He calls any other relation between two texts, where the text in question does not relate to the previous one as a metatext, a *hypertext*.[23] *Dein Name* clearly is both a hypertext and a metatext, a concourse of opposites that Genette himself only finds one example for in all of world literature, namely Virgil's *Aeneid*. James Joyce's *Ulysses*, Genette claims, was 'just' transposing the Odyssey to twentieth century Dublin, while Virgil transformed the actual narrative which is what Genette calls 'imitation' or 'indirect transformation' as opposed to the 'simple transformation'.[24] *Dein Name* relates in 'indirect transformation'-mode to myriad texts, not to one Odyssey alone. Jean Paul's writings are among the many hypo-texts to which Kermani refers, though they constitute the main structural analogy. This is why I propose to call *Dein Name* hyper-textual. As with Jean Paul, Kermani's narrator shifts between first- and third-person narratives while explaining Jean Paul's shifts between first- and third-person narrators and why they make sense.

Kermani therefore rewrites poetic mechanisms as he describes them; the semantic analogies thus weave a self-conscious structural homology that

---

23   Gérard Genette, *Palimpsests. Literature in the Second Degree*, trans. Channa Newman and Claude Dobinsky (Lincoln, NE: University of Nebraska Press, 1982).

24   Ibid., 13–15.

repeats and rewrites the structures of those reviewed analogies. The most important types of analogies then refer to descriptions of religious – often mystical – experiences, to thoughts about the relationship between aesthetic and religious encounters, and to ideas about how metaphors and other figures of speech could approximate those experiences verbally.

All of these analogies form a literary structure themselves in that their interwovenness becomes a viable and significant poetological category. The threads of thought and threads of narrative are woven into a textual tapestry that's speed of weaving and that's thickness become poetic means. *Dein Name* – despite its extraordinary length – relinquishes most figures of speech such as allegory and allusion. It does not strive after a metaphysical approximation to the void or to God in transcendent language. It rather weaves a tapestry consisting of many such efforts of approximation of others that tightens around its ineffable centre. This is what I call a meta-mystical approach. Kermani *en passant* unfolds a typology of mystical approaches.

As the text refers to its own constructedness, the homology-style structure is self-similar and therefore reminds us of Novalis's fractal in *Heinrich von Ofterdingen*.[25] Thus, Kermani's postmodern and hyperrealist autofiction resembles Romanticist writing styles in quite unexpected ways. The reputed hodgepodge of myriad genres called *Dein Name* is a well-structured novel restraining itself from using common poetic means like allusions or vague connotations. It is a mere 'text', an interweaving and superimposing of threads of narrative and discourse.

An example shall illustrate the poetic technique using the thickness of threads of texts as a poetic means: Almost in the middle of *Dein Name*, Kermani describes how one of Harald Bergmann's films about Friedrich Hölderlin depicts the German writer as a prophet-poet in a tradition of Jeremiah and Isaiah. While talking about the film, the narrator attempts to describe the possible essence of descriptions of both religious and aesthetic experience, thus precisely the topic that apparently generates the whole book's poetics. Shortly before he arrives at the aim of this description, which we know represents the void that is so difficult, or rather impossible, to grasp verbally, the narrator abruptly turns away from his effort and says he cannot work anymore because he drank too much whisky while writing. Within the staged present of the book the narrator claims to be about to trot to heaven with the help of 'single malt and wild horses'. Of course, inebriety has always been used as an analogy to spiritual excitement in descriptions of mystical encounters, as readers of Rumi know. But the question of why Kermani talks about wild

---

25   Novalis, *Heinrich von Ofterdingen*.

NAVID KERMANI'S POETIC HERMENEUTICS   133

horses remains. In order to understand this, one should know that Neil Young is Kermani's notorious example for mystic encounters and immersion in contemporary music, or, rather, in contemporary art in general.[26] Young's band is called "Crazy Horse". But there is even more to this short sentence. In the Book of Isaiah, to which Kermani refers via Harald Bergmann just two sentences earlier, chapter 66 describes the Chariot and throne of God as well as the Cherubim, the angels guarding God. This became a *locus classicus* for mystic literature, in fact constituting the beginning of the Hekhalot literature that forms the fundament of Jewish mysticism.[27] Thus, on a micro-logical level, Kermani has bundled threads of thought that on a macro-logical level analogise to the whole topic of the book. This is the fractal structure referred to earlier. What seems to be a wide container of texts lacking any structuring principles other than chronology – *Dein Name* – can thus be understood as a literary experiment relying on the poetics of structure rather than on the poetics of allusions and stylistic devices.

In addition, Kermani's commitment to the genre of autobiography is a restricting frame unleashing creative powers. The constraint is needed in order to provide a level of freedom yet unknown – this is the mystic's foundation: freedom through self-restraint and self-control. Although *Dein Name* is about describing a worldview that does not accept coincidence since it claims the existence of a world-producing force, it confines itself only to the things that allegedly 'really' happened between 2006 and 2009. One would then, of course, expect the kind of contingency and amount of meaningless details contemporary literature knows from other auto-fictions. But Kermani staged and arranged his book meticulously. Nothing is a coincidence in this novel: if it really were unfiltered life, it would be full of redundancy, full of encounters without impact, full of places without significance. But in the book, no detail remains without an ascribed relevance.

Not only the lives and plots within *Dein Name* are interwoven in order to build this world within which nothing is contingent. The text also interacts with all other literary and academic texts Kermani had previously published. For example, just before the close of the novel we find the narrator in Tulsa, Oklahoma.[28] This is the only place he visits without any contextualization and

---

26   See Navid Kermani, *Das Buch der von Neil Young Getöteten* (Zürich: Ammann, 2008).

27   See the chapter on "Merkabah Mysticism and Jewish Gnosticism" in Gershom Scholem, *Major Trends in Jewish Mysticism* (New York: Schocken Books, 1961), 40–79. See also Peter Schäfer, *Die Ursprünge der jüdischen Mystik* (Berlin: Verlag der Weltreligionen, 2011), 50–51.

28   Kermani, *Dein Name*, 1228.

initiation. Now, why would Tulsa be a stopover on the last trip of the narrator? Because of the Neil Young song *Last Trip to Tulsa*. In his book *Buch der von Neil Young Getöteten*, Kermani explains how Young structures his songs with this example. As always, when Kermani writes about others' poetics, he talks about his own:

> Das Brüchige, das Assoziative, das Zufällige ist hier, wie später so oft in seiner Musik und seinen Texten, zum Prinzip erhoben, die herkömmliche Liedstruktur der äußeren Form nach bewahrt, von innen jedoch zertrümmert.[29]

Even the poet Young needs to constrain himself to something, in this case to the traditional structure of a song. The constraint is necessary in order to provide a level of freedom yet unknown, which again is often the mystic's foundation of poetic and mental liberty through rigorous self-control. In *Dein Name* there are dozens of such comparisons with other aesthetic structures that show analogies to the novel itself – from the medium of a blog to other writers' prose to a blue-ray disc with its hyperlink structure.

To summarize, Kermani's webs of text not only reveal their own constructedness but also the approximation to religious, sometimes firmly mystic experiences and revelations with the help of aesthetic means. Three kinds of experiences are being addressed. First, the texts want to approximate the mystic experience of self-aggrandizement through self-transcendence or self-annihilation. Second, they refer to the religious consciousness of a world that is completely pervaded with a structuring force. And third, the texts explore the possibility of understanding and appropriating others' experiences of faith. This threefold approach creates a constant attempt to establish a poetic hermeneutics of religious experience; an attempt that is very much aware of the fact that it will never meet this standard but generates exciting literature on the way, thereby resuming a tradition of mystically inspired literature including its Islamic threads that now, with Kermani, German contemporary literature is also informed about.

---

29 Kermani, *Das Buch der von Neil Young Getöteten*, 11–12: "The broken, the associative and the accidental is turned into a principle here – as it often happens in his music and his lyrics, which conserve the conventional structure of songs on the outside, but shatter it from the inside."

Literature

Abu Zaid, Nasr Hamid, *Ein Leben mit dem Islam* (Freiburg: Herder, 1999).

Abu Zaid, Nasr Hamid, *Refomation of Islamic Thought. A Critical Historical Analysis* (Amsterdam: Amsterdam University Press, 2006).

Abu Zaid, Nasr Hamid, *Rethinking the Qur'ān. Towards a Humanistic Hermeneutics* (Utrecht: University of Humanities, 2004).

Bauer, Thomas, *Die Kultur der Ambiguität. Eine andere Geschichte des Islams* (Berlin: Verlag der Weltreligionen, 2011).

Blumenberg, Hans, *Paradigms for a Metaphorology*, trans. Robert Savage (Ithaca, NY: Cornell University Press, 2010).

Böhme, Jakob, *Aurora*, trans. Andrew Weeks and Günther Bonheim (Leiden: Brill, 2013).

Boyarin, Daniel, *Sparks of the Logos. Essays in Rabbinic Hermeneutics* (Leiden: Brill, 2003).

Celan, Paul, *Threadsuns*, trans. Pierre Joris (Los Angeles, CA: Green Integer, 2006).

Daiber, Jürgen, "Die Suche nach der Urformel. Zur Verbindung von romantischer Naturforschung und Dichtung", *Aurora* 60 (2000), 75–103.

Discher, Gisela, *Das Sichtbare haftet am Unsichtbaren. Mystische Spuren in Kunst und Dichtung der Moderne* (Berlin: Philo, 2005).

Doubrovsky, Serge, "Textes en main", in *Autofictions & Cie*, ed. Serge Doubrovsky, Jacques Lecarme and Philippe Lejeune (Nanterre: Université Paris X, 1993), 207–217.

Franke, William, "Apophasis and the Turn of Philosophy to Religion. From Neoplatonic Negative Theology to Postmodern Negation of Theology", *International Journal for Philosophy of Religion* 60 (2006), 61–73.

Franke, William, "Apophasis as the Common Root of Radically Secular and Radically Orthodox Theologies", *International Journal for Philosophy of Religion* 71 (2012), 57–76.

Gellner, Christoph, and Georg Langenhorst, *Blickwinkel öffnen. Interreligiöses Lernen mit literarischen Texten* (Ostfildern: Patmos, 2013).

Genette, Gérard, *Palimpsests. Literature in the Second Degree*, trans. Channa Newman and Claude Dobinsky (Lincoln, NE: University of Nebraska Press, 1982).

Islam in der deutschen und türkischen Literatur, ed. Michael Hofmann and Klaus von Stosch (Paderborn: Schöningh, 2012).

Jean Paul, *Werke. Historisch-kritische Ausgabe. Vol. I: Hesperus oder 45 Hundsposttage*, ed. Barbara Hunfeld (Tübingen: Max Niemeyer, 2009).

Kermani, Navid, *Das Buch der von Neil Young Getöteten* (Zürich: Ammann, 2008).

Kermani, Navid, *Dein Name. Roman* (München: Hanser, 2011).

Kermani, Navid, *Der Schrecken Gottes. Attar, Hiob und die metaphysische Revolte* (München: Beck, 2011).

Kermani, Navid, *Gott ist schön. Das ästhetische Erleben des Koran* (München: Beck, 1999).

Kermani, Navid, *Offenbarung als Kommunikation. Das Konzept wahy in Nasr Hamid Abu Zaids Mafhum an-nass* (Frankfurt am Main: Peter Lang, 1996).

Kermani, Navid, *Vierzig Leben* (Zürich: Ammann, 2004).

Landy, Francis, "Song of Songs", in *The Literary Guide to the Bible*, ed. Robert Alter and Frank Kermode (Cambridge, MA: Harvard University Press, 1987), 305–319.

Le Fort, Gertrud von, *The Veil of Veronica*, trans. Conrad M. R. Bonacina (New York: AMS Press, 1970).

Lewitscharoff, Sibylle, *Vom Guten, Wahren und Schönen* (Berlin: Suhrkamp, 2013).

Neuwirth, Angelika, "Der Prophet Muhammad. 'Ikone' eines Rebellen im Wahrheitsstreit oder 'Tabula rasa' für den Empfang göttlicher Wahrheit", in *Prophetie und Prognostik. Verfügungen über Zukunft und Wissenschaften, Religionen und Künsten*, ed. Daniel Weidner and Stefan Willer (München: Fink, 2013), 229–239.

Neuwirth, Angelika, *Der Koran als Text der Spätantike. Ein europäischer Zugang* (Berlin: Verlag der Weltreligionen, 2010).

Novalis, 'Die Christenheit oder Europa', in *Schriften. Die Werke Friedrich von Hardenbergs, vol. 3*, ed. Richard Samuel, Hans Mähl and Gerhard Schulz (Stuttgart: Kohlhammer, 1984), 506–524.

Novalis, "Heinrich von Ofterdingen", in *Schriften. Die Werke Friedrich von Hardenbergs, vol. 1*, ed. Paul Kluckhohn and Richard Samuel (Stuttgart: Kohlhammer, 1960), 181–369.

Polaschegg, Andrea, and Daniel Weidner: *Das Buch in den Büchern. Wechselwirkungen von Bibel und Literatur*, ed. Andrea Polaschegg and Daniel Weidner (München: Fink, 2012), 9–35.

Roth, Patrick, *Ins Tal der Schatten* (Frankfurt am Main: Suhrkamp, 2002).

Sachs, Nelly, *Collected Poems 1944–1949*, trans. Michael Hamburger and Ruth Mead (Los Angeles, CA: Green Integer, 2011).

Schäfer, Peter, *Die Ursprünge der jüdischen Mystik* (Berlin: Verlag der Weltreligionen, 2011).

Schneider, Reinhold, *Imperial Mission*, trans. Walter Oden (New York: The Gresham Press, 1948).

Scholem, Gershom, *Major Trends in Jewish Mysticism* (New York: Schocken Books, 1961).

Sells, Michael, *Mystical Languages of Unsaying* (Chicago: University of Chicago Press, 1994).

The Qur'an as Text, ed. Stefan Wild (Leiden: Brill, 1996).

Wagner-Egelhaaf, Martina, "Mystische Diskurse. Mystik, Literatur und Dekonstruktion", *Modern Austrian Literature* 28 (1995), 91–109.

Wilder, Amos Nive, *Theopoetic. Theology and the Religious Imagination* (Philadelphia, PA: Fortress, 1976).

Wolfson, Harry A., *The Philosophy of the Kalam* (Cambridge, MA: Harvard University Press, 1972).

CHAPTER 8

The Complexity of Hermeneutical Experience: Transcendence and Transformation

Werner G. Jeanrond

When I was a doctoral student at the University of Chicago Divinity School, every Wednesday in term time there was a lunch for students and staff with a speaker. However, once a year in May instead of a speaker a student band played traditional American revival music while beer and pretzels were served, sponsored by a major American publishing house. We very much loved this relaxed event towards the end of a compact academic year.

In May 1980 we were happily singing along to tunes such as *Glory, Glory Hallelujah, How Great Thou Art, The Old Country Church,* and *The Little Old Church in the Valley* when the world-famous history of religion professor Mircea Eliade (1907–1986) suddenly appeared in the doorway of the hall listening with great attention to the band playing and us singing. To those of us who spotted him it became instantly clear that, while we were having a merry time with these songs, consuming them, so to speak, at our beer-supported end-of-term gaudy, something rather different was going on in Eliade. He seemed transfixed by the same event, visibly encountering what I would label a religious experience. I shall never forget the complexity of what was going on at the same time: Eliade appeared to have a religious experience caused by the same musical event which provided us students with an experience of end-of-term pleasure. After listening for a while Eliade left the entrance of the hall again when the music stopped.

My fellow students of hermeneutics at Chicago and I were puzzled by this radically different reaction to the same event. Of course, we were well aware of Eliade's theory of religion which highlighted the distinction between the sacred and profane.[1] He had argued that every aspect of our life could become an experience of the sacred. However, we were ill prepared to experience the very author of this famous theory interpreting now our own merry sing along in such obviously religious terms. He did not utter a word, but his transfigured face clearly manifested his religious interpretation of our event. We

---

1 Mircea Eliade, *The Sacred and the Profane: The Nature of Religion,* trans. Willard R. Trask (New York: Harcourt Brace Jovanovich, 1959).

© KONINKLIJKE BRILL NV, LEIDEN, 2016 | DOI 10.1163/9789004328600_010

beer-drinking, pretzel-eating and singing students became the stuff out of which religious experience could be made. This was an experience of a higher kind for us.

We had heard and read of various stories of similar encounters between Eliade and aspects of reality, including how he could see religious dimensions in a circus performance where a lion sprang through a fire wheel, how he got lost in trance at a meeting with a shaman during a study tour of Japan, and how he was over-awed when encountering one of the many grey squirrels on campus. Hence, we knew that his perception of reality was generally more open to seeing religion at work where others might not see any trace of religion at all. But we students were genuinely taken aback by the realization that at an obviously secular festivity we ourselves could become the occasion of a religious experience for Eliade. This did surprise us and left us with a host of questions. Here I wish to take up three of them.

My first question concerns the nature of religious interpretation: What kind of horizon allows for religious interpretations of reality? My second question concerns differences within theological hermeneutics: Which kind of hermeneutics is appropriate to the interpretation of religious texts? And my third question concerns the importance of attending to shifting functions of interpretative acts: Who interprets what, in what circumstances, and for what purpose?

Horizons of Religious Interpretation

In academia, we are used to defining phenomena and perceptions. Part of the mistrust levelled at theological interpretations has to do with the seemingly endless horizon of theological reflection. And yet, in literary hermeneutics we have learned that it does make a difference whether we interpret a text solely in terms of its individual sub-units, i.e. its sentences, words, syllables, or letters, or in terms of the larger units of textuality and intertextuality. A text is more than the sum of its sentences. Perspectives and horizons clearly matter in interpretation not least in terms of establishing the very materiality for interpretation.[2] What then may count as a religious horizon?

Before entering into this debate I need to say a few words about my own theological approach to religion. I propose to understand religion in terms of a dynamic network of relationships: every human person seems called to

---

2   See Werner G. Jeanrond, *Text and Interpretation as Categories of Theological Thinking*, trans. Thomas J. Wilson (Eugene, OR: Wipf and Stock, 2005 [reprint]).

THE COMPLEXITY OF HERMENEUTICAL EXPERIENCE 139

engage in a fourfold relationship: to her or his fellow humans (past, present, and future), to the universe(s), to God or ultimate reality, and to her or his own emerging self. The religious horizon is large enough to comprise all four relationships as well as their inner dynamics and tensions.

Of course, it makes sense to consider the universe in decidedly cosmological and evolutionary terms; it is perfectly reasonable to entertain the question of God or of a god in philosophical discourse; it has become a massive industry to examine the needs, desires, and fears of men, women, and children in their different phases of maturing and troubled subjectivity; it is a feature of all known cultures to encourage various forms of altruism and attention to otherness. However, what makes a horizon *religious* in my proposal has to do with the broader attention to this multi-relational dynamics, which to be sure includes a concern not only for otherness, but even for radical otherness. However, different scholars have offered different approaches to the horizon of religious hermeneutics.

Friedrich Schleiermacher (1768–1834) helped to shape the modern approach to religion after Immanuel Kant by distinguishing religion sharply from dimensions of morality and metaphysics. Religion had to do with human *Gefühl* (feeling). Schleiermacher recommended a larger and more inclusive horizon through which to approach the 'universe'.

> Religion's essence is neither thinking nor acting, but intuition and feeling. It wishes to intuit the universe, wishes devoutly to overhear the universe's own manifestations and actions, longs to be grasped and filled by the universe's immediate influences in childlike passivity. Thus, religion is opposed to these two in everything that makes up its essence and in everything that characterizes its effects. Metaphysics and morals see in the whole universe only humanity as the center of all relatedness, as the condition of all being and the cause of all becoming; religion wishes to see the infinite, its imprint and its manifestation, in humanity no less than in all other individual and finite forms.[3]

Schleiermacher himself offers the following summary: "Praxis is an art, speculation is a science, religion is the sensibility and taste for the infinite."[4] Of course, the passivity to which the young Schleiermacher refers here points to Lutheran and Pietist attempts of protecting God from any human impositions.

---

3 Friedrich Schleiermacher, *On Religion: Speeches to Its Cultured Despisers*, trans. Richard Crouter (Cambridge: Cambridge University Press, 1988), 22–23.

4 Ibid., 23.

The mature Schleiermacher became rather more conscious of the need for human subjectivity to engage hermeneutically with all reality, including the manifestations of religion, in a non-dogmatic approach to interpretation.[5]

Rudolf Otto (1869–1937) set out to clarify further this aspect of *Gefühl*, or as he put it, the irrational in the understanding of God.[6] By irrational he did not understand the simplistic approach that defies any thinking and merely relates to a non-rational life of instincts or closed-mindedness.[7] Rather, Otto argued that any rational approach to the idea of God needs to be complemented by an awareness of the darker dimensions of the numinous which cannot be reduced to any sort of conceptual level. Thus, Otto was concerned not to rationalize the irrational, which is impossible, but to grasp and order the moments of the irrational in order to counter any kind of irrational "enthusiasm (*Schwärmerei*)".[8] Otto wanted to grasp and protect the "experience (*Erlebnis*)" of the "totally different (*Ganz Andere*)".[9] Although in basic agreement with Schleiermacher's approach to religion, Otto was less afraid than Schleiermacher to speak here of "recognition (*Erkenntnis*)" and keen to demonstrate that in our temporality a sense of eternity might become manifest.[10] However, Otto went somewhat beyond the Schleiermacher of the *Speeches* when he identified a human capacity to see the holy, the sacred in life and cosmos,[11] and to claim that true divination springs from religious intuition.[12] The dynamics between being endowed with the potential for intuition and the self-manifestation of the sacred in the process of history presupposes a certain "giftedness (*Begabung*)" which characterises the prophet.[13] For Otto, then, the prophet was the religious subject *par excellence*. While according to this theory every human being is religiously

---

5 See Werner G. Jeanrond, "Friedrich Schleiermacher", in *Klassiker der Religionsphilosophie: Von Platon bis Kierkegaard*, ed. Friedrich Niewöhner (Munich: Beck, 1995), 285–299; 380–384; Jörg Lauster, *Die Verzauberung der Welt: Eine Kulturgeschichte des Christentums* (Munich: Beck, 2014), 476–479.

6 Rudolf Otto, *Das Heilige: Über das Irrationale in der Idee des Göttlichen und sein Verhältnis zum Rationalen* (Munich: Beck, 1979). To stick to the original as closely as possible, I am following the German text. For the English translation see *The Idea of the Holy: An Inquiry into the Non-Rational in the Idea of the Divine and its Relation to the Rational*, trans. John W. Harvey (London: Oxford University Press, 1924).

7 Otto, *Das Heilige*, 75.

8 Ibid., 77.

9 Ibid., 28.

10 Ibid., 176.

11 Ibid., 189.

12 Ibid., 197.

13 Ibid., 204–205.

THE COMPLEXITY OF HERMENEUTICAL EXPERIENCE   141

endowed, some persons possess a particular potential to intuit this inner voice. For Otto, religious genius becomes manifest first in the prophet, and then, on a higher level, even more so in the Son.[14] Thus, Jesus Christ, the Son of the heavenly Father, represents the fullness of spiritual manifestation on earth.

Mircea Eliade continues the Schleiermacher-Otto line of thinking about religious experience, but now in a much more 'democratic' perspective: every human person, and not just the particularly endowed religious genius, is able to experience a *hierophany*: every phenomenon, every aspect of our cosmos and life is capable of becoming a manifestation of the sacred.[15] Eliade thus is not concerned with Otto's distinction between the rational and the nonrational; rather, he is concerned with the manifestation of the sacred in opposition to the profane.[16]

> Man becomes aware of the sacred because it manifests itself, shows itself, as something wholly different from the profane. To designate the act of *manifestation* of the sacred, we have proposed the term *hierophany*. It is a fitting term, because it does not imply anything further; it expresses no more than is implicit in its etymological content, *i.e.*, that *something sacred shows itself to us*.[17]

Eliade stresses that a hierophany does not change the actual object which gives rise to it. Rather, by manifesting the sacred, "any object becomes *something else*, yet it continues to remain *itself*, for it continues to participate in its surrounding cosmic milieu".[18] In this sense, a sacred stone remains a stone. "But for those to whom a stone reveals itself as sacred, its immediate reality is transmuted into a supernatural reality."[19] For people who have a religious experience, "all nature is capable of revealing itself as cosmic sacrality. The cosmos in its entirety can become a hierophany."[20]

Eliade knew, of course, that the very concept of a desacralized world was a modern phenomenon. A completely profane world would have been unthinkable in archaic and premodern societies. Hence, in our time, he could observe two kinds of human beings: those with and those without religious feeling.

---

14   Ibid., 205.
15   Eliade, *The Sacred and the Profane*, 11.
16   Ibid., 10.
17   Ibid., 11 (original italics).
18   Ibid., 12 (original italics).
19   Ibid.
20   Ibid.

'Sacred' and 'profane' are two modes of being in the world, two existential situations assumed by men and women throughout history. The sacred mode of being in the world, i.e. the *homo religiosus*, in spite of all its variations and differences, is open to religious experience.[21] Ultimately, Eliade considered every human being to be a religious being, although not all people choose to embrace a religious hermeneutics of reality.

> Strictly speaking, the great majority of the irreligious are not liberated from religious behaviour, from theologies and mythologies. They sometimes stagger under a whole magico-religious paraphernalia, which, however, has degenerated to the point of caricature and hence is hard to recognize for what it is.[22]

Eliade's approach to religion has been criticised for a number of different reasons.[23] But here I am not concerned with Eliade's detailed interpretations of specific religious phenomena. Rather, I wish to show that he clearly saw and acknowledged the need for a hermeneutics of religious experience.

David Tracy (b. 1939) has been influenced both by Eliade and by William James in his approach to the need for a hermeneutics of religious experience.

> The truth of religion is, like the truth of its nearest cousin, art, primordially the truth of manifestation. Hermeneutical thought, with its defense of this notion, is well-suited to defend anew this primal insight of both art and religion. In that sense, hermeneutics (with its attendant criteria) is useful for reopening the highly complex questions of mysticism, revelation, and enlightenment.[24]

Tracy immediately adds: "To understand at all is to understand differently."[25] Here, in this acknowledgement of interpretative pluralism, the role of the interpreting subject comes into much clearer focus than in either Schleiermacher, Otto, or Eliade. There is no religious experience that is not at the same time

---

21 Ibid., 18.

22 Ibid., 205–206.

23 See, for instance, Jonathan Z. Smith, *To Take Place: Toward Theory in Ritual* (Chicago: The University of Chicago Press, 1987), 1–23.

24 David Tracy, *Dialogue with the Other: The Inter-Religious Dialogue* (Louvain: Peeters Press, 1990), 43. The contribution of William James to the debate on the nature of religious experience is discussed in some detail in this volume by other authors. See esp. Ulrich Schmiedel's and Tobias Tan's articles.

25 Ibid., 44.

THE COMPLEXITY OF HERMENEUTICAL EXPERIENCE 143

an act of interpretation.[26] However, the hermeneutical character of religious experience does not reduce such experience to a mere rationalistic enterprise. Rather, Tracy's stress on truth as manifestation pays tribute to the more than rational acts of the interpreter and resumes Schleiermacher's, Otto's, James's and Eliade's insights into the complex nature of religious experience. Truth as manifestation is presented here not in competition to truth as correspondence and to truth as coherence. Rather, it claims that any serious approach to truth ought to include the *possibility* of the manifestation of the whole by the power of the whole.

> Reality is what we name our best interpretation. Truth is the reality we know through our best interpretations. Reality is constituted, not created or simply found, through the interpretations that have earned the right to be called relatively adequate or true.... Reality is constituted by the interaction between a text, whether book or world, and a questioning interpreter.[27]

Tracy thus confirms the necessity of attention to language – there is no unmediated experience, either religious or otherwise. "We understand in and through language."[28] Language is not an instrument which we can pick up and put down at will; "it is always already there, surrounding and invading all I experience, understand, judge, decide, and act upon."[29] Language is discourse, and to study language as discourse means to discover difference and plurality. There is no short cut to meaning – or, for that matter, to revelation. Meaning emerges always in a web of form, genre, style, convention, semantic shifts, or intertextuality – in difference and plurality. This is not to suggest that ultimately there is no meaning. But it is to underline that meaning cannot be arrived at through simplistic measures and strategies. Meaning, especially in religious contexts, is always complex.

Searching for an overarching concept that enlightens this work on religious and inter-religious hermeneutics, Tracy looks for a way out of the dilemma of being forced to choose between a rationalism in the interpretation of religion that claims too much and overlooks the specificities of particular religious experiences and traditions, on the one hand, and a fideism that articulates

---

26 See also Jörg Lauster's article in this volume.

27 David Tracy, *Plurality and Ambiguity: Hermeneutics, Religion, Hope* (San Francisco, CA: Harper & Row, 1987), 48.

28 Ibid., 49.

29 Ibid., 50.

these traditions at the cost of any claim to public warrant or an interpretation of reality as a whole, on the other hand. Having explored the idea of the classic and then of the religious classic, Tracy later turned to what he calls the religious "fragment" or "frag-event".[30] 'Prophetical' and 'mystical' have become central categories for him, as indeed for Otto and James before him. Tracy is developing – as yet merely in fragments – a concept at once apocalyptic and mystical, resistant to totality systems, to authoritarianism, and to technologies of manipulation and control. Religious experience and its truth have to be approached mindful of the ever-present danger of dogmatist and ideological reductionisms. A hermeneutics of religious experience, therefore, calls for both a hermeneutics of retrieval and a hermeneutics of suspicion. Hence, with regard to Christian theology, Tracy concludes:

> Every Christian theological hermeneutic today – no matter how powerful and believable its retrievals of its authoritative passion narratives, no matter how fierce and unrelenting its suspicions of the history of the effects of its own readings of those narratives – must now endure as not merely unfinished but as broken. Yet theology is broken only in order for some new beginning of a retrieval of hope.[31]

Hence, religious experience and its interpretations have emerged as fragile phenomena – always calling for re-consideration, re-thinking, re-interpreting. No single person is ever able to achieve these hermeneutical acts on their own. Communities of interpreters are called to aim at as adequate interpretations as possible. However, Tracy has not yet developed an analysis of the nature of such communities of interpreters beyond his appeal for strategies of dialogue or conversation, culminating in what he has named as "analogical imagination".[32]

Authentic analogical language is a rare achievement, since it attempts the near impossible: an articulation of real differences as genuinely different but also similar to what we already know. On a more existential level, an analogical imagination suggests a willingness to enter the conversation, that unnerving place where one is willing to risk all one's present self-understanding by facing

---

30   See David Tracy, "Form and Fragment: The Recovery of the Hidden and Incomprehensible God", in *The Concept of God in Global Dialogue*, ed. Werner G. Jeanrond and Aasulv Lande (Maryknoll, NY: Orbis, 2005), 98–114.

31   Tracy, *Dialogue with the Other*, 121.

32   David Tracy, *The Analogical Imagination: Christian Theology and the Culture of Pluralism* (New York: Crossroad, 1981).

THE COMPLEXITY OF HERMENEUTICAL EXPERIENCE

145

the claims to attention of the other. In any conversation we may find ourselves called to change either radically, as suggested by the religious language of conversion, or less completely but genuinely, as in any acknowledgment of the once merely different as now genuinely possible.[33]

What, then, are religious classics for Tracy? In his search for truth as revealed through interpretative action, Tracy had defined classics as such: "what we mean in naming certain texts, events, images, rituals, symbols and persons 'classics' is that here we recognize nothing less than the disclosure of a reality we cannot but name truth."[34] Thus, for Tracy, the classic is a category of reception.[35] The hermeneutical struggle with the sense of a text, event or person confronts the interpreter with a claim to attention which cannot easily be resisted. Truth manifests itself in hermeneutical experiences. The religious classic does not differ in this respect. Rather, according to Tracy it offers yet further levels of intensity. "The believer will sense in the religious classic the interruptive presence of Ultimate Reality empowering a way of life otherwise thought impossible."[36] Hence, the difference in the act of reading a sonnet by William Shakespeare and the Gospel of Mark does not relate to the possible experience of truth manifestation as such; rather, it calls the interpreter to a transformed mode of existence which might hit the believer differently than the non-believer. Tracy insists, of course, that the religious classics must be open to interpretation by all – believers and nonbelievers alike. "To claim that only believers can interpret the religions ... is a position that ultimately robs the religious classics of their claims to truth."[37] However, believers bring a different horizon to the hermeneutical experience; they carry different expectations when approaching a religious classic: "Believers will converse with the tradition in order to be transformed. The ones who partly succeed are named the witnesses, the just, the enlightened ones, the saints."[38]

At this point it might be helpful to take stock. Schleiermacher, Otto, Eliade, and Tracy have all been in some sort of agreement that religious experiences

---

33   Tracy, *Plurality and Ambiguity*, 93–94.

34   Tracy, *The Analogical Imagination*, 108. See also David Tracy, "On Thinking with the Classics", *Criterion* 22 (1983), 9–10 (10): "we sense ourselves recognizing something both important and true, some claim to our attention we cannot easily shirk, some reality which lures us into civilized discourse, some question which demands conversation. In experiencing a classic in any discipline, we recognize that some disclosive and transformative truth seems to be at stake."

35   See Jeanrond, *Text and Interpretation*, 142.

36   Tracy, *Plurality and Ambiguity*, 108.

37   Ibid., 110.

38   Ibid., 108.

involve interpretative horizons. For the young Schleiermacher, religion meant contemplation of the whole "in childlike passivity", as distinct from thinking and acting. For Otto, religious experience added a larger perspective to one's relationship to the cosmos which could not be reduced to mere rational calculation. Religion demanded intuition for the whole in terms of opening oneself towards experiencing the totally different (*das Ganz Andere*). The human subject needed to cultivate its endowment for intuition and proper divination. For Eliade, the universe could be looked at through radically different eyes: either as merely profane or as potentially disclosing its sacred dimensions in every human encounter with aspects of reality. Here religious experience meant experience of the sacred. For Tracy, religious experience does not differ in structure from any other experience of truth, as disclosed in the encounter with classic expressions in tradition and the present. But it differs in terms of its existential significance: Religious experience might lead to conversion, transformation, and liberation.

All four thinkers witness to the irreducible nature of the religious experience of reality. The young Schleiermacher stresses the necessary passivity; Otto highlights the non-rational nature of religious experience; Eliade refers to the auto-presence of the sacred; and Tracy underlines the impossibility of mastering any genuine discourse on Ultimate Reality.[39] However, our four thinkers somewhat disagree with regard to the level of subjective involvement required in the hermeneutics of religious experience. First, for Schleiermacher, religion manifests itself in the struggle (*Auseinandersetzung*) of the person with the whole. Second, the person may or may not be particularly endowed with a particular religious sensibility as in Otto's approach. A religious genius can be imagined, such as Jesus Christ outclassing them all in terms of being the Son. Third, for Eliade, everybody can approach any aspect of reality through the horizon of the sacred. Fourth, for Tracy, the religious interpreter approaches the religious classic – be it as fragment or frag-event – ready to be challenged and transformed. Thus, for Tracy, interpreting the religious classic leads to the possibility of a transformed praxis of being in the world in pursuit of liberation, solidarity, and hope.

Horizons matter as they shape particular hermeneutical expectations, perspectives, and the level of attention to the material conditions of religious experience. The horizon of Eliade through which he entered into our Wednesday sing-along in Chicago differed from the horizon of us students singing along.

---

39   Ibid., 109.

Transcendence: Gift and Act

The hermeneutical encounter of radical otherness charges theological discourse with approaching the question of transcendence. So far we have seen how the four thinkers discussed here have located and organised their respective hermeneutical approach to religious experience. Moreover, all religious experience is hermeneutically mediated. Space, time, and language condition all human experience of the sacred, of the non-rational, of the universe, or of Ultimate Reality. Religion cannot escape hermeneutics. But which type of hermeneutics might be most appropriate to approaching religious experience?

Theological answers to this question have varied depending on the particular horizon through which particular theologians aimed to approach religious experience. Is passivity the best human starting point in terms of approaching God's self-revelation? Or, if not, to what degree would the interpreter and the community of interpreters need to be involved in the praxis of interpretation which in turn continues to shape their horizon?

Karl Barth, Anders Nygren, Hans Frei, and many others have opted for a hermeneutics firmly submitted to particular theological interpretations. Only God can reveal God. The human person submerged in sin is unable to do anything in terms of getting to know God other than through fully submitting to God's Word. Human desire for God, therefore, remains suspicious. In other words, a particular approach to human experiences of God, in this case a christological interpretation, was selected in order to facilitate a clearly limited hermeneutical exercise – limited thematically as well as by its lack of respect for and discussion of the necessarily linguistic nature of all hermeneutical activity.

It is important to appreciate that the hermeneutical question for Karl Barth did not originally arise from a conscious methodological concern about how to devise an appropriate theory of text-understanding with regard to religious experience mediated by the Scriptures. Rather, for him, the hermeneutical question entailed the ultimate material question of theology: who is God and who am I?[40] Barth's hermeneutics was not a methodological reflection before actual theological thinking starts. Rather, it was part of theology proper, and thus part of dogmatics. Barth's hermeneutics was a hermeneutics of revelation, whereas Tracy's is a hermeneutics of signification. Both theologians are, of course, passionately interested in God and in God's revelation. However, they differ with regard to their assessment of human possibilities to relate to God and with regard to the nature and function of religious experience. Both theologians

---

40   For Barth's hermeneutics see Werner G. Jeanrond, *Theological Hermeneutics: Development and Significance* (London: SCM, 1994), 127–137.

respect God's radical otherness: Barth proclaimed: "'God is in heaven and you on earth.' *This* God's relationship to *this* human being, *this* human being's relationship to *this* God is for me the theme of the Bible and the sum of philosophy at once."[41] Tracy argued that the primary theological task is naming God, thus acknowledging the human linguistic condition from the start.

> Incarnation, cross, resurrection, and second coming are the central Christian symbols for understanding who Christ is and thereby for Christians who God is and how God is to be named and who we might become. Christian theology is better described not as christocentric, but as theocentric, and christomorphic. It is the *form* of Christ that allows for the naming Christianly of God, of humanity, of cosmos. And if the christologized form is reduced to just incarnation or just resurrection, or just cross, or just the second coming without the full complexity of fragmenting and disclosive symbols, then we may be depriving ourselves of the full Christian naming of God.[42]

Both Barth and Tracy wish to protect the divinity of God; Barth with reference to God's sovereignty, and Tracy with reference to God's ultimate incomprehensibility. That is why Barth calls for hermeneutical subordination and Tracy for hermeneutical self-critique as exemplified by the apophatic and mystical traditions of Christianity.[43] Both theologians embrace the Bible as classic – Barth as a christocentric classic and Tracy as a theocentric classic. However, the decisive difference concerns Tracy's trust in the human possibility of a hermeneutics of religious experience, however fragmentary and ambiguous, whereas Barth does not encourage trust in human communicative or naming capacities with regard to the divine. Moreover, Barth does not ultimately share Tracy's interest in religion or religious experience as such.

For Tracy, then, transcendence is linked to human language and communication. This is not to say that it emerges from human initiative and may be produced at will. Rather, for Tracy as for Barth, transcendence will always be gift and grace, an incalculable surprise. Yet for Tracy it remains possible precisely

---

41   Karl Barth, *Der Römerbrief* (1922) (Zurich: Theologischer Verlag, 1978), xiii (italics according to the German original). English translation: *The Epistle to the Romans*, trans. Edwyn C. Hoskyns (Oxford: Oxford University Press, 1968), 10.

42   Tracy, "Form and Fragment", 107 (original italics).

43   Ibid.

THE COMPLEXITY OF HERMENEUTICAL EXPERIENCE   149

as the Impossible. "The Impossible may happen. Or it may not."[44] Arguing in
the context of interreligious dialogue, Tracy illustrates further:

> One example of a religious Impossible: the prophetic religious tradi-
> tions in Judaism, Christianity, and Islam, preach resistance to injustice –
> especially injustice to the outcasts of society. We can call this reality, with
> Derrida, the Impossible as Justice to come. The meditative and mystical
> traditions also await the Impossible; they are more likely to name the
> Impossible Love or Wisdom or Bliss.[45]

The experience of transcendence can lead to many reactions, including awe,
unease, paralysis, conversion, social action, and love. It also includes the possibility of transformation and thus of further impacting on our hermeneutical horizons. In any case, this experience will always be mediated through
human language, through human speech acts. God's gift of transcendence thus
requires human acts of reception.

Experiencing Mircea Eliade's experience of transcendence in Chicago has
impacted on many of us students of hermeneutics – most powerfully, because
he left the hall when the music stopped. We were left behind after his experience of transfiguration.

The Functions of Interpreting Experience and of Experiencing
Interpretation

Barth favoured the experience of biblical interpretation whereas Tracy has
remained committed to the interpretation of religious experience – including,
in his case, the experience of biblical interpretation, theological interpretation of all forms of Christian expression, but also the different experiences of
religion in and beyond the Christian context. Both theologians, used here para-
digmatically, have been participants, often critical participants, in particular
communities of interpretation. And both have accepted the challenges of different functions of interpretation. However, it is not only significant who interprets which text, event, experience, symbol, ritual, person, tradition, but also
when and for what function. Using here the example of text-interpretation,

---

44   David Tracy, "Western Hermeneutics and Interreligious Dialogue", in *Interreligious
      Hermeneutics*, ed. Catherine Comille and Christopher Conway (Eugene, OR: Cascade
      Books, 2010), 1–43 (22).

45   Ibid., 23.

I would like to emphasize first the material challenge of every interpretative act and then to reflect upon the different functions of interpretation.

Hans-Georg Gadamer proposed the "fusion of horizons (*Horizontverschmelzung*)" and the analogy of the "play (*Spiel*)" as crucial metaphors that might help us to understand what happens when we interpret.[46] In full agreement with Gadamer's elaboration of the function of pre-judgements in the hermeneutical act, but critical of Gadamer's refusal to accept the necessity of methodological reflection on what happens when we interpret a text as text and do so critically and self-critically, Paul Ricœur challenged hermeneutical reflection to pay much more attention to the matter at stake, the forms of text and the strategies of a text's communicative perspective. In his famous work *Time and Narrative*, he proposed a threefold approach to interpretation consisting of "prefiguration", "configuration", and "refiguration".[47] In the always prefigured act of reading, the inner dynamics of the text, its configuration, is transformed into refiguration. Reading, therefore, can lead to refiguration: "the passage from configuration to refiguration required the confrontation between two worlds, the fictive world of the text and the real world of the reader".[48] This approach paid tribute to the necessary framework in which the interpreter meets a text; to the textuality of the text; and to the necessary engagement of the interpreter with the text, an involvement which might lead to a form of transformation.

Ricœur's hermeneutics is particularly suitable as a conceptual framework for understanding the process of interpreting experience as well as for the process of interpreting the experience of interpretation. It pays adequate attention to the communal and personal dimensions of interpretation, but it also acknowledges and respects the material challenge of all interpretation: there *is* a text in this class![49] However, this text does not meet its interpreters in a vacuum. Rather, every interpretation of an experience or of a text fulfils some sort of function which co-conditions the interpreter's overall choice of genre of interpretation. There are religious functions that call for a religious genre of interpretation, and there are non-religious functions which might lead to the

---

46　For a discussion of Gadamer's hermeneutics, see Jeanrond, *Theological Hermeneutics*, 64–70.

47　Paul Ricœur, *Time and Narrative*, 3 vols, trans. Kathleen McLaughlin and David Pellauer (Chicago: University of Chicago Press, 1984–1988).

48　Ibid., vol. 3, 159.

49　For my engagement with Stanley Fish, *Is There a Text in This Class? The Authority of Interpretive Communities* (Cambridge, MA: Harvard University Press, 1982), see Jeanrond, *Text and Interpretation*, 110–113.

THE COMPLEXITY OF HERMENEUTICAL EXPERIENCE   151

call for a religious genre of interpretation, as my introductory story of Eliade's experience has tried to document. By returning to Barth and Tracy, I hope to clarify further this consideration of religious functions in hermeneutics.

The religious function which shaped Barth's interpretative genres starting with the second edition of his *Römerbrief* was an attempt to reconfirm God's sovereignty in the aftermath of liberal theology and its fiasco in the experience of the First World War. The function of Barth's dogmatics was to readjust the place of the Christian church under the sovereignty of God. The function of Tracy's interpretation of Christian texts, experiences, and symbols has been the articulation of God's mysterious presence in the world – as classic, religious classic, fragment, and frag-event. Tracy's interpretative genres needed to be shaped accordingly. Although Barth and Tracy have interpreted the same interpretative experiences, namely the biblical texts, and paid careful attention to the textuality of the text, they have been motivated by different functions and thus arrived at different interpretations. Moreover, when selecting different functions both the particular perspective and the levels of attention may change – not totally, but at times significantly. The configuration of the object of interpretation remains the same, but the prefiguration and refiguration of the reader are shaped by the demands of the particular function. There is no interest-free interpretation. All interpretation of complex experiences and texts is by nature pluralistic.

There is a clear difference, for example, between functions of reading which are inspired by the inner perspective of a particular religious tradition and functions of reading which are inspired by concrete inter-religious encounter. Again, the spectrum of prefiguration and refiguration can be great. Transcendence, when it happens, will also be figured differently even though it will always be related to material conditions – however, material conditions can only be approached through particularly shaped horizons, perspectives, and functions.

We have seen that religious interpretations of reality always presuppose a particular horizon and involve hermeneutical choices which, in turn, either are prepared to go the long way through linguistic forms and the interpretative requirements or prefer theological short cuts according to prefigured theological aims. Finally, concrete interpretative functions help to disclose religious worlds in front of the text, although the experience of transcendence can never be produced at will. Transcendence, however different an experience, is always an experience of human beings in concrete circumstances. It is always a hermeneutical experience.

I owe Mircea Eliade not only innumerable insights into a variety of religions, their history, and their differences as well as common patterns, but also a particular hermeneutical experience of refiguration which entailed hermeneutical challenges on many different levels so that I am still wrestling with all that complexity. Since I experienced Eliade's transfiguration in May 1980 in Chicago, listening to American revival songs keeps confronting me with particular hermeneutical challenges.

Literature

Barth, Karl, *Der Römerbrief* (1922) (Zurich: Theologischer Verlag, 1978).

Barth, Karl, *The Epistle to the Romans*, trans. Edwyn C. Hoskyns (Oxford: Oxford University Press, 1968).

Eliade, Mircea, *The Sacred and the Profane: The Nature of Religion*, trans. Willard R. Trask (New York: Harcourt Brace Jovanovich, 1959).

Fish, Stanley, *Is There a Text in This Class? The Authority of Interpretive Communities* (Cambridge, MA: Harvard University Press, 1982).

Jeanrond, Werner G., "Friedrich Schleiermacher", in *Klassiker der Religionsphilosophie: Von Platon bis Kierkegaard*, ed. Friedrich Niewöhner (Munich: Beck, 1995), 285–299; 380–384.

Jeanrond, Werner G., *Text and Interpretation as Categories of Theological Thinking*, trans. Thomas J. Wilson (Eugene, OR: Wipf and Stock, 2005 [reprint]).

Jeanrond, Werner G., *Theological Hermeneutics: Development and Significance* (London: SCM, 1994).

Lauster, Lauster, *Die Verzauberung der Welt: Eine Kulturgeschichte des Christentums* (Munich: Beck, 2014).

Otto, Rudolf, *Das Heilige: Über das Irrationale in der Idee des Göttlichen und sein Verhältnis zum Rationalen* (Munich: Beck, 1979).

Otto, Rudolf, *The Idea of the Holy: An Inquiry into the Non-Rational in the Idea of the Divine and its Relation to the Rational*, trans. John W. Harvey (London: Oxford University Press, 1924).

Ricœur, Paul, *Time and Narrative*, 3 vols, trans. Kathleen McLaughlin and David Pellauer (Chicago: University of Chicago Press, 1984–1988).

Schleiermacher, Friedrich, *On Religion: Speeches to Its Cultured Despisers*, trans. Richard Crouter (Cambridge: Cambridge University Press, 1988).

Smith, Jonathan Z., *To Take Place: Toward Theory in Ritual* (Chicago: The University of Chicago Press, 1987).

Tracy, David, "Form and Fragment: The Recovery of the Hidden and Incomprehensible God", in *The Concept of God in Global Dialogue*, ed. Werner G. Jeanrond and Aasulv Lande (Maryknoll, NY: Orbis, 2005), 98–114.

Tracy, David, "On Thinking with the Classics", *Criterion* 22 (1983), 9–10.

Tracy, David, "Western Hermeneutics and Interreligious Dialogue", in *Interreligious Hermeneutics*, ed. Catherine Comille and Christopher Conway (Eugene, OR: Cascade Books, 2010), 1–43.

Tracy, David, *Dialogue with the Other: The Inter-Religious Dialogue* (Louvain: Peeters Press, 1990).

Tracy, David, *Plurality and Ambiguity: Hermeneutics, Religion, Hope* (San Francisco, CA: Harper & Row, 1987).

Tracy, David, *The Analogical Imagination: Christian Theology and the Culture of Pluralism* (New York: Crossroad, 1981).

CHAPTER 9

"Mediated Immediacy": Karl Rahner and Edward Schillebeeckx on the Non-Reflective Element of Experience

Marijn de Jong

The Linguistic Turn and Religious Epistemology

"It is the text so to speak, which absorbs the world, rather than the world the text."[1] This quotation from George Lindbeck's *The Nature of Doctrine* forms the starting point for my consideration of the consequences of the turn to language for contemporary theology. The so-called 'linguistic turn' signifies modern philosophy's growing recognition of the fundamental role of language and its consequent formative and de-formative powers. Hence it also has important repercussions for the way in which we conceive of experience and interpretation. Paying proper attention to the role of language leads to a 'break with immediacy'. Language is now seen as deeply influencing, differentiating, and shaping experience.[2]

The linguistic turn has forced theologians to reconsider religious epistemology and theological method. Lindbeck's post-liberal approach has been particularly influential, giving rise to the so-called 'Yale School' of theology.[3] Drawing primarily on insights from Ludwig Wittgenstein and Clifford Geertz, Lindbeck proposes a "cultural-linguistic" paradigm for understanding religion as an

---

1 George Lindbeck, *The Nature of Doctrine: Religion and Theology in a Post-Liberal Age* (Louisville, KY: Westminster John Know Press, 1984), 104.

2 Steven Shakespeare, "Language", in *The Oxford Handbook of Theology and Modern European Thought*, ed. Nicholas Adams, George Pattison and Graham Ward (Oxford: Oxford University Press, 2013), 105–126. 'Linguistic relativism' or 'determinism', also known as the Sapir-Whorf hypothesis, holds that perception and experience are determined by language. The strength of the attributed influence of language varies depending on either weaker or stronger forms of this position. See *The Oxford Dictionary of Philosophy*, s. v. "Sapir-Whorf hypothesis."

3 For a more comprehensive overview of the characteristics of the 'Yale School' in relation to the 'Chicago School', see Werner G. Jeanrond, "The Problem of the Starting-Point of Theological Thinking", in *The Possibilities of Theology: Studies in the Theology of Eberhard Jüngel in his Sixtieth Year*, ed. John Webster (Edinburgh: T&T Clark, 1994), 70–89.

© KONINKLIJKE BRILL NV, LEIDEN, 2016 | DOI 10.1163/9789004328600_011

"MEDIATED IMMEDIACY" 155

alternative to what he calls the "experiential-expressivist" model.[4] Lindbeck associates this model with liberal theology since Friedrich Schleiermacher and considers thinkers like Bernard Lonergan, Karl Rahner, David Tracy and Paul Ricoeur as its representatives.[5] The experiential-expressivists assume the existence of a common 'core experience'. This core experience is deemed to be pre-reflexive, preceding the stage of its expression. Accordingly, various religious traditions are viewed as different ways of symbolizing and conceptualizing the same original core experience.[6] Lindbeck objects to this prioritizing of experience over expression and advocates a reversal: "Instead of deriving external features of a religion from inner experience, it is the inner experiences which are viewed as derivative".[7] Experience thus is *constituted by* culture and language.[8] Consequently, individual subjectivity is shaped by the community rather than vice versa.[9] Applying these insights to theology, Lindbeck concludes that the texts of religious communities are the regulative principle of religion.[10] Religious experiences therefore can be considered as "by-products of linguistically or conceptually structured cognitive activities".[11]

While there are good grounds for Lindbeck's call for attention to the central role of language and culture, his alternative proposal also has various problematic aspects. These concerns are well articulated in David Tracy's review of *The Nature of Doctrine*.[12] First, Tracy questions the adequacy of Lindbeck's assessment of the shortcomings of the experiential-expressive paradigm. Hermeneutical theologians belonging to this 'tradition' have anything but ignored the linguistic turn and yet they strive to combine the new understandings of the role of language with a deeper and broader understanding of experience.[13] Hence Lindbeck's distinction between two fundamentally different models seems inaccurate. Second, Tracy also draws attention to the fact

---

4 Lindbeck, *The Nature of Doctrine*, 1–11. Lindbeck also distinguishes a third model, the cognitive-propositionalist model. However, in the discussion which interests us here he focuses on the differences between the experiential-expressivist and the cultural-linguistic model.

5 Lindbeck, *The Nature of Doctrine*, 24; 30; 122.

6 Ibid., 7; 17–18.

7 Ibid., 20.

8 Ibid.

9 Ibid., 19.

10 Ibid., 98–124.

11 Ibid., 22.

12 David Tracy, "Lindbeck's New Program for Theology: A Reflection", *The Thomist* 49 (1985): 460–472.

13 Ibid., 462–464.

that Lindbeck's emphasis on the inner logic of the language of a particular ecclesial community seems inadequate to account publicly for the truth claims of a tradition. When the only possible 'apologetics' is an 'ad-hoc- apologetics', it becomes difficult to conceive of the truth claims, transcending particular cultural-linguistic discourses. As a result, the cultural-linguistic approach runs the risk of turning into relativism, confessionalism, or fideism.[14]

This critique of Lindbeck's theological appropriation of the linguistic turn serves to illustrate the difficulties involved in rethinking the relation between experience and interpretation. Focusing on cultural-linguistic factors may lead to a unilateral determination of experience by interpretation. Surprisingly, notwithstanding the unilateral tendency in his thought, Lindbeck also characterizes the relation between experience and interpretation as reciprocal.[15] Yet since his own theory seems unable to develop this dialectical relationship, I propose to reconsider the role of experience in theological epistemology by turning to two experience-oriented theologians: Karl Rahner and Edward Schillebeeckx. Following Tracy, my aim is to show that their experience-orientated approaches are far from hermeneutically naïve or inattentive to the conditioning role of language. Moreover, Rahner's and Schillebeeckx's opposition to a complete usurpation of experience by language provides a valuable perspective to rethink the dialectical relation between experience and interpretation. I will develop this argument by focusing on their accounts of a non-reflective element in their theological epistemology.[16] My goal is to show that the 'mediated-immediacy' position of Rahner and Schillebeeckx allows for a dimension of commonality in human experience that enables the public discussion of particular religious truth claims. I argue that the commonality thus established can work both negatively by relativizing every concrete expression of experience, as well as positively by enabling and encouraging to transcend the cultural-linguistic limitations of particular traditions.

Karl Rahner's Epistemology

Rahner's *Foundations of the Christian Faith*[17] opens with a methodological introduction in which several epistemological presuppositions of his

---

14   Ibid., 469–470.

15   Lindbeck, *The Nature of Doctrine*, 19.

16   It is interesting to note that Lindbeck rejects uninterpreted experience, but that he does affirm the existence of so-called non-reflective experience. See ibid., 22.

17   Karl Rahner, *Grundkurs des Glaubens: Einführung in den Begriff des Christentums* (1976), Sämtliche Werke Band 26, ed. Nikolaus Schwerdtfeger and Albert Raffelt (Freiburg: Herder,

"MEDIATED IMMEDIACY" 157

philosophy and theology are explained.[18] One key principle introduced reads as follows: "There is in man [sic] an inescapable *unity in difference between one's original self-possession and reflection*."[19] With the assertion of this unity in difference, Rahner seeks to distance himself from two extremes that he characterizes as "rationalism" and "modernism".[20] Whereas rationalism stresses conceptual reflection at the expense of experience, modernism favors experience to such an extent that it disregards the role of reflection. Yet this initial emphasis on the unity of experience and interpretation is immediately problematized by the subsequent claim that "there is also a more original unity, not indeed for everything and anything, but certainly for the actualization of human existence, and this is a unity of reality and its 'self-presence' [*Bei-sich-selber-Sein*] which is more, and is more original, than the unity of this reality and the concept which objectifies it".[21] This dense statement must be read in light of the metaphysics that Rahner develops in *Spirit in the World* and *Hearer of the Word*.[22] One of its central principles is the unity of being and knowing which is established via a phenomenological analysis of the universal question about the meaning of being. Rahner observes that the metaphysical question about being as such emerges necessarily in human existence, yet the fact that we need to question also shows that the meaning of being eludes us. "We know

---

      1999). Translated by William V. Dych as *Foundations of Christian Faith: An Introduction to the Idea of Christianity* (New York: Crossroad, 1978).

18   Rahner's uses various terms to refer to experience, such as 'basic knowledge' or 'original self-possession'. Similarly, he also uses the term 'reflection' rather than 'interpretation' in relation to experience. See for instance Karl Rahner, "Experience of Self and Experience of God", in *Theological Investigations*, vol. XIII, trans. David Bourke (London: Darton, Longman & Todd, 1975), 123–124, in which Rahner explains his decision to use the term 'experience' rather than the term 'knowledge', even though both terms are closely related at the so-called transcendental level. In presenting Rahner's epistemology, I will follow his use of these various terms.

19   Rahner, *Foundations*, 15.

20   Ibid., 15.

21   Ibid.

22   See Karl Rahner, *Geist in Welt: Zur Metaphysik der endlichen Erkenntnis bei Thomas von Aquin* (1939), Sämtliche Werke Band 2, ed. Albert Raffelt (Freiburg: Herder, 1996). Translated by William Dych as *Spirit in the World* (New York: Continuum, 1994); and Karl Rahner, *Hörer des Wortes: zur Grundlegung einer Religionsphilosophie* (1941), Sämtliche Werke Band 4, ed. Albert Raffelt (Freiburg: Herder, 1997). Translated by Joseph Donceel as *Hearer of the Word: Laying the Foundation for a Philosophy of Religion*, ed. Andrew Tallon (New York: Continuum, 1994). A full discussion of Rahner's metaphysics is beyond the scope of this paper. For a more elaborated account, see Peter Eicher, *Die anthropologische Wende: Karl Rahners philosophischer Weg vom Wesen des Menschen zur personalen Existenz* (Freiburg: Universitätsverlag, 1970), esp. 172–180.

158   DE JONG

of it (*bekannt*) but we do not really know it (*erkannt*)".[23] Here we find an indication of Rahner's recognition of the circular nature of human understanding. Rahner connects this analysis of human questioning with the scholastic axiom *omne ens est verum* (all being is truth) to conclude that intelligibility is an essential characteristic of every being: "the original meaning of knowing is self-possession [bei-sich-sein], and being possesses itself to the extent that it is being".[24] Thus, according to Rahner, knowing is in the first place self-knowing. He stresses the identity between the knowing subject and the known object. Hence, Rahner conceives of an initial experiential level where experiencing subject and experienced object are in unity.

However, this poses the question whether interpretation plays any role at all in his epistemology. Rahner takes up this question in an attempt to delineate his own position from German idealism.[25] He does so by emphasizing the analogical nature of knowing as 'Bei-sich-sein' (being-present-to-oneself). Only pure being – God – is fully present to itself. The fact that human beings continually question shows that we are not fully present to ourselves. As finite beings, our (self-)knowledge is limited.[26] Here Rahner's metaphysics of knowledge offers an interesting point of connection with a more hermeneutical approach. Rahner does not extensively problematize the conditioning role of language for human understanding.[27] Yet, in the *Grundkurs*, his remark on the original unity of reality and its self-presence is followed by the assertion that there is a moment of "reflection" operative even in this original knowledge. The original unity is possible only "in and through language".[28] For Rahner, therefore, the mediating role of language does not merely occur after a prior experiential moment, but rather forms a constitutive element of the most basic unity that characterizes human experience.

Rahner's reflections on the role of language are not comprehensive, and he uses various terms interchangeably when discussing this role.[29] When

---

23   Rahner, *Hearer*, 28.
24   Ibid., 30.
25   Ibid., 35–36.
26   Ibid., 35–39.
27   Paul Ricoeur noted the absence of any specific attention to language in Rahner's work, yet did not judge Rahner's theory faulty for this reason. Instead he advocated to complement Rahner's approach with a stronger focus on the role of language. See Paul Ricoeur, "Response to Karl Rahner's Lecture: On the Incomprehensibility of God", *The Journal of Religion (Supplement)* 58 (1978): 126–131.
28   Rahner, *Foundations*, 16.
29   Ibid. See also Rahner, "The Experience of God Today", in *Theological Investigations*, vol. XI, trans. David Bourke (London: Darton, Longman & Todd, 1974), 152.

"MEDIATED IMMEDIACY" 159

asked about language, Rahner stated that "Language is always about something, which is distinct from language and which cannot be expressed fully by language".[30] His recognition of the indispensable mediatory role of language is continually combined with a deep concern to retain at least an analytical distinction between the experiential and the interpretative level. To complicate matters, he even states that basic experiences such as love, joy, or trust are in principle independent from processes of conceptual objectification and interpretation. Yet this statement must be read in conjunction with the foregoing assertion that experience and interpretation cannot be absolutely separated.[31] Rahner, then, is seeking to maintain a difficult balance, a precarious tension between experience and interpretation. On the one hand, experience includes a process of conceptual articulation towards theoretical knowledge. On the other hand, there is also a reverse movement from conceptualization back to original experience.[32] Rahner's unity in difference of experience and interpretation is best illustrated by turning to his analysis of the transcendental and categorical dimensions of experience.

Transcendental experience is a central concept for Rahner's theology. He defines transcendental experience as "the subjective, unthematic, necessary and unfailing consciousness of the knowing subject that is co-present in every spiritual act of knowledge, and the subject's openness to the unlimited expanse of all possible reality".[33] This definition combines a Kantian understanding of the transcendental, that which concerns the a priori conditions for the possibility of experience, with an understanding of transcendental as going beyond or above individual finite objects.[34] Analyzing the act of knowing, Rahner observes that we have an ability to put everything – including ourselves – into question. In this questioning we reach beyond finiteness and experience ourselves as beings of unlimited transcendence. Our radical questioning reveals an infinite mysterious horizon. This horizon forms a necessary condition for all human acts of knowledge. Only by having a so-called pre-apprehension (*Vorgriff*) of the totality of possible objects of knowledge – in short, absolute

---

30 Karl Rahner, *Karl Rahner im Gespräch. Band 2: 1978–1982*, ed. Paul Imhof and Hubert Biallowons (München: Kösel, 1983), 229.

31 Rahner, "The Experience of God Today," 151–152.

32 Rahner, *Foundations*, 16–17. See also Rahner, "Experience of Self and Experience of God," 124.

33 Rahner, *Foundations*, 20.

34 It is important to distinguish the various meanings of 'transcendental' that are at play when Rahner uses this adjective. See Karen Kilby, *Karl Rahner: Theology and Philosophy* (London: Routledge, 2004), 32–37.

being – can we recognize an object given in sensory intuition as an individual finite object. As the transcendental condition for human knowledge, the *Vorgriff* of absolute being is co-present in every act of human knowing and is as such a universal experience.[35]

However, transcendental experience is never available apart from its historical and categorical mediation.[36] We have no immediate vision of the infinite horizon of being. Rather, we only experience this horizon in the sensory experience of historical worldly objects. Transcendental experience and historical-categorical experience are therefore mutually related.[37] This returns us to the relation between experience and interpretation. For Rahner, human persons can transcend the world in knowledge (transcendental experience), but only via worldly and categorical mediation (categorical experience). The human person is a finite spirit.[38] The self-transcending capacity is located by Rahner at the unthematic experiential level.[39] Yet this capacity is always actualized within the concrete conditions of world and history, and therefore, we might add, also always conditioned by language. Since transcendental experience is always mediated categorically, experience is necessarily interpreted experience. "Experience always involves at least a certain incipient process of reflection".[40] Hence, it would be wrong to conceive of transcendental experience (experiential moment) and categorical experience (interpretative moment) as two distinct and separated moments in time, the latter following the former. Although we cannot avoid the abstract term experience, we should always use this term in relation to a historical context.[41]

---

35 Rahner, *Foundations*, 33–34.

36 Ibid., 140–142. See also the article Karl Rahner, "Thomas Aquinas on Truth", in *Theological Investigations*, vol. XIII, trans. David Bourke (London: Darton, Longman & Todd, 1975).

37 Rahner, "Thomas Aquinas on Truth", 20–28.

38 Rahner, *Hearer*, 47–50. Accordingly, Rahner names the human person a "spirit in the world", the "mid-point suspended between the world and God" and argues that anthropological reflections become necessarily theological reflections: "man encounters himself when he finds himself already in the world and when he asks about God; and when he asks about his essence, he always finds himself already in the world and on the way to God. He is both of these at once, and cannot be one without the other." (Rahner, *Spirit*, 406–407).

39 There is much debate about the precise meaning of 'unthematic' in Rahner's thought. He usually uses the term in opposition to 'thematic' or 'conceptual'. The implicit, unthematic becomes explicit, thematic through reflection. See Rahner, *Foundations*, 18.

40 Rahner, "The Experience of God Today", 152.

41 Rahner, "Experience of Self and Experience of God", 124. The English translation of this passage is incorrect. It suggests that Rahner denies that the interpretation of transcen-

"MEDIATED IMMEDIACY" 161

Rahner, standing in the Christian tradition of interpretation, identifies transcendental experience as a universal unthematic experience of God. Yet he acknowledges that this experience can also be interpreted in different religious or non-religious terms, be denied or suppressed, or left unexplored. The key fact is that every person is somehow engaged in a dynamic process of interpreting a universal, unthematic, transcendental experience.[42] Rahner distinguishes gradual stages in the history of interpretation of transcendental experience. He calls this the history of revelation and salvation.[43] The conceptual systems that are used in this reflective process of interpretation are dependent on the respective religious, cultural, and historical milieux. No matter how much we reflect on our experiences, however, we will never be able to capture the transcendental experience in a definitive interpretation. The horizon which becomes present in transcendental experience always remains ineffable mystery.[44] Rahner warns repeatedly against the identification of experience and interpretation. The inability to articulate and conceptualize the transcendental element of experience pushes us to revisit our experience continually.[45] We find here again – at least implicitly – a recognition of the hermeneutical nature of human understanding. However, for an explicitly hermeneutical account of theological epistemology we turn to a contemporary of Rahner.

---

dental experience is part of the concrete human history of experience whereas he actually says the very opposite in the German original. See Karl Rahner, "Selbsterfahrung und Gotteserfahrung", in *Schriften zur Theologie*, Band X (Einsiedeln: Benziger, 1972), 135. This mistranslation might have contributed to the impression that Rahner considers transcendental experience and categorical experience as two separately existing realities. See for instance Derek Simon, "Rahner and Ricoeur on Religious Experience and Language. A Reflection on the Mutuality between Experience and Language in the Transcendental and Hermeneutical Traditions", *Église et Théologie* 28 (1997): 77–99, esp. 82.

42   Karl Rahner, "Experience of Transcendence from the Standpoint of Catholic Dogmatics", in *Theological Investigations*, vol. XVIII, trans. Edward Quinn (New York: Crossroad, 1983), 177. See also Rahner, "The Experience of God Today", 152–153.

43   Rahner, *Foundations*, 153–170. For Rahner, the event of Jesus Christ provides the ultimate hermeneutical principle for the interpretation of this history of revelation and salvation.

44   See Karl Rahner, "The Hiddenness of God", in *Theological Investigations*, vol. XVI, trans. David Morland (London: Darton, Longman & Todd, 1979), 227–243; and Rahner, *Foundations*, 21–23.

45   Rahner, "The Experience of God Today", 152; Rahner, *Foundations*, 16–17.

162   DE JONG

Edward Schillebeeckx' Epistemology

In *The Understanding of Faith*, Edward Schillebeeckx observes that all human understanding, including theological understanding, is caught in the hermeneutical circle as a result of the historicity of human existence. Consequently, no definitive, timeless understanding is possible.[46] This raises the question whether such an acknowledgment of historicity leads to relativism. Schillebeeckx' response to this issue entails a prioritizing of questions of 'meaning' over questions of 'truth'. Traditional theological language is considered 'meaningless' by many contemporaries because it has lost its connection to the experiences of daily life. Schillebeeckx therefore proposes to take "the relationship with lived experience" as the criterion for theological interpretation. To be sure, the meaning of the Christian faith cannot simply be deduced from experience. Yet, in order to claim meaningfulness and intelligibility, a hermeneutics of the Christian tradition must be related to a hermeneutics of experience.[47]

This programmatic call to connect the tradition with experience finds application in *Jesus: An Experiment in Christology* and *Christ: The Christian Experience in the Modern World*.[48] In this contribution, however, I will focus on *Interim Report*, in which Schillebeeckx offers a concise reflection on the theological

---

46   Edward Schillebeeckx, "Naar een katholiek gebruik van de hermeneutiek", in *Geloofsverstaan: Interpretatie en kritiek* (Bloemendaal: Nelissen, 1972), 15. Translated by N. D. Smith as "Towards a Catholic use of hermeneutics", in *God the Future of Man*, The Collected Works of Edward Schillebeeckx, vol. III, Schillebeeckx, *Interim Report*, 11. (London: Bloomsbury, 2014), 7–8.

47   Edward Schillebeeckx, "Ervaringscontext en de doxologische waarde van het gelovige spreken", in *Geloofsverstaan: Interpretatie en kritiek* (Bloemendaal: Nelissen, 1972), 57–62. Translated by N. D. Smith as "The context and value of faith-talk", in *The Understanding of Faith: Interpretation and criticism*, The Collected Works of Edward Schillebeeckx, vol. V, ed. Ted Mark Schoof and Carl Sterkens with Erik Borgman and Robert J. Schreiter (London: Bloomsbury, 2014), 14–18. For a more comprehensive overview of the role of experience in Schillebeeckx' theology, see Lieven Boeve, "Experience according to Edward Schillebeeckx: The Driving Force of Faith and Theology," in *Divinising Experience. Essays in the History of Religious Experience from Origen to Ricoeur*, ed. Lieven Boeve and Laurence P. Hemming (Leuven: Peeters, 2004), 199–225.

48   Edward Schillebeeckx, *Jezus, het verhaal van een levende* (Baarn: Nelissen, 1974). Translated by Hubert Hoskins and Marcelle Manley as *Jesus: An Experiment in Christology*, The Collected Works of Edward Schillebeeckx, vol. VI, ed. Ted Mark Schoof and Carl Sterkens with Erik Borgman and Robert J. Schreiter (London: Bloomsbury, 2014); Edward Schillebeeckx, *Gerechtigheid en liefde, genade en bevrijding* (Bloemendaal: Nelissen, 1977). Translated by John Bowden as *Christ: The Christian experience in the Modern World*, The

"MEDIATED IMMEDIACY" 163

epistemology used in these two christological books.[49] Schillebeeckx recalls his central claim that God's revelation takes place through human experience.[50] Yet to counter the suggestion that this experiential focus turns into a subjectivization of revelation, Schillebeeckx explains his view on the relationship between experience and interpretation. He argues that we must distinguish between "the way which things really are" and "the way they appear" to the experiencing subject.[51] The thing which appears within our particular perspective simultaneously transcends our observation. Hence, our experience is determined not only by our personal perspective, but also in part by "the unique contribution" of the experienced thing itself.[52] Schillebeeckx uses the term "interpretandum" to signify this objective dimension of the experience.[53]

However, this is not to suggest that there is a moment of uninterpreted experience in concrete life; there is no such thing as raw experience. Interpretation does not start at the moment when one begins to reflect on one's experience, but rather is an inner moment of experience itself, first unexpressed and later deliberately reflected upon.[54] Schillebeeckx analyses the interpretative dimension of experience, distinguishing 'inner' experiential interpretative elements and 'outer' reflective interpretative elements". Inner interpretative elements have their "basis and source directly in what is experienced, as content of a conscious and so somewhat clear experience".[55] Schillebeeckx thus again emphasizes the unique contribution that the object experienced provides to our experience and argues that this objective influence extends to interpretation. There are also interpretative elements which are "handed to us from elsewhere, outside at least this experience".[56] These interpretative elements do not derive from the object experienced, but from cultural-linguistic elements that have formed the experiencing subject. Schillebeeckx illustrates this with the example of love.

Collected Works of Edward Schillebeeckx, vol. VII, ed. Ted Mark Schoof and Carl Sterkens with Erik Borgman and Robert J. Schreiter (London: Bloomsbury, 2014).

49   Edward Schillebeeckx, *Tussentijds verhaal over twee Jezus boeken* (Bloemendaal: Nelissen, 1978). Translated by John Bowden as *Interim Report on the Books Jesus and Christ*, The Collected Works of Edward Schillebeeckx, vol. VIII, ed. Ted Mark Schoof and Carl Sterkens with Erik Borgman and Robert J. Schreiter (London: Bloomsbury, 2014).

50   Schillebeeckx, *Interim Report*, 9–11.

51   Ibid., 10.

52   Ibid., 11.

53   Schillebeeckx, *Jesus*, 746.

54   Schillebeeckx, *Interim Report*, 11.

55   Ibid.

56   Ibid.

For example, an experience of love contains interpretative elements within the experience itself, suggested by the concrete experience of love. The love that is experienced knows what love is, and it even knows more about it than it can express at the moment. This interpretative identification is therefore an intrinsic moment of the love that is experienced. Afterwards, it is possible that one may also express the experience of love in language taken from *Romeo and Juliet,* from the biblical *Song of Songs,* from St. Paul's hymn to love or from all kinds of modern poetry. This additional thematizing in no way means a nonchalant or superfluous elaboration. *Interpretation and experience have a reciprocal influence on one another.* Real love lives on the love experience and on its own progressive self-expression... However, this growing self-expression makes it possible to deepen the original experience; based on the experience, it reveals that experience more explicitly to itself.[57]

Accordingly, Schillebeeckx tries to maintain the close connection between experience and interpretation, yet also distinguishes them analytically. Like Rahner, he argues that there is a surplus of meaning present in experience. We become aware of this surplus of meaning in the realization that every expression and conceptualization of our experience remains incomplete and fails to articulate this experience exhaustively. Whereas Rahner connects the inadequacy of articulations and conceptualizations primarily with the imperfect subjectivity of the experiencing person, Schillebeeckx instead emphasizes the objective side of experience. Yet, like Rahner, Schillebeeckx distinguishes between an original interpretative experience, brought to expression in so-called first-order statements, and an advanced, reflexive interpretative experience, brought to expression in so-called second-order statements.[58]

Schillebeeckx returns to the objective element of experience in his reflections on the notion of the 'contrast experience'. In his *Theological Testament,* he argues that human persons share a radical basic experience, an experience which is pre-religious and universally accessible.[59] This so-called contrast experience has two inter-related dimensions. On the one hand, there is a negative experience of indignation in the face of the omnipresence of suffering, evil, and injustice in the world. This calls for a 'No' to the inhumanity in our history. On the other hand, in the negative experience of the rejection of the

---

57 Ibid., 12 (emphasis added).

58 Ibid.

59 Edward Schillebeeckx, *Theologisch testament. Notarieel nog niet verleden* (Baarn: Nelissen, 1994), 128.

"MEDIATED IMMEDIACY" 165

inhumane, a positive dimension becomes apparent: trust in humanity and hope that the world can be changed. This hope actually enables the resistance that the negative contrast experience brings about.[60] Schillebeeckx argues that a Christian could interpret such contrast experiences as a divine call to engage in the praxis of liberation. However, such a religious interpretation is not the only interpretation possible.[61] This dynamic between a universal experience and a variety of interpretations is taken up again in the book *Church: The Human Story of God*.[62]

In this book, Schillebeeckx connects the contrast experience with a basic experience of radical finitude and contingency. This experience of an absolute limit is a universal experience. It differs, however, from Schleiermacher's notion of 'absolute dependence' because it is never experienced directly, but always as mediated by particular experiences of limits.[63] This description does certainly call to mind Rahner's distinction between the transcendental and the categorical. Schillebeeckx repeats his conviction that the absolute limit experience can be interpreted either religiously or atheistically. Yet given his emphasis on the close connection between experience and interpretation, this raises the question of whether it is still licit to speak of a common experience in this regard. Schillebeeckx responds by admitting that a believer's and an agnostic's experience of contingency are indeed fundamentally different experiences. He rejects something like a common uninterpreted experience which is subsequently interpreted in different ways. Interpretation is part of the experience itself. However, he maintains that we can still speak of the same sort of shared experience, because there is a pre-linguistic element in experience that is universally human: although "interpretations are an intrinsic part of the experience of contingency and thus colour this experience as a whole, the experiential aspect of contingency *qua* contingency is not itself identical with the interpretative element and is thus human and universal".[64]

Instead of distinguishing objective and subjective interpretative elements in experience, Schillebeeckx now chooses to locate the universality at the experiential level. Moreover, this is the only instance where he speaks specifically

---

60 Schillebeeckx, *Theologisch testament*, 129–130.

61 Ibid., 132.

62 Edward Schillebeeckx, *Mensen als verhaal van God* (Baarn: Nelissen, 1989). Translated by John Bowden as *Church: The Human Story of God*, The Collected Works of Edward Schillebeeckx, vol. X, ed. Ted Mark Schoof and Carl Sterkens with Erik Borgman and Robert J. Schreiter (London: Bloomsbury, 2014).

63 Schillebeeckx, *Church*, 75–76.

64 Ibid., 80.

about a pre-linguistic element in experience. It could be asked whether this choice of words is consistent with his plea that all experience is interpreted. The next paragraph will make clear though that the particular use of the prefix 'pre-' here must be seen within the context of a double distinction that is at work in the epistemologies of Rahner and Schillebeeckx.

Mediated Immediacy: Through Language Beyond Language

An evaluation of the theological epistemologies of Rahner and Schillebeeckx reveals that both approaches, although distinctive, lead to remarkably similar outcomes. Rahner approaches the topic of experience and interpretation primarily from the standpoint of human subjectivity, whereas Schillebeeckx focuses on the specific role of objective reality. Both authors acknowledge that language fundamentally conditions human knowing and therefore eschew the notion of uninterpreted or immediate experience. Nevertheless, these epistemologies also uphold an unthematic or non-reflective element in experience. Rahner and Schillebeeckx are able to maintain these seemingly oppositional positions by using two distinctions in their work. I will refer to these distinctions as 'analytical' and 'actual' respectively.

Both authors maintain an analytical distinction between an experiential dimension and an interpretative dimension of the single event of interpretative experience. This analytical distinction is employed to clarify that our experience consists of elements that are beyond our interpretative control. Rahner uses the term transcendental experience to describe the unthematic nature of this experiential dimension, whereas Schillebeeckx speaks of a pre-linguistic element in experience. However, this experiential dimension is never available in pure form because it is intrinsically related to the interpretative dimension of experience. The necessary mediatory role of language ensures that there is always an initial level of reflection or interpretation at work in every experience. Rahner argues that the transcendental dimension, while analytically distinct from the categorical dimension, only occurs in union with the categorical dimension. Similarly, Schillebeeckx's analytical distinction between inner and outer interpretative elements must be read against the background of his assertion that all experience is interpretative.[65]

A closer examination of the interpretative dimension leads to a second distinction between what we might call 'original experience' and 'reflected

---

65   See Edward Schillebeeckx, "Theologie der Erfahrung – Sackgasse oder Weg zum Glauben? Ein Gespräch mit Prof. Edward Schillebeeckx", *Herder Korrespondenz* 32 (1978): 392.

"MEDIATED IMMEDIACY" 167

experience'. It can be called an actual distinction because both types of experience can be encountered in real life. Strictly speaking, however, the distinction between original and reflected experience is gradual in nature. Rahner and Schillebeeckx use the concept original experience to describe an experience which entails only a very basic level of interpretation, reflection, or articulation. To be sure, there is linguistic mediation and interpretation operative at this level, but it is merely basic and unreflective. At this original level, the role of the unthematic experiential element is much larger than the interpretative element. Additional reflection using categories from a specific cultural-linguistic or religious framework increases the role of interpretation. The subsequent articulation and conceptualization seeks to clarify the original experience, thus transforming it into a reflected experience. Yet reflection can never exhaust the original experience. Specific conceptualizations and articulations therefore always refer back to the original experience, which contains a surplus of meaning. For Rahner and Schillebeeckx, the origin of this surplus of meaning is located at the non-reflective experiential level. As a result, experience retains a logical – though not a temporal – priority over interpretation.[66]

This double distinction serves to clarify how Rahner and Schillebeeckx reconcile a non-reflective element in experience with a hermeneutically sensitive approach. It is clear that these epistemologies are not unaffected by the linguistic turn. Experience is fundamentally conditioned by language insofar as our access to experience is always linguistically mediated. Language therefore can be considered a transcendental condition of experience. Yet Rahner and Schillebeeckx argue that the conditioning role of language does not mean that experience is completely determined by language. They use the notion of the unreflective element of experience to highlight the limitations of the mediatory role of language. Language refers us back to something more, which asks for further reflection, but can never be fully articulated. Both Rahner and Schillebeeckx use the term '"mediated immediacy"' to describe how *through* the mediation of language we also move *beyond* language.[67] The finite medium

---

66 See Rahner, *Karl Rahner im Gespräch*, 257, for Rahner's comments on the logical priority of experience over expression; and Schillebeeckx, *Church*, 26–27, where Schillebeeckx discusses the logical priority of the transcendental over against the categorical in the context of revelation.

67 Philip Kennedy writes that it is not clear who is to be credited with the term 'mediated immediacy' and notes that the term appears in the writings of Rahner, Schillebeeckx, and John Baillie. See Philip Kennedy, "God and Creation", in *The Praxis of the Reign of God: An Introduction to the Theology of Edward Schillebeeckx*, ed. Mary Catherine Hilkert and Robert J. Schreiter (New York: Fordham University Press, 2002), 52. The epistemological use of the term 'mediated immediacy' to characterise the nature of human knowing goes

168   DE JONG

of language is necessary to bring us in relation to reality, most eminently in relation to God. Yet precisely in this finite mediation immediacy becomes present – immediacy which needs language, but is also richer than any linguistic expression.[68] The concept of "mediated immediacy" calls for a critical reconsideration of Lindbeck's critique of experiential-expressivism.

Retrieving the Commonality of Human Experience

Contrary to Lindbeck's suggestion, an experience-orientated epistemology does not necessarily conceive naïvely of a preliminary stage of experience that subsequently leads to interpretation. Both Rahner and Schillebeeckx clearly reject the notion of uninterpreted experience. Lindbeck is right, however, insofar as Rahner and Schillebeeckx do indeed prioritize experience in their attempts to avoid a reduction of experience to interpretation. Yet he overlooks the fact that this priority is logical rather than temporal. To explain this logical prioritization, Rahner and Schillebeeckx develop a double distinction: one analytical distinction between the unthematic experiential level and the reflected interpretative level, and one actual distinction between original experience and reflected experience. The question remains whether the epistemological accounts of these theologians are relevant for contemporary theology.[69] To address this question, I take up Tracy's criticism of the confessionalist and fideistic tendency of Lindbeck's position. The epistemological frameworks of Rahner and Schillebeeckx offer a more promising avenue for the public discussion of theological truth claims than Lindbeck's cultural-linguistic model.

The mediated-immediacy position of Rahner and Schillebeeckx provides a way of combining an awareness of the hermeneutical imperative,

---

back to Georg W. F. Hegel, see Michael Inwood, *A Hegel Dictionary* (Oxford: Blackwell, 1992), 183–186.

68   For Rahner's use of the term, see *Foundations*, 83–84. Rahner develops this notion of mediated immediacy further in his reflections on God as mystery, see for instance Rahner, "The Hiddenness of God". For Schillebeeckx' use of the term, see *Christ*, 806–813.

69   In an essay reviewing Lindbeck's critique of Rahner, Nicholas Adams states that the theories of truth Rahner uses "fail to persuade contemporary theologians" and argues that his philosophical shortcomings need to be repaired. However, apart from a short account of Rahner's indebtedness to and deviation from the German philosophical tradition, Adams fails to explain adequately why he deems Rahner's epistemology unpersuasive. See Nicholas Adams, "Rahner's reception in twentieth century Protestant Theology", in *The Cambridge Companion to Karl Rahner*, ed. Declan Marmion and Mary E. Hines (Cambridge: Cambridge University Press, 2005), 211–224.

"MEDIATED IMMEDIACY" 169

without reducing experience to the particularities of culture and language. Acknowledging the conditioning role of language implies a recognition that truth claims of different religious traditions cannot be easily assimilated. The concepts and symbols that religions use to express past and present experiences are colored by the cultural-linguistic particularities of these various traditions of interpretation. A hermeneutical focus on the particularities of religious discourse is therefore required to understand what these religious traditions have to say. However, Rahner and Schillebeeckx would reject Lindbeck's claim that the text 'absorbs' the world. Their epistemologies allow for an unreflective or non-conceptual experiential engagement with reality. Such a non-reductive view of experience is essential if articulations of experience, especially religious experience, are to be discussed publicly. This has been observed more recently by, for instance, Charles Taylor in an article on the epistemology of Maurice Merleau-Ponty.[70]

Taylor takes up Merleau-Ponty's analysis of 'everyday coping' to argue for a non-conceptual and corporeally embedded pre-understanding which forms the condition for the possibility of reflective and conceptual thought.[71] Through their bodies human beings are in contact with a common world and it is "in virtue of this contact with a common world that we always have something to say to each other, something to point to in disputes about reality".[72] Of course, it cannot be denied that different people express their relation to reality in different ways. However, according to Taylor the realist epistemology of Merleau-Ponty maintains the important distinction between reality and the human grasp of reality. Hence the existence of "different, mutually untranslatable cultural 'takes' on reality" must be recognized, yet given their grounding a shared embodied contact with the world these different takes cannot be "insurmountable or inescapable".[73]

---

70 Charles Taylor, "Merleau-Ponty and the Epistemological Picture", in *The Cambridge Companion to Merleau-Ponty*, ed. Taylor Carman and Mark B. N. Hansen (Cambridge: Cambridge University Press, 2005), 26–49. Finding a familiarity between Rahner and Schillebeeckx in the thought of Merleau-Ponty is not particularly surprising, given the fact that the influence of Merleau-Ponty on Schillebeeckx' thinking is generally recognized (see Phillip Kennedy, *Schillebeeckx*, [Collegeville, MN: The Liturgical Press, 1993]). However, to date this influence, especially in the context of epistemology, has not been studied extensively. Comparisons between Rahner and Merleau-Ponty likewise are scarce, but for one contribution, see Robert D. Doud, "Sensibility in Rahner and Merleau-Ponty", *The Thomist* 44 (1980): 372–389.

71 Taylor, "Merleau-Ponty," 32–38.

72 Ibid., 40.

73 Ibid., 40.

Rahner's and Schillebeeckx's epistemologies similarly emphasize the shared horizon of experience by maintaining a dialectical tension between the particular cultural-linguistic interpretative elements and universal non-reflective experiential elements of experience. To be sure, such a shared horizon does not provide a meta-perspective or meta-language. Yet, contrary to the cultural-linguistic approach, it does retain a common reference point for discussions between different traditions of interpretation. This reference point works negatively insofar as it relativizes every concrete expression as being an incomplete articulation of experience. This introduces humility into inter-religious engagements and allows otherness – the otherness of reality, the otherness of revelation, mystery itself – to break into established convictions. The non-reflective element also works positively insofar as it impels us to transcend the cultural-linguistic limitations of our own traditions. It makes manifest that we are conditioned, yet not determined, by the particularities of our cultures and languages. This insight invites us not only to continually revisit the expressions of our experiences, but also to find ways to communicate our experiences to people outside our own cultural-linguistic community. Such communication will inevitably be colored by the particularity of our context. Nevertheless, the non-reflective element of experience provides a potential element of commensurability necessary for intra- and inter-religious engagements.

Literature

Adams, Nicholas, "Rahner's reception in twentieth century Protestant Theology", in *The Cambridge Companion to Karl Rahner*, ed. Declan Marmion and Mary E. Hines (Cambridge: Cambridge University Press, 2005), 211–224.

Boeve, Lieven, "Experience according to Edward Schillebeeckx: The Driving Force of Faith and Theology", in *Divinising Experience. Essays in the History of Religious Experience from Origen to Ricoeur*, ed. Lieven Boeve and Laurence P. Hemming (Leuven: Peeters, 2004), 199–225.

Doud, Robert D., "Sensibility in Rahner and Merleau-Ponty", *The Thomist* 44 (1980), 372–389.

Eicher, Peter, *Die anthropologische Wende: Karl Rahners philosophischer Weg vom Wesen des Menschen zur personalen Existenz* (Freiburg: Universitätsverlag, 1970).

Jeanrond, Werner G., "The Problem of the Starting-Point of Theological Thinking", in *The Possibilities of Theology: Studies in the Theology of Eberhard Jüngel in his Sixtieth Year*, ed. John Webster (Edinburgh: T&T Clark, 1994), 70–89.

Kennedy, Phillip, *Schillebeeckx* (Collegeville, MN: The Liturgical Press, 1993).

"MEDIATED IMMEDIACY" 171

Kennedy, Philip, "God and Creation", in *The Praxis of the Reign of God: An Introduction to the Theology of Edward Schillebeeckx*, ed. Mary Catherine Hilkert and Robert J. Schreiter (New York: Fordham University Press, 2002), 37–58.

Kilby, Karen, *Karl Rahner: Theology and Philosophy* (London: Routledge, 2004).

Lindbeck, George, *The Nature of Doctrine: Religions and Theology in a Post-Liberal Age* (Louisville, KY: Westminster John Know Press, 1984).

Rahner, Karl, "Selbsterfahrung und Gotteserfahrung", in *Schriften zur Theologie*, Band X (Einsiedeln: Benziger, 1972).

Rahner, Karl, "The Experience of God Today", in *Theological Investigations*, vol. XI, trans. David Bourke (London: Darton, Longman & Todd, 1974), 149–165.

Rahner, Karl, "Thomas Aquinas on Truth", in *Theological Investigations*, vol. XIII, trans. David Bourke (London: Darton, Longman & Todd, 1975).

Rahner, Karl, "Experience of Self and Experience of God", in *Theological Investigations*, vol. XIII, trans. David Bourke (London: Darton, Longman & Todd, 1975).

Rahner, Karl, *Grundkurs des Glaubens: Einführung in den Begriff des Christentums*, Sämtliche Werke Band 26, ed. Nikolaus Schwerdtfeger and Albert Raffelt (Freiburg: Herder, 1999).

Rahner, Karl, *Foundations of Christian Faith: An Introduction to the Idea of Christianity* (New York: Crossroad, 1978).

Rahner, Karl, "The Hiddenness of God", in *Theological Investigations*, vol. XVI, trans. David Morland (London: Darton, Longman & Todd, 1979), 227–243.

Rahner, Karl, *Karl Rahner im Gespräch. Band 2: 1978–1982*, ed. Paul Imhof and Hubert Biallowons (München: Kösel, 1983).

Rahner, Karl, "Experience of Transcendence from the Standpoint of Catholic Dogmatics", in *Theological Investigations*, vol. XVIII, trans. Edward Quinn (New York: Crossroad, 1983).

Rahner, Karl, *Hörer des Wortes: zur Grundlegung einer Religionsphilosophie*, Sämtliche Werke Band 4, ed. Albert Raffelt (Freiburg: Herder, 1997).

Rahner, Karl, *Hearer of the Word: Laying the Foundation for a Philosophy of Religion*, trans. Joseph Donceel, ed. Andrew Tallon (New York: Continuum, 1994).

Rahner, Karl, *Geist in Welt: Zur Metaphysik der endlichen Erkenntnis bei Thomas von Aquin*, Sämtliche Werke Band 2, ed. Albert Raffelt (Freiburg: Herder, 1996).

Rahner, Karl, *Spirit in the World*, trans. William Dych (New York: Continuum, 1994).

Ricoeur, Paul, "'Response' to Karl Rahner's Lecture: On the Incomprehensibility of God", *The Journal of Religion* (*Supplement*) 58 (1978), 126–131.

Schillebeeckx, Edward, "Ervaringscontext en de doxologische waarde van het gelovige spreken", in *Geloofsverstaan: Interpretatie en kritiek* (Bloemendaal: Nelissen, 1972), 57–62.

Schillebeeckx, Edward, *Gerechtigheid en liefde, genade en bevrijding* (Bloemendaal: Nelissen, 1977).

Schillebeeckx, Edward, "Naar een katholiek gebruik van de hermeneutiek", in *Geloofsverstaan: Interpretatie en kritiek* (Bloemendaal: Nelissen, 1972), 11–41.

Schillebeeckx, Edward, *Jezus, het verhaal van een levende* (Baarn: Nelissen, 1974).

Schillebeeckx, Edward, "Theologie der Erfahrung – Sackgasse oder Weg zum Glauben? Ein Gespräch mit Prof. Edward Schillebeeckx", *Herder Korrespondenz* 32 (1978), 391–397.

Schillebeeckx, Edward, *Tussentijds verhaal over twee Jezus boeken* (Bloemendaal: Nelissen, 1978).

Schillebeeckx, Edward, *Mensen als verhaal van God* (Baarn: Nelissen, 1989).

Schillebeeckx, Edward, *Theologisch testament. Notarieel nog niet verleden* (Baarn: Nelissen, 1994).

Schillebeeckx, Edward, "The context and value of faith-talk", in *The Understanding of Faith: Interpretation and criticism*, trans. N. D. Smith (London: Bloomsbury, 2014), 14–18.

Schillebeeckx, Edward, "Towards a Catholic use of hermeneutics", in *God the Future of Man*, trans. N. D. Smith (London: Bloomsbury, 2014), 1–30.

Schillebeeckx, Edward, *Christ: The Christian experience in the Modern World*, trans. John Bowden (London: Bloomsbury, 2014).

Schillebeeckx, Edward, *Church: The Human Story of God*, trans. John Bowden (London: Bloomsbury, 2014).

Schillebeeckx, Edward, *Interim Report on the Books Jesus and Christ*, ed. Ted Mark Schoof and Carl Sterkens with Erik Borgman and Robert J. Schreiter, trans. John Bowden (London: Bloomsbury, 2014).

Schillebeeckx, Edward, *Jesus: An Experiment in Christology*, trans. Hubert Hoskins and Marcelle Manley (London: Bloomsbury, 2014).

Shakespeare, Steven, "Language", in *The Oxford Handbook of Theology and Modern European Thought*, ed. Nicholas Adams, George Pattison and Graham Ward (Oxford: Oxford University Press, 2013), 105–126.

Simon, Derek, "Rahner and Ricoeur on Religious Experience and Language. A Reflection on the Mutuality between Experience and Language in the Transcendental and Hermeneutical Traditions", *Église et Théologie* 28 (1997), 77–99.

Taylor, Charles, "Merleau-Ponty and the Epistemological Picture", in *The Cambridge Companion to Merleau-Ponty*, ed. Taylor Carman and Mark B. N. Hansen (Cambridge: Cambridge University Press, 2005), 26–49.

Tracy, David, "Lindbeck's New Program for Theology: A Reflection", *The Thomist* 49 (1985), 460–472.

CHAPTER 10

Supra-Religious? The Concept of Transcendental Experience and the (In-)Accessibility of the Absolute

Knut Wenzel

Richard Schaeffler, a doyen of the German-speaking philosophy of religion, once interrupted the lecture he was giving in response to a festschrift he had been presented. Addressing his audience directly – 'off the record', so to speak – he said: "And when people approach me saying: 'I have had an experience of the Divine', I reply: 'How beautiful for you, I haven't'". We have to imagine the narrator of this anecdote as a religious devotee of Catholic brand. As a religious person as well as a philosopher of religion, Schaeffler is skeptical about both the reality and evidentiality, or conclusiveness, of such an experience. In particular, he is skeptical – and this might be a typically Catholic doubt – about the necessity of experiences of the divine in order to be truly religious or to prove one's religious devotion – one's state of justification or rebirth.

The Catholic type of religion seems to be informed by objectifying tendencies, being church-orientated, ritual-orientated, doctrine-orientated, law-orientated; whereas the Protestant type of religion seems to be informed by subjectifying tendencies, being community-orientated, orientated towards personal experience and confessions of personal experience. Catholic religion is an institutional, ritual, doctrinal, nomological religion; Protestant religion is a relational, testimonial, experiential religion. Catholicism is in danger of trivializing, Protestantism of internalizing religion. But it is the Catholic tradition that keeps alive an intra-religious skepticism: a skepticism concerning the validity of religious experience. Being twofold, it doubts firstly that religion exclusively is grounded on religious experience; secondly, it doubts that religious experience is in any case, or can at all be, an experience of the divine. Religious experience may very well be ascertained as an experience of utmost intensity. Even then, however, there are no criteria at hand to identify this as bridging the sublime gap between the finite and the absolute – and not as the subject's mere encounter with herself or himself. It seems suitable to view this as an update of the Neo-Scholastic distinction between natural and supra-natural experience, the reality of the latter being more a theological postulate than an empirical fact.

© KONINKLIJKE BRILL NV, LEIDEN, 2016 | DOI 10.1163/9789004328600_012

A skepticism of this sort is not so much critical of religion, but sympathetic to it. It proves that attitudes towards religion hold a much higher quality of pluralism, or difference, than the simplistic alternative of the hyper-devotees versus the 'new atheists' suggests. It is a skepticism, however, that comes up with an ambiguous result. Personal religiosity, on the one hand, is relieved from the burden of verification through the display of documents, testimonials or other evidence of a personal experience of the divine. Personal religiosity, instead, expresses itself in religious practice. But the relief comes with its own costs: personal religiosity verified by religious practice inevitably comes under the control of the institutions (or the variety of their implicit presence) of an established religion. On the other hand, through such a skepticism the whole business of religion becomes somewhat unplugged from a 'tight connection' to the divine, the 'Real Absolute'. But what, then, is religion, surrendered to human hands alone, yet strictly confined within the fences of immanence?

Strangely enough, we are confronted with a Protestant-Catholic consensus which distrusts religion at this very point, a consensus so secret that neither of the partners seems to know about it. The Protestant part is clearly spoken out in the critique of 'religion' developed by Karl Barth in his dialectical period. For Barth, religion is a variation of culture and therefore a product of human activity, deeply inked with sin and having revelation as its anti-thesis. The Roman-Catholic position is much more veiled. Roman-Catholic distrust in religion appears disguised by the powerful role the church ascribes to itself. One is tempted to formulate it paradoxically: the Catholic distrust of religion is articulated in terms of religion. For, what is the response to the Neo-Scholastic ir-realization of a 'real' experience of the divine? – To install the church, above all its magisterial authority, as the exclusive legitimate procurator of the 'tight connection' to the divine. The church articulates its distrust of religion by absorbing religion's incapability and by spiriting it off into the brilliance of her proclaimed authority. But by making its procuratorate exclusive through the disconnection from any outside control, the church obscures the ground of its own legitimation. What if the church nourished its power, its dark glamour, from the cumulative energy of the desperate hopes of a multitude of people who do not want to hope in vain? Then, the church would figure as a symbol of the question rather than a symbol of an answer.

The fallacy of this institution-focused, 'objectifying' option is to restrict access to the absolute from human experience, whereas the fallacy of the 'subjectifying' option is to reify the absolute within the finite realm of human conscious, conceptualizing, and thematic experience. All those who emphatically

THE CONCEPT OF TRANSCENDENTAL EXPERIENCE   175

confess to have 'found Jesus', or whatever they would label the holy, might be
aware of Augustine's warning: "God is known better by not knowing him."[1]

But how to escape the dilemma of either reifying the absolute or destroying the relative, or even denying any possible encounter of the two? Friedrich
Wilhelm Joseph Schelling gives a dramatized version of this aporetic situation when he suggests that any recognition of the absolute would have to be
ecstatic. In order to comprehend the absolute, the finite subject would have
to leave itself; it would have to leave its finite constitution behind. In order to
be able to receive the absolute, the finite subject would have to give up its very
capability, which is to say: it would have to give up itself.[2]

Karl Rahner's proposition takes the inverse direction: the finite subject
reaches out to the absolute not by abandoning itself, but by ingressing into
itself. The finite subject proceeds through itself in order to open itself for or
experience the absolute. Such could be described the way of the 'transcendental experience'. The following considerations are not meant as a close exegesis
of Rahner's approach. Rather, they are undertaken within its theoretical framework. The idea of transcendental experience serves the purpose of articulating
the (im-)possibility of 'experiencing' the absolute – a conception exhibiting
vicinity to the mystical experience – *as* hermeneutics of the subject.

In the Realm of Subject-Experience[3]

There are quite a range of concepts of the transcendental experience, none
of them of course without contact to the Kantian tradition. Richard Schaeffler
conceptualizes transcendental experience as the anchor of his philosophy
of experience, conceiving of it as the dimension of experience which has a
changing impact on the transcendental conditions of our ability to experience at all.[4] Even when not following Schaeffler's path, it is worth noting that

---

1 "[Deus] qui scitur melius nesciendo." Augustine, *De Ordine* 11,16,44.
2 Schelling does so in his "Erlanger Vorlesung" (Erlangen lecture) from 1820/21. See Knut
   Wenzel, "Ekstase statt Diskurs? Schelling und die (Un)Möglichkeit, das Absolute zu denken",
   in *Religion und Irrationalität: Historisch-systematische Perspektiven*, ed. Jochen Schmidt and
   Heiko Schulz (Tübingen: Mohr Siebeck, 2013), 41–56.
3 The term is, somewhat helplessly, intended as the equivalent for the German 'Subjekt-
   erfahrung', naming a point of indifference in the ground of experience, where the experiencing subject encounters itself as being a 'content' of the experience.
4 See Richard Schaeffler, *Erfahrung als Dialog mit der Wirklichkeit: Eine Untersuchung zur Logik
   der Erfahrung* (Freiburg: Alber, 1995), 23–34.

transcendental experience has an aspect of altering the very conditions of experience itself.[5] According to the logic of transcendental analysis the ability to have experiences – like the ability to reason and the ability to feel – is a basic dimension of human identity and therefore rooted in the constitutional ground of subjectivity. When, with Schaeffler, the transcendental experience has an altering impact on the constitutional conditions of experience as such, this is so because the experience provides access to the foundations of the subject-existence. Transcendental experience realizes the subject-existence in its radical alterability. And how is that possible? Because through transcendental experience the subject realizes itself in its own conditions. In transcendental experience, the conditions of subjective being assert themselves within the realm of subjective experience. These conditions are, however, the being itself, the absolute. In the focus of its self-realization, the subject opens itself, or experiences its openness, towards being as such, towards the absolute.

Measured by a common understanding of experience, transcendental experience is empty, indefinite, spacious rather than topical. It is the void of a full moon night: not mere nothingness, but an illuminated darkness, infinitely full of possible significance. As not simply another experience alongside others, transcendental experience is utmost profundity; it is the depth dimension of experience as such, rooted in the foundations of self-realization (*subjektiver Selbstvollzug*). It is limited to no specific, thematic content. In transcendental experience, the subject is experientially given to itself – a self-givenness that does not materialize as some kind of knowledge; transcendental experience is not the place or the time of learning; self-givenness not in a materializing but in a transitional mode. In transcendental experience, the subject realizes an internal transition from its instance of activity to its foundational conditions, to reality as such, towards the absolute: a transitional dynamics taking place in complete concealment. The transcendental experience is not a thematic experience among other ordinary experiences but the fundamental dynamics of experience itself. In its depth dimension any object-related experience is an operation not only executed by the subject, but taking place subjectively. The subject *is* the experience it has, albeit not so much in the mode of its content, but rather as indispensable implication of experience. Reality's most indispensable moments disclose beauty, peacefulness, love only implicitly. By way of the dialectics of necessity and implication, reality can realize itself without becoming tautological. In the implicitly self-present subject, reality is present

---

5 A precise overview and evaluation of models of transcendental experience can be found in Bernd Irleborn, "Was ist eine 'transzendentale Erfahrung'? Zu den Entwürfen von Krings, Rahner, Lotz und Schaeffler", *Theologie und Philosophie* 79 (2004), 491–510.

THE CONCEPT OF TRANSCENDENTAL EXPERIENCE   177

by being felt, thought, bespoken – by being experienced – and the subject is
self-given, undetermined by any content, simply as being real. Inasmuch as
transcendental experience is the self-givenness of the subject, its 'being real'
is the content of transcendental experience – not the 'reality' of the subject
as an isolated, identifiable substantial 'something' on its own, but the subject
being real.

Applying what has been said above about the indeterminacy, the empti-
ness, or *Inhaltslosigkeit*, of transcendental experience to the issue of the self-
givenness of the subject as being real (via transcendental experience), the
following conclusion can be reached: in transcendental experience the subject
is discerning, through itself, reality as such. Presumably, the notion of discernment lends a connotation too active to the matter at stake. It might be more
appropriate to say that in the mode of self-presence transcendental experience is, reality ('the' real – 'the' being) asserts itself. In order to gesture towards
this concept with a term that is as false as it might be true (I thus withdraw
it in the very moment of placing it) I might say: transcendental experience is
Seinserfahrung (experience of being).

The segregation between a transcendental sphere and the experiential reality is always in danger of turning it into another double-world concept. Rahner,
being a Catholic theologian, whose life-concern has been to transform the two-
story-worldview of Neo-Scholasticism into a comprehensive modern theology,
could not help reacting sensitively to this. His effort to overcome it seems to be
strikingly plausible. However, it generates consequences. Insofar as the transcendental sphere – as being principal to any particular existence and letting
it become possible – asserts itself within the realm of subjective experience,
it is no longer merely transcendental but crystallizes as 'the real', 'the being'.
The concept of transcendental experience holds that the very conditions of
possibility of the subject can themselves become 'matter' to experience, which
is to say, there is a quality of reality to them: not of a specific reality among
others but of being real as such. Inasmuch as transcendental experience is in
its status qualified by the convergence of indefiniteness and profundity, it is
in its 'content'-dimension defined by the indistinguishable presence of the
subject and 'the real': subject qualified as real; the real being defined through
subject-activities such as the act of reception, the act of realization, the act
of expression.

In transcendental experience the subject is given to itself as uncondition-
ally real; and the real is subjectively present, disconnected from any distinctive
'something'. There is, in a word, an absoluteness to this scene of transcendental
experience. Absoluteness can be identified as a qualifier, an attribute of transcendental experience. However, can we say that it is experiential itself? Is

there such a thing as an experience of the absolute? Perhaps I should stop here, saying that the human economy of experience is, via transcendental experience, capable of an openness towards the absolute. The disproportionateness within the relation of the finite and the infinite does not signify the difference between the subject and the absolute; rather it is a subject-constitutional disproportion. The human *ability* to experience, to discern (in a general, not only cognitive sense) is structured and therefore finite. The subject's *readiness* to experience, however, rendered possible by that finite structure is undetermined, is infinite; an infinitude already implied in a finite structure of experience that allows experience to become reflective: when in subjective experience the experiential subject encounters itself as the mediator of the presence of the real.

When this subject-constitutional disproportion is conceptualized as transcendental experience, it becomes possible to respond to the Neo-Scholastic skepticism concerning religious experience. For any Neo-Scholasticism which discriminates between 'natural' and 'supra-natural' experience, no longer necessarily falls apart. Instead, the latter appears at the horizon of a radical analysis, if not realization, of the former.

Between Religion and Mysticism

Religion is disavowed when the possibility of an absolute experience – if not of an experience of the Absolute – is situated within the range of the subject's capability. Transcendental experience is a supra-religious rather than a religious experience. As a consequence, the relation between the sphere of absolute experience – or the experience of the absolute – and religion has to undergo a process of re-examination. Religion, as a doctrinally, ritually, and nomologically explicit discourse *about* the absolute, whether it be experientially claimed as intimately present or as ungraspably absent, is not in itself the access to the absolute; religion is the talk, not the topic. Religious experience then is, at least at first glance, self-experience of the subject within the significant boundaries of the religious discourse; it is something eminently immanent. Religious experience is urged by religious discourse and not by a transcendent reality. An experience generated by a discourse, a discursive experience, is not particularly 'authentic'.

What, then, is religious discourse? It is the verbalization of an absolute muteness, the signification of a presence without of any significance, the operationalization of the ungraspable real. Religious discourse is dysfunctional, unjustifiable, impossible. Its reference-relation to its signified is unclear, to

THE CONCEPT OF TRANSCENDENTAL EXPERIENCE 179

say the least. There is an obscurity, a moment of indefiniteness that connects an address with an answer – a disconnection rather than a smooth transition. Religious discourse responds to the scene of transcendental experience, which is, as we have seen, a double process: the self-realization of the real within the sphere of subjectivity *and* the self-givenness of the subject as being real. The responsive structure of religious discourse is well known in the "Biblical Code";[6] it can be identified in the New Testament's reports of the resurrection appearances, being narrative responses to an experience we cannot grasp as such; it is the basic structure of the canon of biblical scriptures as a whole, for these scriptures are not *verba Dei* in a simplistic sense but have "true human authors",[7] and only as they are human responses to a divine address that as such is not verbalized, they comprehend the *verbum Dei*.

As a response to and not a result of transcendental experience, religion's reference-relation is not guaranteed. No religious discourse whatsoever can justifiably claim absoluteness for itself, but for the incidence of the real to which it responds. There is also a justifiable claim for the significance of this responsiveness itself, as it is articulated by religious discourses. Perhaps religions would never admit to their mere responsive and therefore secondary status. Confronted with it, they would rather react by self-radicalization or by asserting their nomological and institutional authorities. These official religious discourses, deformed, as it were, by a genuine (that is, discursive) form of power, cannot help but have mystical practices remind them of their secondary status. Regardless of whether it is, more commonly, regarded as a highly affirmative or, with Michel de Certeau,[8] as a specifically negativistic practice: mysticism is a constitutively eccentric practice of articulating the Absolute, because it realizes the impossibility of representing the Absolute discursively. Mysticism is, therefore, a practice relating to the absolute that in principle criticizes any discursive usurpation of the absolute. Therefore, orthodox authorities and forces in all religions persecute mystical groups and individuals and attempt to extinguish mystical traditions and practices. One need only think of Meister Eckhart, Marguerite Porète, Juan de la Cruz, and Theresa of Avila, or of the persecution of Sufi-traditions by orthodox Muslim forces from Turkey, through Iran, to Pakistan, and beyond.

Perhaps religion's aggressive approach to mysticism can be read as a dialectical affirmation of the truthfulness, if not of the mystical practices themselves, then of their concern: to verbalize the insignificant, to shape the immense,

---

6　Alluding to Northrop Frye's *The Great Code* (New York: Harcourt Brace Jovanovich, 1982).

7　See Vatican II, *Dogmatic Constitution on the Divine Revelation* Dei verbum, 11,3.

8　See Michel de Certeau, *The Mystic Fable* (Chicago: University of Chicago Press, 1992).

to represent the absent, to praise the missing, to love the remote … Mystical practices operate with, and within, these tensions that religious discourse can only cope with by taming them. Religious discourse cannot follow mystical practice by losing itself to the absolute. To lose oneself to the absolute is the essence, and not the end, of mystical practice. A discourse defined by office and doctrine, as is the religious, cannot realize that. Religious discourse bears knowledge of the mystical practices being closer to transcendental experience and its concerns. There is merit, however, to the secondary: in the antagonism of mystical practices and religious discourse, the two core dimensions of the absolute come into worldly presence: *reality* and *meaning*.

Mystical practice strives for contact with the absolute in the highest possible intensity: to touch, to unify with, to be touched by the absolute.[9] However, there is no way of producing such an intense contact, no way of communicating it, no way of representation. A contact not done, untold, and unrepresented, has no displayable reality. *Mysticism*, for the sake of the absolute, collapses as practice, and is unable to develop a discourse of the absolute. It instead comes up with an incomplete practice, with a stuttering, non-discursive talk. Its reflexivity does not elaborate as a discourse but rather entangles this mystical talk in itself. *Religion* produces a discourse of enacting, verbalizing, asking, demanding – if not using – the absolute, a discourse that shall not end, as the eternal light in Catholic churches shall not cease burning. As liturgy or cult, religion is expected to operate trouble-free. Its principle of perfection is internal; it is the grammar of this discourse. Religion, it could be said, re-constructs the absolute *as* discourse: as an integral, comprehensive, gapless, operative structure of meaning. This reconstruction, however, follows the inner logic of discourse, and not a presumed 'essence' of the absolute. The (Neo-)Platonist confidence in a stable and realistic relation between the image and the original has long gone astray.[10] In a post-realist and more skeptical era, the notions of representation and realization no longer indicate a natural or self-evident relation of 'real presence',[11] but rather of expectation, if not of hope. The modern soul's disposition is not 'inhibitive' (in the sense of dwelling) but explorative.

---

9   The story of Jacob fighting all through one night with an angel at the river Jabbok, escaping from this struggle with both an injury and a benediction, can be regarded as a paradigmatic narration of such a 'being touched' by the Absolute (Gen 32,23–33).

10   The controversy between Paschasius Radbertus and Ratramnus about the Eucharistic presence of the Body of Christ in the ninth century and a similar quarrel around Berengar of Tours in the eleventh century indicates the end of a (Neo-)Platonist symbolic thinking and the dawn of Nominalist breakup of the sign and a respectively signified reality.

11   See George Steiner, *Real Presences* (Chicago: University of Chicago Press, 1991).

THE CONCEPT OF TRANSCENDENTAL EXPERIENCE

Seemingly self-occupied, this soul invests itself into its quest for a reality to live up to.

The Mediating Gap between the Finite Subject and the Real Absolute

Transcendental experience is devoid of any significant, distinctive, or definite content. This is not to say that it is altogether blank; rather, transcendental experience is related to reality as such, to the subject-for-real, given in transcendental experience: an *in*significant, *in*distinct, *in*definite 'content' most meaningful – unspoken, yet mutefully provoking speech. But mind the metaphysical gap, if not abyss, between the presence's muteness and the discursiveness of representation: in the sphere of transcendental experience, we are doing nothing. Once having become active, we are out there, in the fields of practice and discourse. 'Out there', we have to create the presence, to (re)construct the meaning of 'the real', of its normative vehemence. This, I think, is a proper notion in order to indicate the Real as such to be the 'content' of transcendental experience: the Real in its *vehemence*: inevitable, unreplaceable. There is mere presence in transcendental experience, not a presence of; there is mere reality in transcendental experience, not the reality of; mere being, not a being of. As this purity, however, bears a quality, the quality of vehemence, and as it is this qualified experience intertwined with the self-presence of the subject within the identical act, or incidence, of transcendental experience, it is plausibly received in subject-categories. The subject discerns a normative spin in the vehemence, with which the Absolute attains presence, and interprets it as a desire for articulation. Articulation is the subject's genuine mode of re-*present*-ation.

The being, the absolute given through transcendental experience, no longer simply 'is', but allows itself to become significant in the mode of subject-experience. It has given itself into the dynamics of subjective discernment, interpretation, communication. This Being-Real in the mode of subject-experience does not happen incidentally. Rather, the subject experiences it as a significant givenness, interpreting its significance as intentionality. The consistency of this *syntagma* – the presence of the Absolute in a vehemence that calls for articulation, and all this within the sphere of transcendental experience and in the paradigm of the subject – comes to proper explication within the concept of theism. Theism conceives of the Absolute as a personal God who speaks, acts, wants, and addresses him- or herself. In this act of self-addressing God simultaneously recognizes and creates another subject of (relative) autonomy.

Consequently, we might very well narrate the story of transcendental experience as the story of the constitution of the subject. This narrative might contain the profound significance of the Biblical-Christian religion told in the Western tradition. We might however also stress the absorbing effect of the vehemence, and this would make a different story, that of a subject foundering in the Absolute: a story to be told in the mystical paradigm, or on the trails of Eastern religions. The two- or manifoldness of these explications of transcendental experience signals the secondary status of both religious discourse and mystical practice in relation to transcendental experience. Religious experience is the experiential confirmation of religious discourse; its benchmark is a discourse, not a substantial reality. Accordingly, transcendental experience has to be classified as supra-religious. It is undefined, indistinctive, and may therefore (but need not) trigger articulations, testimonials, explications, interpretations – in short: discourses and significant practices. It may, or may not, trigger them. The articulations of transcendental experience will be plural, diverse, particular, and contingent: that is, they might not happen at all. A world without religion is conceivable, a world which would not necessarily have to be thought of as a world without transcendental experience. A secular world is not necessarily a world without the wells of what we know as religion.

There are other articulations of transcendental experience – the Absolute's presence within the sphere of subject experience – such as literature, poetry, arts, and music (including and pop music). Some Romantics saw a strong continuity, if not identity, between arts and religion in any event. These more secular modes of articulation may not claim a grip on the absolute as rigidly as religion does, which one might weigh as weakness, or as discretion. The close proximity of art and religion confirms a central insight of these considerations: when it comes to articulating transcendental experience, be it in the idiom of religion, of poetry or of pop music, the articulation does not result from a divine utterance, but rather is yielded by *human expressivity*.[12] Revelation is a complex concept, co-coordinating the absolute and its self-realization within the sphere of subject-experience, with the human capability to experience, or openness towards, the Absolute, with the expressive nature of humanity. In order to reconstruct the concept of revelation properly, one would have to start with the latter.

---

12   In the field of pop music, Sean Wilentz has compiled and analyzed an immense amount of material about the historical reference of secular folk music to a culture of religious songs, supporting the above account: Sean Wilentz, *Bob Dylan in America* (London: The Bodley Head, 2010).

THE CONCEPT OF TRANSCENDENTAL EXPERIENCE   183

In terms of expressivity, mysticism appears in the *ecstatic* or *poetic* mode, whereas religion occurs in the *discursive* or *prosaic* mode. Transcendental experience itself ultimately has no mode but merely happens; the proper quality to be ascribed to it would be *intenseness*. Poetic expressivity strives to say it all in one word, to condense a cosmos of significance to one simultaneously uttered word,[13] to widen a word to a whole world of meaning. Prosaic expressivity opens a texture and multi-layered architecture of signification in order to explicate all dimensions and to let come to voice all the interpretations of the reality to be articulated. Transcendental experience – is the principle of human expressivity, prior to any modes of articulation, pre-articulate even, sheer intenseness.

Literature

Augustine, *On Order/De Ordine*. Trans. Silvano Borruso (South Bend, IN: St. Augustine's Press, 2007).

Certeau, Michel de, *The Mystic Fable* (Chicago: University of Chicago Press, 1992).

Frye, Northrop, *The Great Code* (New York: Harcourt Brace Jovanovich, 1982).

Irleborn, Bernd, "Was ist eine 'transzendentale Erfahrung'? Zu den Entwürfen von Krings, Rahner, Lotz und Schaeffler", *Theologie und Philosophie* 79 (2004), 491–510.

Schaeffler, Richard, *Erfahrung als Dialog mit der Wirklichkeit: Eine Untersuchung zur Logik der Erfahrung* (Freiburg: Alber, 1995).

Steiner, George, *Real Presences* (Chicago: University of Chicago Press, 1991).

Wenzel, Knut, "Ekstase statt Diskurs? Schelling und die (Un)Möglichkeit, das Absolute zu denken", in *Religion und Irrationalität: Historisch-systematische Perspektiven*, ed. Jochen Schmidt and Heiko Schulz (Tübingen: Mohr Siebeck, 2013), 41–56.

Wilentz, Sean, *Bob Dylan in America* (London: The Bodley Head, 2010).

---

13   See Augustine's concept of the *verbum Divinum* in *Confessiones* 11.

PART 4

Performing the Unperformable?

∴

CHAPTER 11

The Trouble with Trust in the Transcendent: Ernst Troeltsch's Reception of William James

Ulrich Schmiedel

Complaints about the collapse of community have haunted the humanities.[1] In theology, these complaints commonly compare present and post-modern churches to past and pre-modern churches, imagining community as a lost paradise in which Christianity offered a firm foundation for personal and political praxis.[2] But the paradise is either past or potential, never present.[3] As the concept of experience allegedly announces the priority of the individual over the social, 'experience' is sidestepped by the theologians who complain about the collapse of community: it is branded as hollow or hazardous.[4]

Drawing on George R. Lindbeck's seminal study on *The Nature of Doctrine*, John Milbank's theology exemplifies the sidestepping of 'experience': Milbank advocates the turn from 'liberalism' to 'postliberalism' – a turn which is inextricably interwoven with the conceptualization of community.[5] Liberals examine how religious experiences are expressed; postliberals examine how religious expressions are experienced. What is at stake here is the conceptualization of religion: for liberals, religious experiences provoke expressions of religion; for postliberals, expressions of religion provoke religious experiences. The alternative between experience and expression mirrors the alternative between the individual and the social. Liberal theology utilizes 'individuality' as its core category, because religion is experienced individually; postliberal theology utilizes 'sociality' as its core category, because religion is expressed socially. Empirically, however, experience and expression are entangled. The empirical entanglement implies that one cannot decide what comes first: experience

---

1 For a succinct summary see Gerard Delanty, *Community* (London: Routledge, 2004), 7–23.

2 John Milbank, *Theology and Social Theory: Beyond Secular Reason* (Oxford: Blackwell, 2006), 9: "Once, there was no 'secular'.... Instead, there was the single community of Christendom".

3 Zygmunt Bauman, *Community: Seeking Safety in an Insecure World* (Cambridge: Polity Press, 2001), 1–20.

4 Milbank, *Theology and Social Theory*, 384–385.

5 Ibid., 384–391, drawing on George R. Lindbeck, *The Nature of Doctrine* (London: SPCK, 1984), esp. 30–45.

© KONINKLIJKE BRILL NV, LEIDEN, 2016 | DOI 10.1163/9789004328600_013

or expression? Hence, one can confidently criticize the liberal for whom individual experience is primary or the postliberal for whom social expression is primary. Since one's argument always already assumes the priority of this or that, it is unlikely that the conundrum can be solved and settled.

In what follows, I will argue that the alternative between the individual experience of religion and the social expression of religion is a *false* alternative. I will advocate a conceptualization of religion as trust in the transcendent which conceives of religion as neither simply individual nor simply social, but relational. With the concept of trust, I aim to assert that both the experience and the expression of religion are crucial for the construction of community.

However, my argument comes with caveats about both the description and the definition of trust.[6] Trust is commonly conceived of as an attitude:[7] when I trust the other, I adopt an attitude about her which is rooted in my evaluation of her trustworthiness in the past and my expectation of her trustworthiness in the present. My attitude allows for a praxis in which I entrust myself to the other. The issue with the conceptualization of trust as attitude is that it cannot get to grips with the fact that trust occurs *in-between* trusting persons rather than *in* trusting persons.[8] It turns trust into a matter of evaluations and expectations rather than a matter of engagements with the other, thus concealing the *risk* which is involved in trust.[9] Although my evaluation and expectation of the other's trustworthiness is vital for the trust in-between us, trust is neither

---

6 The literature on trust fills libraries. For a comprehensive overview which considers disciplinary as well as interdisciplinary approaches see the trilogy edited by Ingolf U. Dalferth and Simon Peng-Keller, *Kommunikation des Vertrauens* (Leipzig: EVA, 2012), *Gottvertrauen: Die ökumenische Diskussion um die* fiducia (Freiburg: Herder, 2012), and *Grundvertrauen: Hermeneutik eines Grenzphänomens* (Leipzig: EVA, 2013). See also my review article Ulrich Schmiedel, "Vertrauen Verstanden? Zur Vertrauenstrilogie von Ingolf U. Dalferth und Simon Peng-Keller", *NZSTh* 56 (2014), 379–392.

7 As far as I can ascertain, there is no consensus on the description or the definition of trust. However, the conceptualization of trust as practical attitude has become increasingly important in the humanities. See Ingolf U. Dalferth and Simon Peng-Keller, "Kommunikation des Vertrauens verstehen – Hermeneutische Annäherung", in *Kommunikation des Vertrauens*, 10–32.

8 Ibid., 19–21.

9 Trust in-between persons is to be distinguished from trust in situations or trust in traditions which could be captured with the concept of reliance (Ibid.). If trust is reduced to evaluations and expectations – which is to say, if it is equated with the absence of distrust or mistrust – trust "is trivialized, denoting nothing more than the fact that people keep out of each others' way". Claudia Welz, "Trust as Basic Openness and Self-Transcendence", in *Trust, Sociality and Selfhood*, ed. Claudia Welz and Arne Grøn (Tübingen: Mohr Siebeck, 2010), 45–64 (53).

THE TROUBLE WITH TRUST IN THE TRANSCENDENT 189

captured nor confined by evaluations and expectations. When I trust the other, I take the risk to be disappointed by her because she might act differently than I evaluated or expected her to. The other is other: ultimately undetermined and ultimately undeterminable. Accordingly, I define trust as a *relation* to the other which is characterized by openness to the other's otherness. Openness to otherness allows the other to transcend my evaluations and expectations of her in the relation of trust.[10] Hence, transcendence breaks in whenever I trust the other. If transcendence is registered in my engagement with the other, the praxis of trust might be crucial for both the experience and the expression of religion.

In order to analyze and assess the centrality of trust for experiences and expressions of religion, I will explore Ernst Troeltsch's reception of William James's concept of religion.[11] Both liberals and postliberals interpret James's research on religion as the epitome of experientialism.[12] Troeltsch concurs with their interpretation. However, he does not fall for the alternative of experience or expression which makes his work particularly promising for the conceptualization or re-conceptualization of community through the concept of

10   For the centrality of alterity for trust, see Claudia Welz, *Vertrauen und Versuchung* (Tübingen: Mohr Siebeck, 2010). See also the contributions by Arne Grøn and Claudia Welz to *Trust, Sociality and Selfhood*, 13–30 and 45–64.

11   Troeltsch repeatedly refers to James's approach to religion. Initially, he discusses James's philosophy in reviews from 1896 as well as 1897 (Ernst Troeltsch, *Kritische Gesamtausgabe*, vol. 2, ed. Friedrich Wilhelm Graf [Berlin: De Gruyter, 2007], 213–309 and 366–486), and James's psychology of religion in a review from 1904 (Ernst Troeltsch, *Kritische Gesamtausgabe*, vol. 4, ed. Friedrich Wilhelm Graf [Berlin: De Gruyter, 2004], 364–371), even before James's studies were translated into German. These articles are taken up in Ernst Troeltsch, *Psychologie und Erkenntnistheorie in der Religionswissenschaft: Eine Untersuchung über die Bedeutung der Kantischen Religionslehre für die heutige Religionswissenschaft* (Tübingen: Mohr Siebeck, 1905). If not stated otherwise, all translations are my own. For a succinct summary in English, see Troeltsch's obituary for James, "Empiricism and Platonism in the Philosophy of Religion: To the Memory of William James", *The Harvard Theological Review* 5 (1912), 401–422. Troeltsch concentrates on the epistemology of James's approach to religion. The issues of individual experience and social expression on which I focus are merely mentioned in passing. Maren Bienert, *Protestantische Selbstverortung: Die Rezensionen Ernst Troeltschs* (Berlin: De Gruyter, 2014), 173n. 735, emphasizes that Troeltsch discusses neither James's philosophy nor James's psychology in detail. As a consequence, my account of Troeltsch's reception of James will have to look between the lines of Troeltsch's oeuvre in order to fill in the gaps which he left open.

12   Charles Taylor, *Varieties of Religion Today: William James Revisited* (Cambridge, MA: Harvard University Press, 2002), 1–29.

trust. In a first step, I will analyze James's psychology of religion in order to demonstrate that his definition of religion as trust in the transcendent prioritizes experience over expression. For James, religion is anchored in a solitary subject. In a second step, I will analyze Troeltsch's reception of James's psychology of religion. It is not trust itself, but the way in which James conceptualizes trust which Troeltsch criticizes. His critique pinpoints the (mis)prioritization of experience over expression, drawing vital consequences for the concept of community. For Troeltsch, religion is not anchored in a solitary subject, but in-between social subjects. Finally, in a third step, I will combine my analyses in conversation with Graham Ward's astute account of (un)belief,[13] outlining a concept of religion as trust in the transcendent which allows for the combination of experience and expression within what I call the open(ed) community.

To be sure, my exploration of Troeltsch's reception of James is organized systematically rather than historically. Without diving too deeply into the conversation between pragmatism and historicism,[14] I aim to retrieve the concept of experience for the construction of religious and non-religious community.[15] Because trust involves the openness to otherness which causes trouble in any community, my retrieval goes against the grain of those theologies which sidestep experience for the sake of community. But the trouble with trust is a constructive rather than a destructive trouble: it opens community to the experience of the transcendence of the other. Hence, a community which facilitates and fosters trust might escape the nostalgias for community which haunt the humanities.

A Solitary Subject

The current controversy about the uses and the abuses of 'experience' has its origins in James. His Gifford Lectures introduced the concept of religious as opposed to non-religious experience into the study of religion. Published as *The*

---

13 Graham Ward, *Unbelievable: Why We Believe and Why We Don't* (London: I. B. Tauris, 2014).

14 Wilhelm Hennis, "The Spiritualist Foundation of Max Weber's 'Interpretative Sociology': Ernst Troeltsch, Max Weber and William James's Varieties of Religious Experience", *History of the Human Sciences* 11 (1998), 83–106, analyzes how Troeltsch introduced James's concept of religion to Max Weber. But his analysis takes no account of Troeltsch's reception of James's concept.

15 I will return to the distinction between what counts as religious and what counts as non-religious. To be sure, I argue that it is a *relative* distinction because openness to the transcendence of the other is crucial for both religious and non-religious relations.

THE TROUBLE WITH TRUST IN THE TRANSCENDENT 191

Varieties of Religious Experience: A Study in Human Nature, these lectures have been avidly read by theologians past and present.[16] Where does the immense interest in these lectures come from? Troeltsch points to the turn to experience which is anticipated by Friedrich Schleiermacher's *Speeches on Religion*.[17] But he criticizes that Schleiermacher's turn strands in "stiff scholasticism": the essentialism in his definition of religion cannot capture historical or cultural flux.[18] But, according to Troeltsch, James can. By drawing on his empirical explorations, James defines religion as the experience of a relation between the immanent and the transcendent.[19] He conceives of this relation through a concept which he had introduced in his philosophy of religion: "trust".[20]

For James, trust is circular. He alludes to the attraction between persons in order to elaborate on the circle.[21] Does she fancy him or does she not fancy him? If he acts as if she does fancy him, he can wake her fancy; if he acts as if she does not fancy him, he cannot wake her fancy. Similarly, the investment of trust into a relation provokes the relation of trust and the relation of trust provokes the investment of trust into a relation.[22] Hence, the relation of trust implies that I entrust myself to the other because whether the other is or is not trustworthy cannot be answered *prior* to our relation. I cannot wait

---

16 William James, *The Varieties of Religious Experience: A Study in Human Nature. Being the Gifford Lectures on Natural Religion Delivered at Edinburgh in 1901–1902*, The Works of William James, vol. 15, ed. Frederick H. Burkhardt, Fredson Bowers, and Ignas K. Skurupskelis (Cambridge, MA: Harvard University Press, 1987).

17 Friedrich D. E. Schleiermacher, *On Religion: Speeches to its Cultured Despisers*, trans. Richard Couter (Cambridge: Cambridge University Press, 1988). See also Hans Joas, "Schleiermacher and the Turn to Experience in the Study of Religion", in *Interpreting Religion: The Significance of Friedrich Schleiermacher's "Reden über die Religion"*, ed. Dietrich Korsch and Amber L. Griffioen (Tübingen: Mohr Siebeck, 2011), 147–161.

18 Ernst Troeltsch, "Rezension zu William James's *The Varieties of Religious Experience*", *Kritische Gesamtausgabe*, vol. 4, 364–371 (365).

19 James, *The Varieties of Religious Experience*, 34.

20 For trust as a core concept of James's philosophy of religion, see esp. William James, *The Will to Believe and Other Essays in Popular Philosophy*, The Works of William James, vol. 6, ed. Frederick H. Burkhardt, Fredson Bowers, and Ignas K. Skurupskelis (Cambridge, MA: Harvard University Press, 1979), 19; 28–29; 40–42; 50–54. The concept is taken up in *The Varieties of Religious Experience*, esp. 229–230; 261; 287–286; 413.

21 James, *The Will to Believe*, 28–29. See Hans Joas's analysis in *The Genesis of Values*, trans. Gregory Moore (Cambridge: Polity Press, 2000), 43.

22 Joas, *The Genesis of Values*, 43, stresses the significance of the advance in faith for interpersonal relations. With 'advance in faith' Gregory Moore renders the German concept of 'Vertrauensvorschuss'. See Hans Joas, *Die Entstehung der Werte* (Frankfurt: Suhrkamp, 1997), 71.

until I have evidence of the other's trustworthiness. Trust is "previous"[23] or "precursive"[24] – which is to say, trust creates trust. According to James, the creative circle of trust pertains to both trust in the finite other and trust in the infinite other.[25] Arguably, what James has in mind here is the mystery of alterity. The other always already escapes the ways in which I think and talk about her. Otherwise, the other would not be other. Hence, to trust the other is risky – a risk which is involved in non-religious trust in the finite other as well as in religious trust in the infinite other. James refers to a "jump" – a jump into the relation with the other.[26] As Charles Taylor puts it, "James is our great philosopher of the cusp".[27]

Troeltsch summarizes James's conceptualization of religion succinctly: religion is the experience of a relation to the transcendent which can be described but not dissected.[28] The other remains mysterious. James avoids the dogmatic dissection (vivisection?) of transcendence because the existence or non-existence of the transcendent is irrelevant for him.[29] He is not interested in transcendence, but in the *experience* of transcendence.[30]

Considering the centrality of experience for James, it is puzzling that there is no definition of the concept in the Gifford Lectures (as far as I can ascertain, a puzzle strictly and studiously avoided by scholarship).[31] However, James's

---

23   James, *The Will to Believe*, 28.

24   See William James, *Some Problems of Philosophy*, The Works of William James, vol. 7, ed. Frederick H. Burkhardt, Fredson Bowers, and Ignas K. Skurupskelis (Cambridge, MA: Harvard University Press, 1979), 116, where James offers a succinct summary of the creative circle of trust.

25   James, *The Will to Believe*, 32.

26   James, *Some Problems of Philosophy*, 116.

27   Taylor, *Varieties of Religion Today*, 59. In *A Secular Age* (Cambridge, MA: Harvard University Press 2007), Taylor speaks of James's "open space where you can feel the winds pulling you, now to belief now to unbelief" (Ibid., 549).

28   Troeltsch, "Rezension zu William James's *The Varieties of Religious Experience*", 366–367.

29   James, *The Varieties of Religious Experience*, 30–49. See Jörg Lauster, *Religion als Lebensdeutung: Theologische Hermeneutik heute* (Darmstadt: Wissenschaftliche Buchgesellschaft, 2005), 19–21.

30   James's critique of dogmatics responds to the obsession with dogmas in the contemporary study of religion.

31   One of the exceptions is Richard R. Niebuhr, "William James on Religious Experience", in *The Cambridge Companion to William James*, ed. Ruth A. Putnam (Cambridge: Cambridge University Press, 1997), 214–236, who stresses that *The Varieties of Religious Experience* employs the concept of experience "rather loosely" (Ibid., 202). He argues that a variety of threads from James's writings have to be tied together in order to arrive at James's concept of experience.

THE TROUBLE WITH TRUST IN THE TRANSCENDENT   193

The Principles of Psychology comes close to a definition of experience.[32] The concept of experience is at the core of his notion of consciousness. For James, consciousness is a "stream" which continuously captures a subject's internal and external sensations.[33] Either consciously or unconsciously, the subject selects a subset from the set of the data of her consciousness in order to experience. Experience is not without consequences – neither for what the subject does select (and thus experience) nor for what the subject does not select (and thus not experience):

> The mind works on the data it receives...as the sculptor works on his block of stone. In a sense the statue stood there from eternity. But there are a thousand different ones beside it, and the sculptor alone is to thank for having extricated this one...Other sculptors, other statues from the same stone.[34]

Accordingly, experience is simultaneously a reaction and a construction.[35] James stresses that the simultaneity is structured through language which he defines as a system of signifiers in which a signifier signifies a signified in spite of the difference between signifier and signified.[36] Hence, language allows the subject to select a subset of data from the set of data in her stream of consciousness: 'signifier' captures the subset of the data of consciousness; 'signified' captures the set of the data of consciousness. However, James is strikingly suspicious of this linguistic selection. "Language was made by men...who were not psychologists", because psychologists are interested in the signified, not the signifier, the set of data, not the subset of data.[37] James explains that when a subject is angry, she is simply angry. But – to paraphrase James – when a subject says 'I am angry', language introduces a difference between her and her anger. She is not in the state of 'I-am-angry'; she is in the state of 'I-say-I-am-angry'.[38] In his posthumously published *Essays on Radical Empiricism*,

---

32   William James, *The Principles of Psychology*, 3 vols, The Works of William James, vols 8–10, ed. Frederick H. Burkhardt, Fredson Bowers, and Ignas K. Skurupskelis (Cambridge, MA: Harvard University Press, 1981).

33   James, *The Principles of Psychology*, vol. 1, 233.

34   Ibid., 278.

35   See Lauster, *Religion als Lebensdeutung*, 20–21.

36   James, *The Principles of Psychology*, vol. 2, 980.

37   James, *The Principles of Psychology*, vol. 1, 193. In ibid., 193–196, James discusses language as a source of error in psychology. His discussion revolves around 'introspection', *the* method in contemporary psychology and psychology of religion.

38   See ibid., 191.

James refers to pure and impure experience to capture both of these subjective states: the one with and the other without a distinction between signifier and signified.[39] What the metaphors of (im)purity demonstrate is that James defines language as a source of contamination: it turns the pure un-expressed experience into the impure expressed experience.[40]

In his Gifford Lectures, the suspicion towards language is pushed to the extreme. The core characteristic of mysticism – the center of religion for James – is that it is "ineffable".[41] Hence, trust in the transcendent can be experienced, but trust in the transcendent cannot be expressed: the state of 'I-say-I-trust-in-the-transcendent' contaminates the state of 'I-trust-in-the-transcendent'; expression contaminates experience. According to James, ineffability and individuality are connected so closely that his definition of religious as opposed to non-religious experience contains the concept of solitude. To experience religion is a matter of "individual men [sic] in their solitude".[42] Scornfully, he characterizes community as "second-hand".[43] Trust in the transcendent is experienced by a solitary subject. It cannot be transmitted because transmission from solitary subject to solitary subject would require the contamination of experience through expression. Religion is trapped within individuality; it is private as opposed to public. With the privatization of religion, James attempts to defend the individual against the social because he sees churches as structures of religious suppression rather than structures of religious support. Through their dogmatic domestications of trust, churches

---

39   William James, "A World of Pure Experience", in *Essays in Radical Empiricism*, The Works of William James, vol. 3, ed. Fredson Bowers and Ignas K. Skurupskelis (Cambridge, MA: Harvard University Press, 1976), 21–44.

40   In his article "Experience", in *Essays in Philosophy*, The Works of William James, vol. 5, ed. Frederick H. Burkhardt, Fredson Bowers, and Ignas K. Skrupskelis (Cambridge, MA: Harvard University Press, 1977), 95, James defines experience as "the entire process of phenomena, of present data considered in their raw immediacy, before reflective thought has analyzed them into subjective and objective aspects". For the implications of James's "Reinlichkeitsmetaphorik", see Matthias Jung, *Erfahrung und Religion: Grundzüge einer hermeneutisch-pragmatischen Religionsphilosophie* (München: Alber, 1999), 172–175 (172).

41   James, *The Varieties of Religious Experience*, 302–303. Although mysticism is ineffable as opposed to effable, it has a "noetic quality" for the mystic (ibid.).

42   Ibid., 34.

43   Ibid., 15; 33; 270. Jeremy Carrette, "Passionate Belief: William James, Emotion, and Religious Experience", in *William James and the Varieties of Religious Experience: A Centenary Celebration*, ed. Jeremy Carrette (London: Routledge, 2005), 79–93, traces James's acknowledgement of the sociality of religious experiences and religious emotions. However, he points out that James's concern is individual psychology as opposed to social psychology.

THE TROUBLE WITH TRUST IN THE TRANSCENDENT 195

invent orthodoxies and heterodoxies in order to "excommunicate those whose trust is different".[44] Hence, the prioritization of experience over expression implies the prioritization of individuality over sociality. Both are anchored in the solitary subject.

Overall, James conceives of religion as the experience of trust in the transcendent. Trust revolves around a transcendence which is implied by the exposure to both the finite and the infinite other. Since language turns the experience of trust in the transcendent from the pure to the impure, the experience cannot be expressed. Accordingly, religion is a matter of ineffability as much as it is a matter of individuality. It is here where Troeltsch's critique comes in.[45]

A Social Subject

Troeltsch is fascinated by James's turn to experience. Reading his rhapsodizing reviews of the Gifford Lectures, a magnifying glass is needed to spot critique. "Die Selbständigkeit der Religion" – Troeltsch's debut in both the philosophy of religion and the psychology of religion – might fulfill the function of the magnifying glass. Published prior to James's Gifford Lectures, it is a series of articles which amount to a monograph.[46] Hans Joas excavated the study prior to its re-publication in the critical collection of Troeltsch's oeuvre.[47] The title

---

44 James, The Will to Believe, 51.

45 Joel D. S. Rasmussen, "Mysticism as a Category of Inquiry in the Philosophies of Ernst Troeltsch and William James", in Exploring Lost Dimensions in Christian Mysticism: Opening to the Mystical, ed. Louise Nelstrop and Simon D. Potmore (Aldershot: Ashgate, 2013), 51–68, analyzes the impact of James's concept of experience on Troeltsch. Rasmussen argues that James's concept of experience is crucial for Troeltsch's concept of mysticism (ibid., 62–63). But since Troeltsch criticizes James for the individualization and interiorization of experience, Rasmussen concludes: "Somewhat incongruously, then, Troeltsch apparently comes under his own critique here" (ibid., 63). See also Joel D. S. Rasmussen, "Empiricism and Mysticism in Ernst Troeltsch's Philosophy of Religion", Mitteilungen der Ernst-Troeltsch-Gesellschaft 13 (2000), 48–65. However, what Rasmussen does not take into account is that Troeltsch is critical of the individuality and interiority of mysticism.

46 Ernst Troeltsch, "Die Selbständigkeit der Religion", ZThK 5 (1895), 361–436; ZThK 6 (1896), 71–110, and 167–218. I follow the recent re-publication of Troeltsch's study in Kritische Gesamtausgabe, vol. 1, ed. Christian Albrecht (Berlin: De Gruyter 2009), 359–535.

47 Hans Joas, "Die Selbständigkeit religiöser Phänomene: Ernst Troeltsch als Vorbild der Religionsforschung", Fuge 6 (2010), 15–28. See also Jörg Lauster, "Die Selbständigkeit der Religion", in Aufgeklärte Religion und ihre Probleme, ed. Ulrich Barth, Christian Danz, Wilhelm Gräb, and Friedrich Wilhelm Graf (Berlin: De Gruyter, 2013), 431–445.

of the study is (as often or all-too-often the case with Troeltsch's titles) impossible to translate. What "Die Selbständigkeit der Religion" – literally: the self-standing-ness of religion – suggests is a non-reductionist concept of religion, a concept which Troeltsch applies in diachronic and in synchronic perspective.[48] I will refer to the study in order to examine the critique of James's concept of religion which lurks between the lines of Troeltsch's reviews.

In his reviews of James's philosophy and psychology of religion, Troeltsch exposes how James ignores the "conjunction (*Verknüpfung*)" between experience and expression.[49] He marshals a myriad of concepts to argue that the event of religion (in James's terminology, pure experience) and the expression of religion (in James's terminology, impure experience) *co-constitute* the experience of religion.[50] The event of trust in the transcendent cannot be experienced without language, because language is what allows a subject to draw the distinction between transcendence and immanence in the first place. Transcendence is done with language.[51] In contrast to James, Troeltsch concludes that mystical experiences are *simultaneously* ineffable and effable.[52] He stresses the significance of "imagination (*Phantasie*)" for religion.[53] Since the content of religion is inextricably intertwined with the "media (*Medien*)" through which the content comes to the subject's consciousness, these media are "imbibed (*einverleibt*)" into religion.[54] Thus, the media are "indispensable" for the actualization or the self-actualization of the event in the experience.[55] By 'imagination', Troeltsch refers to the subject's engagement with the media which have been transmitted to her. She might engage these media either more productively or more reproductively.

However, Troeltsch admits that actualization or self-actualization through expression does not imply a one-to-one correspondence between the event

---

48 Joas, "Die Selbständigkeit religiöser Phänomene", esp. 17–18.

49 Troeltsch, *Psychologie und Erkenntnistheorie in der Religionswissenschaft*, 17. As mentioned above, the study ties in with Troeltsch's critical comments on James in "Rezension zu William James's *The Varieties of Religious Experience*", 371.

50 Troeltsch, "Die Selbständigkeit der Religion", 399; 419–420; 423; 448. See Lauster, "Die Selbständigkeit der Religion", 434–435.

51 See Lauster, *Religion als Lebensdeutung*, 24–25. See also Lauster's contribution to this compilation. However, 'language' must not be defined too narrowly. When Troeltsch stresses the significance of imagination for religion, he points out that language might include verbal and non-verbal modes of expression.

52 Troeltsch, *Psychologie und Erkenntnistheorie in der Religionswissenschaft*, 16–17.

53 Troeltsch, "Die Selbständigkeit der Religion", 388.

54 Ibid.

55 Ibid.

THE TROUBLE WITH TRUST IN THE TRANSCENDENT   197

and the experience. In accordance with James, he highlights that (self-) actualization is always already alteration.[56] He coins the concept of "das Unaussprechlichste".[57] Troeltsch's (substantially and stylistically incorrect) superlative of 'the ineffable' highlights that the event cannot be captured completely in the experience. The triangle of event, expression, and experience counters the binary distinction between what is expressed and what is experienced without collapsing experience and expression. Troeltsch combines apophatic and cataphatic theology because event and expression are *equiprimordial* for him.[58]

Incidentally, his characterization of religion captures the empirical explorations of James's Gifford Lectures more properly and more pointedly than James himself, for James's survey is indeed not a survey of experiences but a survey of expressions of experiences.[59] When James admits that he himself has not had mystical experiences,[60] he admits that his Gifford Lectures are dependent on (in his terminology) impure as opposed to pure experiences. Troeltsch can account for the dependency – beyond the liberal and the postliberal definition of religion. His account is instructive because it frees the subject from her solitude.

Troeltsch turns James on his head (or from his head back onto his feet). Building on what I identified as the triangle of event, expression, and experience he concludes that the transmission of religion "always already (*stets*)" occurs through "the transfer of religious imaginations (*Vermittelung der religiösen Vorstellungswelt*)".[61] Hence, he appears to shift from the liberal expression of experience to the postliberal experience of expression. But appearances might be deceptive. Troeltsch concurs with James's critique of churches, stressing the rigidity with which churches put pressure on Christians and non-Christians alike to conform to dogmatically domesticated orthodoxies and heterodoxies.[62] He continues, however, that churches can impact religion either constructively or destructively, depending on the ecclesiology of the respective church: churches can be structures of support as much as structures of suppression. Eventually, he cautions against two ecclesiological risks which I call the 'postliberal' and the 'liberal'.

---

56   Ibid., 395.

57   Ibid., 436.

58   Lauster, "Die Selbständigkeit der Religion", 442–443.

59   Niebuhr, "William James on Religious Experience", 232.

60   James, *The Varieties of Religious Experience*, 301.

61   Troeltsch, *Psychologie und Erkenntnistheorie in der Religionswissenschaft*, 17.

62   Troeltsch, "Die Selbständigkeit der Religion", 436.

As for the ecclesiological risk in postliberalism, Troeltsch – like James – argues that if the social expression is prioritized over the individual experience, the prioritization results in communal "fossilization (*Versteinerung*)" or communal "ossification (*Verknöcherung*)".[63] In order to avoid the postliberal risk, the community must allow the subject to challenge the traditions of the church. Otherwise, the community would separate the experience of trust in the transcendent from the expression of trust in the transcendent, thus perverting religion from a relation into a reflection. The subject would be concerned with the traditions which represent the transcendent instead of the transcendent; she would trust in the tradition but not in the transcendent. Religion would be nothing but rational assent, "*Fürwahrhalten*".[64] Here, the social would drain the individual.

As for the ecclesiological risk in liberalism (the inversion of the postliberal risk to which Troeltsch alludes), Troeltsch – unlike James – argues that if the individual experience is prioritized over the social expression, the prioritization results in individual fossilization or individual ossification.[65] In order to avoid the liberal risk, the subject must allow the community to challenge her challenges of the traditions of the church. Otherwise, the subject would separate the experience of trust in the transcendent from the expression of trust in the transcendent. Thus, she would lose the ability to express and experience the event of trust in the transcendent. Eventually, the subject would misinterpret her expressions of the event for the event because her interpretation would not be challenged.[66] Here, the individual would drain the social.

I have structured these ecclesiological risks in parallel: postliberalism as well as liberalism turn religion into bones (ossification) or into stones (fossilization). To avoid the bones and stones of religion, Troeltsch's characterization of the event of religion in-between experience and expression is instructive. Religion is neither simply a matter of the individual, nor simply a matter of the social: it is a matter of relations between social subjects.

Overall, Troeltsch criticizes the interpretation of trust in James's philosophy and psychology of religion.[67] He stresses that experience and expression

---

63   Ibid., 427.

64   Ibid., 436.

65   Ibid., 427–428.

66   Ibid., 435–436.

67   Trust is *not* a core concept for Troeltsch. He criticizes its individualization and its interiorization in Ernst Troeltsch, *The Christian Faith: Based on Lectures Delivered at the University of Heidelberg in 1912 and 1913*, trans. Garett E. Paul (Minneapolis, MN: Fortress, 1991), 48–50 where 'Vertrauen' has been rendered as 'confidence'. Troeltsch's distrust or mistrust in

THE TROUBLE WITH TRUST IN THE TRANSCENDENT   199

cannot be nicely and neatly distinguished because both are dependent on the subject's imagination. To trigger religious imagination, a dynamics between experience and expression is crucial. If a church evokes a dynamics in which the individual can challenge the social as much as the social can challenge the individual, the church is turned from a structure of religious suppression to a structure of religious support. Countering James's privatization of religion, Troeltsch anchors trust in the transcendent not in a solitary subject but in-between social subjects. Trust is a relation. Thus, 'trust' is a particularly pertinent concept to account for the combination of the individual experience of religion and the social expression of religion in a community which is open(ed) to the other.

Trust in-between Social Subjects

As Graham Ward argues in *Unbelievable*, relationality is at the core of religion.[68] He identifies "the going out of oneself" which is evoked and entailed by relationality as the "origin" of belief.[69] Pushing Ward's analysis further, I argue that religion originates in the praxis of trust because the praxis of trust *is* a praxis in which the subject goes out of herself in order to open herself to the other.[70] Since the trustworthiness of the other cannot be established prior to the trust in the other – recall James's "jump" – trust requires that I entrust myself to the other. If transcendence is interpreted in *functional* rather than *substantial* terms, the function of transcendence pertains to both non-religious trust in the finite other and religious trust in the infinite other. The transcendent is that which transcends. Through the praxis of trust, the other transcends how

---

     the terminology of trust might be traced to his discussions with Wilhelm Herrmann for whom the concept of trust was crucial. For these discussions see Mark D. Chapman, *Ernst Troeltsch and Liberal Theology: Religion and Cultural Synthesis in Wilhelmine Germany* (Oxford: Oxford University Press, 2001), 89–110.

68   Ward, *Unbelievable*, 54–55, 58–59.

69   Ibid., 54 Strictly speaking, Ward identifies "the going out of oneself" as the origin of conscious as opposed to unconscious belief. The distinction is indispensable for his analysis which traces beliefs in the biological make-up of humanity.

70   See, again, the contributions by Grøn and Welz in *Trust, Sociality and Selfhood*, 13–30 and 45–64. See also Arne Grøn, "Grenzen des Vertrauens: Kritische Bemerkungen zur Rede von Grundvertrauen", in *Grundvertrauen: Hermeneutik eines Grenzphänomens*, 145–158, where Grøn conceptualizes the going out of oneself as "eccentricity (*Exzentrizität*)". Ward alludes to trust and trusting in *Unbelievable*, 54–55. "Belief ... concerns that which we can come to trust. ... Belief is a relational category" (Ibid., 55).

I think and talk about her; the other transcends me. Hence, the contradistinction between non-religious trust and religious trust is *not* a categorical contradistinction: both the finite other and the infinite other transcend how I think and talk about them.[71] In the case of the finite other, the transcendence of the other is a routine matter: it is ordinary. In the case of the infinite other, the transcendence of the other is a radical matter: it is extraordinary.

In order to assess how the event of transcendence can be characterized as simultaneously effable and ineffable, I suggest a differentiation between two dimensions in the concept of expression – *articulation* and *interpretation*. According to my distinction, the experience of trust implies that the subject articulates trust in the other. But if trust in the other means that the other transcends the subject's articulation, her *interpretation* of trust relativizes her *articulation* of trust. Described differently, the subject articulates trust in the other. But simultaneously she interprets her articulation as inadequate because the articulation cannot completely characterize the other. The other would not transcend me if she could be characterized completely. When I trust her, I accept that she is ultimately undetermined. Hence, in order to account for the effability and for the ineffability of mystical experience, Troeltsch's triangle of event, expression, and experience requires a dialectical concept of expression: articulation and interpretation.[72]

The difference between the dimension of articulation and the dimension of interpretation is instructive for religious and non-religious trust. Trust requires what Ward assesses as the simultaneity of consciousness and consciousness-of-consciousness:[73] the subject articulates her trust in the other (consciousness) and the subject interprets her articulation of her trust in the other (consciousness-of-consciousness) at the same time. Through the simultaneity of consciousness and consciousness-of-consciousness, the subject can register that the other transcends her. The distinction between religious and non-religious trust is *not* drawn by the

---

71   Accordingly, it would be incorrect to refer to the finite other as simply immanent and to the infinite other as simply transcendent. Both others might transcend me.

72   By 'articulation', I mean the way in which the subject registers that she is exposed to the other. Hence, articulation might capture different forms of language as well as different forms of protolanguage which is exemplified by what neuroscientists refer to as "limbic speech": utterances like 'oh' or 'uh' of 'ah' relating to stimuli which the limbic sphere processes directly as opposed to indirectly. In limbic speech, the event is registered, but not reflected (Ward, *Unbelievable*, 58–59). Crucially, even limbic speech is oriented towards the other. As Ward puts it, because it is immediate as opposed to mediate, "limbic speech is 'infective'" (Ibid., 59).

73   Ibid., 215.

THE TROUBLE WITH TRUST IN THE TRANSCENDENT 201

engagement with transcendence – both the finite and the infinite other transcend me. Instead, it is drawn by the degree to which the articulation differs from the interpretation: as mentioned above, in the case of non-religious trust it is a routine difference, in the case of religious trust it is a radical difference. Consequently, the boundary between the religious and the non-religious is blurred. Religion is rooted in the radical dissonance between the articulation and the interpretation of trust: religious experience is the *hermeneutical experience* in which one's interpretation highlights the radical inadequacy of one's articulation.[74]

Dissonance causes psychological and physiological reactions; it might make the subject literally shiver or sweat.[75] But when a subject registers dissonance in cognitive or non-cognitive modes, her imagination is triggered.[76] Through imagination, the subject engages with transcendence which is why, as Troeltsch already anticipated, imagination is indispensable for religion.[77] Accordingly, experience might be evoked from both ends: events might call for expressions as much as expressions might call for events.[78] With such a dynamics in the concept of experience, religion is located beyond liberalism and postliberalism *in* the praxis of trust. Here, the other is not seen as a total or totalized other, for if the other – finite or infinite – was totally other, relations to her would be impossible.[79]

The differentiation between articulation and interpretation which holds for the expression of the events of religious and non-religious trust alike is crucial for the conceptualization or re-conceptualization of community beyond the alternative of liberalism and postliberalism. It allows theologians to assess the correlation between religious and non-religious trust. Troeltsch describes and defines these inter-related relations as the "double character (*Doppelcharakter*)" of Christianity.[80] In Christianity, the relation to the finite other intersects

---

74   For the concept of hermeneutical experience see Werner G. Jeanrond's contribution to this compilation.

75   Ward, *Unbelievable*, 95.

76   Ibid.

77   For the significance of imagination see esp. Amber L. Griffioen's and Graham Ward's contributions to this compilation.

78   See Hans Joas, "On the Articulation of Experience", in *Do We Need Religion? On the Experience of Self-Transcendence*, trans. Alex Skinner (Boulder, CO: Paradigm Publishers, 2008), 37–49, esp. 46–47.

79   Ward, *Unbelievable*, 216.

80   Ernst Troeltsch, *The Social Teachings of the Christian Church[es]*, vol. 1, trans. Olive Wyon (London: Macmillan, 1931), 57, translation altered. Olive Wyon's translation of *Doppelcharakter* with "double aspect" is deceptive because Troeltsch argues that the

with the relation to the infinite other. How a subject relates to the finite other influences how she relates to the infinite other and how she relates to the infinite other influences how she relates to the finite other – admittedly not much more than a complicated conceptualization of the double-commandment of love. Christianity itself is concern for the infinite other and concern for the finite other; it challenges the absolute distinction between what counts as religious and what counts as non-religious. But what are the consequences of such a double character for the concept of community?

If trust in the finite other and trust in the infinite other are correlates, religion requires both individuality and sociality without reducing sociality to a function of individuality (the liberal tendency) or reducing individuality to a function of sociality (the postliberal tendency). The issue is that these reductions exclude alterity – the otherness of the other – from religion by falling into the traps of the liberal ecclesiological risk or the postliberal ecclesiological risk. If divorced from the social, the individual prevents openness to otherness. If divorced from the individual, the social prevents openness to otherness. Both become self-enclosed. Since transcendence comes in through the exposure of the subject to the otherness of the other, liberalism and postliberalism cannot cope with transcendence. In both cases the other is controlled by constructs of her, either individual constructs or social constructs. Trust is turned into its opposite: closure and control. To avoid such a turn, a community must be structured in ways which provoke and preserve the possibility of trust; community is to be opened to the other. Although one has to be careful not to cause a short circuit by sliding from correlation to causation, it is crucial to stress that exposure to the finite other might allow for encounters with the infinite other and that exposure to the infinite other might allow for encounters with the finite other.

Community cannot be reduced to a shelter for the insecure. Instead, community entails engagements with alterity, 'jumps' towards the finite and the infinite other. In the nostalgias for community which haunt the humanities, openness to otherness is rejected. Countering these nostalgias (the rejection of which leads James to reject community altogether), Troeltsch's reception of James is instructive. Following Troeltsch, the social contributes to the individual as much as the individual contributes to the social. Conceptualized as trust in the transcendent, religion causes trouble – a trouble which exposes the compulsion for closure and control in the nostalgias for community. Therefore, the trouble with trust in the transcendent is constructive, not destructive.

---

inter-related relations to the finite and the infinite other are the *characteristics* (not only *aspects* of the characteristics) of Christianity.

THE TROUBLE WITH TRUST IN THE TRANSCENDENT   203

To conclude, Troeltsch's reception of James's concept of trust in the transcendent clarifies that the concept of experience is not necessarily rooted in individualism. If the binary distinction between experience and expression which characterizes James's concept of religion is broken up through the triangle of event, expression, and experience, then the individual and the social can be arranged or rather re-arranged in the concept of the open(ed) community. Trust captures this (re-)arrangement: relations to the other – finite and infinite – entail a transcendence which is registered in the routine difference or the radical dissonance between the subject's articulation and the subject's interpretation of trust. Thus, a community which aims to foster religious trust ought to facilitate non-religious trust, and a community which aims to foster non-religious trust ought to facilitate religious trust. The relation to the finite other and the relation to the infinite other are inextricably interwoven.

But what about the specter of the 'collapse of community' mentioned at the outset? Are the complaints about it factual or fictional? Considering its creative circularity, the experience of trust is more an experience of being chosen than an experience of choosing.[81] Trust might be demanded or commanded, but one cannot force it. I cannot even force myself to trust: sometimes, I *do not* trust the other although I decided to trust her and sometimes I *do* trust the other although I decided not to trust her.[82] Hence, in order to foster and facilitate trust, a community must allow for the subject's exposure to the otherness of the other from which recognition of the other might follow – a recognition which is crucial for trust.[83] What such recognition would look like is a matter of praxis. But it would *not* look like the nostalgias for coherent and consistent community. These nostalgias operate with clear-cut concepts of identity which separate and segregate the insider from the outsider such that the encounter with the other is not permitted let alone provoked and preserved. Thus, the nostalgic complaint about the collapse of community might be precisely what is contributing to the very collapse.

---

81   Grøn, "Trust, Sociality and Selfhood", 13–14, 26–29.

82   Ibid., 24.

83   Ibid., 13–14, 26–29. Grøn defines 'recognition' as a way of seeing: "If we think that we can see the other as she is 'in herself', we fail to recognize her as a self relating to herself. By contrast, to see that she is 'in herself', beyond that as which we see her, is to recognize her in the strong sense of seeing her as standing on her own feet, being independent of our relation to her. The other is beyond our relation to her already in responding on her own to what we do to her" (Ibid., 22). Described differently, recognition means to register and respect the otherness of the other which transcends our evaluations and expectations of her.

Literature

Bauman, Zygmunt, *Community: Seeking Safety in an Insecure World* (Cambridge: Polity Press, 2001).

Bienert, Maren, *Protestantische Selbstverortung: Die Rezensionen Ernst Troeltschs* (Berlin: De Gruyter, 2014).

Carrette, Jeremy, "Passionate Belief: William James, Emotion, and Religious Experience", in *William James and the Varieties of Religious Experience: A Centenary Celebration*, ed. Jeremy Carrette (London: Routledge, 2005), 79–93.

Chapman, Mark D., *Ernst Troeltsch and Liberal Theology: Religion and Cultural Synthesis in Wilhelmine Germany* (Oxford: Oxford University Press, 2001).

Dalferth, Ingolf U. and Simon Peng-Keller (eds.), *Gottvertrauen: Die ökumenische Diskussion um die* fiducia (Freiburg: Herder, 2012).

Dalferth, Ingolf U. and Simon Peng-Keller (eds.), *Grundvertrauen: Hermeneutik eines Grenzphänomens* (Leipzig: EVA, 2013).

Dalferth, Ingolf U. and Simon Peng-Keller (eds.), *Kommunikation des Vertrauens* (Leipzig: EVA, 2012).

Delanty, Gerard, *Community* (London: Routledge, 2004).

Grøn, Arne, "Trust, Sociality, Selfhood", in *Trust, Sociality and Selfhood*, ed. Claudia Welz and Arne Grøn (Tübingen: Mohr Siebeck, 2010), 13–30.

Hennis, Wilhelm, "The Spiritualist Foundation of Max Weber's 'Interpretative Sociology': Ernst Troeltsch, Max Weber and William James's Varieties of Religious Experience", *History of the Human Sciences* 11 (1998), 83–106.

James, William, "A World of Pure Experience", in *Essays in Radical Empiricism*, The Works of William James, vol. 3, ed. Fredson Bowers and Ignas K. Skurupskelis (Cambridge, MA: Harvard University Press, 1976), 21–44.

James, William, "Experience", in *Essays in Philosophy*, The Works of William James, vol. 5, ed. Frederick H. Burkhardt, Fredson Bowers, and Ignas K. Skrupskelis (Cambridge, MA: Harvard University Press, 1977), 95.

James, William, *Some Problems of Philosophy*, The Works of William James, vol. 7, ed. Frederick H. Burkhardt, Fredson Bowers, and Ignas K. Skurupskelis (Cambridge, MA: Harvard University Press, 1979).

James, William, *The Principles of Psychology*, 3 vols, The Works of William James, vols 8–10, ed. Frederick H. Burkhardt, Fredson Bowers, and Ignas K. Skurupskelis (Cambridge, MA: Harvard University Press, 1981).

James, William, *The Varieties of Religious Experience: A Study in Human Nature. Being the Gifford Lectures on Natural Religion Delivered at Edinburgh in 1901–1902*, The Works of William James, vol. 15, ed. Frederick H. Burkhardt, Fredson Bowers, and Ignas K. Skurupskelis (Cambridge, MA: Harvard University Press, 1987).

THE TROUBLE WITH TRUST IN THE TRANSCENDENT 205

James, William, *The Will to Believe and Other Essays in Popular Philosophy*, The Works of William James, vol. 6, ed. Frederick H. Burkhardt, Fredson Bowers, and Ignas K. Skurupskelis (Cambridge, MA: Harvard University Press, 1979).

Joas, Hans, "Die Selbständigkeit religiöser Phänomene: Ernst Troeltsch als Vorbild der Religionsforschung", *Fuge* 6 (2010), 15–28.

Joas, Hans, "On the Articulation of Experience", in *Do We Need Religion? On the Experience of Self-Transcendence*, trans. Alex Skinner (Boulder, CO: Paradigm Publishers, 2008), 37–49.

Joas, Hans, "Schleiermacher and the Turn to Experience in the Study of Religion", in *Interpreting Religion: The Significance of Friedrich Schleiermacher's "Reden über die Religion"*, ed. Dietrich Korsch and Amber L. Griffioen (Tübingen: Mohr Siebeck, 2011), 147–161.

Joas, Hans, *Die Entstehung der Werte* (Frankfurt: Suhrkamp, 1997).

Joas, Hans, *The Genesis of Values*, trans. Gregory Moore (Cambridge: Polity Press, 2000).

Jung, Matthias, *Erfahrung und Religion: Grundzüge einer hermeneutisch-pragmatischen Religionsphilosophie* (München: Alber, 1999).

Lauster, Jörg, "Die Selbständigkeit der Religion", in *Aufgeklärte Religion und ihre Probleme*, ed. Ulrich Barth, Christian Danz, Wilhelm Gräb, and Friedrich Wilhelm Graf (Berlin: De Gruyter, 2013), 431–445.

Lauster, Jörg, *Religion als Lebensdeutung: Theologische Hermeneutik heute* (Darmstadt: Wissenschaftliche Buchgesellschaft, 2005).

Lindbeck, George R., *The Nature of Doctrine* (London: SPCK, 1984).

Milbank, John, *Theology and Social Theory: Beyond Secular Reason* (Oxford: Blackwell, 2006).

Niebuhr, Richard R., "William James on Religious Experience", in *The Cambridge Companion to William James*, ed. Ruth A. Putnam (Cambridge: Cambridge University Press, 1997), 214–236.

Rasmussen, Joel D. S., "Empiricism and Mysticism in Ernst Troeltsch's Philosophy of Religion", *Mitteilungen der Ernst-Troeltsch-Gesellschaft* 13 (2000), 48–65.

Rasmussen, Joel D. S., "Mysticism as a Category of Inquiry in the Philosophies of Ernst Troeltsch and William James", in *Exploring Lost Dimensions in Christian Mysticism: Opening to the Mystical*, ed. Louise Nelstrop and Simon D. Potmore (Aldershot: Ashgate, 2013), 51–68.

Schleiermacher, Friedrich D. E., *On Religion: Speeches to its Cultured Despisers*, trans. Richard Couter (Cambridge: Cambridge University Press, 1988).

Schmiedel, Ulrich, "Vertrauen Verstanden? Zur Vertrauenstrilogie von Ingolf U. Dalferth und Simon Peng-Keller", *NZSTh* 56 (2014), 379–392.

Taylor, Charles, *A Secular Age* (Cambridge, MA: Harvard University Press, 2007).

Taylor, Charles, *Varieties of Religion Today: William James Revisited* (Cambridge, MA: Harvard University Press, 2002).

Troeltsch, Ernst, "Die Selbständigkeit der Religion", in *Kritische Gesamtausgabe*, vol. 1, ed. Christian Albrecht (Berlin: De Gruyter, 2009), 359–535.

Troeltsch, Ernst, "Empiricism and Platonism in the Philosophy of Religion: To the Memory of William James", *The Harvard Theological Review* 5 (1912), 401–422.

Troeltsch, Ernst, "Rezension zu William James's *The Varieties of Religious Experience*", *Kritische Gesamtausgabe*, vol. 4, 364–371.

Troeltsch, Ernst, *Psychologie und Erkenntnistheorie in der Religionswissenschaft: Eine Untersuchung über die Bedeutung der Kantischen Religionslehre für die heutige Religionswissenschaft* (Tübingen: Mohr Siebeck, 1905).

Troeltsch, Ernst, *The Christian Faith: Based on Lectures Delivered at the University of Heidelberg in 1912 and 1913*, trans. Garett E. Paul (Minneapolis, MN: Fortress, 1991).

Troeltsch, Ernst, *The Social Teachings of the Christian Church*, 2 vols, trans. Olive Wyon (London: Macmillan, 1931).

Ward, Graham, *Unbelievable: Why We Believe and Why We Don't* (London: I. B. Tauris, 2014).

Welz, Claudia, "Trust as Basic Openness and Self-Transcendence", in *Trust, Sociality and Selfhood*, ed. Claudia Welz and Arne Grøn (Tübingen: Mohr Siebeck, 2010), 45–64.

Welz, Claudia, *Vertrauen und Versuchung* (Tübingen: Mohr Siebeck, 2010).

CHAPTER 12

The Corporeality of Religious Experience: Embodied Cognition in Religious Practices

Tobias Tan

William James opens his Gifford Lectures, *The Varieties of Religious Experience*, with a blistering critique of what he calls "medical materialism".[1] When applied to religious experiences, medical materialism locates the cause of these experiences entirely in certain bodily conditions, thereby attempting to provide reductive physiological explanations. Given that *The Varieties* is *the* classic on 'religious experience', it is with some trepidation that I seek to argue that bodily factors contribute to shaping the meaning of religious experience. My aim, however, is neither to rehabilitate the theories which James rejects nor to offer an account which reductively explains religious experience entirely in terms of physiological factors. Rather, I argue that James's total rejection of corporeal factors is too extreme and a more nuanced account, which recognizes physiological elements as one factor among others, can steer a middle way between reduction to and rejection of bodily factors.

To make this case I shall proceed in three sections. First, I shall revisit James's circumscription of religious experience to uncover the reasons for his rejection of physiological explanations. By restricting his treatment to 'personal' rather than 'institutional' religion and to ecstatic rather than quotidian experiences, James excludes the experience of rituals, one of the aspects of religious practice in which bodily activity is most prominent. Second, having enlarged the ambit of religious experience to include embodied practices, I shall look to recent developments in cognitive science which reveal how bodily factors participate in our cognitive processes, namely the field of 'embodied cognition'. Third, the meaning implicit in bodily practices can be integrated into a larger hermeneutical framework of a 'tradition' to avoid the reductionism which James fears. By integrating corporeal factors into a larger account of religious meaning-making, I aim to recover the role of the body as both a source of religious experience and a form of its expression.

---

1 William James, *The Varieties of Religious Experience: A Study in Human Nature* (London: Longmans, Green and Co., 1902), 6–19.

© KONINKLIJKE BRILL NV, LEIDEN, 2016 | DOI 10.1163/9789004328600_014

James's Circumscription of Religious Experience

James observes that religion resists any essentialist definition, arguing that no monolithic essence captures the full gamut of what might be predicated as religious.[2] He therefore begins *The Varieties* by carefully delimiting his field of inquiry. His working definition of religion is "the feelings, acts and experiences of individual men [*sic*] in their solitude, so far as they apprehend themselves to stand in relation to whatever they may consider the divine."[3] In order to analyze such experiences, he argues that one must study the most obvious examples: "such a quality will be of course most prominent and easy to notice in those religious experiences which are most one-sided, exaggerated, and intense."[4] He therefore makes the methodological decision of selecting extreme accounts of personal and private experiences. As a result, it is the most intense mystical experiences which are paradigmatic for James.

James readily acknowledges that his choice to focus on extreme instances of personal experience is somewhat arbitrary.[5] However, given the unruly nature of the term 'religion' and the lack of a unifying essence, he argues that a delimitation of the territory which he intends to cover is necessary. This move is not intended to provide a definitive definition, but is merely "for the purpose of these lectures".[6] It is thus sold as a "practical convenience",[7] rather than an ideological assertion. This rather humble and winsome strategy seems laudable at first glance: it aims to bring clarity and precision to the otherwise unmanageable task of analyzing religion. Numerous critics, however, have argued that James's definition is far from innocent. Nicholas Lash offers a particularly incisive critique, with which I shall briefly engage by way of two (classes of) criticism of James.[8]

The first criticism questions the *neutrality* of James's circumscription. James not only focuses on the individual's experience, but also contrasts it favorably

---

2   Ibid., 26–28. See Nicholas Lash, *Easter in Ordinary: Reflections on Human Experience and the Knowledge of God* (London: University of Notre Dame Press, 1990), 38–40.

3   James, *Varieties*, 31.

4   Ibid., 45.

5   In a later lecture, however, James intimates that this definition was more deliberate and calculated: "You see now why I have been so individualistic throughout these lectures, and why I have seemed so bent on rehabilitating the element of feeling in religion and subordinating its intellectual part. Individuality is founded in feeling", ibid., 501.

6   Ibid., 28.

7   Lash, *Easter in Ordinary*, 43, 51.

8   Ibid., 1–104. See also Charles Taylor, *Varieties of Religion Today: William James Revisited* (Cambridge, MA: Harvard University Press, 2002), 20–29.

THE CORPOREALITY OF RELIGIOUS EXPERIENCE 209

with institutional religion. For James, personal religious experience is "original" whilst institutional religion is a "second-hand" and a "dull habit".[9] If religious institutions are to be understood, one must trace their origins back to the experience of a religious "pattern-setter", in the figure of their founder.[10] As Lash points out, James is not so much distinguishing between two facets of religion, as he is demarcating two types of religion: one mystical and the other institutional, one for the founders and another for the adherents.[11] Given that the intense, first-hand experiences of the pattern-setters are both infrequent and confined to the privileged few, Lash tersely asks "where does that leave the rest of us?"[12] James is not simply identifying two aspects of religion, but is also making a *judgment* about which religious experiences are legitimate and which are not. 'Personal' experiences are authentic, direct, powerful, and effective, whereas experiences in institutional contexts are derivative, mediated, imitative, and dull.

James's valuation is clearly open to contestation. Not only does it restrict 'pure' religion to the few, but it is also far from obvious that mystical experiences are inherently superior. Even on James's own criteria for evaluating religious experiences, namely that they ought to be judged by their fruits, the picture is rather ambiguous.[13] As James himself admits, there are circumstances in which the psychological dispositions and attributes of the 'saintly', namely devoutness, purity, tenderness and charity, and asceticism, can yield negative consequences.[14] Moreover, as James is again aware, the memory of intense experiences fades over time and quotidian life must recommence.[15] Conversely, could not the ritual and institutional aspects of religion bear good fruit? Surely the regular and repetitive nature of rituals makes them capable of forming character and inculcating virtues, if exercised correctly. James's chosen focus and rhetoric gives the impression of an ingrained prejudice against institutions rather than a casual emphasis on personal religion.

A second criticism of James's circumscription of religious experience questions its *plausibility*. Recall that James defines religious experience as something which individuals have "in their solitude". There is, to my mind, an ambiguity here with the concept of solitude. While it is clear that one can achieve

---

9   James, *Varieties*, 6.

10   Ibid., 30.

11   Lash, *Easter in Ordinary*, 54.

12   Ibid., 73.

13   James, *Varieties*, 18.

14   Ibid., 340–368.

15   Ibid., 257–258.

physical solitude by withdrawing to a space in which one is alone, it is less clear whether *psychological* solitude is possible. As Lash argues, "our 'private' experiences are never entirely 'naked'",[16] since "[t]he symbolic, linguistic, affective resources available to us are given by prior experience, and by the culture, the traditions, the structures, institutions, and relationships that bring us to birth and give us such identity as we have".[17] In other words, physical solitude does not entail psychological solitude; even in moments of physical solitude we are not isolated individuals, but remain social beings shaped by institutions and traditions.

This entanglement is also apparent in the opposite direction, since our experiences in corporate settings are equally *our* experiences and thus equally personal. Lash again: "[i]f there was this 'one great partition' between human institutions and individual personal experience, then (for example) birthday parties and rituals of courtship could never be said to be 'personal experiences' for their participants".[18] Experiences which occur in corporate or institutional settings have the capacity to be equally as 'first-hand' as those which do not. Who is to say that receiving a sacrament is not as personal, as legitimate, as direct, and, indeed as 'religious' as, say, receiving a mystical vision?

Thus, on the one hand, our social world impinges on our thoughts even when we are alone; and on the other hand, our experiences in institutional or corporate settings can still be said to be personal. The lack of physical proximity to other human beings seems to be an odd criterion for religious experience. Lash captures this point in his characteristically terse manner: "[i]f James's account were correct, then the best way to prepare someone for the experience of God would seem to be to abandon them, at birth, in some untracked waste far from human habitation".[19] It would seem that James's individualistic bias blinds him to the implausibility of separating personal and institutional religious experiences.

It is within the context of James's prejudice for individual and against institutional religious experience that he considers the *corporeal* dimension of such experiences. He begins his lectures by rejecting "medical materialism", which attempts to explain religious experiences purely in terms of a physiological condition.[20] For James, the reduction of religious experience to physiological

---

16   Lash, *Easter in Ordinary*, 57.

17   Ibid., 57–58.

18   Ibid., 55.

19   Ibid., 58.

20   James, *Varieties*, 10–16. Although James is responding to a particular set of theories from a particular era and context, he can be read as making wider claims about the corporeal

THE CORPOREALITY OF RELIGIOUS EXPERIENCE 211

causes is a "too simple-minded system of thought" and "finishes up St Paul by calling his vision on the road to Damascus a discharging lesion of the occipital cortex, he being an epileptic. It snuffs out Saint Teresa as an hysteric, Saint Francis of Assisi as an hereditary degenerate. George Fox's discontent with the shams of his age, and his pining for spiritual veracity, it treats as a symptom of a disordered colon."[21] The absurd reduction of such profound spiritual experiences to a simple physiological disorder ought to strike any listener as an inadequate, if not downright ridiculous, explanation. Moreover the deployment of seemingly whimsical associations of proposed physiological causes and their experiential results, without any explanation of why one should lead to the other, pours further scorn on such reductionist explanations.

Does this settle the matter then? Are we to occlude all physiological explanations from our attempts to understand religious experience? My contention is that such a total dismissal of corporeal factors is far too hasty on three related counts.

First, James's rejection of corporeal factors is predicated on his problematic circumscription of religious experience to individual and extreme instances. By opting for a single-minded focus on 'personal' rather than institutional experiences, he excludes ecclesial practices, together with their bodily manipulations and material environments.[22] By considering only extreme examples, he likewise has little time for more mundane personal rituals which involve adopting particular bodily postures or engaging with material objects, such as kneeling in solitary prayer or thumbing through a rosary. Thus, by unshackling religion from James's definitional constraints, we can re-evaluate the corporeal dimension of religious experiences within both personal and ecclesial settings.

This is not to say that the intense, personal, and mystical experiences which James recounts do not also have physiological correlates (even if, following James, one cannot reduce such experiences to pure physiology).[23] Indeed these components are on occasion mentioned in the accounts cited by James and his analysis of them (though predominantly as symptoms rather than causes).[24]

---

dimension of religious experience (or lack thereof). Given the classical status of his work, I consider him to be of continuing significance.

21   Ibid., 13.

22   "James cannot avoid acknowledging religious institutions (ecclesiastical systems) or worship in his study, but he never finds a way to integrate these into this model of religious emotion." Jeremy R. Carrette, "Passionate Belief: William James, Emotion and Religious Experience", in *William James and the Varieties of Religious Experience: A Centenary Celebration*, ed. Jeremy R. Carrette (London: Routledge, 2005), 79–93 (90).

23   See Lash, *Easter in Ordinary*, 54.

24   See James, *Varieties*, 200, 251, 296–297, 312, 381, 412, 478.

However, given that such experiences tend to be rare, esoteric, and potentially quite variable, it is difficult to discuss their physiological components outside of individual cases. Ritual practices, by contrast, are far more common, deliberate and structured. This makes their corporeal dimension more amenable to analysis.

Second, if one accepts that physiological factors do not explain religious experience *in their entirety*, it does not follow that they have *nothing* to contribute. James convincingly argues that physiology is hardly capable of providing a comprehensive account of religious experience, such that a religious experience is 'nothing but' a physiological state.[25] He fails, however, to return to the subject to offer a more nuanced account of how corporeal elements may contribute to religious experiences as one factor among others. There is little given by way of justification for James's all-or-nothing approach to the bodily nature of religious experience.

James's blinkered approach to corporeal factors is somewhat surprising. In his earlier work on emotion, James emphasizes the importance of bodily factors for emotional experience, suggesting that changes in body state are constitutive of emotions.[26] In *The Varieties*, James argues that emotions play a crucial role in religious experience.[27] Combine these two insights and one would expect James to allow some place for corporeal factors in religious experience. James, however, fails to make this connection. In *The Varieties*, emotions become "psychic entities".[28] Lash argues that this "gives the impression that religious experience is exclusively a matter of *mental* states".[29] A more nuanced account would allow corporeal elements to enter into considerations of religious experience without attempting to provide exhaustive explanations.

---

25 Ibid., 12–13. Incidentally, the 'nothing but' formula has become emblematic for reductionist accounts. See, for example, Manuel A. Vásquez, *More Than Belief: A Materialist Theory of Religion* (Oxford: Oxford University Press, 2011), 4.

26 William James, "What Is an Emotion?", *Mind* 9/34 (1884), 188–205; William James, *The Principles of Psychology*, ed. Fredson Bowers, Frederick Burkhardt, and Ignas K. Skrupskelis, 2 vols., vol. 2 (Cambridge, MA: Harvard University Press, 1981), 1058–1097; William James, "The Physical Basis of Emotion", *Psychological Review* 1/5 (1894), 516–529.

27 James, *Varieties*, 27–28, 48, 79, 196, 241, 266–267, 271–273, 279, 284, 425–427.

28 Ibid., 28. See Carrette, "Passionate Belief: William James, Emotion and Religious Experience".

29 Lash, *Easter in Ordinary*, 41. Lash also argues that despite James's 'radical empiricism', his wider philosophical position, found in *The Varieties* and in his other works, ultimately fails to extricate itself from a Cartesian dualism. See ibid., 35.

THE CORPOREALITY OF RELIGIOUS EXPERIENCE   213

Third, while James's objection to medical materialism critiques weaknesses in causal physiological explanations, subsequent scientific research has gone some way towards addressing these weaknesses. Critiquing one example of medical materialism (that religion is a result of sexual development) James retorts: "[i]n this sense the religious life depends as much on the spleen, the pancreas, and the kidneys as on the sexual apparatus, and the whole theory has lost its point in evaporating into a vague general assertion of the dependence, *somehow*, of the mind upon the body".[30] The point James seems to be making is that the proposed causal connections from physiology to religious experience are all too vague. The mind may, by all means, be dependent on the body in some general way (by, for example, keeping the brain alive), but this is a far cry from this assertion of the more specific claim that a particular physiological condition causes a determinate religious experience. If one were to make this kind of claim, James might contend, then one would need a far more detailed account of the mechanism by which a physiological state induces a religious experience and far greater evidence that such a relationship exists. Without such evidence the proposed connections are either wild speculation or too general to count as an interesting causal explanation.

This point may well have been a valid critique of the purveyors of medical materialism given the psychological evidence available in James's day. As Gerald Edelman states, "it is not enough to say that the mind is embodied; one must say how".[31] And yet all the medical materialists could offer was a handwaving '*somehow*'. Recent advances in cognitive science, however, have begun to provide new insights into the connection between particular corporeal factors and their cognitive effects, illuminating the previously obscure '*somehow*'. These studies and their broader theoretical syntheses have been collected under the rubric of *embodied cognition*. Although James's lectures have deservedly become a classic, embodied cognition research provides an impetus to reconsider his dismissal of corporeal factors. In particular, by broadening his circumscription of religious experience to include personal and ecclesial practices and then considering these practices in light of embodied cognition, we stand to uncover the more nuanced account of the corporeal dimension of religious experience which was a casualty in James's polemic against medical materialism.

---

30   James, *Varieties*, 12.

31   Gerald M. Edelman, *Bright Air, Brilliant Fire: On the Matter of the Mind* (London: Allen Lane, 1992), 15.

214   TAN

Embodied Cognition and Religious Ritual

'Embodied cognition' groups together research in cognitive science which considers how factors beyond the brain (or beyond the central nervous system) participate in our cognitive processes.[32] It marshals evidence from a wide variety of disciplines, including experimental psychology, affective studies, robotics and animal behavior, to argue that cognition cannot be understood in exclusively neurological terms. To give a complete account of cognition, proponents contend, one must also consider the broader context of the human body and its environmental interactions.

Embodied cognition research illuminates the corporeal dimension of religious experiences in three areas: first, human perception, which is contingent upon the particularities of our embodiment, grounds our concepts; second, certain body states influence cognition; and, third, environmental factors bias cognition.[33] Although relatively few studies explore specifically religious practices (and, indeed, more research on this front would be most welcome), it is not difficult to see how general psychological mechanisms are at work within particular religious contexts.[34]

The Perceptual Grounding of Religious Concepts

Recent studies in cognitive science speak to the question of how abstract symbols become meaningful in human cognition (sometimes known as the 'symbol grounding problem').[35] Lawrence Barsalou et al. attempt to address

---

32   For an overview, see Lawrence A. Shapiro, *Embodied Cognition* (New York: Routledge, 2011).

33   Shapiro categorizes embodied cognition into three hypotheses which he calls 'conceptualization', 'replacement' and 'constitution'. See ibid. The first area I consider corresponds to the conceptualization hypothesis. The second and third areas blend the replacement and constitution hypotheses, while distinguishing between factors within and beyond our skin.

34   Lawrence W. Barsalou et al., "Embodiment in Religious Knowledge", *Journal of Cognition and Culture* 5/1–2 (2005), 14–57; Fraser Watts, "Embodied Cognition and Religion", *Zygon* 48/3 (2013), 745–758. Given that there is no generic religious practice and particular religious practices are enormously diverse, I shall restrict my examples to the Christian ritual practices with which I am most familiar. Religious practices of other faiths, or indeed other expressions of Christianity, could similarly be considered in terms of their corporeality.

35   See John R. Searle, "Minds, Brains, and Programs", *Behavioral and Brain Sciences* 3 (1980), 417–424; Stevan Harnad, "The Symbol Grounding Problem", *Physica D: Nonlinear Phenomena* 42/1–3 (1990), 335–346.

THE CORPOREALITY OF RELIGIOUS EXPERIENCE   215

this question by examining the relationship between symbols and our perceptual experience.[36] To this end, they draw a distinction between 'amodal' and
'modal' theories of knowledge, which aim to describe both the nature of concepts and the process of their acquisition.

Amodal theories of knowledge assert that concepts are represented in the
mind by abstract representations which are detached from the *mode* of perception through which they were acquired. According to amodal theories,
although perception is required to gain knowledge of the outside world, once
knowledge is represented in the mind it becomes divorced from the means by
which it was perceived. For example, although dogs may be perceived through
sight, sound, smell and touch (or, in some cultures, even taste), the concept
'dog' no longer relies on these particular perceptions. Hence concepts are not
related to the sensations from which they arise.[37]

A key aspect of amodal theories of knowledge is the transduction
principle.[38] Since amodal symbols are detached from their modes of perception, amodal theories assume that there is some process which translates – or
transduces – sense perception into amodal symbols for use in conceptual processing. Barsalou et al. note that although the transduction principle is central
to amodal theories, there has been no research into how the process of transduction might occur.[39]

In contrast, *modal* theories argue that concepts remain linked to the mode
of perception through which they are acquired. Thus the concepts do not
become separated from the perceptual systems, but the visual, gustatory, olfac-
tory, auditory, tactile, proprioceptive perception, as well as the motor movements which accompany and support them, also *constitute* these concepts.

Instead of the transduction principle, modal theories explain how perceptual interactions become concepts with the *simulation principle*. Barsalou et
al. summarize, "[w]hereas the transduction principle assumes that amodal
symbols are transduced to represent the experience, the simulation principle
assumes that the original modality-specific states are partially captured to represent it".[40] Thus, when concepts are used for memory, thought or language, the
initial sensory conditions in which they were acquired are simulated and this
simulation constitutes the concept. Barsalou et al. have amassed numerous

---

36   Barsalou et al., "Embodiment in Religious Knowledge".
37   Ibid., 20.
38   Ibid.
39   Ibid., 24.
40   Ibid., 22.

studies from cognitive psychology, social psychology and cognitive neuroscience which provide evidence that certain human concepts are indeed modal.[41]

The implication of this is that human knowledge is more interconnected to perceptions than amodal theories presumed. Given that our modes of perception are contingent on the particularities of our body's configuration and perceptual capacities, it also follows that concepts are grounded in our embodiment. Even if some concepts are amodal, a possibility which is difficult to rule out empirically, this does not undermine the significance of our widespread reliance on modal symbols.[42] If Barsalou et al.'s work is to speak to the symbol grounding problem, then amodal symbols must relate back to modal ones to be *meaningful*.[43]

This general insight about concepts can be applied to theological concepts by considering how they relate back to perceptually-contingent modal representations. Indeed Barsalou et al. suggest that modal representations play a pronounced role in religious experience: "[o]utside the study of religious experience, increasing evidence suggests that mundane knowledge is grounded in the brain's modality-specific systems... Embodiment is likely to be central in religious experience as well".[44]

Metaphors and analogy are an obvious example, since they usually illuminate an abstract concept by relating it to a more concrete vehicle present in our perceptual experience.[45] Moreover, they play a crucial role in biblical texts and other theological writings. Bread, vines, light, wine, water, meat, milk, wheat, yeast, fire, warmth, brightness, height, depth, trees, sheep, bodies, houses, doors, rocks, and fortresses are but a few examples. These objects or qualities, to which we have direct perceptual access, are used to illuminate more abstract theological concepts. Barsalou et al.'s work suggests that we have embodied knowledge of them, since our concepts are likely to be tied to the modes of perception.

---

41   Ibid., 27.

42   Shapiro, *Embodied Cognition*, 105.

43   For a fully-developed theory of concepts which employs Barsalou et al.'s findings, see Jesse J. Prinz, *Furnishing the Mind: Concepts and Their Perceptual Basis* (Cambridge, MA: MIT Press, 2002). For a fuller discussion of empirical evidence and conceptual issues in this area, see Arthur M. Glenberg, Manuel de Vega, and Arthur C. Graesser, eds., *Symbols and Embodiment: Debates on Meaning and Cognition* (Oxford: Oxford University Press, 2008).

44   Barsalou et al., "Embodiment in Religious Knowledge", 48.

45   See George Lakoff and Mark Johnson, *Metaphors We Live By* (Chicago: Chicago University Press, 1980).

THE CORPOREALITY OF RELIGIOUS EXPERIENCE 217

Rituals likewise employ symbols – a cross, bread, or wine – which, like metaphors, ground more abstract concepts in perceptually available objects. The liturgical utterances which accompany these symbols invite participants to engage in particular perceptual tasks or embodied states, such as the imperatives: '*take, eat*, this is my body...', '*drink*...', 'let us pray', '*behold* the lamb of God...' and '*hear* O Israel...' In summary, the theological concepts which articulate and inform our experiences are grounded in the particular perceptual capacities of our bodies.

Body States and Religious Cognition
In addition to the general grounding of theological concepts, the particularities of our embodiment also influence our cognition in religious contexts in a more direct fashion. Various studies have demonstrated that certain bodily manipulations can influence cognition. This implies that body postures and movements in religious practices can contain theological content (albeit inchoate) which is conveyed through embodied participation in these practices.

Crucially, studies have demonstrated a link not only *from* emotional concepts *to* bodily states, but also in the opposite direction. For example, Fritz Strack et al. conducted a study in which participants were asked to hold a pencil in their mouth using their teeth in one condition or their lips in another. Unbeknownst to the participants, holding a pencil with your teeth requires muscles used for smiling whilst using your lips suppresses the use of those muscles. The study found that participants exerting their smile muscles also gave more positive affective responses.[46] Although we often assume that mental states express themselves in bodily movements, such studies demonstrate that bodily states can also influence our cognition.

These general findings from embodied cognition research can be applied to specifically religious settings to reveal how the bodily nature of religious practices participates in our mental lives.[47] More specifically, Barsalou et al. suggest

---

46 Fritz Strack, Leonard Martin, and Sabine Stepper, "Inhibiting and Facilitating Conditions of the Human Smile: A Nonobtrusive Test of the Facial Feedback Hypothesis", *Journal of personality and social psychology* 54/5 (1988), 768–777; Sandra Duclos et al., "Emotion-Specific Effects of Facial Expressions and Postures on Emotional Experience", *Journal of Personality and Social Psychology* 57/1 (1989), 100–108. Nodding and shaking one's head similarly primes positive and negative emotion respectively, see Gail Tom et al., "The Role of Overt Head Movement in the Formation of Affect", *Basic and Applied Social Psychology* 12/3 (1991), 281–289. Barsalou et al., "Embodiment in Religious Knowledge", 31–32.

47 Barsalou et al., "Embodiment in Religious Knowledge", 14, 18–19, 36.

218   TAN

that the mechanism by which body states prime emotion can be deployed in
religious contexts:

> [I]nducing a particular embodiment produced a corresponding mental
> state. Configuring the face into a smile, for example, triggers positive
> emotion, which can similarly result from head nodding and approach
> motions. The embodiments in rituals may have similar effects on mental
> states. Indeed the design of rituals may typically attempt to capitalize on
> such relationships.[48]

Blaise Pascal already intuited this point in the *Pensées*.[49] He recognizes that
participation in embodied religious practices and customs can influence our
'internal' states. The recent studies in cognitive science vindicate this position
and reveal with far greater specificity the way in which bodily states interact
with affective and cognitive processes.

Memory is another domain in which embodiment facilitates religious cognition. Studies show that a memory is more easily recalled when one adopts
the same body posture of the original experience.[50] One study examined how
body posture in religious rituals influences cognition and found that participants who were kneeling (as opposed to sitting) judged events as more miraculous and were more likely to identify objects in photographs as religious.[51] This
suggests that adopting a body posture typically associated with religious ritual
(say kneeling) facilitates memory recall of other experiences in the same posture, reinforcing the continuity of one's religious life. Hence certain religious
bodily manipulations can contribute to cognition both by prompting affective
responses and shaping perception and judgment.

Environmental Factors and Religious Cognition

Not only do religious rituals invite participants to adopt specific body postures, but they can also take place in highly elaborate settings. These rich

---

48   Ibid., 43. See Rebecca Sachs Norris, "Religion, Neuroscience and Emotion: Some
     Implications of Consumerism and Entertainment Culture", in *Religion and the Body:
     Modern Science and the Construction of Religious Meaning*, ed. David Cave and Rebecca
     Sachs Norris (Leiden: Brill, 2012), 105–128 (105,107).

49   Blaise Pascal, *Pensées and Other Writings*, ed. Anthony Levi and Honor Levi (Oxford:
     Oxford University Press, 2008), §250–253.

50   See Katinka Dijkstra, Michael P. Kaschak, and Rolf A. Zwaan, "Body Posture Facilitates
     Retrieval of Autobiographical Memories", *Cognition* 102/1 (2007), 139–149.

51   Michael R. Ransom and Mark D. Alicke, "On Bended Knee: Embodiment and Religious
     Judgements", *Current Research in Social Psychology* 21/9 (2013).

THE CORPOREALITY OF RELIGIOUS EXPERIENCE 219

contexts – including interpersonal interactions, processional patterns, vestments, incense, bells, music, art, and architecture – can also participate in the cognition of those who inhabit them.[52] Given the diversity of these 'environmental' factors of religious practices, one could consider a wide range of material factors and their cognitive dimensions. I shall briefly note a few representative examples which are relevant to ecclesial contexts.

It has long been intuitively held that various types of music have the capacity to elicit different emotions. Empirical studies have borne out this connection and shown that music can modulate affective states in listeners.[53] The affective difference between a funeral dirge and triumphant Easter hymn is readily evident. Researchers have also identified the mechanism by which incense can affect our cognitive states.[54] A study has shown that the burning of frankincense (*boswellia* resin) can contribute to "the euphoric feeling produced during religious functions, due to both positive, presumably mild, emotional effects and the sensation of warmth".[55] A number of studies show that clothes affect both how others perceive someone[56] and the person wearing them.[57] The latter showed that wearing a lab-coat improved performance in attention-related tasks on account of both the symbolic meaning assigned to the coat and the physical experience of wearing the coat. The influence of clothing on cognition suggests that liturgical vestments assist officiants to assume the identity of their office and communicates the office to observers.

In addition to environmental factors impinging on individuals, religious rituals often involve *interactions* between the worshipper and her environment (including other people).[58] The worshipper takes cues from her surroundings

---

52   James, incidentally, comes close to this insight when he strays from his usual focus on the personal and discusses the aesthetic dimension of corporate Christian worship, see James, *Varieties*, 458–460. In this passage, however, he fails to appreciate the ways in which the multi-sensory engagement with the context of worship is contingent on the human body.

53   For a summary of available studies, see John A. Sloboda, *Exploring the Musical Mind: Cognition, Emotion, Ability, Function* (Oxford: Oxford University Press, 2005), 203–224.

54   Arieh Moussaieff et al., "Incensole Acetate, an Incense Component, Elicits Psychoactivity by Activating TRPV3 Channels in the Brain", *The FASEB Journal* 22/8 (2008), 3024–3034.

55   Ibid., 3033.

56   Hajo Adam and Adam D. Galinsky, "Enclothed Cognition", *Journal of Experimental Social Psychology* 48/4 (2012), 918–925 (918).

57   Ibid.

58   In the embodied cognition literature this is sometimes referred to as the 'replacement' hypothesis, which attempts to replace internal mental representations of the external world with interactive models of cognition. See Shapiro, *Embodied Cognition*, 114–157;

and may in turn manipulate them, revealing interdependence between worshipper and environment. Consider a ritually-elaborate Christian Eucharist, for instance. I suspect that most participants, even those who participate in this ritual regularly, would have difficulties writing out a complete and precise order of service from memory. When placed in the ritual context, however, participation becomes second nature after sufficient exposure. This can in large part be ascribed to the interactive dimensions of the liturgy: bells indicate points at which participants make the sign of the cross, the first line of a prayer triggers the remainder of its formulations, verbal cues such as 'let us pray' signal that a kneeling body posture is to be adopted. Much like the way in which drivers can negotiate familiar routes on 'autopilot', performing the required bodily movements without any conscious effort, so too participants 'navigate' a religious ritual using familiar environmental cues. Thus, viewed as a cognitive task, ritual participation is not merely an internal script but an interaction *between* the habituated participant and her environment.

In some instances the cognitive role of the environment is even more pronounced, when cognition can be said to be deferred to an object external to the worshipper.[59] A rosary is an obvious example, as it represents the structure of the prayer in physical form.[60] The number of beads represents repetitions, and the shape of a bead corresponds to a formulation. Hence keeping track of one's stage in the prayer and which formulation comes next is deferred from the working memory to the beads. This allows the person praying to devote their conscious attention elsewhere. Thus the rosary can be said to constitute part of the cognitive task of praying.

If the empirical evidence shows a clear link between practices and our cognition, this connection can nevertheless be a subtle one. The effects are statistically significant across sample groups, and are therefore susceptible to individual variation. The primes introduce biases rather than necessarily being a decisive factor. Moreover, they often influence subjects in an affective or phenomenological manner, which may be difficult to articulate propositionally.[61]

Andrew D. Wilson and Sabrina Golonka, "Embodied Cognition Is Not What You Think It Is", *Frontiers in psychology* 4/58 (2013), 1–13.

59   In the embodied cognition literature this is sometimes referred to as the 'constitution' hypothesis. It attempts to locate physical objects beyond the brain which implement cognition.

60   Barsalou et al., "Embodiment in Religious Knowledge", 48.

61   Mark Wynn, *Faith and Place: An Essay in Embodied Religious Epistemology* (Oxford: Oxford University Press, 2009), 58.

THE CORPOREALITY OF RELIGIOUS EXPERIENCE

All of these factors contribute to the more inchoate nature of the embodied aspects of cognition, in comparison to linguistic articulations. The theological content present in practices may well be less precise and more susceptible to multiple interpretations.[62] Nevertheless, the embodied effects are statistically significant and, although they may only introduce mild biases on their own, we can only assume that if the myriad factors can be deployed harmoniously then the cumulative effect would be profound. Consider, for example, a well 'curated' worship service in which music, architecture, stained-glass windows, movement, gesture, vestments, posture, poise, incense, art, vessels and other liturgical objects are all 'singing off the same hymn sheet', so to speak. In such a context small individual factors can additively create a compelling and holistic experience. What's more, such experiences have the potential to generate pronounced affective changes and even the general resolve for personal transformation. In short, the bodily and environmental dimensions of practices are *meaningful* and can convey theological content.

A Hermeneutics of Embodied Religious Meanings

The science of embodied cognition can clearly provide an insightful hermeneutical tool for understanding how certain embodied forms are appropriated to convey certain meanings or affective content. How then might the meaning derived from the embodied dimension of religious experience fit into a larger meaning-making framework? To address this question I shall consider two contrasting ways in which meaning can attach to embodied practices with a view to exploring their interplay.[63]

The first kind of explanation understands the form of the practice as *symbol*. By symbol, I have in mind the definition of linguistic symbols offered by Ferdinand de Saussure in *Cours de linguistique générale*.[64] De Saussure

---

62 Although one might note that textual theologies are not immune from ambiguities and multiple interpretations, as revealed by disagreements in secondary literature, and thus the difference is one of degree rather than kind. Perhaps this explains why theologians often feel on safer ground engaging with explicit linguistic formulations.

63 See Maia Green, "Medicines and the Embodiment of Substances among Pogoro Catholics, Southern Tanzania", *The Journal of the Royal Anthropological Institute* 2/3 (1996), 485–498. Green notes that in the ritual practices she observes the significance of substances used cannot be reduced to their symbolic representations, but that the physiological and social effect on the participants' bodies must also be considered.

64 Ferdinand de Saussure, *Course in General Lingustics*, ed. C. Bally and A. Sechehaye, trans. A. Riedlinger (New York: McGraw-Hill, 1966).

points out that both written symbols and their spoken phonetic counterparts bear no relation to that which they refer (onomatopoeic words being an obvious exception). Hence the German '*Pferd*', the English 'horse' and the French '*cheval*' can all, despite their total visual and phonetic difference, refer to the same thing. The word comes to refer to its particular referent according to the socially-established linguistic norms. Thus, according to this definition of symbol, the relationship between the symbol and its referent is *arbitrary* and is established by *convention*.

One can then apply this notion of symbol to the meaning of a ritual practice by 'reading' such practices symbolically. This 'reading' attempts to decode the forms of a certain practice, say a body posture, a processional pattern, or the use of an item of material culture, by uncovering the particular symbolic meaning which has been assigned to it. In accordance with our theory of symbols, the connection between the forms of the religious practice and their meanings is arbitrary and is established by convention. To study these symbolic meanings, one therefore needs to interrogate the texts and social institutions which establish and propagate the meaning-making conventions.

In contrast to the symbolic account, a second kind of explanation understands the practice as giving rise to a meaning by virtue of its *embodiment*. These include the corporeal mechanisms for creating meaning which were outlined in the previous section. Unlike the symbolic explanation, according to an embodied explanation the meaning of a religious practice is not arbitrarily attached to its form by convention. Rather it attaches to a particular form by virtue of its bodily manipulation or bodily interactions with the environment. The particularities of the human body determine that certain bodily or environmental states will prompt meanings or ranges of meaning.

To explore the interplay between these two kinds of meaning-making, let us consider the ecclesial practice of kneeling in prayer. Whence does this practice derive its meaning? On the symbolic account, one might suggest that kneeling became associated with humility and submission. This convention is set down by a more general cultural convention, which also, for example, historically saw people kneeling before feudal lords. On the embodied account, however, one observes that kneeling also derives its meaning because of how it configures the human body. By lowering the body and impairing mobility, kneeling embodies submission and vulnerability and thereby communicates humility. If kneeling were exclusively an arbitrary symbol of humility, then presumably doing a handstand would make for an equally apt prayer posture; so long as one were to establish a cultural symbolic convention which associated handstands with humility, the meaning ought to be identical. The bodily effects

THE CORPOREALITY OF RELIGIOUS EXPERIENCE

of kneeling, however, make it the better suited to prayer offered by a humble supplicant.

The example of kneeling demonstrates that the two sets of factors are inexorably intertwined. Although it is helpful to distinguish between these two types of factors to tease out the distinctiveness of embodied meanings, they cannot be definitively considered in isolation from one another in any given context. Both classes of meaning can layer on each other, together participating in the creation of meaning. One can easily imagine situations in which the two kinds of meaning push in opposite directions, a 'conflict of interpretations' as Paul Ricoeur would put it. For example, if someone has endured an experience of abuse in a church context, the negative symbolic associations triggered by an ecclesial setting are likely to override any positive affective valence produced by an embodied presence or practice in such a setting. Conversely, one could imagine a religious ritual involving the consumption of a strong hallucinogenic or psychoactive substance, such that in the first instance the physiological effects of the substance drown out any symbolic meaning one might wish to attach to the ritual.

Given the interplay between these two types of meaning, both symbolic and embodied meanings ought to be considered part of a religious tradition. Moreover, both symbolic and embodied meanings are simultaneously experienced – we can receive and comprehend them – and yet they also count as mediating expressions – they can communicate aspects of our experiences to others. Both are caught up within a social and historical reality of a 'tradition', understood as an epistemic category in the philosophical hermeneutics of Hans-Georg Gadamer.

In *Truth and Method*, Gadamer attempts to rehabilitate the categories of tradition, authority and 'prejudice'.[65] For Gadamer, the enlightenment's suspicion of these categories and its attempt to establish an objective view from nowhere is simply implausible. He argues that we cannot stand totally outside of the authoritative traditions which we inherit, as these traditions supply the prejudices – or, less pejoratively, the pre-judgments – which we use as a framework to make new judgments. This is true "even where life changes violently, as in ages of revolution, far more of the old is preserved in the supposed transformation of everything than anyone knows".[66] For Gadamer, this situation is not to be lamented; the pre-judgments of our tradition are necessary since

---

65 Hans-Georg Gadamer, *Truth and Method*, 2nd, revised ed. (New York: Crossroad, 1989), 277.

66 Ibid., 281.

they provide us with the conditions for the possibility of making decisions; we cannot begin with a blank slate. As a result human knowledge is historically contingent and ensconced in the particularities of our place in history.[67]

Gadamer's emphasis on situating knowledge can be readily extended from the historical to the material and corporeal. Indeed, as is often the case for locutions about time, to say that knowledge is 'historically *situated*' or forms a '*horizon*' is already to employ spatial metaphors to express the historical contingency of knowledge.[68] Embodied cognition (sometimes glossed as 'situated cognition') extends Gadamer's insight to include the way that knowledge is situated in beings in particular bodies and environments. We are not merely disembodied minds floating through time, but are situated in history as embodied creatures.

If we understand embodied ecclesial practices as part of a 'tradition' thus conceived, we begin to appreciate that we not only learn from the embodied practices we engage with, but they also form the context from within which we reason. Embodied practices are not simply specialist exercises in which we, as autonomous individuals, may or may not choose to participate (although one can opt in or out of particular embodied practices, one cannot opt out of all practices and embodiment *tout court*). Rather we are immersed in embodied practices from the outset; they shape and form us and they provide the background against which thinking and theorizing takes place. By integrating embodied practices into the concept of 'tradition', we can extend Gadamer's hermeneutical account of knowledge: our knowledge is not only temporally situated in a specific historical tradition; it is also spatially and corporeally situated in the particularities of our bodies and environments.

By embedding the embodied content present in religious practices within a larger hermeneutical framework, I hope to have avoided two extremes. On the one hand, together with James, I've sought to reject reductionist physiological explanations of religious experience. There is no one-to-one correspondence between a bodily state and a resulting religious experience. Rather, the inchoate content provided by the embodied nature of ritual practices is but one input into a larger context of meaning-making. On the other hand, arguably contra to James, this approach does not reject a physiological contribution to religious experience *tout court*. Instead I have attempted to outline a positive and nuanced account of how corporeal factors may contribute to and be interpreted within our religious experiences.

---

67   Ibid., 276.
68   Ibid., 269–274.

James largely focuses on *mental* experiences which are expressed *textually*. By extending James's category of religious experience to include the ritual and institutional dimensions, we are able to capture the corporeal dimensions of religious experience. Moreover, by providing a thicker description between how practices and meanings interrelate, embodied cognition illuminates the interdependence between experience and expression. Embodied practices both influence the subject and have the potential to publically communicate meaning; they are simultaneously experiences and expressions.

Literature

Adam, Hajo, and Adam D. Galinsky, "Enclothed Cognition", *Journal of Experimental Social Psychology* 48 (2012), 918–925.

Barsalou, Lawrence W. et al., "Embodiment in Religious Knowledge", *Journal of Cognition and Culture* 5 (2005), 14–57.

Carrette, Jeremy R., "Passionate Belief: William James, Emotion and Religious Experience", in *William James and the Varieties of Religious Experience: A Centenary Celebration*, ed. Jeremy R. Carrette (London: Routledge, 2005), 79–93.

De Saussure, Ferdinand, *Course in General Lingustics*, ed. Charles Bally and Albert Sechehaye, trans. Albert Riedlinger (New York: McGraw-Hill, 1966).

Dijkstra, Katinka, Michael P. Kaschak, and Rolf A. Zwaan, "Body Posture Facilitates Retrieval of Autobiographical Memories", *Cognition* 102 (2007), 139–149.

Duclos, Sandra et al., "Emotion-Specific Effects of Facial Expressions and Postures on Emotional Experience", *Journal of Personality and Social Psychology* 57 (1989), 100–108.

Edelman, Gerald M., *Bright Air, Brilliant Fire: On the Matter of the Mind* (London: Allen Lane, 1992).

Gadamer, Hans-Georg, *Truth and Method*, trans. Joel Weinsheimer and Donald G. Marshall (New York: Crossroad, 1989).

Glenberg, Arthur M., Manuel de Vega, and Arthur C. Graesser, eds., *Symbols and Embodiment: Debates on Meaning and Cognition* (Oxford: Oxford University Press, 2008).

Green, Maia, "Medicines and the Embodiment of Substances among Pogoro Catholics, Southern Tanzania", *The Journal of the Royal Anthropological Institute* 2 (1996), 485–498.

Harnad, Stevan, "The Symbol Grounding Problem", *Physica D: Nonlinear Phenomena* 42/1–3 (1990), 335–346.

James, William, "What Is an Emotion?", *Mind* 9 (1884), 188–205.

James, William, "The Physical Basis of Emotion", *Psychological Review* 1 (1894), 516–529.

James, William, *The Varieties of Religious Experience: A Study in Human Nature* (London: Longmans, Green and Co., 1902).

James, William, *The Principles of Psychology*, ed. Fredson Bowers, Frederick Burkhardt, and Ignas K. Skrupskelis., vol. 2 (Cambridge, MA: Harvard University Press, 1981), 1058–1097.

Lakoff, George, and Mark Johnson, *Metaphors We Live By* (Chicago: Chicago University Press, 1980).

Lash, Nicholas, *Easter in Ordinary: Reflections on Human Experience and the Knowledge of God* (London: University of Notre Dame Press, 1990).

Moussaieff, Arieh et al., "Incensole Acetate, an Incense Component, Elicits Psycho-activity by Activating TRPV3 Channels in the Brain", *The FASEB Journal* 22 (2008), 3024–3034.

Pascal, Blaise, *Pensées and Other Writings*, ed. Anthony Levi and Honor Levi (Oxford: Oxford University Press, 2008).

Prinz, Jesse J., *Furnishing the Mind: Concepts and Their Perceptual Basis* (Cambridge, MA: MIT Press, 2002).

Ransom, Michael R., and Mark D. Alicke, "On Bended Knee: Embodiment and Religious Judgements", *Current Research in Social Psychology* 21 (2013).

Sachs Norris, Rebecca, "Religion, Neuroscience and Emotion: Some Implications of Consumerism and Entertainment Culture", in *Religion and the Body: Modern Science and the Construction of Religious Meaning*, ed. David Cave and Rebecca Sachs Norris (Leiden: Brill, 2012), 105–128.

Searle, John R., "Minds, Brains, and Programs", *Behavioral and Brain Sciences* 3 (1980), 417–424.

Shapiro, Lawrence A., *Embodied Cognition* (New York: Routledge, 2011).

Sloboda, John A., *Exploring the Musical Mind: Cognition, Emotion, Ability, Function* (Oxford: Oxford University Press, 2005).

Strack, Fritz, Leonard Martin, and Sabine Stepper, "Inhibiting and Facilitating Conditions of the Human Smile: A Nonobtrusive Test of the Facial Feedback Hypothesis", *Journal of personality and social psychology* 54 (1988), 768–777.

Taylor, Charles, *Varieties of Religion Today: William James Revisited* (Cambridge, MA: Harvard University Press, 2002).

Tom, Gail et al., "The Role of Overt Head Movement in the Formation of Affect", *Basic and Applied Social Psychology* 12 (1991), 281–289.

Vásquez, Manuel A., *More Than Belief: A Materialist Theory of Religion* (Oxford: Oxford University Press, 2011).

Watts, Fraser, "Embodied Cognition and Religion", *Zygon* 48 (2013), 745–758.

Wilson, Andrew D., and Sabrina Golonka, "Embodied Cognition Is Not What You Think It Is", *Frontiers in Psychology* 4 (2013), 1–13.

Wynn, Mark, *Faith and Place: An Essay in Embodied Religious Epistemology* (Oxford: Oxford University Press, 2009).

CHAPTER 13

Religious Experience in Fourteenth-Century Mystical Writing: The Revelations of Elsbeth von Oye

Johannes M. Depnering

Mystical texts contain descriptions of ecstatic visions and auditions, which often directly relate to exceptional experiences of physical pain. Pain, in this context, is conceived as an indication of God's great love, which becomes apparent in the suffering of Christ. This construction of pain as proximity to the divine is particularly prominent in the case of a fourteenth-century nun of the Dominican convent Ötenbach in Zurich, Elsbeth von Oye (c. 1289–1339). She offers explicit descriptions of torment, her self-inflicted mortification, and mystical experiences in a surviving autograph (Zurich, Central Library, Ms. Rh 159) – a rare case for the vernacular. Despite the large number of female biographical and autobiographical texts from medieval Germany, none of the sources possess such a degree of immediacy in their description of sensory experiences as this text. Unusually, it is written in the first person perspective.[1] Furthermore, in contrast to comparable mystical accounts from the same period, such as those of Margareta Ebner (1291–1351) and Dorothea von Montau (1347–1394), there was no involvement of a confessor who might have influenced the content of the descriptions, in order to assure favourable treatment in subsequent canonization processes.[2] By looking at the comparatively

---

1 In this regard, Elsbeth's writing differs from what is considered to be the earliest surviving autobiography in English, *The Book of Margery Kempe*. It is attributed to the mystic Margery Kempe (*c.* 1373–after 1439), whose scribe transferred most of her narration into the third person. See Nicholas Watson, "The Making of 'The Book of Margery Kempe'," in *Voices in Dialogue: Reading women in the Middle Ages*, ed. Linda Olson and Kathryn Kerby-Fulton (Notre Dame, IN: University of Notre Dame Press, 2005), 395–434.

2 See Urban Federer, *Mystische Erfahrung im literarischen Dialog: Die Briefe Heinrichs von Nördlingen an Margaretha Ebner* (Berlin: De Gruyter, 2011), who analyses the written conversation between Margareta Ebner and her confessor, the priest Henry of Nördlingen. Several Latin accounts and one German version of Dorothea von Montau's life were written by her confessor Johannes Marienwerder and later used to support the long-drawn out process of her canonization. See David Wallace, *Strong Women: Life, Text, and Territory, 1347–1645* (Oxford: Oxford University Press, 2011), 1–61, and Almut Suerbaum and Annette Volfing (eds.),

---

© KONINKLIJKE BRILL NV, LEIDEN, 2016 | DOI 10.1163/9789004328600_015

eccentric and lesser known revelations of Elsbeth, this essay seeks to contribute to the ongoing discussion about mystical experience, a specific kind of religious experience, here understood as the immediate contact and union of the soul with the divine in this life.[3] Elsbeth's account is particularly suitable, as it does not exhibit a secondary interpretation of her experience, but rather her own description, where interpretation and experience seem almost intrinsically connected.

Only minimal scholarly work has been undertaken on this text, due to the lack of an edition of the Zurich manuscript,[4] but also because of its problematic, if not confusing, character. When Peter Ochsenbein presented his re-discovery of the revelations of Elsbeth at a conference in 1984, he declared them in the subsequent discussion as pathological and masochistic, and concluded that "a God who wants what is being described here, is no longer a God, but the devil".[5] The first and only major study on the manuscript, an unpublished dissertation by Klaus Haenel from 1958, resulted in the unchallenged hypothesis that it is indeed Elsbeth's own writing.[6] However, Haenel's conclusion to classify the manuscript as a 'diary' has been strongly criticized. As Elsbeth's self-torment and mystical experiences apparently took place in privacy, Peter Ochsenbein generally agreed that her manuscript could be viewed as a private, diary-like document; ultimately, however, he rejected this notion and concluded that it was, from the very beginning, intended for other readers.[7] According to him, Elsbeth was not concerned with verbalizing her mystical experiences, rather with mystical teaching and justification in the context of ascetic exercises.[8]

Dorothea von Montau and Johannes Marienwerder: Constructions of Sanctity (Oxford: Modern Humanities Research Centre, 2010).

3 An excellent overview of the past and recent discourses is provided by Jerome Gellman, "Mysticism", in *The Stanford Encyclopedia of Philosophy* (Spring 2014 Edition), ed. Edward N. Zalta, http://plato.stanford.edu/archives/spr2014/entries/mysticism/ (accessed 30 December 2014).

4 I would like to thank Wolfram Schneider-Lastin who provided me with a draft version of his edition, from which I have taken the quotations.

5 Klaus Kirchert, "Diskussionsbericht zur Vorlage von Peter Ochsenbein," in *Abendländische Mystik im Mittelalter: Symposion Kloster Engelberg 1984*, ed. Kurt Ruh (Stuttgart: Metzler, 1986), 473–475 (473).

6 Klaus Haenel, *Textgeschichtliche Untersuchungen zum sogenannten "Puchlein des Lebens und der Offenbarung Swester Elsbethen von Oye"*, (PhD Diss., University of Göttingen, 1958).

7 Peter Ochsenbein, "Die Offenbarungen Elsbeths von Oye als Dokument leidensfixierter Mystik", in Kurt Ruh, *Abendländische Mystik*, 423–442 (436).

8 Ibid.

RELIGIOUS EXPERIENCE IN FOURTEENTH-CENTURY MYSTICAL WRITING 229

Research of recent years by Burkhart Hasebrink and Gregor Wünsche dissociates itself completely from any biographical reading.[9] Reflecting upon their textual constructedness only, Hasebrink characterizes Elsbeth's revelations as a "construction of an inconstant religious identity, which aims to constitute itself in a literary process of iterativity, comprising narrative and comment simultaneously".[10] Following Hasebrink's approach, Wünsche concludes that leaving any biographical evidence aside, "in some respects frees scholarship from unnecessary dead weight".[11] In contrast to this, the aim of my approach is to restore, to a certain degree, the historicity of this text by differentiating between potentially reality-based experiences and literary motifs. At the same time, I seek to obviate the other extreme, which considers mystical texts as essentially factual report.[12] My argument, rather, is that both Elsbeth's experience and writing have inevitably been influenced by her social and cultural context, and that, for this reason, her account should be seen as more than mere fiction and also considered as an attempt at attributing meaning to her challenging situation as well as self-affirmation.

Elsbeth von Oye: The Manuscript and Revelations

Elsbeth's manuscript, Ms Rh 159, is a small codex with 89 parchment leaves in eight quires that measure approximately 9 × 7 cm, and was written in the third or fourth decade of the fourteenth century – certainly in the later stages of Elsbeth's life. Resulting from the fact that the autograph was composed and written in various stages, the text has no clear structure.[13] It is conspicuous

---

9   Burkhard Hasebrink, "Elsbeth von Oye: Offenbarungen", in *Literarische Performativität. Lektüren vormoderner Texte*, ed. Cornelia Herberichs and Christian Kiening (Zurich: Chronos, 2008), 259–279; Gregor Wünsche, *Präsenz des Unerträglichen: Kulturelle Semantik des Schmerzes in den "Offenbarungen" Elsbeths von Oye*, (PhD Diss., University of Freiburg, 2008); Gregor Wünsche, "Die 'Offenbarungen' Elsbeths von Oye im Kontext der dominikanischen Johannesfrömmigkeit im 14. Jahrhundert", in *Schmerz in der Literatur des Mittelalters und der Frühen Neuzeit*, ed. Hans-Jochen Schiewer, Stefan Seeber, and Markus Stock (Göttingen: V&R Unipress, 2010), 167–190.

10 Gregor Wünsche, *Präsenz des Unerträglichen*, 260.

11 Ibid., 64.

12 This position is particularly represented by Peter Dinzelbacher, "Zur Interpretation erlebnismystischer Texte des Mittelalters", in *Mittelalterliche Frauenmystik*, ed. Peter Dinzelbacher (Paderborn: Schöningh, 1993), 304–331.

13 On the challenges of editing Elsbeth's revelations, see Wolfram Schneider-Lastin, "Das Handexemplar einer mittelalterlichen Autorin: Zur Edition der Offenbarungen Elsbeths von Oye," *editio* 8 (1994), 53–70.

230 DEPNERING

in its constant iteration, both regarding the content and linguistically, with numerous entries using the same arrangement, initially describing the exercise that she had carried out (e.g., hurting herself with the cross), followed by an introductory clause and her audition in direct speech (e.g., "Then it was spoken: 'You have ...'").[14] However, a palaeographical and layout analysis shows that it was certainly not written, nor corrected, in the heat of the moment, but more likely copied from earlier notes written on scrap parchment. Concrete references to time and space are rare, but Christmas is mentioned twice (33,14; 85, margin),[15] and together with the occasionally named saints' days, one can assume that Elsbeth's account covers a period of several years. Based on a later apology, presumably written by a Dominican friar in the margins and blank leaves at the end of the manuscript in the second half of the fourteenth-century (160–178), which refers to several *büchlinen* ('little books'), it has been speculated that several manuscripts of this kind may have existed.[16] However, none have survived.

The main, and only, topic of her writing is Elsbeth striving for compassion with the suffering of Christ and, subsequently, the experience of a mystical union with God. According to her description, Elsbeth wore a cross with nails, which was bound to her body with a belt that, again, has been covered with nails, for several years. She was hardly able to breathe and the nails penetrated deep into her flesh. The following quotation describes the act of wearing the cross. Remarkably, it is preceded by a parallel narration of her scourging

---

14 "Do wart gesprochin also: 'Du hast ...'" (12, 3–5).

15 All references in round brackets relate to the modern pagination and lines in manuscript Zurich, Central Library, Ms. Rh 159.

16 The most convincing argument relates to Elsbeth's *Vita* in the so-called *Ötenbacher Schwesternbuch*, which was written shortly after her death by a Dominican friar who integrated parts of her revelations into it. In view of the extent of the *Vita*, the author must have had at least one, if not several, of her little books at his disposal. The *Ötenbacher Schwesternbuch* survived in a single copy, which was written at St Catherine's convent in Nuremberg around 1460. The second volume, which contains Elsbeth's *Vita*, has only been discovered at the University Library of Wrocław (Breslau) in 1995; see Wolfram Schneider-Lastin, "Die Fortsetzung des Ötenbacher Schwesternbuchs und andere vermißte Texte in Breslau", *Zeitschrift für deutsches Altertum und deutsche Literatur* 124 (1995), 201–210. An edition of the *Vita* has been published by Wolfram Schneider-Lastin, "Leben und Offenbarungen der Elsbeth von Oye: Textkritische Edition der Vita aus dem 'Ötenbacher Schwesternbuch', in *Kulturtopographie des deutschsprachigen Südwestens im späteren Mittelalter: Studien und Texte*, ed. Barbara Fleith and René Wetzel (Berlin: De Gruyter, 2009), 395–467.

RELIGIOUS EXPERIENCE IN FOURTEENTH-CENTURY MYSTICAL WRITING   231

in her childhood or early youth, highlighting the persistence of her self-mortification:[17]

> I was quite young, when I made myself a scourge with needles and scourged myself with it, so that they stuck so deep in my flesh that I could hardly pull them out. I stick my cross mostly ⟨always⟩ so painfully into my flesh, that when I sometimes want to release myself from it, I have to loosen it from the flesh, like you loosen a seal out of wax.[18]

The reference to self-harm during her childhood is also noteworthy in view of psychological studies, which found that hearing voices and traumatic (infantile) experiences, including and particularly child abuse,[19] strongly correlate with each other.[20] Here, however, the physical trauma is self-inflicted and described as a very conscious action of the young persona, in which the lack of any emotions, context, or effect of the scourging, is striking.

In addition to the cross, Elsbeth wears her garment until it begins to rot on her body and worms appear gnawing on her body. When she asks God how it is possible within the divine order that she, being alive, has become food for worms, he replies by quoting Psalm 22:7, "*Ego autem sum vermis, et non homo*" (39,1–2; "but I am a worm, and no man"). Subsequently, she not only resists fighting off the vermin, but, in further imitation of Christ, binds herself with a rope, as Christ was bound when being judged.

Elsbeth has numerous experiences of hearing voices and enters a dialogue predominantly with God and Christ, but also the Holy Spirit, Mary and St John

---

17   The translations are by myself and follow the original very closely, aiming to reflect its style.

18   "Ich was gar jung, do ich mir selber machte ein geisil mit nadeln unt ville mich da mit, also daz si mir gar dike alz tieffe gestekt in dem fleische, daz ich si kum herwider uz geziche. Ich steke min krúze meistlich ⟨alle zit⟩ also pinlich in min fleische, so ich mir selber etwen damitte entlibin wil, daz ich ez uzer dem vleische losen mûs, als man ein in gisigel loset uz einem wachse." (77,13–78,7). The use of angle brackets follows the edition by Schneider-Lastin, indicating text that Elsbeth has added subsequently in the margin or above the line, in order to correct or clarify.

19   Sandra Escher et al., "Determinants of outcome in the pathways through care for children hearing voices", *International Journal of Social Welfare* 13 (2004), 208–222. See also the recent historical and psychological study on auditory verbal hallucinations by Simon McCarthy-Jones, *Hearing Voices: The Histories, Causes, and Meanings of Auditory Verbal Hallucinations* (Cambridge: Cambridge University Press, 2012).

20   Marius A. J. Romme and Alexandre D. M. A. C. Escher, "Hearing Voices", *Schizophrenia Bulletin* 15 (1989), 209–216.

232 DEPNERING

the Evangelist. Wearing the cross stands in direct relation to the imitation of the Passion of Christ and in one of the auditions, she even hears him saying: "You are crucified with me, so that your cross makes mine greening and blooming in the heart of the people who had forgotten about it".[21] We find God stating that he explicitly uses her as an example to show the effect of his divine power and Elsbeth feels internally that he urges her to write everything down (77,1–12) – from a textual perspective, this is clearly also a strategy to attach divine authority to her writing and being urged by God or superiors to write down experiences or thoughts is a rather common topos. Whenever she is struggling with the pain caused by her cross, the divine voices encourage her to endure it. What is more, the pain is directly connected with the perceived presence of God.[22] If she takes off her cross, she distances herself from him and falls into despair, which appears to her even more painful than the physical pain. God's voice explains to her that her physical pain is not her own pain – as Christ has already suffered for her, it is his pain.

Finally, and this is the most controversial aspect of Elsbeth's writing, she describes the repeated exchange of bodily fluids – blood and marrow – with God and Christ. Christ's blood flows into her and her own blood, running from the wounds caused by her cross, runs into Christ, while God, by contrast, pours his marrow (*marc*) into her soul. This exchange of fluids – which can be interpreted as a kind of reciprocal Eucharistic unification – is embedded in metaphorical language of thirst and burning, desert and saturation. Elsbeth, or rather her soul, and Christ celebrate the Eucharist with each other's blood:

> Thus was spoken to me: "I have put my opened/broken open wound into the mouth of your soul, so that it [*the mouth*] always drinks at this place all the desire of your heart".[23]

The divine voice, in return, states that he had a supernatural drink from the innermost blood of her heart (100,12–14) and in a different passage: "Whatever

---

21 "'Du bist mit mir gekruzeget, also daz din krúze min krúze wider grúnende unt blúgende machen sol in der luteherzen, dien ez gar tödmig unt vergezzinlich worden was.'" (81,13–82,3).

22 See Monika Gsell, "Das fließende Blut der 'Offenbarungen' Elsbeths von Oye", in *Deutsche Mystik im abendländischen Zusammenhang: Neu erschlossene Texte, neue methodische Ansätze, neue theoretische Konzepte; Kolloquium, Kloster Fischingen 1998*, ed. Walter Haug and Wolfram Schneider-Lastin (Tübingen: Niemeyer, 2000), 455–482, (463).

23 "Alzo wart gesprochin zů mir: 'Den uf bruch miner wundon hab ich gileitet in den munt diner sele, daz er da alle zit trinke alle die bigirde dines herzen.'" (47aʳ).

RELIGIOUS EXPERIENCE IN FOURTEENTH-CENTURY MYSTICAL WRITING 233

blood I drink ⟨now⟩ from your crucifixion, that shall subsequently become marrow in you".[24]

Erasure Marks

Self-harm and hearing God's and Christ's voice in such a way is controversial, even in a fourteenth-century Dominican convent. An intriguing aspect of the manuscript is, therefore, the erasure marks, which can be found throughout the manuscript and have been exercised systematically with regard to the content, but unprofessionally and in an uncontrolled manner, with the partial omission of words. The deletion of any text implies that it was unwanted and it reflects a subsequent reaction: either the phrases were meant to be rewritten, or they were meant to be extinguished on account of their controversial content. In this case, it was almost certainly the latter.[25] The erased phrases almost exclusively deal with the exchange of fluids with God and Christ, union, and allusions to nourishing and feeding. The contemporary apology at the end of the manuscript, added some years or decades after Elsbeth's death and addressed to her, provides a complete list:

> Four aspects of your reading have been erased, first, where she talks of a re-flowing into the divine nature, second, of union or mixture, third, of the sacrament, fourth, that God had taken meat and drink from her.[26]

---

24 "[Swaz ich ⟨nu⟩ blůtes trinke von diner kruzegunge, daz sol her na zi marge werden in dir.]" (133,7–9).

25 The editor of the text, Wolfram Schneider-Lastin, attributes "numerous cases" of erasing to Elsbeth herself, but without referring to concrete pages or passages. In contrast to the hypothesis that some kind of supervisor was involved, perhaps the prioress, he considers "internal and external circumstances" as reason for Elsbeth to erase certain formulations. See Wolfram Schneider-Lastin, "Das Handexemplar", 58–61. However, while there is clear evidence of rephrasing and editing by Elsbeth, there is no textual or material indication whether the erasures have been executed during or after her lifetime. For this reason, and due to the lack of page references or any external evidence, Schneider-Lastin's interpretation of the erasures as act of revision, reflecting Elsbeth's authorial competence, is not convincing.

26 "An vier sinnen ist din lesen getilget, zem ersten, da si redet von eim wider infliessen in götlich natur, zem andren mal von vereinung oder vermischung, zem dritten von sacrament, zem vierden, daz got von ir spis und trank hab genomen." (164,14–165,7).

The apology, written most likely by a well-educated cleric or friar, reflects that despite the problematic nature of the content of Elsbeth's writing, there was appreciation among contemporaries. He calls her a martyr, compares her with St Gregory and St Augustine whose books were burnt because the world did not understand, and vehemently condemns the erasures. The following selection of quotations shall provide an overview of what exactly has been erased.[27] In the first, God states that it is his eternal will to assimilate Elsbeth with Christ, making Elsbeth's and Christ's nature equal (*vernaturen*):

> It has been my eternal will that my only begotten son would deliver humankind with his death of his cross, as it was my eternal will to impart onto you and equal your nature with his equality.[28]

While it is not completely clear what marrow exactly refers to in the following quotation, it seems to be her blood running from her body, which 'marrows' – perhaps 'nourishes' or 'provides with the innermost essence' – God: "If your cross dismarrows you, then it does marrow me".[29] At a later stage, Elsbeth has adopted the nature of Christ, however the process of Christ's sucking the *inadern* continues. This term usually translates as bowels, but given the context, it might rather refer to her veins:

> You are the purest, most united, similar and incorporated creature, who ever flew from my father's heart, and therefore I am longing forever to suck the innermost veins of your soul. This shall be true.[30]

In the course of the text, God is increasingly heard as strict, demanding and – from a modern perspective – almost cruel and the phrase referring to God's wish (*Got wollte*), which does not appear at the beginning, can later be found numerous times in the text. Furthermore, one can trace an emerging

---

27 Square brackets indicate erasures, the majority of which could be reconstructed by means of a magnifying glass and a UV lamp. See Wolfram Schneider-Lastin, "Das Handexemplar", 59.

28 "Alz daz min ewig wille gewesen ist, daz mir min einborner sun menschelich kunne loste mit dem tode sins krúzes, alz ist daz min ewig wille gewesen, dir eginnen [unt vernaturen] sin glicheit." (11,9–15).

29 "[Entmerget dich din krúze, so merget ez aber mich]" (26,8–9).

30 "[Du bist du luterst, vereintest gilichste ingnaturtest creatur einú, dú von minem] veterlichen herzen ie gevloz, unt darumbe ist mir gar girlich, alle zit [ze sugenne die inresten inadern diner sele]. Diz werde war." (43,13–44,5).

RELIGIOUS EXPERIENCE IN FOURTEENTH-CENTURY MYSTICAL WRITING

pattern in which Elsbeth first hurts herself and subsequently hears a voice speaking to her:

> At one time, I had hurt myself painfully with my cross. Then it was spoken quite endearingly: "I suck all the time from you, should I not again pour the most sweetest marrow of my divine nature into you?"[31]

The phrasing of this last quotation is exemplary for many similar passages. The divine speaks to her only as a result of her 'painful pain' caused by the cross. Extreme sensory stimulation is thus a necessary means to evoke the voices. What is more, the stronger the blood streams, it seems, the higher is the equality with Christ. God's voice accordingly states: "I want from you the most bloody equality with my crucified son".[32] Finally, God even expresses a wish to become actively involved in the nun's self-harm, by opening her vein with the nails of Christ's cross as the instrument: "I want to open the blood flowing vein of your cross with the bloody nails of the cross of my crucified son".[33]

The Experience of God's Voice Speaking

The revelations of Elsbeth are not narratives that provide a model to imitate or inspire other nuns seeking to practice meditation and a contemplative life.[34] This is particularly visible in the second part of the manuscript (125–166),[35] which differs in content and structure and was the original reason for me to consider this text not merely as fiction, but also as the interpretation of real experiences. The former repetitive framework, the dialogue structure and the focus on the cross and exchange of bodily fluids, disintegrates at the same time as the page layout, style and quality of the writing deteriorates and the number of abbreviations increases. Elsbeth's writing becomes almost like a stream of thought and we now find metatextual remarks about it, which can

---

31   "Ich hat mich zi einer zit gar pinlich gepint mit minem krúze. Do wart gesprochen gar minneklich: '[Ich suge doch alle zit] von dir, sollte ich denne nit dir wieder ingiezzin daz allersúzzeste marg miner gottlicher natur?'" (51,15–52,3).

32   "'Ich wil von dir die aller blútigisten [glicheit mins kruzgeten suns].'" (94,12–13).

33   "'[Die blút giezzinden runsader dins krúzes will ich dir uf sliezzin mit dien blútigen nagiln des krúzes mins kruzgeten suns.]'" (98,6–10).

34   One could reach such a conclusion from the use of colour for the initials and the page layout in the first part of the manuscript.

35   See Wolfram Schneider-Lastin, "Das Handexemplar", 56–57.

236 DEPNERING

be understood both as reference to the composition of the text, and as a direct statement reflecting on her experience:

> For a pretty long time, I have had a suffering that was so strange that I cannot describe [*or*: write] it. And whenever I have such particular pain from it, then I feel quite like a human who unknowingly was shot with an arrow or cut with a knife. And then my whole body shivers and shakes, and my hands and arms are beating up and down, so that nobody would believe it, if he would not see in presence the strong change that happens to me at that time. Also, this pain does not touch me as long as I carry my cross, and also when I am alone, and when I suffer this particular pain with rationality, with thought of and desire to God. And the greater the desire is, the more painful is the suffering, and shortly the rationality is being overthrown from the suffering. Currently, I do not feel the pain anymore.[36]

The immediacy of this account is striking, despite the lack of any references to a concrete context, point of time, or space. Elsbeth seems to have achieved what Nikola Grahek has defined as "painfulness without pain", "the full dissociation of affective components of human pain experience from its sensory-discriminative components".[37] According to her description, she has – at least temporarily – lost her sensitivity to pain, as her sensory pain has become distinct from her mental pain and suffering: Elsbeth is in pain, but unable to feel it.[38] The sensation of pain caused by the cross, earlier described as almost punitive, has been transformed into an integrative element of her relationship to God.

---

36 "Ich habe etwie lange ein lidunge gihebt, dů so gar vrômde ist, daz ich ez nit wol gischribin kan. Unt swenne ich sunderlichin pin da von habe, so ist mir recht alz einem menschen, daz unwizzinde gischôzzin wirt mit einem phile oder gistochin mit einem mezzer. Unt denne wirt aller min lib ziternde unt schutinde unt min hende unt arme uf unt nider slaginde, daz ez nieman giloplich ist, wan der geginwertiklich gisehin môchti den starkin wandel, der sich zi der zit ôgit an mir. Ôch girůrit mich dirre pin nit, wan so ich min krúze trage unt ôch so ich alleine bin unt so ich disen pin mit sunderlicher meinunge unt gerunge gotte lide mit vernunst. Unt so du gerunge ie grôzer ist, so du lidunge ie pinlicher wirt, unt alz balde du vernust vellit von der lidunge. Geginwertiklich bivinde ich der pine nicht mere." (157,1–21).

37 Nikola Grahek, *Feeling Pain and Being in Pain* (Cambridge, MA: MIT Press, 2007), 7.

38 On Grahek's distinction between "feeling pain" and "being in pain", and the clinical studies which support bases his concept of "painfulness without pain", see ibid., 95–140.

RELIGIOUS EXPERIENCE IN FOURTEENTH-CENTURY MYSTICAL WRITING   237

What exactly is taking place here on a phenomenological level and how does the social context – the Dominican convent – shape the experiences about which Elsbeth is writing? Ariel Glucklich, in his studies on 'Sacred Pain', refers to a similar account of a mystic and provides a convincing explanation. He draws on the Gate Control Theory by Ronald Melzack and Patrick Wall,[39] according to which "a mechanism in the spinal cord controls the flow of neuronal stimuli from the body's peripheries to the brain, where the pain is registered. The gate mechanism operates by means of signals that "descend" from the brain to the gate and inhibit the incoming signals".[40] In the same way that sensory deprivation can lead to hallucinations, a sensory overload – caused, for example, by strapping a cross to your body – can cause what he terms a "reverse hallucination", that is, the "shrinkage of mental experience and the weakened experience of the body".[41] Although this is a, more or less, intentional manipulation, it takes place subconsciously.[42] Glucklich has further pointed out the significance of culture, in this case the Christian context, in this kind of experience. "A Christian mystic will not experience a vision of Kali or a bodhisattva but will draw on material incorporated through learning and memorization within his or her cultural context. In the absence of incoming stimulation of any sense modality, such stored neuronal information [what we know about religion] begins to overfire and produce the phenomenal experiences, which may be visual, auditory, or consist of other phantoms".[43] McCarthy-Jones and colleagues note similarly: "Voice-hearers' pre-existing spiritual worldviews... may offer a coherent framework to make sense of voice-hearing".[44] If one carries this through, one reaches the conclusion that Elsbeth inevitably would hear the voice of the divine and no other entities, because she conceptualized an imitation of Christ from the beginning; as she says, already as a child. Against this background and despite Elsbeth's struggling, suffering and occasional doubting of her actions, pain – and thus subconscious control over

---

39   Ronald Melzack and Patrick D. Wall: "Pain Mechanisms: A New Theory", *Science* 150 (1965), 971–978.

40   Ariel Glucklich, *Sacred Pain: Hurting the Body for the Sake of the Soul* (New York: Oxford University Press, 2001), 52–53.

41   Ibid., 59.

42   Ariel Glucklich, "Self and Sacrifice: A Phenomenological Psychology of Sacred Pain", *The Harvard Theological Review* 92 (1999), 479–506 (479).

43   Ibid., 494.

44   Simon McCarthy-Jones et al., "Spirituality and Hearing Voices: Considering the Relation", *Psychosis* 5 (2013), 247–258 (248).

238   DEPNERING

her consciousness – becomes a meaningful tool rather than a problem one has
to evade.[45]

At first glance, Glucklich's observations correspond perfectly with the
strong constructivist position among mysticism scholars, according to which
the cultural and religious background forms and determines the experience
of the mystic. As Steven T. Katz has prominently stated: "*There are* NO *pure
(i.e. unmediated) experiences....* [T]he experience itself as well as the form
in which it is reported is shaped by concepts which the mystic brings to, and
which shape, his experience".[46] Katz continues: "Again, the Christian mystic
does not experience some unidentified reality, which he then conveniently
labels God, but rather has at least partially prefigured Christian experiences
of God, or Jesus, or the like".[47] Accordingly, following on from this assumption,
a distinction between experience and interpretation cannot be made, as they
are directly intertwined. While the constructivist position considers mystical
or any other religious experience exclusively as a product of cultural shaping, one of its most recent critics, Ann Taves, proposes a different approach.
While acknowledging that the meaning of an experience is influenced by a
cultural framework,[48] she also considers the option of a multi-stage, 'building-
block' process, in which the person who had an experience reflects upon it –
interprets it – and attributes meaning that may not be directly determined by
his or her culture:

> Things that strike people as special are (among) the basic building blocks
> of religion. Ascriptions of specialness may take place below the threshold
> of awareness; when this happens, it tends to make things seem inher-
> ently special. People can decide, upon reflection, that things that seem
> special are more or less special than they initially seemed. In the process
> of reflection, special things may be caught up in pre-existing systems of
> belief and practice, may generate new or modified beliefs and practices,
> or may lose their specialness and become ordinary.[49]

---

45   See Ariel Glucklich, "Self", 485.

46   Steven T. Katz, "Language, Epistemology, and Mysticism," in *Mysticism and Philosophical
      Analysis*, ed. Steven T. Katz (New York: Oxford University Press, 1978), 22–74 (26).
      Emphases in the original.

47   Ibid.

48   Ann Taves, *Religious Experience Reconsidered: A Building-Block Approach to the Study of
      Religion and Other Special Things* (Princeton, NJ: Princeton University Press, 2009), 118.

49   Ibid., 162.

RELIGIOUS EXPERIENCE IN FOURTEENTH-CENTURY MYSTICAL WRITING 239

Applied to the case of Elsbeth, almost all experiences of hearing voices and their interpretation take place on a non-conscious level, thus making it impossible to ask if this could be considered an interpretation of experience, or an experience of interpretation, constructed and shaped by her cultural background. However, there is one instance which might allow for such a distinction. Following one of her first dialogues with God, Elsbeth states that she took a rest from her crucifixion exercise, aware that this was against God's will.[50] Immediately, she hears God's encouraging voice, which explains that as unnatural as it might seem for her to suffer, as natural and endearing it is for him (28,9–12). Shortly after, we learn about a different concern relating to her practice:

> I have had a lot of fear that this exercise would perhaps not be from God, because it is in many ways completely foreign. I showed this to God. Then it was spoken quite endearingly: 'What have you ever given to me, that I would not take care all the time with paternal affection as endearingly as I ever did to any creature'.[51]

Elsbeth was afraid that her exercise – and therefore the voice speaking to her – was not divine, which implies that it could also have been considered demonic.[52] The situation described neither fits completely with the constructivist nor the attribution model. Elsbeth describes a situation of reflection and interprets her experience in a conscious and causal way. However, instead of drawing a conclusion and attributing the experience to a divine or demonic realm herself, this decision is taken from her and, one could argue, non-consciously externalized: as before, God himself intervenes and resolves all doubt that the voice and the exercise are of divine origin. The impact of Elsbeth's cultural framework is so strong that it does not allow for any attribution process. Her effort to independently interpret her experience fails, and interpretation and experience become coalesced for good. In view of this, and in light of the material evidence (the manuscript) and the textual evidence (the traumatic and mystical experiences), I would argue that this text can be

---

50 "Wan es was nit gottes wille, dez wart ich wol inne" (28,6–8).

51 "Ich han dike vorchte gehebt, daz disù ûbunge vil lichte nit von gotte si, wan si alz gar vrômde ist in etlicher wis. Diz zeigte ich gotte. Do wart gesprochin gar minneklich: 'Waz sache hastu mir ie darzů gegebin, daz ich din nit alle zit hûte mit veterlicher herzeklicheit alz minneklich, alz ich ie getet dekeiner creature?'" (29,15–30,3).

52 For a brief history of hearing voices and the discourse of discerning demonic from divine voices, see Simon McCarthy-Jones, *Hearing Voices*, 11–37.

perceived not merely as a literary phenomenon, but also as an attempt at self-affirmation and meaning-making in a highly stressful situation.[53] On a more general level, it is a significant example of a comparatively immediate account of religious experience, which is so fundamentally shaped by culture that interpretation and experience are virtually indistinguishable. It could, therefore, be argued that we should review in the same way comparable sources of religious expression, which display a similarly complex relationship between the subconscious and conscious, physical and textual, as well as reality and literary topoi.

Literature

Dinzelbacher, Peter, "Zur Interpretation erlebnismystischer Texte des Mittelalters", in *Mittelalterliche Frauenmystik*, ed. Peter Dinzelbacher (Paderborn: Schöningh, 1993), 304–331.

Escher, Sandra et al., "Determinants of outcome in the pathways through care for children hearing voices", *International Journal of Social Welfare* 13 (2004), 208–222.

Federer, Urban, *Mystische Erfahrung im literarischen Dialog: Die Briefe Heinrichs von Nördlingen an Margaretha Ebner* (Berlin: De Gruyter, 2011).

Gellman, Jerome, "Mysticism", in *The Stanford Encyclopedia of Philosophy* (Spring 2014 Edition), ed. Edward N. Zalta, http://plato.stanford.edu/archives/spr 2014/entries/mysticism/ (accessed 30 December 2014).

Glucklich, Ariel, "Self and Sacrifice: A Phenomenological Psychology of Sacred Pain", *The Harvard Theological Review* 92 (1999), 479–506.

Glucklich, Ariel, *Sacred Pain: Hurting the Body for the Sake of the Soul* (New York: Oxford University Press, 2001).

Grahek, Nikola, *Feeling Pain and Being in Pain* (Cambridge, MA: MIT Press, 2007).

Gsell, Monika, "Das fließende Blut der 'Offenbarungen' Elsbeths von Oye", in *Deutsche Mystik im abendländischen Zusammenhang: Neu erschlossene Texte, neue methodische Ansätze, neue theoretische Konzepte; Kolloquium, Kloster Fischingen 1998*, ed. Walter Haug and Wolfram Schneider-Lastin (Tübingen: Niemeyer, 2000), 455–482.

---

53   See Crystal L. Park, "Making Sense of the Meaning Literature: an Integrative Review of Meaning Making and its Effects on Adjustment to Stressful Life Events", *Psychological Bulletin* 136 (2010), 257–301. See also Monika Gsell, "Das fließende Blut", 461, who considers that Elsbeth's writing could have served as mechanism to cope and create meaning of her internal processes.

Haenel, Klaus, *Textgeschichtliche Untersuchungen zum sogenannten "Puchlein des Lebens und der Offenbarung Swester Elsbethen von Oye"*, (PhD Diss., University of Göttingen, 1958).

Hasebrink, Burkhard, "Elsbeth von Oye: Offenbarungen", in *Literarische Performativität. Lektüren vormoderner Texte*, ed. Cornelia Herberichs and Christian Kiening (Zurich: Chronos, 2008), 259–279.

Katz, Steven T., "Language, Epistemology, and Mysticism," in *Mysticism and Philosophical Analysis*, ed. Steven T. Katz (New York: Oxford University Press, 1978), 22–74.

Kirchert, Klaus, "Diskussionsbericht zur Vorlage von Peter Ochsenbein," in *Abendländische Mystik im Mittelalter: Symposion Kloster Engelberg 1984*, ed. Kurt Ruh (Stuttgart: Metzler, 1986), 473–475.

McCarthy-Jones, Simon et al., "Spirituality and Hearing Voices: Considering the Relation", *Psychosis* 5 (2013), 247–258.

McCarthy-Jones, Simon, *Hearing Voices: The Histories, Causes, and Meanings of Auditory Verbal Hallucinations* (Cambridge: Cambridge University Press, 2012).

Melzack, Ronald and Patrick D. Wall: "Pain Mechanisms: A New Theory", *Science* 150 (1965), 971–978.

Ochsenbein, Peter, "Die Offenbarungen Elsbeths von Oye als Dokument leidensfixierter Mystik", in Kurt Ruh, *Abendländische Mystik*, 423–442.

Park, Crystal L., "Making Sense of the Meaning Literature: an Integrative Review of Meaning Making and its Effects on Adjustment to Stressful Life Events", *Psychological Bulletin* 136 (2010), 257–301.

Romme, Marius A. J. and Alexandre D. M. A. C. Escher, "Hearing Voices", *Schizophrenia Bulletin* 15 (1989), 209–216.

Schneider-Lastin, Wolfram, "Das Handexemplar einer mittelalterlichen Autorin: Zur Edition der Offenbarungen Elsbeths von Oye," *editio* 8 (1994), 53–70.

Schneider-Lastin, Wolfram, "Die Fortsetzung des Ötenbacher Schwesternbuchs und andere vermißte Texte in Breslau", *Zeitschrift für deutsches Altertum und deutsche Literatur* 124 (1995), 201–210.

Schneider-Lastin, Wolfram, "Leben und Offenbarungen der Elsbeth von Oye: Textkritische Edition der Vita aus dem 'Ötenbacher Schwesternbuch', in *Kulturtopographie des deutschsprachigen Südwestens im späteren Mittelalter: Studien und Texte*, ed. Barbara Fleith and René Wetzel (Berlin: De Gruyter, 2009), 395–467.

Suerbaum, Almut and Annette Volfing (eds.), *Dorothea von Montau and Johannes Marienwerder: Constructions of Sanctity* (Oxford: Modern Humanities Research Centre, 2010).

Taves, Ann, *Religious Experience Reconsidered: A Building-Block Approach to the Study of Religion and Other Special Things* (Princeton, NJ: Princeton University Press, 2009).

Wallace, David, *Strong Women: Life, Text, and Territory, 1347–1645* (Oxford: Oxford University Press, 2011), 1–61.

Watson, Nicholas, "The Making of 'The Book of Margery Kempe'," in *Voices in Dialogue: Reading women in the Middle Ages*, ed. Linda Olson and Kathryn Kerby-Fulton (Notre Dame, IN: University of Notre Dame Press, 2005), 395–434.

Wünsche, Gregor, "Die 'Offenbarungen' Elsbeths von Oye im Kontext der dominikanischen Johannesfrömmigkeit im 14. Jahrhundert", in *Schmerz in der Literatur des Mittelalters und der Frühen Neuzeit*, ed. Hans-Jochen Schiewer, Stefan Seeber, and Markus Stock (Göttingen: V&R Unipress, 2010), 167–190.

Wünsche, Gregor, *Präsenz des Unerträglichen: Kulturelle Semantik des Schmerzes in den "Offenbarungen" Elsbeths von Oye*, (PhD Diss., University of Freiburg, 2008).

CHAPTER 14

Speaking of God: Ludwig Wittgenstein and the Paradox of Religious Experience

Brian Klug

In their introduction to this volume the editors call religious experience a "puzzle". The puzzle lies in the tension between, on the one hand, the abundance of material that gives expression to religious experience and, on the other hand, the commonplace that it is in the nature of such experience that it is inexpressible. There is a version of this puzzle in Ludwig Wittgenstein's 'A Lecture on Ethics' (1929), where he raises the question of what phrases like 'absolute good' and 'absolute value' mean. His approach to the question focuses on certain experiences in which he himself is liable to use such phrases. They turn out to be, in every case, experiences that can be expressed by speaking of God. His assessment of these experiences is paradoxical. On the one hand, he finds them compelling. On the other hand, he considers the utterances in which they are given expression to be strictly nonsensical. This paradox was a function of his whole approach to the philosophy of logic and language (at the time); or, which comes to the same thing in his case, his whole approach to philosophy.

The essay falls into three parts.[1] In the first part I broach the difficulty of discussing a philosopher who appears to have two personas – one associated with one *magnum opus* and the other associated with another – and explain the angle from which I am examining his thought. This is a prelude to the second and longest part of the essay, where I set out the paradox of religious experience as it presented itself to him in 'A Lecture on Ethics' and discuss

---

1 In this essay I draw on my paper "Grammar from Heaven: The Language of Revelation in Light of Wittgenstein", presented to the Oxford Seminar in Advanced Jewish Studies, June 2013, with thanks to the other participants for their comments. In the background is my five-week seminar "Wittgenstein on Culture and Religion" at the International Centre for Muslim and Non-Muslim Understanding, University of South Australia, Adelaide, August–September 2012. I am grateful to Salman Sayyid and everyone else who took part for their stimulating contribution to discussion. I owe an incalculable debt to Jack Montgomery (Saint Xavier University, Chicago) for illuminating Wittgenstein's thought in innumerable conversations over many years.

© KONINKLIJKE BRILL NV, LEIDEN, 2016 | DOI 10.1163/9789004328600_016

the predicament in which it left him. In the third and final part I ask how we should understand the philosophical task that the ethics lecture sets. I suggest that the task is not to *resolve* the paradox but to *figure* it better: 'better' precisely by way of preserving what, *au fond*, it expresses. This is one of a number of suggestions that, taken together, add up to a starting-point for a rereading of his later work. The essay ends on the brink of this rereading.

Which Wittgenstein?

Some people say that Wittgenstein was the greatest philosopher of the twentieth century. They are wrong. He was the *two* greatest. He was the author of the *Tractatus Logico-Philosophicus*, published in 1921 when he was in his early thirties, and of *Philosophical Investigations*, which appeared in 1953, two years after his death at the age of 62.[2] Both the *Tractatus* and the *Investigations* (which is how they are usually cited and which is how I shall refer to them from now on) are widely regarded by philosophers as seminal works, hugely influential for the course that (analytic) philosophy would take. They also tend to be seen as fundamentally opposed in their approaches to philosophy. Wittgenstein himself appears to take this view. In his preface to the *Investigations* he writes:

> Four years ago I had occasion to re-read my first book … and to explain its ideas to someone. It suddenly seemed to me that I should publish those old thoughts and the new ones together: that the latter could be seen in the right light only by contrast with and against the background of my old way of thinking.[3]

'Old way of thinking' (*ältere Denkweise*) is a slightly understated way of referring to the whole turn of mind in which he tackled philosophy in the *Tractatus*.[4] He adds in the next sentence that over the years he has "been forced to recognize

---

2 Both works were written in German, though the *Investigations* first appeared in an English translation. The first English edition of the *Tractatus* was in 1922. When I cite the *Tractatus* I refer to the translation by David F. Pears and Brian McGuinness (London: Routledge and Kegan Paul, 1961). When I cite the *Investigations* I refer to the translation by Gertrude E. M. Anscombe (Oxford: Blackwell, 1967, third edition), unless I indicate otherwise.

3 Wittgenstein, *Investigations*, viii.

4 *Denkweise* could also be translated as 'style of thought' or 'style of thinking'. Compare Marie McGinn, *Wittgenstein and the* Philosophical Investigations (London: Routledge, 1997), 10, 20, 21, 23. Again, 'style' should not be taken as indicating something superficial – style as opposed to substance.

SPEAKING OF GOD 245

grave mistakes" in his first book.[5] 'Mistakes' is, similarly, misleading if it suggests his treatment of certain questions or problems and not others; it is the entire approach of his early work – his old *Denkweise* – that he came to regard as mistaken. The *Investigations*, from start to finish, subjects the earlier work to a sustained critique. (This is largely implicit, though occasionally he uses the *Tractatus* to illustrate the error of his old ways.) The two works are so divergent in the way they approach philosophy (or so it seems at first sight) that they might almost have been written by two different people.

Furthermore, each book had a separate sphere of influence. The *Tractatus* was praised by philosophers with a scientific cast of mind, such as Bertrand Russell, and was greeted by the logical positivists of the Vienna Circle in the 1920s as a breakthrough.[6] The *Investigations*, in contrast, inspired post-war 'ordinary language' philosophy, which was thoroughly *anti*-positivist and equally hostile to Russell's take on philosophy. Thus, whether judged by content or by reception, the *Tractatus* and the *Investigations* appear to be so diverse that the title of my essay invites the following question: Which Wittgenstein do I mean? The younger or the older? The philosopher of the old *Denkweise* or the new?

I mean both. I mean the *one* Wittgenstein who is, as it were, the substratum of both: the single thinker who persists through the sea change from his earlier to his later 'way of thinking'.

In his book on Wittgenstein, Anthony Kenny, while not denying the *discontinuities*, emphasizes the "continuity of Wittgenstein's thought".[7] Kenny disputes "the idea that Wittgenstein had fathered two wholly dissimilar and disconnected philosophies", a view that he calls "too simple".[8] He devotes the final chapter of the book to refuting this view, enumerating the "many connections between the earlier and the later work, and many assumptions common to both"[9] in Wittgenstein's treatment of topics in philosophy of logic and

---

5 *Investigations*, viii, xxii.

6 Russell was an advocate of 'the scientific outlook', the title of his 1931 book. In his Introduction to the first English edition of the *Tractatus*, Russell said the book was "a work of extraordinary ... importance". Contrast this with his verdict, years later, on the *Investigations*: "Its positive doctrines seem to me trivial and its negative doctrines unfounded. I have not found ... anything that seems to me interesting and I do not understand why a whole school finds important wisdom in its pages", *My Philosophical Development* (London: Allen and Unwin, 1959), 216.

7 Anthony Kenny, *Wittgenstein* (London: Penguin, 1975), vii. Kenny is not alone in emphasizing this.

8 Ibid., 219.

9 Ibid.

language. Moreover, in Kenny's view, there is "the permanence of his general conception of philosophy".[10] But this is not what I am alluding to. By the *substratum* of the younger and older Wittgenstein I do not mean the threads that connect his technical work nor even a view of philosophy that straddles the two periods. I mean something that lies deeper; something at the bottom of his work in technical philosophy; something like the man himself.

What I mean by 'the man himself', along with the bearing that this perspective has on the way that the paradox of religious experience presents itself to Wittgenstein, will emerge in the course of the essay. But the general point I am seeking to make would not be lost on Wittgenstein who, in a number of remarks, looked through the philosopher, as it were, to the person behind or within. His friend and former student Maurice O'Connor Drury tells us that Wittgenstein often applied the words 'deep' and 'shallow' to thinkers, calling Immanuel Kant (for example) deep and Alfred J. Ayer (for example) shallow.[11] Drury thinks that the difference between 'deep' and 'shallow' is implied in Wittgenstein's observation that "the distinction between a philosopher and a very clever man is a real one and of great importance".[12] When (in the same conversation) Drury says that William James is "such a human person", Wittgenstein responds: "That is what makes him a good philosopher; he was a real human being."[13] I am inclined to put these various comments together and to say that for Wittgenstein good philosophy grows from the roots: the *human* roots of thinking. When he says simply "Let us be human", I take him to mean (or at least to imply): *as philosophers* let us be human.[14] It might be relevant

---

10 Ibid., 229.

11 Maurice O'Connor Drury, "Some Notes on Conversations with Wittgenstein", in *Recollections of Wittgenstein*, ed. Rush Rhees, (Oxford: Oxford University Press, 1984), 76–96 (80).

12 Ibid. In a similar vein, he once wrote that "the greatness, or triviality, of a work depends on where its creator stands", Ludwig Wittgenstein, *Culture and Value*, ed. Georg H. von Wright (Oxford: Blackwell, 1998), 56e.

13 Drury, "Conversations with Wittgenstein", in *Recollections of Wittgenstein*, 97–171 (106). By the same token, the young Wittgenstein felt the positive influence of James on him as a person. In 1912, when he was twenty-three, he wrote to Russell to say that he reads *The Varieties of Religious Experience* whenever he has time, a book that he thinks can "improve" him, Letter to Bertrand Russell, 22 June 1912, in *Wittgenstein in Cambridge: Letters and Documents 1911–1951*, ed. Brian McGuinness (Chichester: Wiley-Blackwell, 2012), 30.

14 Wittgenstein, *Culture and Value*, 36e. In a way, this is the obverse of what Socrates says at his trial when he calls the unexamined life *ou biōtos anthrōpō*, no life for a human being (Plato, *Apology* 38a). In other words, *as human beings* let us be philosophers.

SPEAKING OF GOD 247

that Wittgenstein thought that "by far the most profound thinker of the last century" was Søren Kierkegaard.[15]

Speaking Nonsense

To get our bearings with 'A Lecture on Ethics' it helps to go back to the *Tractatus*, the *locus classicus* for Wittgenstein's 'old way of thinking'. Although it is true that, as Ray Monk points out, "There is no consensus on how that book should be interpreted",[16] the standard view is that essentially the *Tractatus* is, as its full name suggests, a treatise on philosophical logic, including the formal properties of language. The text seems to bear this out: almost the entire contents are taken up with giving an account of the nature of a (meaningful) proposition and the formal relationship between language and the world – picturing possible states of affairs – that marks the difference between speaking sense and speaking nonsense (*Unsinn*). The text touches on certain other topics that are familiar from the history of philosophy, such as solipsism, realism and freedom of the will, but only briefly and purely in pursuit of the "aim of the book", which, as the preface states, is "to set a limit to thought, or rather – not to thought, but to the expression of thoughts".[17] The bulk of the book consists in setting out and working through these (purely logical) limits.[18] There is, in particular, no explicit discussion of religion.

---

15 Drury, "Some Notes on Conversations with Wittgenstein", 87. Not that his admiration was uncritical. In a conversation in 1948 he complained to Drury that Kierkegaard "is too long-winded; he keeps on saying the same thing over and over again", Drury, "Conversations with Wittgenstein", 158. This might make Kierkegaard tedious but it does not make him shallow.

16 Ray Monk, *How to Read Wittgenstein* (London: Granta Books, 2005), 1. (See also 29–30.) Monk points out there is also no consensus "on how his later work, *Philosophical Investigations*, ought to be read, or again on the extent to which the later work repudiates the earlier" (1). A similar comment might be made about Plato, Kant and other philosophers of similar stature. While acknowledging the point, a reader must be robust enough to stake an interpretive claim about their works; otherwise there is a danger of being rooted to the spot, unable to utter a critical thought or tender an intelligible reading. The more complex the thought of a philosopher, the more chancy the task of interpretation. You just have to chance your arm.

17 Wittgenstein, *Tractatus*, 3.

18 Famously, or notoriously, Wittgenstein concludes by pulling the rug out from under his own text: "My propositions serve as elucidations in the following way: anyone who understands me eventually recognizes them as nonsensical, when he has used them – as steps – to climb up beyond them" (prop. 6.54). So, the propositions that set the limits

Until, that is, the final sequence of propositions (from 6.4 to 7), which occupy the last few pages of the work. Suddenly, the topic of God appears in its own right for the first time, along with ethics and the mystical (*das Mystische*).[19] On the standard view, this irruption of the transcendent at the end of the *Tractatus* is puzzling: what are God, ethics and the mystical doing in a rigorous treatise on technical questions in the philosophy of logic and language? One explanation is to dismiss the final sequence of propositions as eccentric, an idiosyncrasy of the author tacked on to the end of the work, from which it is detachable. This, more or less, is how Wittgenstein's philosophical admirers at the time, such as the logical positivists, saw the matter, politely discarding the material they could not stomach. But there is another way of seeing these propositions: as the *culmination* of the work rather than as an afterthought; or even as the *mainspring* of the work. The *Tractatus*, I am inclined to say, works its way towards its own source, which lies within the author himself.

I am inclined to say this partly in view of a letter that Wittgenstein sent Ludwig von Ficker, a prospective publisher of the *Tractatus*, in 1919.[20] He wrote: "the point of the book is ethical".[21] As we shall see when we come to 'A Lecture on Ethics', by 'ethical' he meant this: pertaining to *absolute* good and *absolute* value: good or valuable without qualification; and (as we shall also see) the ethical in *this* sense is, for Wittgenstein, ineluctably personal (which emphatically is *not* to say subjective). He might have written to Ficker that the point of the book is religious, as he saw religion and ethics as going hand in hand. "What is good is divine too", he wrote in the same year in which he gave the ethics lecture. "That, strangely enough, sums up my ethics."[22] Or as he remarked to Friedrich Waismann the following year: "If there is any proposition expressing precisely what I think, it is the proposition 'What God commands, that is good'".[23] – The letter to Ficker continued thus:

exceed the limits they set. Much ink has been spilled in writing about this paradox and Wittgenstein's 'throwaway ladder'. But for the purposes of this essay I am passing over it in silence.

19 'God' occurs in proposition 3.031 and 'a god' in 5.123 but purely in the general context of logic. 'God and Fate' are mentioned in 6.372, but only in the context of the status of the laws of nature.

20 Ficker was one of many publishers he approached before the first German edition eventually appeared in *Annalen der Naturphilosophie* in 1921.

21 Letter 23 of "Letters to Ludwig von Ficker" (undated), in *Wittgenstein: Sources and Perspectives*, ed. C. Grant Luckhardt, (Ithaca, NY: Cornell University Press, 1979), 94.

22 Wittgenstein, *Culture and Value*, p. 5e.

23 Wittgenstein quoted in *Ludwig Wittgenstein and the Vienna Circle: Conversations Recorded by Friedrich Waismann*, ed. Brian McGuinness (Oxford: Blackwell, 1979), 115.

SPEAKING OF GOD   249

> I once wanted to give a few words in the foreword which now actually
> are not in it, which, however, I'll write to you now because they might
> be a key for you: I wanted to write that my work consists of two parts: of
> the one which is here, and of everything which I have *not* written. And
> precisely the second part is the important one.[24]

The 'second part', the 'important one', would have been the part on ethics (or
religion). If he did not write it, this is because (as the *Tractatus* itself clarifies)
it *could* not be written but only, as it were, indicated. The upshot of propositions 6.4 to 7 is that regarding ethics and God nothing can be said: ethical
and religious propositions do not describe or picture states of affairs in the
world (and there are no states of affairs *except* in the world) as they contain
signs to which no meaning is assigned. They are examples of what happens
when someone wants "to say something metaphysical":[25] what they utter is
nonsense. So, taken as a whole, the logico-philosophical treatise that constitutes the *Tractatus* is like an index finger pointing to the unwritten – and non-
writable – part, the part on ethics; this pointing being the point of the book.[26]

If this is the light in which to see the propositions on God, ethics and the
mystical then Wittgenstein appears to be left, at the end of the work, in the
following position. On the one hand, his general account of the nature of language and the world, set out in the body of the *Tractatus*, renders religious
and ethical propositions nonsensical. On the other hand, ethics and religion
are what are most important. It seems to follow that the things that are most
important are nonsensical; which itself seems nonsensical. It is a paradox.

This paradox pervades 'A Lecture on Ethics', which Wittgenstein gave at a
time when his thought was still constrained by the overall framework of the
Tractatus,[27] and which closes with these words:

---

24   Letter 23, 94.

25   *Tractatus*, proposition 6.53.

26   Compare Paul Engelmann, *Letters from Wittgenstein with a Memoir*, trans. L. Furtmüller,
     ed. Brian McGuinness (New York: Horizon Press, 1967), 94–99. See also Allan Janik and
     Stephen Toulmin in their *Wittgenstein's Vienna* (New York: Simon and Schuster, 1973),
     where they refer to the *Tractatus* as an "ethical deed" (24).

27   I say 'overall' because he had changed his mind on certain points under pressure of objec-
     tions from Ramsey and others. In particular, as Rush Rhees points out, by the time he gave
     the lecture he no longer thought that it was possible to give "a general account of proposi-
     tions in terms of truth functions", "Some Developments in Wittgenstein's View of Ethics",
     Philosophical Review, 74 (1965), 17–26 (19). Nonetheless, he continued to think of language
     "primarily as description" (Ibid.) and, as far as I am aware, description continues to mean
     for him what it means in the *Tractatus*: the formal picturing of (possible or actual) facts.

My whole tendency and I believe the tendency of all men who ever tried to write or talk Ethics or Religion was to run against the boundaries of language. This running against the walls of our cage is perfectly, absolutely hopeless. Ethics so far as it springs from the desire to say something about the ultimate meaning of life, the absolute good, the absolute valuable, can be no science. What it says does not add to our knowledge in any sense. But it is a document of a tendency in the human mind which I personally cannot help respecting deeply and I would not for my life ridicule it.[28]

Before engaging with the image of language as a cage, we need to be clear about his use of the term 'science' for that realm of discourse which does *not* give rise to a sense of imprisonment by words. Wittgenstein wrote the lecture in English, but usually he wrote in German, his mother tongue. *Wissenschaft* has a wider meaning than the English word 'science'. It denotes, roughly, learning or scholarship in general: any systematic pursuit of knowledge in accordance with established methods of research. *Die Wissenschaften* include not only 'sciences' in the narrow sense but branches of learning and enquiry in general. So, when Wittgenstein refers to science it is safe to assume that he is using the word in the wider sense of *Wissenschaft* unless he indicates differently. In *this* case, he indicates that this *is* how he is using the word, for after saying that ethics "can be no science" he adds at once: "What it says does not add to our knowledge *in any sense*" (emphasis added).

If ethical and religious discourses do not add to our knowledge, what *do* they do? Or rather, what do they *try* but *fail* to do? For, in the image of the cage with which he closes his lecture, Wittgenstein depicts the efforts of ethics or religion in "running against the boundaries of language" or "the walls of our cage" as "perfectly, absolutely hopeless". It is a striking image but a cage is precisely what language, as he himself conceived it at the time, is not. He knew this full well. He says so himself in a conversation with Waismann the following year: "Running against the limits of language? Language is, after all, not

---

So, any departure from the original framework of the *Tractatus* does not affect the argument of this essay.

28 Wittgenstein, "A Lecture on Ethics" in Ludwig Wittgenstein, *Philosophical Occasions: 1912–1951*, ed. James C. Klagge and Alfred Nordmann (Indianapolis, IN: Hackett, 1993), 36–44 (44). First published in *Philosophical Review* 74/1 (1965), 3–12. The lecture, which was given to a general audience of the Heretics Club in Cambridge on 17 November 1929, was, "the only 'popular' lecture he ever gave in his life", Ray Monk, *Ludwig Wittgenstein: The Duty of Genius* (London: Vintage, 1991), 277.

SPEAKING OF GOD 251

a cage."[29] Why not? Because if it *were* a cage there would be an inside and an outside and both would be *in* the world; whereas the 'boundaries' or limits of language are (according to the *Tractatus*) the limits *of* the world. That is to say, the logical form of propositions mirrors the form of the world (or of reality, *Wirklichkeit*). So, if there is no going beyond the world – beyond possible or actual states of affairs – this is not because of iron bars or walls but because of an iron necessity: the necessity of the *a priori*.

One word for this *a priori* necessity – my word not his – is finitude. The *Tractatus* is suffused with a sense of a limit that does not lie within the limits of the finite; and which therefore is inexpressible. "The aim of this book", he wrote in the preface, "is to set a limit to thought, or rather – not to thought, but to the expression of thoughts; for in order to be able to set a limit to thought, we should have to find both sides of the limit thinkable (i.e. we should have to be able to think what cannot be thought)."[30] If language were really a kind of cage then we would be able to think what cannot be thought; for we could 'see' – think – outside it: we would be able (if only in our mind's eye) to gaze upon the open range beyond our reach. He continues: "It will therefore be in language that the limit can be set, and what lies on the other side of the limit will simply be nonsense."[31]

In the ethics lecture Wittgenstein uses another image to express the inexpressibility of ethics (and, along with ethics, religion). It involves a contrast between two books. One book contains "the whole description of the world".[32] This is the 'world-book'.[33] In it, "all propositions stand on the same level": they are all about facts: "facts, facts and facts but no Ethics".[34] The other book is the ethics book. "It seems to me obvious", he says, "that we cannot write a scientific book, the subject matter of which could be intrinsically sublime and above all other subject matters."[35] And then comes the image: "I can only describe my feeling by the metaphor that, if a man could write a book on Ethics, this book would, with an explosion, destroy all the other books in the world."[36] The 'could', I take it, is logical rather than psychological, and the 'explosion',

---

29   McGuinness, *Ludwig Wittgenstein and the Vienna Circle*, 117.

30   Wittgenstein, *Tractatus*, 3.

31   Ibid.

32   Wittgenstein, "A Lecture on Ethics", 39.

33   Ibid.

34   Ibid., 39, 40. Compare proposition 6.4 in the *Tractatus*: "All propositions are of equal value." Also, the book called *The World as I found it* in 5.631, which contains facts but no subject, no I.

35   On 'scientific', see above.

36   Wittgenstein, "A Lecture on Ethics", 40.

likewise, logical rather than physical. Imagine the explosion this way: after the logical dust settles, all the other books in the world (including the world-book) contain nothing but gibberish, their pages littered with meaningless combinations of letters – combinations that previously were meaningful. Meaning falling out of words: this would be the logical fallout of a logical explosion. For the ethics book, if it could be written, would be a unique book in which the normal bipolarity of sense and nonsense is reversed.

Wittgenstein at once tries to elucidate the metaphor of the explosive ethics book, using yet another metaphor to do so:

> Our words used as we use them in science, are vessels capable only of containing and conveying meaning and sense, *natural* meaning and sense. Ethics, if it is anything, is supernatural and our words will only express facts; as a teacup will only hold a teacup full of water [even] if I were to pour out a gallon over it.[37]

So, given the logical limits inherent in language, given that our words are mere teacups, the ethics book *could* not be written. Which prompts a question that Wittgenstein goes on to ask and then answer: "Then what have all of us who, like myself, are still tempted to use such expressions as 'absolute good,' 'absolute value,' etc., what have we in mind and what do we try to express?"[38] This brings us to the version of the puzzle of religious experience as I find it in the lecture.

Wittgenstein introduces his answer to his question this way: "Now whenever I try to make this clear to myself it is natural that I should recall cases in which I would certainly use the expressions".[39] He describes these cases via certain experiences and, significantly, he identifies the experiences via the things he is inclined to say when he has them. I say 'significantly' because this is a departure from the *Tractatus*. Proposition 6.45 mentions a mystical experience: "Feeling the world as a limited whole – it is this that is mystical." But the text does not provide a way of *identifying* this 'feeling' (*Gefühl*), of picking it out from other 'feelings' or experiences. In 'A Lecture on Ethics' we are, so to speak, given a handle on such experiences; and the handle is verbal.

There are three cases in point. The first he calls "my experience *par excellence*".[40] Here is the account he gives of it: "I believe the best way of

---

37   Ibid.
38   Ibid.
39   Ibid.
40   Ibid., 41.

SPEAKING OF GOD 253

describing it is to say that when I have it *I wonder at the existence of the world*. And I am then inclined to use such phrases as 'how extraordinary that anything should exist' or 'how extraordinary that the world should exist'."[41] The second experience is that of "feeling *absolutely* safe"; and again he identifies the experience via the words with which he gives utterance to it: "I mean the state of mind in which one is inclined to say 'I am safe, nothing can injure me whatever happens.'"[42] The third case (which he does not elaborate) is the experience "of feeling guilty".[43] In each case, he equates the utterances he is inclined to make with an utterance about God. The first experience, wondering at the existence of the world, "is exactly what people were referring to when they said that God had created the world".[44] The author of the book of Genesis, for instance. The second, feeling absolutely safe, "has been described by saying that we feel safe in the hands of God".[45] Psalm 23 comes to mind: "Though I walk through a valley of deepest darkness, I fear no harm, for You are with me".[46] The third, feeling guilty, is "described by the phrase that God disapproves of our conduct".[47] Here I think of Eve and Adam in Eden, hiding from God in the early evening (Gen. 3:8–10). Thus the three cases meet in speaking of God.

In giving expression to the three experiences, Wittgenstein is, so to speak, writing the ethics book – or the second part of the *Tractatus*, the part that he told Ficker in his letter is "the important one", the part that is unwritten, unwritten because non-writable. But if it is non-writable, how can he be writing it? It is a paradox; and what Wittgenstein gives with one hand he takes away with the other. The handle he gives us on these three experiences turns out to be an illusion, for the experiences are inexpressible. Consider again the metaphor of the explosive ethics book: the book that explodes the world-book along with every other book in the world. The point of the metaphor is the opposite of what it says. It says the book is explosive, but actually the ethics book *im*plodes. And so, when Wittgenstein steps back from the three experiences that he has put into words, he *rounds* on those words: "the first thing I have to say is, that the verbal expression which we give to these experiences is nonsense! If I say

---

41   Ibid.
42   Ibid.
43   Ibid., 42.
44   Ibid.
45   Ibid.
46   Translation as in *JPS Hebrew-English Tanakh* (Philadelphia, PA: The Jewish Publication Society, 1999), 1436.
47   Wittgenstein, "A Lecture on Ethics", 42.

'I wonder at the existence of the world' I am misusing language."[48] Thus, before the ink can dry on the page, the utterances are drained of their meaning.

And yet the experiences are compelling: this is what I understand him to mean when he says, "Now the three experiences which I have mentioned to you (and I could have added others) seem to those who have experienced them, *for instance to me*, to have in some sense an intrinsic, absolute value".[49] In each case he is *inclined* to say such-and-such; but more than a mere inclination seems to be involved. Take his "experience *par excellence*", the one he uses as his "first and foremost example".[50] This is the experience that inclines him to say: 'how extraordinary that the world should exist'. The utterance seems to demand an exclamation mark. It is more like a cry that is drawn from him involuntarily than an opinion or judgment.[51] He is *struck* by the existence of the world: it hits him with the force of a revelation.

The fact that he finds the three experiences *compelling* is crucial, for otherwise there would be no paradox: since the utterances associated with them are nonsensical, he could have dismissed the experiences as vivid emotions signifying nothing. The fact that *he* finds them compelling is crucial too. In a conversation with Waismann the following year he remarked: "At the end of my lecture on ethics I spoke in the first person: I think that this is something very essential. Here there is nothing to be stated any more; all I can do is to step forth as an individual and speak in the first person."[52] I had this in mind when earlier I said that for Wittgenstein the ethical, in the sense in which he means it, is ineluctably personal. Actually, he 'speaks in the first person' not only at the end of the lecture but also when he describes his three key experiences, the ones that he says could also be expressed by speaking of God. It is because he cannot dismiss these experiences as trivial that he cannot dismiss the utterances in which he gives them expression. And yet, given his conception of language and logic at the time, these utterances are precisely nonsensical. It is a paradox.

The paradox places him in a predicament. For at the end of the lecture he attests to "a tendency in the human mind which I personally cannot help respecting deeply", the tendency to try to overreach the limits of language and

---

48   Ibid., 41.

49   Ibid., 43 (emphasis added).

50   Ibid., 41.

51   Compare this remark from 1937 – written long after the 'turn' in his thought from his old *Denkweise* to the new – about 'election by grace': "It's less a theory than a sigh or a cry", Wittgenstein, *Culture and Value*, 34e–35e.

52   McGuinness, *Ludwig Wittgenstein and the Vienna Circle*, 117.

SPEAKING OF GOD 255

speak of the sublime, even though his framework of analysis in the lecture seems to pull the rug out from under his feet, undermining the respect he professes. To be sure, depending on who is speaking, the utterance 'how extraordinary that the world should exist' *could* be highfalutin hogwash deserving of contempt. But on Wittgenstein's lips it is language that commands respect: language that is inexorable and that will not be silenced by being told it is nonsense.

So, on the one hand, he attaches the utmost importance to certain experiences that lead him (or others) to speak of God. On the other hand, he considers the utterances that give expression to these experiences to be, strictly speaking, nonsensical. On this note, his lecture on ethics ends; and, we could almost say, so does the whole of his 'old way of thinking'. It ends in crisis.

Wittgenstein's Turn

A crisis is a turning-point; and Wittgenstein turns.[53] The year after the ethics lecture he prepared a text, subsequently published posthumously as *Philosophical Remarks*, which is on the cusp.[54] Three years later he was dictating the Blue Book, the first full text that reflects the turn in his thought, which reaches maturity in the *Investigations*.[55] Since the *Investigations* is to his later *Denkweise* what the *Tractatus* is to his earlier, it is natural to look to the former for guidance on how to deal with the paradox of religious experience generated by his earlier work. But the book contains even less material on religion than the *Tractatus*. It does not touch on the subject apart from one parenthetical remark about theology and a few allusions to a divinity – which are made in passing or in the course of investigating some other topic.[56] So, any guidance that we find in its pages must be derived by extrapolation. We can assume that

---

53   To be clear: I am not suggesting that it was the ethics lecture that precipitated his turn, nor that the paradox of religious experience which emerges in the lecture was at the forefront of his mind when he began to doubt his old *Denkweise*, nor even that it was anywhere in his consciousness at all when his whole approach to philosophy began to change. The claim I am making is not, in *this* sense, biographical.

54   The book did not appear in German until 1964 and in English until 1975.

55   Not that the turn was complete. 'The Blue Book', together with 'The Brown Book', was first published in 1958.

56   Wittgenstein, *Investigations*, par. 373: "Grammar tells what kind of object anything is. (Theology as grammar.)" God is mentioned in passing in par. 342. See pars. 346 ('God'), par. 426 ('a god') and 217 and 226 where he is investigating some other topic. There is also an aside about ethics in par. 77.

256   KLUG

the book contains resources for rethinking the status of those utterances that are left dangling paradoxically at the end of the ethics lecture. But the question is this: what use should we make of those resources?

This depends, in the first place, on what we understand to be the philosophical task that the ethics lecture sets. On the face of it, the task is to *make sense* of those utterances: to turn what he calls a *mis*use of language into a *different* use of language, different from – but no less legitimate than – the *wissenschaftlich*: the scientific or theoretical. Ultimately there is nothing wrong with formulating the task this way. But it carries with it a temptation to extract a general formula from the *Investigations* and apply it to religious language. Here (italicising the key phrases taken from the text) is the gist: religion is a *form of life*, and when people say such things as 'God created the world' or 'I feel safe in the hands of God' they are playing a distinctive *language-game* in which the use of their words is governed by a set of rules – a *grammar* – that stipulate the practical contexts in which those words and phrases can be legitimately employed. So, applying the formula: to understand the language of religious experience plot the moves that can be made with it on, as it were, the game board of religion.

The trouble with this solution is that it is facile: it makes something difficult look easy when it is not. That is why I call it a temptation. Or you could say that it gives the *illusion* of a solution: it is nothing more than a reshuffling of cards from the pack of phrases supplied by the text. For, with a little ingenuity, it is of course possible to fit the language of religious experience into the frame of this formula; for it is possible to fit *any* use of language into the frame. But what does this achieve in the end other than showing that the formula can be made to fit anything? It is as if you viewed the world through spectacles that had a grid painted on the lenses and said, 'See: everything fits into the grid!'[57] Now, this is an image that I have purloined from Wittgenstein; he uses it in the *Investigations* when critiquing his own presupposition in the *Tractatus* that language has an essence: "Where does this idea come from?" he asks, "It is like a pair of glasses on our nose through which we see whatever we look at. It never occurs to us to take them off".[58] He sums it up thus: "We predicate of the

---

57   Stephen Mulhall makes much the same point, even making it in a similar way, in "Realism, Modernism and the Realistic Spirit: Diamond's Inheritance of Wittgenstein, Early and Late", *Nordic Wittgenstein Review*, 1 (2012), 7–33. Mulhall refers to the phrases 'language-game', 'grammar' and 'forms of life' as a set of "signature concepts" (10). I am grateful to him for drawing my attention to this essay.

58   Wittgenstein, *Investigations*, par. 103.

SPEAKING OF GOD

thing what lies in the method of representing it".[59] My point in borrowing his simile is this: if we extract from the *Investigations* a one-size-fits-all formula then the same criticism that the *Investigations* makes of the *Tractatus* can be leveled at the *Investigations* itself. For then we are back to something like an essence.[60] If we stipulate *a priori* that religion is a 'language-game' among others, with its own set of rules, including rules governing utterances like 'God created the world' or 'how extraordinary that the world should exist', what are we doing if not predicating of the thing what lies in the method of representing it?

The temptation to settle for a solution of this kind comes from a misunderstanding of the philosophical task set by the ethics lecture. This misunderstanding in turn arises from a misconception about the place of the lecture (or the subject of the lecture) in the larger context of his thinking. Let me explain.

I said that it is natural to look to the *Investigations* for guidance on how to deal with the paradox of religious experience generated by his earlier work. But there is no point in looking to the *Investigations* if we do not see the text in what (in the preface) he calls 'the right light': seeing it "by contrast with and against the background of" his "old way of thinking". What does this mean? One way of taking it is to think it calls for juxtaposing the things he says earlier and the things he says later on a given philosophical topic and then describing similarities and differences. But this is to lose the plot. Throughout his work, from early to late, he is insistent on the point that philosophy, unlike (any) science, "may not advance any kind of theory".[61] Philosophy, for Wittgenstein, is "not a body of doctrine but an activity".[62] The activity is not theoretical but reflexive.[63] I suggest that in order to grasp the relationship of the *Investigations* to the *Tractatus* we must understand the relationship of both works to the author who is their common denominator: 'the man himself', as I put it earlier. This is what seeing the *Investigations* against the background of his 'old way of thinking' calls for us to do. Only then can we see the text 'in the right light' and thus be in a position to obtain from it the guidance that we seek.

---

59   Ibid., par. 104.

60   Compare Wittgenstein, *Investigations*, par. 65: "Instead of producing something common to all that we call language, I am saying that these phenomena have no one thing in common which makes us use the same word for all".

61   Ibid., par. 109. For *Tractatus*, see next footnote.

62   *Tractatus*, proposition 4.112.

63   "Work on philosophy ... is really more work on oneself. On one's own conception. On how one sees things", Wittgenstein, *Culture and Value*, 24e. This remark is from 1931, around the time when his overall thought – or way of seeing things – was changing.

It is 'the man himself' who steps forward at the end of 'A Lecture on Ethics' and speaks in the first person singular.[64] The same singular voice is heard in the 1919 letter to Ficker where he says that the point of the *Tractatus* is "ethical" and that the work consists of two parts, the written part and a part that he has *not* written, the latter being the part that is "important".[65] 'Important' downplays its importance: it is, so to speak, the heart and soul of the work: the part that is the *point* of the work: ethics (or religion). Then what about the *Investigations*, in which religion and ethics are even more conspicuous by their absence? I suggest this is another case where absence speaks louder than words. I follow the lead given by Drury, the friend and former student who knew Wittgenstein well, who generalizes from Wittgenstein's letter to Ficker. Drury suggests that "all the subsequent writings continue this fundamental idea. They all point to an ethical dimension."[66] Thus, what Wittgenstein said about the *Tractatus* applies also to the *Investigations*: "the point of the book is ethical", which is to say, religious. Drury recalls a remark that Wittgenstein made to him near the end of his life: "'I am not a religious man but I can't help seeing every problem from a religious point of view'". Wittgenstein added: "'I would like my work to be understood in this way.'"[67]

The Wittgenstein whom I mean in the title of my paper is the one whose work, from start to finish, from early to late, is understood in this way.[68] If the *Tractatus* and *Investigations* represent different approaches to philosophy

---

64 See above and footnote 52.

65 Letter 23, 94.

66 Drury, "Some Notes on Conversations with Wittgenstein", 81. I cannot think of any other commentators who make the move Drury makes, applying Wittgenstein's remark to Ficker to the whole of his work, early and late. I expect this betrays either my ignorance or my forgetfulness. Monk, referring to the same letter to Ficker, calls the *Tractatus* "a curious hybrid of a book, a treatise on logic *and* the expression of a deeply mystical point of view", *How to Read Wittgenstein*, 23. I do not see it as any more hybrid than a coin with two sides.

67 Wittgenstein, quoted according to Maurice O'Connor Drury, "Letters to a Student of Philosophy II", ed. Desmond Lee, *Philosophical Investigations* 6/3 (1983), 171 (Letter 15). Compare "Some notes on Conversations with Wittgenstein", 79, where Drury reproduces the same remark by Wittgenstein, omitting the final 'sentence' ("I would like my work to be understood in this way"). It should be noted that in 1966 Drury wrote to Rush Rhees expressing uncertainty as to whether his perspective on Wittgenstein's work was right: see the extract appended to "Letters to a Student of Philosophy II", 174.

68 There is a literature on what Wittgenstein meant when he spoke about "seeing every problem from a religious point of view". See especially Norman Malcolm, *Wittgenstein: A Religious Point of View*, ed. Peter Winch (London: Routledge, 1993). Malcolm's essay is followed by a response by Winch.

SPEAKING OF GOD

they nonetheless share the same depth. The same substratum – the same *man* – underlies both works, both phases of his thinking, the early and the later.[69] At first sight the change in his thinking is linear: progress along a line that leads from A (early) to B (late). But it is more like going from A to A. As he put it in 1930 (when his thought was turning): "For the place to which I really have to go is one that I must actually be at already."[70] Eighteen years later he reiterated this thought: "Where others go on ahead, I remain standing".[71] What I am suggesting is that he remained standing on the same spot throughout his work. What changed was how he plotted its coordinates.

I suggest that the three experiences that he describes in 'A Lecture on Ethics' are experiences that, so to speak, come from the depths of the spot on which he stood; they come from 'the man himself', Ludwig Wittgenstein, who steps forth "as an individual" and speaks in the first person singular. Furthermore, the *radicality* of those experiences is expressed by the fact that they are uttered in sentences that do not make sense. If so, and if he remains standing on that same spot throughout his work, then the philosophical task set by the ethics lecture *cannot* be to turn nonsense into sense. The task, I suggest, is to make sense of the uttering of nonsense; to make sense of the utterances in question *as* nonsense; to make room for them in the life of a person who has the kinds of experiences that Wittgenstein describes, experiences that lead them to speak of God. The task, then, is not to *resolve* the paradox of religious experience but to *figure* it better: 'better' precisely by way of preserving what, *au fond*, it expresses.[72]

---

69   Nothing in my essay is intended to suggest that Wittgenstein had a settled religious con-
      viction. On the contrary, his remarks in texts such as *Culture and Value* show that his
      relationship to faith was both ambiguous and fraught, though perhaps his doubts need
      to be read in the light of this observation (from 1950): "If you want to stay within the reli-
      gious sphere, you must *struggle*", *Culture and Value*, 98e. The *depth* that religion or ethics
      had for Wittgenstein is not captured by the question of what he did or did not *believe*. In
      his work, from beginning to end, he was at pains to protect the *dignity* of the *language* of
      ethics and religion from various depredations. These range from superstition to bombast
      to the hegemony of the scientific outlook – itself a kind of superstition.

70   Wittgenstein, *Culture and Value*, 10e.

71   Ibid., 75e.

72   Compare Stephen Mulhall: "Wittgenstein's view of ethico-religious utterances (early
      and late) is that they are sheerly nonsensical" (emphasis added), *The Great Riddle:
      Wittgenstein, Nonsense, Theology and Philosophy* (Oxford: Oxford University Press, 2015),
      21. Mulhall makes this point in the context of his own interpretive project and pursues it
      in his own direction. But I am obliged to him for this extremely suggestive remark, which
      has had a crucial influence on the argument of this essay.

The predicament in which Wittgenstein finds himself at the end of the ethics lecture is this: given his old 'way of thinking', he has no way of valorizing the utterances that give expression to the three experiences that he finds compelling. The philosophical task set by the lecture is to account for the fact that they command respect. There is no point in looking to the *Investigations* for guidance if we do not look in this light.

I have concluded the essay with a number of suggestions that, taken together, add up to a starting-point – no more than that – for a rereading of Wittgenstein's later work. I would have liked to take the argument further by speaking about Wittgenstein's abiding sense of finitude, the sense of finitude that pervades the *Tractatus*, the sense of a limit that does not lie within the limits of the finite; *this* being what is expressed by speaking of God. But the essay ends here.

Literature

Drury, Maurice O'Connor, "Letters to a Student of Philosophy II", ed. Desmond Lee, *Philosophical Investigations* 6/3 (1983), 171.

Drury, Maurice O'Connor, *Recollections of Wittgenstein*, ed. Rush Rhees (Oxford: Oxford University Press, 1984).

Engelmann, Paul, *Letters from Wittgenstein with a Memoir*, trans. L. Furtmüller, ed. Brian McGuinness (New York: Horizon Press, 1967).

Janik, Allan, and Stephen Toulmin, *Wittgenstein's Vienna* (New York: Simon and Schuster, 1973).

Kenny, Anthony, *Wittgenstein* (London: Penguin, 1975).

Luckhardt, C. Grant (ed.), *Wittgenstein: Sources and Perspectives* (Ithaca, NY: Cornell University Press, 1979), 94.

Malcolm, Norman, *Wittgenstein: A Religious Point of View*, ed. Peter Winch (London: Routledge, 1993).

McGinn, Marie, *Wittgenstein and the* Philosophical Investigations (London: Routledge, 1997).

McGuinness, Brian (ed.), *Ludwig Wittgenstein and the Vienna Circle: Conversations Recorded by Friedrich Waismann* (Oxford: Blackwell, 1979).

McGuinness, Brian (ed.), *Wittgenstein in Cambridge: Letters and Documents 1911–1951* (Chichester: Wiley-Blackwell, 2012).

Monk, Ray, *How to Read Wittgenstein* (London: Granta Books, 2005).

Monk, Ray, *Ludwig Wittgenstein: The Duty of Genius* (London: Vintage, 1991).

Mulhall, Stephen, "Realism, Modernism and the Realistic Spirit: Diamond's Inheritance of Wittgenstein, Early and Late", *Nordic Wittgenstein Review*, 1 (2012), 7–33.

Mulhall, Stephen, *The Great Riddle: Wittgenstein, Nonsense, Theology and Philosophy* (Oxford: Oxford University Press, 2015).

Rhees, Rush, "Some Developments in Wittgenstein's View of Ethics", *Philosophical Review*, 74 (1965), 17–26.

Russell, Bertrand, *My Philosophical Development* (London: Allen and Unwin, 1959).

Wittgenstein, Ludwig, "A Lecture on Ethics", in *Philosophical Occasions: 1912–1951*, ed. James C. Klagge and Alfred Nordmann (Indianapolis, IN: Hackett, 1993), 36–44.

Wittgenstein, Ludwig, *Culture and Value*, ed. Georg H. von Wright (Oxford: Blackwell, 1998).

Wittgenstein, Ludwig, *Philosophical Investigations*, trans. Gertrude E. M. Anscombe (Oxford: Blackwell, 1967).

Wittgenstein, Ludwig, *Tractatus Logico-Philosophicus*, trans. David F. Pears and Brian McGuinness (London: Routledge and Kegan Paul, 1961).

Conclusion: Experience or Expression? Preserving the Puzzle

Thomas Hardtke, Ulrich Schmiedel and Tobias Tan

To arrive at a hermeneutics of religion, we argued in the introduction, experience and expression cannot be pitted against each other. Only if religion is explored through both its experiences *and* its expressions, is it extricated from the confining circumscriptions exemplified by William James on the one hand and by the critics of William James on the other. However, in order to explore religion through the categories of experience and expression, these categories need to be examined.

In what follows, we will return to the questions which were raised in the introduction. What constitutes a religious experience? What constitutes a religious expression? And, crucially, how are these concepts related? Considering James's caution against the "pedantry" of "definitions" and "would-be definitions", we have not stipulated conceptualizations of experience and expression in the introduction, because these conceptualizations are at stake throughout the compilation.[1] Yet, predictably, we cannot escape from the task of defining our core concepts. The point of our "pedantry" is not to finally fix 'experience' and 'expression' in order to exorcize the dilemma of their entanglement which has haunted the study of religion since James. Rather, the point is to map the territories through which a hermeneutics of religion might have to navigate to take *both* religious experiences and religious expressions into consideration. Revisiting the concepts 'experience' and 'expression', then, offers us the occasion to survey the cumulative contribution which the contributions to our compilation make in response to the (Jamesian) puzzle.

Putting Expression Back into Experience

What constitutes a religious experience? James has had a significant impact on the conceptualizations of experience in the study of religion. His *The Varieties*

---

1   William James, *The Varieties of Religious Experience: A Study in Human Nature. Being the Gifford Lectures on Natural Religion Delivered at Edinburgh in 1901–1902*, The Works of William James, vol. 15, ed. Frederick H. Burkhardt, Fredson Bowers, and Ignas K. Skurupskelis (Cambridge, MA: Harvard University Press, 1987), 30.

CONCLUSION 263

of Religious Experience has been so influential that the (Jamesian) puzzle of experience and expression casts a shadow over both disciplinary and interdisciplinary approaches.[2] Taking extreme examples as the point of departure,[3] James's Gifford Lectures allocated the experience of religion to the extraordinary rather than the ordinary. But the contributions to our compilation call James's confinement of 'experience' into question. Here, those contributions which put expression back into experience are crucial.

When *Jörg Lauster* explores the experience in the example of a dancing plastic bag in Sam Mendes's film *American Beauty* (1999), he expands the horizon for experience. What he assesses as experience of transcendence can be found in everyday life.[4] *Johannes Kleine* describes the close analogy between the mystical and the aesthetical, suggesting that transcendence might be experienced through literature. Similarly, *Amber L. Griffioen*'s account stresses the similarities between religious and non-religious experience by identifying the ways we relate to fictional characters. *Graham Ward* points to perception as a mode of experience which could be qualified as a root of religion because acts of perception involve transcendence. Accordingly, the distinction between religious and non-religious experience is relativized. Ward quasi-quarantines the terminology of religious and non-religious experience.[5] Echoing Mircea Eliade, *Werner G. Jeanrond* affirms that any subject or any object might manifest a transcendence which needs to be approached indirectly rather than directly through the detour of its manifestations. *Marijn de Jong* employs Karl Rahner's notion of the experience of "self-presence (Bei-Sich-Selber-Sein)", including the ramifications such a notion has for our accounts of experience and expression. Correspondingly, *Knut Wenzel* advocates the Rahnerian category of transcendental experience, anchored as it is in the structure of subjectivity, which he conceives of as "supra-religious" because it can be filled religiously and non-religiously. *Ulrich Schmiedel* argues that relations to what he calls "the finite other" and relations to what he calls "the infinite other" are structured similarly. Hence, relations to any other involve moments of transcendence which is

---

2   For succinct summaries, see the contributions to *William James and the Varieties of Religious Experience: A Centenary Celebration*, ed. Jeremy Carrette (London: Routledge, 2005). See also Jeremy Carrette, *William James's Hidden Religious Imagination: A Universe of Relations* (London: Routledge, 2013).

3   William James, *The Varieties of Religious Experience*, 5, 40, 44.

4   See also Jörg Lauster, *Religion als Lebensdeutung: Theologische Hermeneutik Heute* (Darmstadt: Wissenschaftliche Buchgesellschaft, 2005), 17–18.

5   See Graham Ward, *Unbelievable: Why We Believe and Why We Don't* (London: I. B. Tauris, 2014), 220.

why transcendence can be found both in the ordinary and in the extraordinary. Following up on Schmiedel's critique of the interiorization and the individualization of experience, *Tobias Tan* likewise loosens James's circumscription of experience by rehabilitating ritualistic and religious practices which James dismissed as "second-hand".[6]

Our short summary of the sites of experiences of transcendence dramatically and drastically expands upon the range of experiences which James is willing to countenance as religious. Accordingly, the fictional, the aesthetical, the perceptual, the social, and the ritual can be conceived of as sources or as seeds for the experience of transcendence. Subjectivity itself might provoke religious rather than non-religious expressions. Considering the vast variety of experiences, James ought not to be blamed for restricting his 'Varieties' in order to make his already ambitious twenty-lecture project more manageable.[7] But manageability comes at a significant cost: it excises any but the most extreme experiences from the study of religion.

What is at stake here is the consequence(s) of qualifying experiences as either 'religious' or 'non-religious'. For James, such a qualification implies the demarcation of the subset of extraordinary religious experiences from the set of ordinary non-religious experiences. In contrast to James, the (re)turn to a more expansive view of experience implies the democratization of experiences of transcendence. These experiences, then, are no longer confined to extravagant elites, mystical minorities who happen to be gifted or graced with the encounter with transcendence.[8] Instead, they become the purview of potentially each and every person.

What, then, makes these experiences religious rather than non-religious? A number of contributions conceive of 'transcendence' as the core characteristic

---

6 James, *The Varieties of Religious Experience*, 15, 33, 270.

7 See ibid., 34, where James stresses that he defines religion for the purpose of his lectures. It is not a comprehensive conceptualization which fits each and every case. See again Carrette, *William James's Hidden Religious Imagination*, 1–20.

8 Ann Taves category of 'the special' fulfils a similar function. Her account of singularization allows scholars to cast the net of experience so wide that it catches religious and non-religious phenomena within one category. Thus, comparisons between experiences which are deemed religious and experiences which are deemed non-religious are facilitated. See Taves, *Religious Experience Reconsidered: A Building-Block Approach to the Study of Religion and Other Special Things* (Princeton, NJ: Princeton University Press, 2009), 28–55. See also the introduction to our volume. Tacitly, however, Taves's use of the concept of singularization still identifies 'the religious' with 'the special' and 'the non-religious' with 'the non-special'. Accordingly, she argues along the lines of James who allocates religion to the extraordinary and non-religion to the ordinary.

CONCLUSION 265

of religious in contrast to non-religious experience. *Jörg Lauster* points to the "breaking-in of transcendence" as a classic conceptual marker which distinguishes the religious from the non-religious. Following up on Lauster's pointer, the contributors to our volume argue that transcendence is itself relative. Since it gestures towards that which is 'before', 'behind' or 'beyond', the question is not *whether* transcendence is experienced but *which* transcendence is experienced. *Graham Ward* notes that the phenomenologies of perception point to the invisible which is co-present in the visible. He argues that phenomenologists are ultimately unable to distinguish between 'immanent', intentional transcendence and 'transcendent', non-intentional transcendence, thereby leaving the doors of the world open for divine encounter. Building on Ward, *Ulrich Schmiedel* defines transcendence functionally rather than substantially – as that which transcends the subject's evaluations and expectations. He sketches a spectrum of experiences of transcendence which reaches from routine to radical otherness. Working in the wake of Rahner, *Marijn de Jong* and *Knut Wenzel* find transcendence in the subject's experience of subjectivity, whereby it is not used as a marker that distinguishes between the religious and the non-religious. *Werner G. Jeanrond* sketches the history of 'experience' in the theological and the non-theological study of religion, contextualizing the concept in a variety of sometimes overlapping and sometimes non-overlapping "interpretive horizons", different frameworks for interpreting the world which might or might not give rise to religion. Theologically, he stresses the otherness of God which transcends and transforms whom it 'hits'.

These contributions, then, share the analogical logic which can be found in James's *The Will to Believe*, published prior to his Gifford Lectures in 1898. Here, James pointed to the analogies between trust in the creature and trust in the creator.[9] Incidentally, it is a logic that is already apparent in Friedrich D. E. Schleiermacher, who argued that the absolute dependence which denoted the creator was analogically related to partial dependence which denoted the creature.[10] The corollary of such an analogical logic is the critique of the concentration on belief as a marker to distinguish between what is religious and what is non-religious. For Schleiermacher, religion could not be confined to cognitive assent or dissent. *Tobias Tan's* contribution also – albeit from a

---

9   See William James, *The Will to Believe and Other Essays in Popular Philosophy*, The Works of William James, vol. 6, ed. Frederick H. Burkhardt, Fredson Bowers, and Ignas K. Skrupskelis (Cambridge, MA: Harvard University Press, 1979), 19, 28–29, 40–42, 49, 51–54, 76. See also Schmiedel's contribution to our volume.

10 See Friedrich Schleiermacher, *The Christian Faith*, ed. Hugh R. Mackintosh and James S. Stewart (Edinburgh: T&T Clark, 1928), 14–16.

physiological rather than a psychological angle – calls into question definitions of religion which privilege belief.[11] Since cognition is embodied, bodily and environmental factors can influence belief. This calls for a renewed focus on embodied religious practices, rather than an exclusive obsession with beliefs. *Amber L. Griffioen* even questions the need or the necessity of belief for religion by entertaining the possibility that those who lack belief can equally share in experience which we would qualify as religious rather than non-religious.

Overall, the contributions which concentrate on putting expression back into experience enlarge the territory of experience of transcendence. Crucially, they explain the difficulties with demarcating between experiences, thus identifying the sites where the religious fades into the non-religious and vice versa. Admittedly, the territory of experiences mapped out throughout our volume is far less manageable than James's neatly encircled fiefdom. But by disturbing and disrupting convenient or all-too-convenient demarcations, our compilation resists the ways in which 'experience' has been used, as *Yvonne Sherwood* argues, to police religion. What runs through our contributions is the realization that the experience cannot be studied without its expressions if one takes the experiencing subjects – entangled as they are in their historical and cultural contexts – seriously.

Putting Experience Back into Expression

What constitutes a religious expression? The complaint voiced against James is that he mistakes experiences for expressions and expressions for experiences. On the one hand, he argues that inexpressibility marks religious in contrast to non-religious experiences. But, on the other hand, he takes religious expressions as representations of religious experiences. Interestingly, James simply copies snippets from his sources into his Gifford Lectures. For James, then, expressions are *transparent* windows into experience. The contributions to our volume depart from the assumption that expressions simply and straightforwardly convey experiences. Instead, the ways in which expressions are both fascinatingly and frustratingly opaque inform their accounts. Here, the contributions which put experience back into expression are crucial.

Yvonne Sherwood catalogues the semantics and the pragmatics of experience, considering the subtle and the striking ways in which 'experience' has been put to work in academic and public discourses, together with all

---

11   See also Manuel A. Vásquez, *More Than Belief: A Materialist Theory of Religion* (Oxford: Oxford University Press, 2011).

CONCLUSION

its connotations. For her, 'experience' has become prominent in modernity because it is able to traffic between scientifically respectable "fact-objects" and scientifically unrespectable "fairy-objects", between the private and the public. As she concludes, "'Experience' manages irruptions of religion in the modern space." Through her account of Abraham's attempt to sacrifice his son, she demonstrates that even the expression of an experience *as* an experience has consequences for both the act of experiencing and the act of expressing. To label experiences as experiences might sterilize the experience at stake. Similarly, *Hannah M. Strømmen*'s reading of John's Revelation conceives of expression as both that which conveys experience and that which constructs experience. What Strømmen calls "John's apocalyptic experience" is simultaneously veiling and un-veiling, conceived of through Jacques Derrida's notion of autoimmunity. As a result, interpretation includes an intra- and inter-textual dynamic where a variety of textual layers interact. Therefore, the Jamesian assumption of a straight-forward connection between experience and expression turns out to be rather more complicated.

Continuing with the concentration on texts, *Catherine Lewis-Smith* argues that texts do more than mediate experiences, using the analytic tools provided by Mikhail Bakhtin's toolbox. Texts can contain records of mediation as exemplified in the 'double voice' identified by Lewis-Smith, which establishes an ambiguity between a messenger of YHWH and YHWH, the mediated and the unmediated. *Johannes Kleine* provides a detailed analysis of the literary mechanisms which Navid Kermani employs to convey mystical experience, on the one hand, and to convey how to convey mystical experience, on the other. The ineffability of mysticism is not absolute, since it can be gestured towards using distinct and diverse literary devices. Ineffability, then, is experienced in the way it is simultaneously made effable and ineffable through the text. Attention to the "theopoetics" of literature brings the operations performed by the text into the foreground. In concert with the recent surge in scholarship on the materiality of texts, *Johannes M. Depnering* demonstrates that close attention to the material form of the text sheds much light on its status as an expression. He employs a paleographic analysis to show how aspects of the experience are conveyed by the physical form of the text. Moreover, subsequent alterations – erasures and explanations – included into the manuscript, reveal layers of interpretation added to the text. The materiality of texts, then, constitutes its expressiveness alongside its semantics and its pragmatics. *Brian Klug* widens the horizon from textual to non-textual expression through the concentration on Ludwig Wittgenstein's philosophy of language. Here, linguistic expressions of experiences are interpreted as that which allows us to make sense of these experiences, although they are, strictly speaking, nonsensical. "The task", Klug argues, "is to make sense of the uttering of nonsense", where persons say nonsense in order to make sense of "experiences that lead them to speak of God". Accordingly, those contributions which put experience back into expression point to the semantics, the pragmatics and the materiality of language.

As is the case in everyday language, the contributions do not explicitly raise the question of what makes expressions religious rather than non-religious. *Yvonne Sherwood* points to the text(s) about Abraham, *Hannah M. Strømmen* to those of John of Patmos and *Catherine Lewis-Smith* to those about Gideon in the Bible. Similarly, *Johannes M. Depnering*'s contribution attends to a 'canonical' rather than a 'non-canonical' text when he concentrates on the "Revelations" of the medieval mystic Elsbeth von Oye. Accordingly, these texts are read as religious rather than non-religious texts, albeit without presuming that such a reading would be the only possible reading. *Johannes Kleine*'s interpretation of Kermani's *Dein Name* problematizes any clear-cut differentiation between the canonical and non-canonical status of texts, pointing to the ways in which classical mystical themes can be found in the contemporary and the contemporary can be found in classical mystical themes.[12] As *Brian Klug*'s contribution concludes, what lies behind the question of what makes an expression religious rather than non-religious is the question of making sense of what seems to militate against such sense-making.

Overall, these contributions dispel the Jamesian illusion that one can look through the expression onto the experience in the way one can look through a window. There may well be experiences 'behind' the text, experiences 'within'

---

12   Examples of aesthetic experiences which include moments of transcendence abound throughout our volume. *Jörg Lauster*'s example of the plastic bag explores how an aesthetic experience is interpreted in mystical terms; *Amber L. Griffioen* uses experiences of fiction as a model for experiences of religion which suspends questions of belief; *Johannes Kleine* describes how mysticism encroaches on art and art encroaches on mysticism in the oeuvre of Navid Kermani; and *Knut Wenzel* identifies continuities between religion and the arts as well as the arts and religion in Romanticism. Considering how close aesthetics comes to religion (and religion to aesthetics), it is not surprising that the imagination is discussed in more than one contribution. *Graham Ward* argues that the encounter with the transcendent is rooted in our cognitive capacity for imagination. *Amber L. Griffioen* notes that, regardless of one's metaphysical commitments, imaginative engagement is necessary for understanding religions since they exceed empirical 'facts'. Imagination is also a key concept for Ernst Troeltsch, and *Ulrich Schmiedel* expounds how imagination is required to engage with the Troeltschian triangle of event, experience and expression. Imagination, then, proves to be a particularly promising point of departure for further studies on the relation between experience and expression.

CONCLUSION 269

the world of the text, and experiences 'before' (or in front of) the text. By attending carefully to the textual expressions themselves, these intertwined layers of experience are seen diffusely. What runs through our contributions is the realization that the expression cannot be studied without its experience if one takes the expressing subjects – entangled as they are in their historical and cultural contexts – seriously.

Exploring the Entanglements of Experience and Expression

Having surveyed the territories of the central concepts, we are yet to get to our core concern. The puzzle of experience and expression upon which our volume focuses cannot be considered by revisiting each concept *in isolation*. How, then, are experience and expression entangled?

As mentioned above, the boundary markers of the debate concerning experience and expression are found in the extremes which privilege *either* experience at the cost of expression *or* expression at the cost of experience. Crucially, the false alternative implies a disciplinary privilege. On the one hand, the defenders of experience argue that religious experience is *sui generis*, and it is phenomenal rather than epiphenomenal. The result is that the 'religious' core of the experience is emphasized by pitting religious experience against religious expression. Accordingly, the study of these experiences is confined to the disciplines concerned with religion because any other discipline would run the risk of *anti-religious reductionism* by analyzing expression instead of experience.[13] On the other hand, the despisers of experience argue that religious experience is not *sui generis*, and it is epiphenomenal rather than phenomenal. The result is that the 'religious' core of the experience is eroded by pitting religious expression against religious experience. Accordingly, the study of these experiences is confined to the disciplines not concerned with religion because any other discipline would run the risk of *religious reductionism* analyzing experience instead of expression.[14]

---

13 For a detailed discussion, see Taves, *Religious Experience Reconsidered*, 16–22, esp. the concise chart on p. 18. Taves points out that although the *sui generis* approach is associated with the isolation of the religious from the non-religious, such isolationism is not suggested by all of its proponents.

14 It is noteworthy that the discussion is commonly conceived of as a discussion about the nature of the study of religion. Here, religious reductionism is characterized as a theological take-over attempt; non-religious reductionism is characterized as anti-theological take-over attempt. Timothy Fitzgerald's *The Ideology of Religious Studies* (Oxford: Oxford

Unsurprisingly, the contributors to our volume avoid the excesses which either of these extremes entails. The *sui generis* approach ignores the fact that culture provides the vocabulary through which experiences must be strained to be expressed. The anti-*sui generis* approach ignores that even if subjects use the vocabulary of their culture to express their experiences, they must nevertheless recognize their experiences in the vocabulary that the culture provides if they are to bring it to expression. As a result, our volume seeks to interrogate the *entanglement* of experiences and expressions. If one approach confines itself to the 'religious disciplines' while the other confines itself to the 'non-religious disciplines', the entanglement requires an interdisciplinary hermeneutics.

What would an interdisciplinary hermeneutics of religion which takes both experience and expression seriously look like? One promising way of probing how the two relate is by considering alternative models. Stated negatively, we not only reject the extremes of 'experience versus expression' and 'expression versus experience', but we also disavow a *linear* progression from experience to expression or from expression to experience. On the one hand, the linear model from experiences to expression assumes the priority of experience. This approach gave thinkers such as James the flexibility to argue that variation between religious expressions are of secondary concern, since the divergent expressions can be related back to the same underlying experience.[15] A by-product of declaring that experience is the essence of the religion is that experience and expression become estranged. On the other hand, the linear model from expression to experience assumes the priority of expression. This

---

University Press, 2000) excellently exemplifies the approach which suggests to quarantine the category of religion.

15 The Jamesian 'flexibility' is the point of departure for the critics of the *sui generis* approach who argue that it tacitly transports a theological agenda. See the influential study by Tomoko Masuzawa, *The Invention of World Religions: Or, How European Universalism was Preserved in the Language of Pluralism* (Chicago: University of Chicago Press, 2005). It should be noted, however, that theologians like Friedrich D. E. Schleiermacher, who concentrate on the concept of experience, complicate the picture considerably. In his *Speeches on Religion*, which are not mentioned in Masuzawa's account, Schleiermacher also assumes that experience precedes expression. However, esp. in the fifth speech, he calls for a return to the particularities of expression. See Friedrich Schleiermacher, *On Religion: Speeches to Its Cultured Despisers*, ed. Karl Ameriks and Desmond M. Clarke, trans. Richard Crouter (Cambridge: Cambridge University Press, 1996), 95–124. Accordingly, there is a tension in Schleiermacher's account. Disciplinary (self)definitions which completely disconnect theology from religious studies and religious studies from theology run the risk of losing track of such tensions.

CONCLUSION 271

approach gave thinkers such as the critics of James the flexibility to argue that the variation between religious expressions is of primary concern, since the divergent expressions cannot be related back to the same underlying experience. There are a number of strategies which contributors to our volume employ in order to criticize the linear progression model.[16] These criticisms short-circuit the linear model by proposing that expressions feed (back) into religious experiences as much as religious experiences feed (back) into religious expressions. Whatever is experienced needs to be expressed in order to be experienced. Whatever is expressed needs to be experienced in order to be expressed. If one takes the position of a person who has had experiences of transcendence seriously, then it is difficult to distinguish between experience and expression. The distinction is indeed analytical. But as analytical distinction, it fulfills important and instructive functions in the analysis of religion.

The negative task of dispelling the linear models already provides the central clues for how they might be replaced with a *reciprocal* model in which expressions and experiences mutually infuse each other. A two-way analysis runs through the contributions to our volume, where 'new' experiences call for 'new' expressions and 'new' expressions call for 'new' experiences.[17] Albeit through decidedly different approaches, the two theoretical and meta-theoretical studies which open our volume in the section "Grasping the Ungraspable?" point to such a reciprocal approach. They are taken up in the sections on "Imagining the Unimaginable?" and "Interpreting the Uninterpretable?" which approach the reciprocal relationship between experience and expression in terms of their production (imagination) and in terms of their reception (interpretation) respectively. The fourth and final section "Performing the Unperformable?" suggests 'practice' as a concept which connects experience and expression.

---

16   *Jörg Lauster* and *Marijn de Jong*, for instance, invoke theories of 'linguistic relativity' to examine the way in which the language used in expressions might shape experience. *Tobias Tan* similarly argues for a 'bodily relativity', since bodily states can shape cognition. Moreover, *Hannah M. Strømmen, Amber L. Griffioen* and *Johannes Kleine* observe ways in which expressions are themselves experienced in the reception of texts. As *Strømmen* argues, "In John's apocalypse there is little sign of a prior, originary experience of an unmediated ... revelation; rather, the entire experience is caught up in a mesh of traces ..., as if every experience is always already mediated, caught up in a system of signs ..." Accordingly, a skepticism that one can ever get behind a text to its author seems to be applicable to a parallel skepticism that one can ever get behind an expression to an experience.

17   See also Hans Joas, "Do We Need Religion?", in Hans Joas, *Do We Need Religion? On Experiences of Self-Transcendence*, trans. Alex Skinner (Boulder, CO: Paradigm Press, 2008), 3–20 (12).

Practices have a liminal character as potentially both expression and experience: the performance of a practice might imply both a religious expression (such that the practice co-constitutes a religious expression) and a religious experience (such that the practice co-constitutes a religious experience). The question of what makes a practice religious rather than non-religious might be at stake in the practice itself. Practice, then, is a concept which brings the issues which have been raised throughout our compilation into sharp relief.

The analytic assumption that experience and expression are entangled allows for a look at practices from different disciplinary angles. But, first and foremost, the exploration of the entanglement of experience and expression requires *interdisciplinary* accounts: against a non-religious reductionism which tries to reduce what persons experience in manifold modes into a mere monolithic concept of expression (which, by definition, can have nothing to do with the transcendent); against a religious reductionism which tries to reduce what subjects express in manifold modes into a mere monolithic experience (which, by definition, can have nothing to do with the immanent). If the relationship between experience and expression is reciprocal, then religious experiences cannot be studied in isolation from expressions and religious expressions cannot be studied in isolation from experiences. Interdisciplinary studies are crucial to removing experiences and expressions from their mutual isolation. Therefore, our volume has not been content with exploring and elaborating on the conceptual argument that expression and experience are entangled. Rather, it has attempted to respond to the entanglement of religious experiences and religious expressions by provoking and pursuing an interdisciplinary conversation which opens the possibility that both can be examined in their interrelations by bringing together scholars with a diverse array of disciplinary tools at their disposal. How, then, are experience and expression entangled? The (Jamesian) puzzle of experience and expression cannot be studied by removing one of the partners in the experience-expression pair. Instead, the puzzle is itself the point of departure. When the interlocking pieces – experience and expression – are assembled together, a more comprehensive picture comes into view.

Literature

Carrette, Jeremy (ed.), *William James and the Varieties of Religious Experience: A Centenary Celebration* (London: Routledge, 2005).

Carrette, Jeremy, *William James's Hidden Religious Imagination: A Universe of Relations* (London: Routledge, 2013).

CONCLUSION 273

Fitzgerald, Timothy, *The Ideology of Religious Studies* (Oxford: Oxford University Press, 2000).

James, William, *The Will to Believe and Other Essays in Popular Philosophy*, The Works of William James, vol. 6, ed. Frederick H. Burkhardt, Fredson Bowers, and Ignas K. Skrupskelis (Cambridge, MA: Harvard University Press, 1979).

James, William, *The Varieties of Religious Experience: A Study in Human Nature. Being the Gifford Lectures on Natural Religion Delivered at Edinburgh in 1901–1902*, The Works of William James, vol. 15, ed. Frederick H. Burkhardt, Fredson Bowers, and Ignas K. Skurupskelis (Cambridge, MA: Harvard University Press, 1987).

Joas, Hans, *Do We Need Religion? On Experiences of Self-Transcendence*, trans. Alex Skinner (Boulder, CO: Paradigm Press, 2008).

Lauster, Jörg, *Religion als Lebensdeutung: Theologische Hermeneutik Heute* (Darmstadt: Wissenschaftliche Buchgesellschaft, 2005).

Masuzawa, Tomoko, *The Invention of World Religions: Or, How European Universalism was Preserved in the Language of Pluralism* (Chicago: University of Chicago Press, 2005).

Schleiermacher, Friedrich, *On Religion: Speeches to Its Cultured Despisers*, ed. Karl Ameriks and Desmond M. Clarke, trans. Richard Crouter (Cambridge: Cambridge University Press, 1996).

Schleiermacher, Friedrich, *The Christian Faith*, ed. Hugh R. Mackintosh and James S. Stewart (Edinburgh: T&T Clark, 1928).

Taves, Ann, *Religious Experience Reconsidered: A Building-Block Approach to the Study of Religion and Other Special Things* (Princeton, NJ: Princeton University Press, 2009).

Vásquez, Manuel A. *More Than Belief: A Materialist Theory of Religion* (Oxford: Oxford University Press, 2011).

Ward, Graham, *Unbelievable: Why We Believe and Why We Don't* (London: I. B. Tauris, 2014).

Index of Names

Abu Zaid, Nasr Hamid 127
Adam, Hajo 219n
Adams, Nicholas 168n
Agamben, Giorgio 33
Alicke, Mark D. 218
Alston, William 76, 85
Al-Thaʿlabī, Ahmad ibn Muhammad 128
Ankersmit, Frank 45
Ansari, Khwaja Abdullah 130
Aristotle 22, 30
Ashley Cooper, Anthony *see* Shaftesbury, 3rd Earl of
Augustine of Hippo 128, 175, 183n, 234
Ayer, Alfred J. 246

Bach, Johann Sebastian 27
Badiou, Alain 123
Bakhtin, Mikhail 8, 89–90, 93–104, 267
Barr, James 91
Barsalou, Lawrence W. 214–217, 220
Barth, Karl 147–149, 151, 174
Bauer, Thomas 127
Bauman, Zygmunt 187n
Bayle, Pierre 52
Beckett, Samuel 34
Bellah, Robert 21, 28
Bergmann, Harald 132, 133
Biddle, Mark E. 99n
Bienert, Maren 189n
Blanton, Ward 45n
Block, Daniel 91n, 96n, 98
Blumenberg, Hans 124n
Boeve, Lieven 162n
Böhme, Jakob 124
Bonds, Mark Evan 23n
Boyarin, Daniel 124n
Brosses, Charles de 31
Brown, Wendy 37n, 38
Bultmann, Rudolf 27–28, 66n
Bunyan, John 23
Burney, Charles F. 99
Butler, Judith 106
Butler, Trent C. 98n, 99n

Carlyle, Thomas 24
Carrette, Jeremy 1n, 194n, 211n, 212n, 263n, 264n
Carroll, Robert 60
Celan, Paul 126
Certeau, Michel de 179
Chenu, Marie-Dominique 108
Chrétien, Jean-Louis 109
Chubb, Thomas 53n
Collins, John J. 62
Cox, James 34

Dahlhaus, Carl 23n
Daiber, Jürgen 125n
Damasio, Antonio 82–83
Dawkins, Richard 38
Deacon, Terrene W. 114n
Defoe, Daniel 23
Dennett, Daniel 116–117
Derrida, Jacques 7, 43n, 44n, 48n, 50n, 59, 61–62, 64–71, 149, 267
Dijkstra, Katinka 218
Dilthey, Wilhelm 43
Dinzelbacher, Peter 229n
Discher, Gisela 124n, 125n
Döring, Sabine 20n
Dorothea von Montau 227
Dostoevsky, Fyodor 94, 99n
Doud, Robert D. 169n
Drury, Maurice O'Connor 246–247, 258
Duclos, Sandra 217

Ebner, Margareta 227
Eckhart von Hochheim *see* Meister Eckhart
Edelman, Gerald 213
Edwards, Jonathan 16
Eicher, Peter 157n
Ekman, Paul 116
Eliade, Mircea 8, 36, 137–138, 141–143, 145–147, 149, 151–152, 263
Elsbeth von Oye 10, 227–240, 268
Emerson, Ralph Waldo 16, 50
Engelmann, Paul 249n

INDEX OF NAMES

Escher, Alexandre 231n
Escher, Sandra 231n
Eshleman, Andrew 75n

Farmer, Frank M. 90n, 93n
Federer, Urban 227n
Fenves, Peter 31
Ficker, Ludwig von 248–249, 253, 258
Fish, Stanley 150
Fitzgerald, Timothy 34, 269n
Fox, George 41, 43, 211
Francis of Assisi 211
Franke, William 123n
Frei, Hans 147
Friedrich, Caspar David 24
Frye, Northrop 179n

Gadamer, Hans-Georg 10, 31, 150, 223–224
Galinsky, Adam D. 219n
Gallup, Gordon G. 114n
Geertz, Clifford 154
Gellman, Jerome 228
Gellner, Christoph 127
Genette, Gérard 131
Giotto 22
Glucklich, Ariel 237–238
Golonka, Sabrina 220n
Gorman, Michael 60
Grahek, Nikola 236
Green, Garrett 74n, 87n
Green, Maia 221n
Gregory of Nyssa 109, 234
Grøn, Arne 189n, 199n, 203n
Gsell, Monika 232n, 240n

Habel, Norman C. 98n
Haenel, Klaus 228
Hafez 129
Hardenberg, Friedrich von see Novalis
Harnad, Stevan 214n
Harrison, Victoria 76n
Hasebrink, Burkhart 229
Hegel, Georg Wilhelm Friedrich 20–21, 123, 168n
Heidegger, Martin 31n, 109, 110, 123
Heinrich von Nördlingen 227n
Hennis, Wilhelm 190n
Herzel, Roger W. 92n

Hitchens, Christopher 38
Hölderlin, Friedrich 132
Howard-Snyder, Daniel 77
Husserl, Edmund 107, 109

Inwood, Michael 168
Irleborn, Bernd 176n
Ismhael ben Elisha, Rabbi 48

James, William 1–4, 6, 9, 10, 16–17, 20, 40–50, 63, 85n, 142–144, 189–199, 202–203, 207–213, 219, 224–225, 246, 262–272
Janik, Allan 249n
Jay, Martin 31, 33n, 34, 35n, 37n, 40, 52n
Jean Paul 130, 131
Jesus 63, 65n, 141, 146, 148, 161–163, 227, 230–235
Joas, Hans 24n, 34, 53, 191n, 195–196, 201n, 271n
John of the Cross 179
Johnson, Mark 216n
Joyce, James 131
Juan de la Cruz see John of the Cross
Jung, Matthias 18–19, 194n

Kant, Immanuel 43, 44, 47, 48, 52, 116, 117, 125n, 139, 159, 175, 189n, 246, 247n
Kaschak, Michael P. 218n
Katz, Steven T. 238
Kearny, Richard 70
Kempe, Margery 227n
Kennedy, Philip 167n, 169n
Kenny, Anthony 245–246
Kermani, Navid 8, 123–134, 267–268
Kermode, Frank 59, 128
Kierkegaard, Søren 53, 247
Kilby, Karen 159n
Kirchert, Klaus 228n
Klein, Lillian 96n, 97n
Koester, Craig R. 60
Kopytoff, Igor 4
Kovakovich, Karson 82–83
Kuschel, Karl-Josef 127

Lakoff, George 216n
Landini, Greg 77n
Landy, Francis 124n
Langenhorst, Georg 127

INDEX OF NAMES

Lash, Nicholas 208
Latour, Bruno 31–32
Le Fort, Gertrud von 126
Le Poidevin, Robin 75n
Legaspi, Michael C. 43n
Lessing, Gotthold Ephraim 51
Lewitscharoff, Sibylle 126n
Lindbeck, George 154–156, 168–169, 187
Locke, John 37
Lonergan, Bernard 155
Lubac, Henri de 108
Luhrmann, Tanya M. 87n
Luther, Martin 50, 128

MacDonald, Graham 113n
Mahmood, Saba 38n, 48n
Malcolm, Norman 258n
Manoussaki, John P. 62
Marienwerder, Johannes 227n
Martin, Craig 2–4
Martin, Leonard 217
Masuzawa, Tomoko 32n, 270n
McCarthy-Jones, Simon 231n, 237, 239n
McCutcheon, Russell T. 2–3, 34
McGilchrist, Iain 110n
McGinn, Marie 244n
McLuhan, Marshall 22
Meier, Samuel 91
Meister Eckhart 25, 179
Melanchthon, Phillip 113
Melzack, Ronald 237
Mendes, Sam 25–26, 263
Merleau-Ponty, Maurice 8, 106–110, 113, 116, 119, 169
Midgely, Warren 93n
Milbank, John 187
Millikan, Ruth 113
Monk, Ray 247, 250n, 258n
Montau, Dorothea von see Dorothea von Montau
Moore, Gregory 191n
Moore, Stephen D. 52n
Moussaieff, Arieh 219n
Mulhall, Stephen 256, 259n
Muyskens, James 77

Naas, Michael 67
Nagel, Thomas 114n, 118

Neuwirth, Angelika 127, 128n
Niebuhr, Richard R. 192n, 197n
Nietzsche, Friedrich 53, 123
Novalis 124–125, 132
Nygren, Anders 147

Oakeshott, Michael 40
Oatley, Keith 81n
Ochsenbein, Peter 228
Otto, Rudolf 8, 16–17, 36, 59, 61n, 73n, 79, 84, 140–146
Özdamar, Emine Sevgi 127

Papineau, David 113n
Park, Crystal 240n
Pascal, Blaise 128, 218
Paul 22, 36, 41, 112–114, 211
Petrarca, Francesco 22
Pippin, Tina 60
Plato 22, 180, 246n, 247n
Polaschegg, Andrea 128n
Poovey, Mary 106
Porète, Marguerite 197
Povinelli, Daniel J. 114
Prinz, Jesse J. 216
Proudfoot, Wayne 2n, 73n, 85

Radford, Colin 82–83
Rahner, Karl 9, 155, 156–161, 164–170, 175, 177, 263, 265
Ramsey, Frank P. 249n
Ransom, Michael R. 218
Rasmussen, Joel D. S. 195n
Rhess, Rush 249n, 258n
Richter, Johann Paul Friedrich see Jean Paul
Riesebrodt, Martin 15n
Romme, Marius A. J. 231n
Roth, Patrick 126n
Royle, Nicholas 65
Russell, Bertrand 245, 246n
Ryan, Roger J. 96n

Sachs Norris, Rebecca 218n
Sachs, Nelly 126
Sahagún, Bernardino de 30n
Sartre, Jean-Paul 111, 115
Saussure, Ferdinand de 221–222
Savran, George W. 92

INDEX OF NAMES

Schaeffler, Richard 173, 175–176
Schäfer, Peter 133n
Schelling, Friedrich Wilhelm Joseph 175
Schillebeeckx, Edward 9, 156, 162–170
Schlegel, Friedrich 124
Schleiermacher, Friedrich Daniel Ernst 8, 16, 17, 45, 79, 83n, 84, 139–146, 155, 165, 191, 265, 270n
Schmidt, Leigh Eric 53n
Schneider, Reinhold 126
Schneider-Lastin, Wolfram 228n, 229n, 230n, 231n, 233n, 234n, 235n
Scholem, Gershom 133n
Schreber, Daniel Paul 44
Searle, John R. 214n
Sells, Michael 123n
Shaftesbury, 3rd Earl of 52
Shakespeare, Steven 4n, 154n
Shantz, Colleen 97n
Shapin, Steven 44
Shapiro, Lawrence A. 214n, 216n, 219n
Sharf, Robert H. 3n
Sidnell, Jack 90n
Simon, Derek 161n
Slater, Peter 90n, 94n, 101, 103,
Sloboda, John A. 219n
Smart, Ninian 36
Smith, Jonathan Z. 142n
Smith, Les W. 96
Smith, Wilfred Cantwell 43n
Socrates 246n
Soggin, J. Alberto 99, 101n
Sommer, Benjamin D. 91n
Spivak, Gayatri Chakravorti 68
Staël, Germaine de 24
Steiner, George 28
Stepper, Sabine 217
Strack, Fritz 217
Suerbaum, Almut 227n
Szabó Gendler, Tamar 82–83

Tallis, Raymond 115, 118
Taves, Ann 2n, 4–5, 34, 238, 264n, 269n
Taylor, Charles 169, 189n, 192, 208n
Teresa of Ávila see Theresa of Ávila
Theresa of Ávila 41–42, 179, 211

Thomas Aquinas 23, 28
Thompson, Leonard 63
Tillich, Paul 83n
Tom, Gail 217n
Toulmin, Stephen 249n
Tracy, David 8, 142–151, 155–156, 168
Troeltsch, Ernst 9, 16, 17, 189–192, 195–203, 268n
Tull, Patricia K. 95n

Ulfgard, Håkan 66n

Van der Leeuw, Gerardus 36
Vásquez, Manuel A. 212n, 266n
Vergilius Maro, Publius see Virgil
Virgil 131
Volfing, Annette 227n
Vries, Hent de 123

Wach, Joachim 36
Wagner-Egelhaaf, Martina 123n
Waismann, Friedrich 248, 250, 254
Wall, Patrick D. 237
Wallace, David 227n
Walton, Kendall 82
Ward, Graham 190, 199
Watson, Nicholas 227n
Watts, Fraser 214n
Webb, Barry G. 91n, 100
Weidner, Daniel 128n
Welz, Claudia 188n, 189n, 199n
Wild, Stefan 127
Wilder, Amos Nive 126n
Wilentz, Sean 182n
Williams, William Carlos 114
Wilson, Andrew D. 220n
Wittgenstein, Ludwig 10, 154, 243–260, 267
Wolfson, Harry A. 128n
Wünsche, Gregor 229
Wynn, Mark 220n
Wyon, Olive 201n

Young, Neil 128–129, 133–134

Zaimoglu, Feridun 127
Zwaan, Rolf A. 218n

Index of Subjects

absolute 9, 21, 22, 70, 108–109, 113, 125, 159–160, 173–183, 243
aesthetics 40, 46, 52, 75n, 95, 99, 124, 127–134, 219n, 263, 264, 268n
alterity 9, 34–35, 70, 117, 139, 147, 170, 189–192, 199–203, 265
analogy 49, 108, 129–132, 216
anthropology 18–19, 106, 160n
apophatic theology *see* negative theology
approximation 124–126, 129, 131–132, 134
articulation 2, 8–11, 15–28, 43, 60, 85, 118, 125, 129, 129, 143–144, 146, 149, 151, 154–156, 159, 161, 163–164, 167–170, 175, 117, 179, 181–183, 187–190, 194–203, 207, 217, 221, 223, 225, 240, 243–244, 247–248, 251–260, 262–272; *see also* cataphatic theology, inexpressibility, negative theology
authenticity 2–3, 45, 53, 100, 144, 178, 209
autobiography *see* self-account

beauty *see* aesthetics
belief 7–8, 37–40, 45, 46, 53, 73–87, 110–116, 145, 165, 190, 199, 259n, 265–266, 268n; *see also* faith, non-believers

cataphatic theology 28, 86n, 197; *see also* articulation
church 151, 156, 173–174, 194, 197–199, 202, 211, 213, 219–224; *see also* community
community 9, 42, 50, 51, 59, 97, 117, 144–150, 155–156, 173, 187–190, 194–195, 198–199, 201–203; *see also* church
consciousness 5, 15, 17, 19, 41–42, 100, 109–118, 134, 159, 163, 193, 196, 199n, 200, 231, 237–240
constructivism *see* culturalism
conversion 41, 48–49, 128, 145–146, 149
corporeality 10, 44, 106–119, 169, 207–226, 266
culturalism 2–5, 9, 18–21, 26–28, 45, 154–156, 187–189, 197–198, 201–202, 238–239, 262, 269–272; *see also* linguistic relativity

disbelief *see* non-believers

ecclesiology *see* church
embodiment *see* corporeality
emotion 7–8, 73–74, 80–87, 110, 114–116, 130, 194n, 211n, 212, 217–219, 254
enthusiasm 47, 49, 124, 140
epiphany *see* revelation
ethics 40–41, 46–47, 50–53, 75n, 81n, 83–84, 128, 139, 248–260
evidence 30, 90, 99, 111–112, 192, 213–216, 220
evolution 20–23, 113, 118, 139
experiential-expressivism *see* realism
expression *see* articulation

faith 8, 48, 75, 77, 87, 107–108, 111–113, 134, 162, 191n, 259n; *see also* belief
fetish 31–33
fictionalism 8, 75–87, 263, 268n
freedom 30–32, 36, 40, 111, 117–118, 133–134, 247

hallucination 85, 223, 231, 237, *see also* pathologization
hierophany 141; *see also* holy
holy 17, 36, 73n, 140, 175; *see also* hierophany
homology 131–132
hope 75n, 77–78, 111–112, 117, 165

imagination 6–8, 20, 22, 61, 73–87, 91, 110–111, 115, 118, 144–145, 196–197, 199, 201, 268n, 271
immediacy *see* mediacy
individuality 3, 9, 10, 33–34, 38, 63, 97n, 187–188, 194–195, 198–199, 202–203, 208–211, 224, 254, 259, 264
ineffability *see* inexpressibility
inexpressibility 1–2, 9, 22, 27, 33, 37, 63, 123–126, 129, 131–132, 161, 194–197, 200, 243, 251, 253, 266–267, *see also* negative theology
interiorization 9, 10, 195n, 198n, 264
interreligious dialogue 76n, 79, 149

invisibility   8, 22, 109–116, 124, 265
Islamic Studies   127–128

language   9, 10, 18, 19, 44–45, 62, 67, 89, 94n,
        97, 125, 129, 132, 143–145, 147–149,
        154–156, 158–160, 162, 166–170, 193–196,
        200n, 215, 243–260, 267–268, 271n
liberalism   43, 50, 51, 151, 155, 187–189,
        197–198, 201–202; *see also* realism
linguistic relativity   15, 154n, 271n; *see also*
    culturalism
linguistic turn   4, 9, 154–156, 167; *see also*
    language
literature   8, 20, 23–25, 59–71, 89–104,
        123–134, 227–240, 263, 267; *see also*
        theopoetics
liturgy   *see* performance of religion

mediacy   7, 9, 19, 22, 62–64, 67, 68, 70–71,
        89–94, 103, 116, 143, 147, 149, 154–170,
        178, 181–183, 194n, 196, 200n, 209, 223,
        227–228, 236–238, 240, 267, 271n
medical approaches *see* pathologization
metaphor   77n, 124, 131–132, 216–217, 224, 232
moral *see* ethics
music   22–23, 128–129, 133–134, 137, 182, 219
mysticism   2, 8, 10, 25, 34, 35, 79, 85n, 108,
        123–134, 144, 148–149, 175, 178–183,
        194–197, 200, 208–211, 227–240,
        248–249, 252, 258n, 263, 264, 267, 268;
        see also unification

negative theology   25, 28, 86n, 108, 123, 129,
        148, 197; *see also* inexpressibility
neuroscience   15, 33, 106, 115, 200n
non-believers   74–87
numinous   17, 36, 73n, 98, 123, 140

objectivism   15, 16, 31, 173–174
otherness *see* alterity

pain   10, 52–53, 227, 230–232, 235–237
paradox   8, 10, 113, 123, 125–131, 243–259
passivity   69, 86, 139, 146, 147
pathologization   41–44, 81, 207, 210–211, 213,
        228; *see also* hallucination
perception   85, 91, 103, 106–107, 110–111,
        115–118, 125, 154n, 215–217, 232, 263, 265;
        see also hallucination

performance of religion   9–10, 20, 22, 50, 74,
        174, 179–182, 207–225, 271–272
phenomenology   8, 36, 106–111
poetry *see* literature
postliberalism   154–155, 187–189, 197–198,
        201–202; *see also* culturalism
psychology of religion   190, 195–199

Quran   127–128, 130

realism   2–5, 9, 18–21, 26–28, 154–156,
        187–189, 197–198, 201–202, 262, 269–272
revelation   8, 10, 18, 25–27, 32–33, 38, 59–71,
        100, 103, 124, 127, 134, 142, 143, 147, 161, 163,
        167n, 170, 174, 182, 228–230, 254, 271n; *see
        also* theophany
ritual *see* performance of religion
Romanticism   24, 124–125, 129, 132, 182, 268n

sacrality *see* holy
Sapir-Worf hypothesis *see* linguistic
    relativism
secularization   23–25, 27, 35–40, 54, 118, 182
self-account   90–91, 95–104, 130, 133, 227
self-transcendence   8, 34n, 118, 134, 160
sensual perception *see* perception
skepticism   173–174, 178, 180, 271n
sociality *see* community
subconscious *see* consciousness
subjectivity   9, 16–17, 33, 48, 54, 73, 139–140,
        146, 155, 159, 163–166, 176–179, 194, 248,
        263–265
Sufism   123n, 129–130, 179
symbol   17, 20, 37, 71, 115, 117, 155, 169, 180n,
        214–217, 221–223

textuality   45–46, 62–64, 138, 150, 151
theophany   8, 91–92, 98–99, 102; *see also*
    revelation
theopoetics   126, 267
tolerance   37–38
tradition   10, 22, 24–26, 77–80, 85, 143–144,
        146, 155–156, 162, 169, 198, 210, 223–224
transcendence   5, 7–9, 16–28, 34, 39, 46, 54,
        62–64, 74, 83, 86n, 106–119, 147–151,
        159–161, 166–167, 175–183, 188–203, 248,
        263–266, 268n, 271–272; *see also*
        self-transcendence
transcendentalism   50, 107, 111

INDEX OF SUBJECTS

truism *see* truth

trust   9, 46, 85–86, 90, 92, 96, 114, 159, 165,
    187–203, 265

truth   9, 16, 34, 44–45, 49, 54, 62, 64–65,
    74–75, 78, 87, 102, 142–146, 156, 158, 162,
    168–169, 179

unification   124, 232

visual arts   20, 22, 25–26, 219, 221

wahy *see* revelation

Printed in the United States
By Bookmasters